# Augsburg and Constantinople

JRR
South Hamilton
2008

# Augsburg and Constantinople

The Correspondence between the Tübingen Theologians
and Patriarch Jeremiah II of Constantinople
on the Augsburg Confession

## George Mastrantonis

HOLY CROSS ORTHODOX PRESS
Brookline, Massachusetts

ISBN 1-916586-82-0

LIBRARY OF CONGRESS CATALOGING–IN–PUBLICATION DATA

Augsburg and Constantinople
    Translation of : Acta et scripta theologorum Wirtembergensium
    et Patriarchae Constantinopolitani D. Hieremiae
Bibliography: p. 320
Includes index.
    1. Augsburg Confession—Addresses, essays, lectures.
    2. Lutheran Church—Doctrinal and controversial works—
    Addresses, essays, lectures. 3. Lutheran Church—Relations—
    Orthodox Eastern Church—Addresses, essays, lectures.
    4.Orthodox Eastern Church—Relations—Lutheran Church—
    Addresses, essays, lectures. 5. Orthodox Eastern Church—
    Doctrinal and controversal works—Addresses, essays, lectures.
    I. Ieremias II, Patriarch of Constantinople. 1536-1594. II.
    Mastrantonis, George. III. Title: Augsburg and Constantinople.
    IV. Series: Archbishop Iakovos library of ecclesiastical and
    historical sources; no. 7.
    BX8069.A313            231'.41            81-7038

*Dedicated to*
*His Eminence Archbishop Iakovos*
*in recognition of his outstanding leadership*
*as Primate of*
*the Greek Orthodox Church in the Americas;*
*for his personal charisma and fortitude which brought*
*the Eastern Orthodox Church to the forefront*
*among the Christian Community.*

# TABLE OF CONTENTS

## PART ONE
## HISTORICAL BACKGROUND

## PART TWO
## THE CORRESPONDENCE BETWEEN PATRIARCH
## JEREMIAH II AND THE TÜBINGEN THEOLOGIANS

# PREFACE

The Very Reverend George Mastrantonis, a priest of the Greek Orthodox Church in America, in addition to his long, exemplary and admirable pastorate, his founding of the OLOGOS publications, and his authorship of hundreds of very useful and informative religious articles and tracts, has presented us with a most erudite study and critique of the famous correspondence exchanged between Patriarch Jeremiah II of Constantinople and the Tübingen theologians.

The present volume elucidates further the questions raised by the Augsburg Confession vis-à-vis Roman Catholic abuses and theological errors, and constitutes a truly great contribution to the ecumenical studies of our times.

It is, therefore, with great pleasure that I recommend this extraordinary book to all those who would like to avail themselves of the opportunity to understand better both Lutheranism and the Protestant Reformation, as well as the Orthodox response to them.

*Archbishop Iakovos*

# FOREWORD

The Very Reverend Father George Mastrantonis has rendered long and distinguished service as priest, author, and publisher not only to the Greek Orthodox Archdiocese of North and South America, but to all the Orthodox churches in the western hemisphere.

His present study, *Augsburg and Constantinople*, the crowning point of his outstanding career, is a labor of love which has occupied his time for a number of years, despite the absence of good health. His heroic persistence and perserverance in completing this study is an additional tribute to him and an example for all of us.

The Holy Cross Orthodox Press is proud to include Father George Mastrantonis' *Augsburg and Constantinople* in its series, "The Archbishop Iakovos Library of Ecclesiastical and Historical Sources."

N. M. Vaporis
General Editor

# INTRODUCTION

The three *Answers* of Patriarch Jeremiah II of Constantinople (1572-1579), sent to the Lutheran theologians of Tübingen, have taken a place among the symbolics of the Orthodox Church. However, these *Answers* are not documents of faith officially ratified by the Church; they are not in the same category as the symbols, especially those of the Nicaeo-Constantinopolitan Creed and the dogmatic decrees issued or ratified by the seven Ecumenical Synods of the Orthodox Church. Jeremiah's discourses, along with other confessions, occupy a secondary place compared to the forementioned symbols and creeds. The Orthodox Church recognizes confessions written from the ninth century on as merely symbolic texts, known also as symbolic books or symbolic monuments. These confessions, issued by local synods or by individual hierarchs or taken from minutes and encyclicals of synods, contain, at least in part, the Orthodox Faith according to their own particular interpretation. They often defend the truths of Orthodoxy against heterodox churches.

The well-written discourses of Jeremiah II in the form of dialogue are considered to be such symbolic texts. They are not to be considered on the same level as the decrees or symbols, or the dogmatical utterances known as *horoi* of the seven Ecumenical Synods. This distinction between symbols and symbolic books does not mean that the content of the latter may not be Orthodox in character, but only that they are pending *probable* acceptance and ratification by an Orthodox Ecumenical Synod. They are not considered authorized catechisms. In the Orthodox Church there is no official catechism. The official expressions of faith are the symbols and the *horoi* issued by Ecumenical Synods. The symbolic books are scholarly with important theological content, written at the time of a specific event or circumstance.

The symbolic books of the Orthodox Church lack the absolute, eternal, catholic, and obligatory validity of the symbols and *horoi* of the Ecumenical Synods. Nevertheless, their importance is not to be diminished. These books are valuable contributions to the history of dogma; they also are important and timely in answering the challenge of the various churches of the West. Thus the symbolic books are not of the same validity as the symbols and *horoi,* which are obligatory teachings of the Orthodox Church.

The symbolic books of the Eastern Orthodox Church should not be equated in validity to the Roman symbolic books (especially of the Council of Trent), nor to the Lutheran symbolic books (such as the Lutheran *Book of Concord*). Moreover, the number of symbolic books in the Orthodox Church differs from time to time, depending on who compiles them. For instance, the list of symbolic books is different among I. Masolora, J. Michalcescu, I. Karmires, and others.

The *Answers* of Patriarch Jeremiah II, which are included in the symbolic books of the Orthodox Church, should be studied along with the Augsburg Confession of the Lutheran Church and the *Replies* of the Tübingen theologians to Jeremiah's *Answers*. In such a context, the truths of the Orthodox Church and the position of the Lutheran Church can be better understood. The Lutheran Church at that particular time was struggling to consolidate its confessions while continuing to oppose the abuses which it observed among the supporters of the bishop of Rome, about fifty years prior to making contact with the Orthodox Church.

The three *Answers* of Jeremiah cannot be fully understood without relating them to the Augsburg Confession of the Lutheran Church and to the three *Replies* of the Lutheran theologians. Jeremiah's discourses are important in that they are the first contact of Orthodoxy with the Lutheran Church and are, at the same time, a well-prepared presentation of Orthodox teachings. They are especially important today when a movement toward better understanding among churches is taking place, requiring that one know the views of the other. It is imperative that problems be faced with a clear mind and feelings of brotherhood. This is what convinced me to translate from the original Greek into English the three *Answers* of Patriarch Jeremiah II, the *Replies* of the Lutheran theologians, and the personal letters which accompanied them.

The first part of this study is, therefore, concerned with the historical setting, while the second deals with the correspondence.

George Mastrantonis

# THE ARTICLES OF THE AUGSBURG CONFESSION

# PART ONE

# HISTORICAL BACKGROUND

*Chapter 1*


# THE FIRST CONTACT BETWEEN THE

# LUTHERANS AND THE EASTERN ORTHODOX

The sixteenth century Western reforming movements and their literature are significant because they brought to the attention of the people the demoralizing characteristics of the Western Church of that time. This movement started as an internal attempt to renovate the Western Church. Its outcome was the Lutheran Reformation, whose leadership was forced out from the Roman Church and developed a theology based primarily on the Scriptures. It disavowed the source of ecclesiastical tradition and the innovations of the Roman Catholic Church, especially the dogma of the primacy of the pope.[1] The proponents of this movement vigorously reconstructed their teachings and practices. They also organized a movement for expansion of their principle methods and theology to other Christians. They attempted to achieve this goal despite internal problems and struggles against the Calvinistic and Zwinglian movements which arose shortly afterward.

The mission of this movement, which afterward became known as the Lutheran Church, was that of spreading its doctrines to others. An outgrowth of this mission was its desire to establish cordial relations with the Orthodox Church which was known to Lutherans as an ancient Church. This desire materialized late in the sixteenth century in contact between the Lutheran Church and the Eastern Orthodox Patriarchate of Constantinople which was, and still is, the primary spiritual see of all the autocephalous branches of the Orthodox Church.[2]

The first fruitful contact between Orthodox and Lutherans was an exchange of personal letters and discourses between Lutheran theologians at the University of Tübingen and the Ecumenical Patriarch of Constantinople, Jeremiah II, with his theologian-advisers.[3] To understand fully the correspondence, which occurred between 1573-1581, an understanding of the era during which it occurred is neccessary. During the fifteenth century there emerged a movement for free expression in science, philosophy, art, and religion. This freedom broke the bonds of religious domination. With the awakening of this spirit, the religious movement,

3

both within the Church and from without, blossomed. In this spirit of religious freedom an opportunity presented itself for an approach between East and West, and it materialized in the aforementioned correspondence.

## The Background

The classic studies, which began in the thirteenth century in Europe, flourished in the fifteenth century as "handmaids" to Christian theology. Contributing to this intellectual awakening were some learned persons who fled from Constantinople after its fall in 1453.[4] The spirit of the classics sowed the "seeds of truth" for the fruits of growing freedom in men. This spirit of freedom encouraged philosophy and sciences to grow free of ecclesiastical domination. This trend also had a dramatic impact in religion and art. The classic studies and spirit cultivated the soil on which civilization blossomed and improved.

This freedom from ecclesiastical dominance penetrated the spirit of man, liberating it from its bondage. For hundreds of years, darkness shadowed the human mind, preventing man from undertaking the disciplined research of the potentialities of nature as well as his own spirit. This movement in the middle of the fifteenth century was an awakening of the whole man in every facet of his life. This spirit of freedom was a rebirth of the human mind, opening the avenues of direct communion with nature and God.

In this era of the renaissance and humanism which characterized the Christian religion in its awakening, there were many who contributed to the spiritual liberation of man. Johann Reuchlin (1455-1522), a learned leader in the humanities; his grandnephew, Philip Melanchthon (1497-1560), a prominent humanist and theologian of the Lutheran movement; and Desiderius Erasmus (1466-1536), a noted humanist who taught in various cities of England, Italy, and the Netherlands, and gained the title, a "citizen of all Europe," were among the many illuminators of humanism who emancipated the mind from the darkness of superstition, corruption, and error often perpetuated by Church and state as well as the monastic life.

There are many men who at various times raised their voices for the reformation of the Church in reaction to this spirit of freedom which was kindled in their hearts. William of Occam (c.1349), John Huss (1369-1415), and others were punished because they dared to set forth new concepts consistent with the evangelical spirit. The development of this spirit of freedom occupied the hearts and minds of devout laymen. They were prepared to accept and cultivate such an evangelical spirit against the deviating teachings of the established Church of Rome. Rome's power of excommunication was a strong weapon which seldom failed to burn at the stake leaders of such new teaching and intimidated devout laymen who adhered to them. Most of those subjected to such pressures did not intend to separate themselves from the Roman Church; they intended only to restore the teachings and practices of the ancient Church.

## Luther's Reaction to Ecclesiastical Freedom

One of these personalities who set forth various renovations and restorations to update the Roman Church according to the Scriptures and practices of the early Church was the renowned Martin Luther. Luther's attitude reflected his personal experiences within the Roman Church where he was a monk of the order of Augustinian hermits of strict observance. He proposed his renovations as would a member of a family who looked for the betterment of his own house. He was not against the foundation of the Church. On the contrary, he sought to reinforce this foundation. What initially motivated his thoughtful renovations for the Church was his opposition to the theory and practice of indulgences, especially the manner in which they were sold. But the heart of his discontentment was justification, that is, the forgiveness of sins before God.[5]

Luther was well-learned in the spirit of the Scriptures. He was sincere in complying with the strictness of the monastic life which never became for him a mere routine. The meaning of this strict manner of life was rather the object of a dialogue within himself. It seems that he was not alone in his thoughts and feelings. They were shared by other monks of the Augustinian Order. The difference between Luther and the others was that he followed his conscience and raised the question with his superiors. Luther presented ninety-five theses, that is to say, topics for discussion on indulgences. He also sent informative letters to various persons. Whether or not Luther affixed or nailed to the doors of the church a scroll containing his ninety-five theses is debated.

31 October 1517, is counted as the beginning of a new era of the Western Church. It was a protest against the unjust and unbecoming actions of the popes; a protest spread among a large number of Roman Catholics, a protest which embodied the frustrations of the conscientious, devout believer. Within a short time word of his protest spread throughout Germany which welcomed it. The reaction of the hierarchy of the Roman Church was an immediate attempt to prevent him from spreading his rebellious attitude and innovations. Luther was officially rebuked by the pope and warned against the consequences of his action. However, Luther was not to be intimidated and stressed his position all the more strongly. Luther was confronted by John Eck, a renowned papalist professor in Ingolstadt, Germany, in a disputation which

resulted in Luther winning many to his cause. Luther's movement soon
became a reality despite his trial in Rome *in absentia*. He was accused of
spreading heretical doctrines. He refused the demand of Cardinal Ca-
jetan at Augsburg to recant. In 1519 at Leipzig, Luther denied the
primacy of the pope and the infalibility of the general councils. He later
dramatized his position by burning the book of canon law in 1520 at Wittenberg. Before an imperial court which summoned him in 1521 in
Worms, Luther once more refused to recant. In 1529, the supporters of
the Lutheran movement affirmed their right to reform their territories
according to the word of God, and were called "Protestants" in consequence.

## The Formulation and Presentation of the Augsburg Confession

A confession of faith, later known as the Augsburg Confession, was
read to the Diet summoned by Emperor Charles V.[6] The writer of this
Confession was Philip Melanchthon. It was presented in an inoffensive
manner at the emperor's request, and, therefore, its language is
moderate. It was presented on 25 June 1530, in Augsburg. Apart from an
introduction, this document is presented in two parts. One includes the
first twenty-one articles which refer to doctrines. The second part of this
Confession refers to practical views on abuses. These abuses include
communion in one element for the laity, clerical celibacy, private masses,
monastic vows, and compulsory confession, among others. The
Augsburg Confession originally was written in Latin, but it was
translated and read in German.[7] The representatives of the papalist party, headed by the theologian, John Eck, were expected to present their
views following the presentation of the Augsburg Confession. But having secured a copy of the Confession, they sought to reconstruct their
thoughts and postponed their presentation until August 3. The papalist
party during this time composed their views in *confutatio pontificia*.
Melanchthon, foreseeing that the papalist representative would receive
permission to delay their answer, wrote the Apology of the Augsburg
Confession in order to answer their confutation, but the emperor refused
to receive it.

## Lutheranism Organized

The forces of Lutheranism were strong convictions and expanding
missions. Their convictions of the truths, as stated in the Scriptures,
disregarded the traditions of the Roman Church which consisted of
customs, arbitrariness, and external habits rather than genuine apostolic
sacred tradition. The Lutherans' mission, also, was an effort to spread the
truths as they interpreted them in the Scriptures in order to win over ad-

herents and to provide spiritual guidance for the leaders of the new movement which later became a great church. Nevertheless, Lutheranism was confronted with confusion on the part of its own leaders and some of their own teachings. Luther found himself both fighting the Roman Church and mediating among leaders of the Lutheran Church. This church created its own house by studying, teaching, preaching, consulting, guiding, and formulating a whole spiritual movement in the new life through its interpretation of Christian truths. Luther was a gifted person armed with courage, an inspiring preacher and prolific writer, a worthy leader of the new movement. He translated the Scriptures into German so that people would have the opportunity to read them for themselves. Among his most gifted colleagues was Philip Melanchthon, the writer of the Augsburg Confession (and its Apology). Lutheran leaders of a later generation include Jacob Andreae, who wrote and arranged with Martin Chemnitz and four other theologians[8] the *Formula of Concord* and its preface, which later was adopted as the preface of the whole *Book of Concord*.

## The Unforeseen Prominence of the Augsburg Confession

The Augsburg Confession of the Lutheran Church is the expression of the main beliefs and practices of the Lutheran Church. It is considered the basic confession from which all the rest of the writings in *The Book of Concord* sprang.[9] It is the basic exposition of the beliefs of the Lutheran movement. During the fiftieth anniversary of its presentation to Emperor Charles V, the closing of *The Book of Concord* took place, and an era of expansion began. In this spirit the contact between the Lutherans and the Orthodox Patriarch of Constantinople took place. The Augsburg Confession was translated into Greek in the hope of eventual establishment of cordial relations with the ancient Church in the East.

The Lutherans pursued their relationship with the Patriarchate of Constantinople, first through Melanchthon, who in 1559 is believed to have sent a personal letter to Patriarch Joasaph II (1555-1565).[10] Later, the Tübingen theologians followed a well-planned approach to the same Patriarchate. This latter communication resulted in an exchange of correspondence that is highly appraised for its theological insights and discourses. This literature was written in Latin and Greek and issued later under the title of *Acta et Scripta Theologorum Wirtembergensium et Patriarchae Constantinopolitani D. Hieremiae*. These writings, now translated from the Greek into English, are the subject of this study.

The translation of the Augsburg Confession into the Greek language reflects the hope of the Lutherans to illuminate other people with Lutheran scriptural theology. Lutheranism as a reforming religious movement had zeal and vigor. This Church established its own definitions and theology, both in theory and practice. The leaders of this Church were members of the old Church who intended initially to correct the misdoings of the Roman Church without any plan to separate themselves from it. They fought against the mishandling of the practical and personal affairs of the old Church. This Church created a spirit of mission and expansion among some members of the old Church and others.[11]

It was logical, then, that the leaders of the Lutheran movement would approach the Eastern Orthodox Church. The concept of mission caused Lutheran leaders to strive to spread their doctrines, and to establish cordial relations with the ancient Eastern Church[12] which had its beginning with Christ and His Apostles. That Church was the Orthodox Church, whose ecumenical see has been in Constantinople since the fourth century. The Lutheran leaders made a special effort to present their own views in such a way as to convince the venerable ancient Church to accept them. The fact that they were approaching a Greek-speaking Church, which at that time had been under Turkish domination for about one hundred years, made the mission all the more momentous. Most of the Lutheran theologians involved were scholars in the Greek language and versed in both New Testament Greek[13] and that of the sixteenth century.

## Contact Between Lutheranism and Orthodoxy

First contact between Lutheran theologians and the Orthodox Church took place when the Patriarch of Constantinople, Joasaph II (1555-1565), sent Deacon Demetrios Mysos to meet the leaders of the Lutheran movement so he could study their teachings, but also the personalities behind the movement. Mysos spent approximately six months as Melanchthon's guest in Wittenberg. From the beginning a warm, sincere friendship was established between the two. During this short period of time it is believed that the translation of the Augsburg Confession into the Greek language was completed and a copy supposedly given to Deacon Mysos to present to Patriarch Joasaph. Melanchthon sent a personal letter in which he expressed his delight in his friendship with Mysos and his respect and reverence for the Patriarch in Constantinople.[14] It is surprising to note that before the arrival of Mysos, Melanchthon was unaware that the ancient Church in Constantinople had survived one hundred-odd years under Turkish domination. It was natural that Mysos be prepared for the encounter with instructions from Patriarch Joasaph, and also with his own keen knowledge of theology and a knowledge of the language used in the dialogue. It is probable that Melanchthon could have used the spoken Greek language, as he was fluent in writing Greek.

It seems that Melanchthon and Mysos decided to present to Patriarch

Joasaph the original Augsburg Confession, which contained the Lutheran teaching as it was accepted by all the leaders and adherents of the Lutheran Church at that time. The Augsburg Confession was written originally in Latin and German. It also seems that they decided to translate the Augsburg Confession into Greek. Melanchthon was capable of this task and Mysos probably helped him in its literal composition into Greek. The translation of the Augsburg Confession into Greek is a free translation, but without a change of meaning. The assumption that the Augsburg Confession was translated into Greek by Paul Dolscius, whose name appeared on the Greek text, is not substantiated. Dolscius may have assisted in copying the translation as a secretary or copyist. It is doubtful that a third person translated it while Melanchthon and Mysos were studying its content together. The claim that the Augsburg Confession was a free translation into Greek, without changing its meaning, tends to support the belief that Melanchthon was the translator. Only the original writer of this document could be prepared to translate it freely into Greek. Because Melanchthon was subsequently (although unjustly) accused of being a crypto-Calvinist, his name may have been replaced by that of one who assisted him as a copyist.[15] It is not the intent of this study to review the controversy on this matter of the translator.

After the completion of Mysos' mission, he left Melanchthon, who gave him a warm personal letter for Patriarch Joasaph. But there is no evidence that Mysos returned to Constantinople and presented the Patriarch with the documents. The silence of Patriarch Joasaph was interpreted by Professor Ioannes Karmires to mean that the Patriarch received the letter and the Greek Augsburg Confession, discussed the matter with Mysos, and found that the Lutherans accepted many interpretations foreign to the ecumenical teaching of the ancient Church. But this interpretation concerning Mysos has no historical basis. On the contrary, Professor Ernst Benz traced the return journey of Mysos and showed that Mysos did not return to Constantinople, nor did he give the Patriarch the Augsburg Confession in Greek. During the time that Mysos was with Melanchthon (1558) in Wittenberg, he became acquainted with a Dr. Peucer, the son-in-law of Melanchthon, a Slavophile, who was able to converse in Slavonic. Previously, Hans von Ungnad had approached Mysos and promised him a position as a translator of the writings of the reformers into Slavonic. Meanwhile, Prince Heraclides had retaken Romania from the Turks and established a Christian kingdom, reforming it after the pattern of the Reformation. Professor Benz established that Mysos decided to serve Prince Heraclides, and remained there after the Prince's death. Therefore, Melanchthon's letter never reached Constantinople.[16]

The leaders of the Lutheran Church had some knowledge of the teachings of the Orthodox Church, although they had no knowledge of

contemporary Orthodoxy because of the conquest of Greece and sur-
rounding countries by the Ottoman Empire from 1453 with the fall of the
Byzantine Empire. Luther invoked the teachings of the Orthodox
Church in his discussion with theologian Eck in Leipzig (in 1519) and
elsewhere. Also, the Greek Church was mentioned in the Apology of the
Augsburg Confession in 1530 and in 1537 in the Smalcald Articles.

After the first endeavor in 1559 to establish cordial relations between
the Lutheran movement and the Orthodox Church, a silence prevailed
between the two. The death of Melanchthon in 1560, and Mysos' failure
to return to Constantinople to complete his mission were events which
contributed to this silence. With the death of Melanchthon, the Greek
translation of the Augsburg Confession vanished, and its fate is
unknown; it is not to be found in the archives of the Patriarchate. Nor
are there any traces of its existence in the hands of other clergymen or
laymen who shared the responsibility of the Patriarchate in Constantinople at that time. Even Martin Crusius had a difficult time in locating a
copy of the Augsburg Confession in Greek.

## NOTES

1. In a letter to George Spalatin (1484-1545), a German humanist, on 20 July 1519, after
the debate with Roman Catholic theologian, John Eck in Leipzig, Luther wrote that he
vigorously defended the Orthodox Church against Eck's slanderous remarks that the Greek
Church had lost the Christian faith after the fall of the Byzantine Empire. See Martin
Luther, *Dr. Martin Luthers Werke: Kirtische Gesamtausgabe* (Weimar, 1884), 2, 227,
272-73; Ioannes Karmires, 'Ορθοδοξία καί Προτεσταντισμός (Athens, 1937), p. 25; Ernst
Benz, *Die Ostkirche im Lichte der protestantischen Geschichtsschreibung von der Reformation bis zur Gegenwart* (Munich, 1952), pp. 10-14. Luther stressed that the ancient
Fathers never held the idea of the primacy of any church leader. Luther also wrote Spalatan
on 7 November 1519, that the Greek Church rejected literally the Latin theory of purgatory; see letter 218 in *Werke*, 1, p. 25; see also Karmires, 'Ορθοδοξία, p. 27. Another innovation of the Roman Catholic Church regarding Communion is mentioned in the
Apology of the Augsburg Confession, 22. 4, asserting that the clergy, as well as the laity,
should receive both elements of the Eucharist, according to the practice of the undivided
Church. Furthermore, the Apology (24. 6) refers to the Greek Church as being against the
practice of private liturgies, that is to say, without anyone in attendance. Again, in ibid.,
24. 78-83, 88, 93, on the substance of the Divine Liturgy, the Lutherans state that the Greek
Church teaches that the Eucharist is only for a sacrifice of praise and thanksgiving, but not
a sacrifice of propitiation.

2. Although Melanchthon in his letter in 1559 to Patriarch Joasaph was not aware of the
condition of the Greek Church which, at that time, was under the domination of the Turks,
nevertheless, the Lutherans were aware of the teachings of the Greek Church in the writings
of the Fathers.

3. The answers of Jeremiah include large segments of the writings of many of the
Fathers. It seems that his theologian-advisers acted merely as researchers in locating the
proper passages of the Fathers used by him. Jeremiah composed the answers on the basis of
the writings of the Fathers, and stated that he was not presenting any new thoughts and interpretations.

4. John Herman Randall, *Making of the Modern Mind* (Boston and New York, 1926), p. 119. The dawn of the Renaissance appears before the fifteenth century with personalities such as Petrarch (1304-74), Boccaccio (1313-75), and Dante (1265-1321). It flourished after three generations, for "glorious was the day when a learned Byzantine, Chrysoloras, accepted a chair at Florence," as Bruni stated in his book, *History of His Own Times in Italy,* quoted in H. O. Taylor, *Thought and Expression in the 16th Century* (2nd ed.; New York, 1959), 1, p. 36. Bruni wrote: "At the coming of Chrysoloras, I was torn in mind. . . I gave myself to Chrysoloras, with such zeal to learn that what through the wakeful day I gathered, I followed after in night, even when asleep"; ibid.

5. Indulgences were given to the faithful primarily to collect funds for the programs of the popes. The worst aspect of selling indulgences was the false teaching of the existence of a state of purgatory. Also false was the teaching that the pope's church was the depository of the abundance of divine grace, dispensed through the sale of indulgences. See "Apology of the Augsburg Confession," *The Book of Concord,* ed. Theodore G. Tappert (Philadelphia, 1959), Article 21. 232, #23-24. See also Roland H. Bainton, *Here I Stand. A Life of Martin Luther* (New York, 1950), chapters 4 and 5.

6. Preface, *The Book of Concord,* p. 5, n. 5. This preface explains that the confession is offered because the emperor had invited both Lutheran theologians and those in communion with the bishop of Rome to present their respective views on the controversy that had broken out. Unfortunately, neither the German nor the Latin text is extant in the exact forms officially submitted. However, more than fifty copies, dating from 1530, have been found, including drafts which represent various stages in its preparation before 25 June 1530.

7. *Augsburg Confession,* Introduction of Part 2, articles 22-28 and conclusion. The *Augsburg Confession* consists of an introduction, two sections and a conclusion. The first part, 1-21, includes the Lutheran doctrines; the second part discusses the abuses that had been corrected in the Lutheran imperial cities and territories.

8. Preface, *The Book of Concord,* p. 3, n. 1. The translation of the *Formula* into English by Arthur Carl Piepkorn.

9. J. L. Neve, *Introduction to the Symbolical Books of the Lutheran Church,* 2nd ed. (Columbus, Ohio, 1956).

10. It is doubtful that Melanchthon sent the Augsburg Confession in Greek to the Patriarch.

11. Philip Melanchthon sent a letter in 1559 to Patriarch Joasaph II; Ioannes Karmires, Ὀρθοδοξία, p. 33. See also Gerlach in Martin Chrusius, *Turcograecia* (Basel, 1684), p. 559.

12. *Acta et Scripta Theologorum Wirtembergensium et Patriarchae Constantinopolitani D. Hieremiae: quae utrique ab Anno MDLXXVI usque ad Annum MDLXXXI de Augustana Confessione inter se miserunt: Graece & Latine ab ijsdem Theologis edita* (Wittenberg, 1584), First *Reply* of Tübingen theologians, pp. 148-49. In the Latin text the whole paragraph is underlined and numbered from 1-19, tabulating subjects in agreement, according to their opinion.

13. Ioannes Karmires, Ὀρθοδοξία, p. 20.

14. Ibid., pp. 33-34.

15. "There are strong reasons for believing that the actual initiative belongs to no lesser than Melanchthon"; see Georges Florovsky, "The *Greek Version* of the Augsburg Confession," *Lutheran World,* 6 (1959), 153.

16. Berthold F. Korte, "Early Lutheran Relations with Eastern Orthodoxy," *Lutheran Quarterly,* 9 (1959), 55-56. This article attempts to summarize the finding of Ernst Benz, *Wittenberg und Byzanz* (Morburg, 1949).

*Chapter 2*

# THE SECOND ATTEMPT BY THE LUTHERANS

# TO ESTABLISH CORDIAL RELATIONS

# WITH THE EASTERN ORTHODOX

Fourteen years after the unsuccessful first attempt at unity between the Lutheran Church and the Orthodox Church another effort was made. It also sought relations of the Lutheran Church with the Patriarchate of Constantinople. This endeavor was undertaken with greater originality, interest, and preparation and more consistent method of contact. It resulted in a friendly dialogue of personal letters and discourses. This monumental mission took place while an involved group of theologians at the University of Tübingen was headed by Jacob Andreae, Professor of Theology and Chancellor of the University, assisted by Martin Crusius, Professor of Classics. The Patriarch of Constantinople, Jeremiah II, shared the dialogue with the German theologians of Tübingen.[1] The events and correspondence of a decade are presented herein.

In 1583, a book was published in Wittenberg under the title, *Acta et Scripta Theologorum Wirtembergensium, et Patriarchae Constantinopolitani D. Hieremiae.* It consists of the correspondence between the Lutheran theologians of the University of Tübingen and the Patriarch of Constantinople, Jeremiah II. This correspondence of personal letters and discourses took place between 1574 through 1582. The purpose of this new effort was the unity and cordial relations between these two Churches: the Church of the Lutherans, which had achieved autonomy from the Roman Catholic Church fifty years previously, and the ancient Eastern Orthodox Church, which had its beginning at the start of the Christian era. The editor of this book was Martin Crusius. He also was the translator of the correspondence therein (Latin into Greek and Greek into Latin), and wrote the preface of this book in Latin.

In the year 1584 another book was published in Basel entitled *Turcograecia,* and written by Martin Crusius. This book, which contains valuable information about the contents of *Acta et Scripta,* is as rare as the *Acta et Scripta* itself.

## *The Efforts of Jeremiah II and Andreae for Unity*

Patriarch Jeremiah II is considered an extraordinary personality whose activities were decisive both in the administration of the church and in the confession of the Christian faith.[2] His nickname was *Tranos* (meaning a person of penetrating intellect). He was elected and re-elected Patriarch of Constantinople three times: 1572-1579, 1580-1584, 1586-1595. He was well versed in theology and revitalized the role of the Ecumenical Patriarchate in inter-ecclesiastical affairs in the sphere of pan-Orthodox activities and with the Lutheran Church. He protested against Pope Gregory XIII over the change of the calendar (1582) from the Julian to the new Gregorian. As Ecumenical Patriarch, Jeremiah journeyed to Russia in 1589. In January of the following year, he installed Iov, elected by the synod of Russian bishops, as the first Patriarch of the Russian Church.[3]

Jacob Andreae (1528-1590), German Lutheran reformer and theologian, was ordained at the age of 18, and had a Masters of Arts degree from Tübingen University. In 1553, Andreae received a theological doctor's degree and became special superintendent. In 1561, he became Professor of Theology, Provost and Chancellor of Tübingen University, a post which he held for thirty years until his death. In 1568, he joined Martin Chemnitz (1522-1586) in order to restore unity to the Lutheran movement. In 1572, Andreae helped to draft the theologians' statement against the supposed crypto-Calvinistic christology.

Andreae took a leading role in the correspondence of the Lutheran theologians of Tübingen with Ecumenical Patriarch Jeremiah II (1536-1595). His famous six sermons became the basis of the Swabian Concordia. He was extensively occupied with the negotiations for the unity of Lutherans which resulted in the Formula of Concord (1577), wrote its epitome and, later, its preface.[4]

At this time Tübingen became one of the theological centers of Lutheranism where many teachers in theology and the classics elevated the academic status of this university to a high plane. It is certain that both centers, the Patriarchate and the University of Tübingen, with their activities and scholars, were known to one another, even without a direct line of communication such as Gerlach later provided.

The German embassy in Constantinople asked the theologians of the University of Tübingen to send a theologian to Constantinople to serve as embassy chaplain. Undoubtedly, the ambassador himself, David Ungnad, reported to the theologians in Tübingen concerning the conditions of the Eastern Orthodox Church in Constantinople, and also probably explained the role a chaplain would play. The Tübingen theologians sent to Constantinople a distinguished, young colleague to

hold this new position of chaplain and to act as liaison between them and
the Patriarch, with the goal of winning over the Eastern Church "to the
Gospel."[5]

This mission was entrusted to the well-known theologian, Stephen
Gerlach. He promptly established friendly relations with the theologians
of the Patriarchate and with the Patriarch himself. The theologians in
Tübingen were represented by Jacob Andreae and Martin Crusius, who
dispatched letters of recommendation for Gerlach. The letters of recommendation were handed to Patriarch Jeremiah by Gerlach on 15 October
1573.[6] Crusius sent another letter with a short homily by Andreae on
Luke 10:9 concerning the kingdom of God. While Patriarch Jeremiah II
was making an extensive pastoral journey which lasted nine months
(starting 19 October 1573), letters from the theologians arrived. Unaware
of the Patriarch's absence from Constantinople, Andreae and Crusius
sent the Patriarch, on 15 September 1574, the Greek translation of the
Augsburg Confession, which they called a *Confession of the Orthodox
Faith*. This copy was accompanied by a letter written by Andreae and
Crusius and sent through Stephen Gerlach. Gerlach handed the copy of
the Augsburg Confession in Greek and the letters to the Patriarch on 24
May 1575.

This copy of the Augsburg Confession in Greek seems to be the same
translation as that of Melanchthon. Patriarch Jeremiah had already
received the two letters previously sent to him by Andreae and Crusius,
and the two short homilies on John 10:11 and Luke 10:9 were well-
received by him.[7] The Patriarch answered those two homilies with kindness and paternal love. However, he properly rejected their interpretations, stating the Orthodox views on the verses from John and Luke.[8]
The Patriarch's *Answer* to these two homilies was sent to the theologians
before he wrote the first discourse (*First Answer*) on the Augsburg Confession, stating that no other foundation of the Father is acceptable than
that which is the cornerstone, Christ the self-truth.

Andreae and Crusius answered this letter of the Patriarch by stating
that they accepted his admonition as wise and paternal. However, they
stated that some innovations had been made, though not in the main articles pertaining to salvation. On the contrary, they claimed that they had
followed the teachings of the Apostles, Prophets, Fathers, and seven
Ecumenical Synods, which they cherished and kept.[9] The Patriarch sent a
second letter on 16 November 1575, saying that he was preparing the
answer to the Augsburg Confession, asserting that he would depend
upon Scripture and Tradition, especially regarding the subject of
justification by faith and good works.[10]

Patriarch Jeremiah's knowledge of the main sections of Lutheran
theology was extensive because of the letters he received from Andreae
and Crusius, and their personal explanation by Gerlach. With such a

background Jeremiah accepted the text of the Augsburg Confession in Greek, which was presented to him by Gerlach with explanations as the first serious step in his dialogue.

The Patriarch, in his *First Answer* to the theologians of Tübingen pertaining to the Augsburg Confession, answered its articles one by one. Jeremiah's *Answer* was very extensive and written with clarity and paternal admonition to the theologians. He urged them to accept the doctrines of the Eastern Orthodox Church. In his *Answer,* Patriarch Jeremiah followed the enumeration of the articles of the Augsburg Confession (without the titles, which were a later addition). He answered not only the first twenty-one articles pertaining to the faith and doctrine, but also all the articles concerning matters in dispute (articles 22-28 and the conclusion). There were many points of agreement, but also points of disagreement, such as the *filioque* phrase in the Nicene Creed, original sin, the priesthood, the confession of sins, free will, justification through faith and good works, and invocation of the saints. In the second part of the Augsburg Confession, starting with the twenty-second article, the Patriarch touched upon the disagreements on Holy Communion, fasting (distinction of foods), monastic vows, and the power of the bishops.[11]

## The Publication of 'Acta et Scripta' and its Description

The publication of the *Acta et Scripta* was made necessary because the opponents of the Lutheran theologians made public the *First Answer* of Jeremiah without their knowledge.[12] This *First Answer* was translated into German and had a wide circulation. Even the Romans, through Pope Gregory himself, interfered by sending a special messenger to congratulate Patriarch Jeremiah for his answer to the Lutherans. This was the reason that the Lutherans, in all sincerity, published all the correspondence between Patriarch Jeremiah II and the Tübingen theologians. This correspondence, discourses, and letters, were published in two languages (Greek and Latin) in Wittenberg in 1582 with a preface in Latin by Martin Crusius. It was titled *Acta et Scripta Theologorum Wirtembergensium, et Patriarchae Constantinopolitani.* The Roman Catholics attempted to use this document against the Lutherans. Nevertheless, this document was an important step which broke the silence between the Eastern Church and the West.

In the Latin text of *Acta et Scripta* there are many words and phrases in Greek which were not translated into Latin. No titles appeared in any articles of the original Augsburg Confession. Titles of some of the articles were inserted in 1553, but were not printed in the *Acta et Scripta.* However, the articles were enumerated and followed by Jeremiah as he answered each. The correspondence in *Acta et Scripta* follows the articles of the Augsburg Confession.

Passages from the Fathers and Scriptures are quoted by both sides. The selection of verses of the Scriptures on the same subject used by both sides varied through emphasis of their own points of view. Frequently, they appear to be in disagreement, although in reality they are not, or not as much as it might appear. It seems each had special techniques and presuppositions for interpreting the Scriptures which governed their minds for the interpretation of a variety of subjects.[13] Passages of the Fathers used by Jeremiah, both direct and indirect, are numerous.[14]

Throughout the correspondence, marginal notes on the pages appear pertaining to paragraph titles, scriptural verses and to the Fathers in both the Latin and Greek text, but they are not complete.

Some pages are incorrectly numbered with some duplicate numbers appearing, but the sequence of the text is correct. References are made to the original and incorrect pages.

The style of writing used in both Latin and Greek produces lengthy sentences. For this reason the writers used the colon sign to break up the lengthy phrases. The abbreviations and ligatures that appear in the text are the usual ones for the Greek language at that time.

There are underlined words and phrases in both texts which do not always correspond with each other.

The writers of the *Acta et Scripta* refer to their own previous writings or those of the others. But many times the passages they quote are not literally the same as the original. Therefore, these passages should not be accepted as exact quotations from the original.

It seems that this correspondence was created by individuals.[15] Patriarch Jeremiah II did not act in response to a synodical decree, but as the spokesman of the Orthodox Faith, he claims unoriginality as a virtue. In fact, the Patriarch used the advice and scholarly assistance of a group of theologians of whom the most noted was Protonotarios Theodosios Zygomalas. On the other side, the German theologians, of whom Jacob Andreae was the most noted, do not appear to represent officially the Lutheran Church. For this reason they tried to keep the correspondence private and confidential. But it is obvious that had the correspondence borne fruit, ways would have been found to bring this to the attention of the Lutheran Church for its approval.

The real promoter of this correspondence seems to be Martin Crusius who took it upon himself to contact, as an individual, the Patriarchate of Constantinople (letters in *Turcograecia*).[16] Crusius' name is the only one that is officially mentioned in connection with the translation of the Latin text of the Lutherans into Greek, and the Greek text of the Patriarchate into Latin.

This correspondence started at the time when both sides were occupied with many internal problems. The Lutherans were involved in the restoration of unity to the various factions that had developed in the

Lutheran community after the death of Martin Luther, while Jeremiah was occupied with problems of the Orthodox Church in Poland and the archbishopric in Russia while under constant pressure from the Turks.

The Lutherans appealed to the Orthodox Church because the latter held the doctrines of the undivided ecumenical Church intact without the many innovations of the Roman Church. Luther himself referred often to the Orthodox Church as keeping the faith and orders in their original function, although he attributed infallibility neither to the Fathers nor to the synods as such.

The Lutheran theologians exclusively maintained the respected Augustana of 1530 as their main confession. They apparently regarded this Augsburg Confession as sufficient and self-explanatory, especially with the presence of the theologian, Stephen Gerlach, at the embassy of the Holy Roman Empire in Constantinople as a liaison officer who would be able to explain any passage that might require comment.

In reality, the Patriarch's *Answers* are considered the last Byzantine patristic presentation of the Eastern Orthodox Church to be succeeded by the scholastic method. The correspondence constituted a dialogue between an ancient traditional Church and a newly autonomous Church.

As a matter of fact, this translation into Greek, as noted by Professor Ernst Benz and cited by Georges Florovsky, "was not an accurate rendering of the final and official text of the Augustana, but a document of a very peculiar character."[17] According to Florovsky, this Greek translation was not the later revision but a special version of the Variata, the altered Augsburg Confession of 1540.[18] A comparison of the Greek translation on hand with the original languages indicates that the translation was made from the Latin text; there are some omissions and additions, but apparently without substantially changing its meaning. Also, there are differences in the Latin text between *Acta et Scripta* and the *Book of Concord.*[19]

Were there actually many differences — essential differences — which caused the termination of this dialogue? Or was it a misunderstood emphasis which hammered a particular side of the discussion, and not the whole discussion itself? Was the Patriarch's loyalty to Sacred Tradition and the Lutheran's to *Sola Scriptura* the real cause of disagreement and termination of the correspondence? It appears that the Orthodox underestimated the importance of Scripture and that the Lutherans underestimated Sacred Tradition.

## NOTES

1. Persons who served as advisors to Patriarch Jeremiah II were Ioannes Zygomalas, Theodosios Zygomalas, Physician Leonardos Mindonios from Chios, Bishop Damaskenos Stoudites of Naupaktos and Arta, Bishop Metrophanes of Verroia, Priest-monk Matthew,

Grand Logothetes Hierax, and probably Gabriel Severos. Jeremiah II himself was the principal composer of the *Answers*.

On the other hand, the persons who wrote the *Replies* to the *Answers* of Patriarch Jeremiah II, and whose signatures appeared on one or more of the *Replies* and letters of the Tübingen theologians, were Jacob Heerbrand, Lucas Osiander, Eberhard Bidembach, John Mageirus, Theodore Schneff, John Brentius, Stephen Gerlach, William Holderer, John Schoppsius and Martin Crusius, all under the leadership of Jacob Andreae.

2. Principal writer of the *Answers* is Patriarch Jeremiah II himself, contrary to the theory that the writers were subordinate theologians, especially Theodosios Zygomalas, who was the Protonotarios (the first of the ecclesiastics of the Synod). A letter written by Theodosios to Crusius dated 15 November 1575, appears in *Turcograecia* saying that the Patriarch is studying "your book which has been sent [to him] which contains the articles of faith, and, as you say, the catechisms. When he [the Patriarch] so desired, he called upon me, my lord father and some wise-men Chion. . . ." Theodosios Zygomalas, in reference to the third *Answer*, wrote to Gerlach that "the Patriarch Jeremiah composes the answer," *Turcograecia*, p. 103. The Patriarch would hardly have entrusted to his subordinates, especially Ioannes Zygomalas who was not a theologian, the presentation of such theological answers. Theodosios Zygomalas in his letter to Gerlach (March, 1581) wrote that the Patriarch "composes the answer which, as I see and as I read it continuously, does not agree with your people," *Turcograecia*, p. 432. Patriarch Jeremiah II "was one of the great personalities of the Greek Orthodox Church in the 16th century," Bergilius Germ, ed., *Encyclopedia of Religion* (New York, 1945), p. 389.

3. For the details of this important event, see George Vernadsky, *The Tsardom of Moscow 1547-1682. Part 1* (New Haven, 1969), pp. 191-92.

4. Arthur Carl Piepkorn, "Andreae, Jacob," *Encyclopedia of the Lutheran Church*, 1, p. 73.

5. A. Landenberger, *Die Reise zweier württembergischer Gesandtschaftsprediger nach Constantinopel im Jahre 1573 und 1577, nach ihrem Tagebücher erzählt* (Wittenberg, 1888), p. 194, cited by Karmires, 'Ορθοδοξία, p. 88, n. 2.

6. *Turcograecia*, pp. 29-30.

7. Ibid., pp. 416-19 and 488.

8. Ibid., p. 422.

9. This reply was received by the Patriarch on 20 March 1575; cf. *Turcograecia*, pp. 423-24, and *Acta et Scripta*, pp. 2-4.

10. *Turcograecia*, pp. 440-41. References to these letters are to be found in *Acta et Scripta*, p. 56; and in Gedeon Kypriou, Βιβλίον καλούμενον Κριτῆς τῆς 'Αληθείας (Leipzig, 1758), 1, 8; I. Mesoloras, Συμβολική τῆς 'Ορθοδόξου 'Ανατολικῆς 'Εκκλησίας (Athens, 1883-1901), 1, p. 124.

11. *Acta et Scripta*, pp. 148-49. The most accurate text and fullest critical apparatus of the Augsburg Confession and the other writings in *The Book of Concord* in the original languages (Latin and German) from which the other translations were derived, is to be found in the second (1952) and later editions of the *Die Bekenntnisschriften der evangelish-lutherischen Kirche,* (4th ed.; Göttingen, 1959). These symbolic writings have been translated into English many times.

The last translation of the symbolic writings of the Lutheran Church into English, which appears in the *Book of Concord,* has been translated directly from the original languages, Latin and German. *The Book of Concord,* ed. T. G. Tappert (Philadelphia, 1959).

12. Georges Florovsky, "An Early Ecumenical Correspondence of Patriarch Jeremiah II and the Lutheran Divines," in *World Lutheranism of Today, A Tribute to Anders Nygren* (Stockholm, 1950). p. 99. Florovsky states: "A copy of the first Patriarchal reply...came into the hands of a Polish priest, Stanislaus Socolovius, and he published it with his comments under an offensive title in Latin" [1582]. The Lutherans, to vindicate their cause, published

all the documents, the Greek replies in full and their own letters," in the *Acta et Scripta*.

13. *Acta et Scripta*, pp. 200, 301. Patriarch Jeremiah points out that there are many aspects upon which they agree and discusses the point of disagreement.

14. Philip Meyer, *Die Theologische Literatur der Griechischen im 16. Jahrundert*, in Bonwetsch-Seeberg, Studien (Leipzig, 1899), 3, pp. 6, 97-100, discerns passages of the Fathers in Jeremiah's *First Answer* in *Acta et Scripta*, pp. 56-57, introduction; pp. 57-58 concerning the Nicene Creed; pp. 58-64 (chs. 2 and 3) according to Symeon of Thessalonike; pp. 64-65, according to St. Basil; pp. 65-71 according to Basil and Chrysostom; pp. 71-77, in part, according to Chrysostom; pp. 77-81, according to Gabriel Severos; pp. 78-79 again according to Symeon of Thessalonike; pp. 81-85, in part, according to Chrysostom; pp. 85-89, independent statement by Jeremiah and, in part, according to Basil; pp. 89-95 according to Ioseph Vryennios, in part; pp. 95-104, according to Nicholas Kabasilas; pp. 104-19 independent statement by Jeremiah with patristic references; pp. 119-27, according to Basil; pp. 127-43, independent statement by Jeremiah with patristic references. In the *Second and Third Answers* of Jeremiah independent statements are contained with much fewer passages from the Fathers, except from Ioseph Vryennios, pp. 200-24, 229-37, 350-64 (cf. G. Steitz, "Die Abendmahlslehre der Griechischen Kirche in ihrer geschichtlichen Entwicklung," in *Jahrbücher für deutsche Theologie*, 13 [1868], 679. The dependence of Jeremiah on the Fathers of the Church does not diminish the validity of his *Answers*, because the Orthodox conception, especially in dogmas, holds that the genuine teaching of the Eastern Orthodox Church depends upon Scriptures and Tradition. Cf. Karmires, 'Ορθοδοξία, pp. 93-94, n. 1.

15. Florovsky, "An Early Ecumenical Correspondence," p. 98. The correspondence "are ecumenical documents of great importance and interest."

16. Martin Crusius, *Turcograecia* (7 April 1573), p. 410.

17. Florovsky, "An Early Ecumenical Correspondence," p. 104. A comparison of the Augsburg Confession in Greek with the accepted text in Latin proves this claim.

18. Ibid., p. 14.

19. The difference between the Greek and Latin text of the Augsburg Confession is difficult to analyze because there are differences in the Latin text itself. For instance, in Article 2 of the Latin text in *Die Bekenntnisschriften der Evangelisch-Lutherischen Kirche*, (4th ed. Göttingen, 1959), p. 53. The original Latin text of the Augsburg Confession consists of seventy-nine words. The *Acta et Scripta* text has 185 words in the Latin and 305 words in the Greek.

*Chapter 3*

# COMMON BELIEFS, ADIAPHORA,

# AND MATTERS IN DISPUTE

## *Areas of Agreements and Disagreements*

There were many beliefs in common among Patriarch Jeremiah II and the Tübingen theologians. It is interesting to note that on the vital beliefs of the Christian faith, on which both sides were in agreement, only a few lines were written to confirm their common belief. Points of disagreement were stressed by each side's emphasis on its own claim. For instance, Tradition, one of the most disputed subjects, was given heavy emphasis by Jeremiah, giving the misimpression that the Scriptures are on a secondary level. He emphasized Tradition because it was in dispute, while the Scriptures, not in dispute, were taken for granted as being the first and main source of Christian belief. On the other hand, the Lutheran theologians claim they used the Tradition of the Orthodox Church (Nicene Creed and utterances of the Synods and the Fathers of the Church) in such a manner as to indicate their acceptance of Tradition. Of special importance was the qualifying clause that the theologians used in connection with Tradition, "if tradition agrees with the Scriptures," as (probably) Martin Crusius later noted in the margin of Jeremiah's *First Answer* concerning Tradition.

Another subject in disagreement was the *filioque* phrase in the Nicaeo-Constantinopolitan Creed. This phrase was a later Western insertion (sixth century) into the Creed, and constituted a vital disagreement between the Eastern Orthodox and the Western Churches.[1]

Another disagreement was over the spiritual and ethical state of man after the fall of Adam. According to Patriarch Jeremiah, following the opinions of the Fathers, man did not lose his free will entirely, and thus the absolute predestination of man is rejected. According to the Lutheran theologians, man, after Adam's fall, lost his free will in spiritual and divine things; and while he retains a passive capacity for freedom, he can accept the redemption obtained by Christ only through the operation of the Holy Spirit.

One of the main subjects of disagreement was over the means of justification. The Lutherans taught that justification is wrought by faith alone, and not by faith and good works; but they emphatically stated that good works are indispensable as fruits of the life-giving faith. According to Jeremiah, good works contribute to justification, although they are not in themselves absolutely worthy of salvation; and, therefore, salvation does not depend upon them, but mainly in faith in God.

As for the sacraments, the theologians disagreed first on the number of sacraments and second, on their effect. Jeremiah stated the Orthodox belief that the sacraments are seven in number, and the Lutherans claimed only two, baptism and Eucharist. They stressed the point that only these two are recorded in Scripture and also that Chrysostom and other Fathers mention only these two. For the sacrament of baptism, Jeremiah stressed the point of immersion, a very ancient practice of the early Church which the Lutherans of the period still followed, thus rejecting the method of pouring, although the Orthodox Church accepts the validity of baptism by pouring provided that the churches confess and baptize in the name of the Holy Trinity. Concerning the Eucharist, Jeremiah stressed the point that, in substance, the Eucharist is both a sacrament and a sacrifice; also he stated the belief in the *metavole,* change of the two elements, bread and wine, into the very body and blood of Christ, an awesome and miraculous change of the elements. The Lutheran belief is that the consecrated bread and wine are the body and blood of Christ.[2] Jeremiah mentioned, also, the use of the leavened bread for Holy Communion, and the giving of the Eucharist to infants after baptism. On the sacrament of repentance (penance) both sides agreed to the rejection of indulgences (as practiced in the Roman Church), purgatory, and the theory that the saints left to the Church the excess of grace by which the pope could free souls from purgatory. Points of disagreement were penances as a remedy, and confession to the priest in detail. In general, Orthodox and Lutherans agree that the absolution of sins is the act of Almighty God who has empowered the sacrament of penance.

There were differences in detail with the Lutherans on the priesthood as a sacrament; also, on the Orthodox teaching concerning the Church and the Eucharist as a sacrifice. Nevertheless, the Lutherans accepted the general idea that the administrator of the word and the sacraments has to be "called," which implies ordination. The Lutherans held that when no bishop was available, any pastor could ordain, and they justified their position by pointing out that the sacred Scriptures and the primitive Church did not differentiate between bishops and priests. Jeremiah stated that "all the officiations are wrought and there is nothing sacred without (the office of) the priest."

The sacraments of chrismation and unction were not accepted as such by the Lutherans. Celibacy of the clergy was rejected by both the Orthodox and Lutherans; although the Orthodox require that bishops be unmarried by ethos pending an official change. Marriage is allowed before ordination by the Orthodox. However, Jeremiah defended the monastic life, which the Lutherans accepted only with many reservations.

The Lutherans agreed that the head of the Church is Christ. Therefore, both sides rejected the primacy of the pope and other innovations of the Roman Church. The Patriarch stressed the infallibility of the Church as a whole, as the interpreter of the divine revelation, stating that supreme authority is bestowed to the "conscience of the Church." While the Lutherans accepted the principle, they balked at the Orthodox formulation.

Concerning eschatology, both sides agreed on the second coming of Christ, the last judgment, and divine reward in the future life.

Ceremonies, the *epiklesis* in the Eucharist, the invocation of the saints, icons, relics, fasting, and other customs and traditions received some attention in the first part of the Augsburg Confession (Articles 15,20,21) and especially in the second part on the disputed subjects. In the statement concerning the above-mentioned beliefs, Jeremiah stressed the teaching of the Orthodox Church in substance and the manner of practice. The Lutherans appear to have misinterpreted the Orthodox Church's position as being that of the Roman Church; this resulted in disagreement between the Lutherans and the Orthodox.

## Enumeration of Subjects in Agreement and Disagreement

It seems that both sides, Jeremiah and the theologians, were in agreement, as a whole, on the following: the truth and inspiration of the Scriptures; God, Holy Trinity; ancestors' sin and its transmission to all men; evil as caused by creatures and not God; Christ's two natures in a single person; Jesus Christ as head of the Church; second coming of Christ, last judgment, future life, endless reward, endless punishment; Eucharist, two species, bread and wine (the body and blood) given to the faithful; the rejection of indulgences, the excess of grace from the saints and Christ which an individual can bestow on other Christians; purgatory, and obligatory celibacy of the clergy.

Points of disagreement, as a whole or in part, were the following: Sacred Tradition; the insertion of the *filioque* in the Nicaeo-Constantinopolitan Creed; the free will of man; the question of predestination; justification, in substance and means; sacraments, their substance and number; the propriety of pouring in baptism, chrismation, and the age at which the Eucharist may be taken; the meaning of "change" in the holy Eucharist leavened bread, and the nature of eucharistic sacrifice; the infallibility of the Church and of the Ecumenical Synods; celebration; invocation of saints; icons; relics; fasts, and other ecclesiastical traditions and customs. There are many subjects that were not treated at all. Some subjects were only partially touched on.

## A Renewal of Discussions Is Imperative

This correspondence between the Patriarchate of Constantinople and the theologians of the University of Tübingen should not be accepted as final. Negative factors were: the confusion at that particular time regarding the split of the Christian Church in the West; the barrier of language and lack of personal experience with each other's worship and convictions; the confusion over some terms and definitions; certain political and ecclesiastical circumstances; and, especially, the emphasis upon points of disagreement rather than agreement. There is the opportunity for both parties to reopen again the discussion in the light of today's perspective without the external forces and influences which prevailed at that time between the Patriarch and the Lutheran theologians. A prominent Orthodox theologian, Georges Florovsky, has stated:

> An extensive study of this friendly exchange of convictions between the Eastern Church and the emerging world of the Reformation yields more than matter for historical curiosity. There was an attempt to discover some common ground and to adopt a common idiom...And all controversial points, dividing the East and the non-Roman West, should be analyzed again in the larger perspective of Patristic tradition.[3]

The movement toward unity of the Church of Christ, dating from the turn of the century, is an unprecedented phenomenon. This effort is fostered by an understanding of the destructive scandal of separation within the Church and, especially, by an approach to unity filled with humility by the leaders of the various Christian bodies. Some recent steps that have been taken toward this goal are: the establishment of the World Council of Churches; the merging of some Protestant churches; the creative efforts through dialogue for future mergers; the new attitude of the Roman Catholic Church started by Pope John XXIII and continued by Paul VI, culminating in the Vatican II Council; and the personal meetings of various church leaders, especially the meetings between Ecumenical Patriarch Athenagoras I and Pope Paul VI.

This personal communication between Pope Paul and Patriarch Athenagoras in Jerusalem and their "embracing of peace," which led to the lifting of the anathemas and excommunications by both sides, the visit of Pope Paul with Patriarch Athenagoras in Constantinople and the return visit of Patriarch Athenagoras to the Vatican are the most significant events in recent times. The vision of unity of the Churches has been strengthened by the Patriarchate of Constantinople through its Encyclical Letter of 1920 to all Christian Churches urging the creation of a league of Churches on the basis of sincere fellowship and love. The spirit by Patriarch Athenagoras, who initiated the first step toward unity in practical terms, and his exchanges of brotherly affection with other church leaders, provide preparation for ultimate union and are the lightposts that shine brightly toward the accomplishment of God's will.

The unity of all Christians should be the first and foremost objective and should be fostered by the spiritual insight of Christians. It is in the nature of the Christian Church to be one entity, for it was founded to be one, as its founder and head is one, remaining forever its Lord and Savior. "Oneness" is the life of the Church and is worthy of the Lord's calling for the awakening of Christians to this need for unity. The attainment of this unity of the Church depends upon the attitude of the people "with all lowliness and meekness" and

> with patience, forbearing one another in love, eager to maintain the unity of the spirit in the bond of peace. There is one body and one Spirit, just as you were called to the one hope that belongs to your call, one Lord, one baptism, one God and Father of us all, who is above all and through all and in all (Eph 4:2-6).

## NOTES

*Part One is from a thesis titled: "The Correspondence of the Tübingen Theologians and Jeremiah II on the Augsburg Confession..." by the Reverend George Mastrantonis, presented for the degree of Master of Sacred Theology at Concordia Seminary, St. Louis, Missouri.

1. See Patriarch Photios' encyclical in Ioannes Karmires, Τά δογματικά καί συβολικά μνημεῖα τῆς Ὀρθοδόξου Καθολικῆς Ἐκκλησίας (Athens, 1953), 1, p. 271. This encyclical is the first symbolic book after the decrees of the Ecumenical Synods and the first official protest against the Western Church. Patriarch Photios used the incident of the insertion into the Nicene Creed of the filioque phrase by the Western Church to protest against its interference in the missionary activities of the Eastern Church, especially in Bulgaria, while also touching on theological and philosophical disagreements in reference to the Holy Trinity.

2. The Book of Concord, ed. Theodore G. Tappert (Philadelphia, 1959), p. 311.

3. Georges Florovsky, "An Early Ecumenical Correspondence," p. 110.

# PART TWO

# THE CORRESPONDENCE BETWEEN PATRIARCH JEREMIAH II AND THE TÜBINGEN THEOLOGIANS

*Chapter 1*

## PRELIMINARY CORRESPONDENCE

*[A.] The Letter from the Tübingen Theologians to Patriarch
Jeremiah [II] Accompanying the Augsburg Confession*

To the Most Honorable Lord, the All-Holy Patriarch of the Christian
Church in the City of Constantinople and surrounding area.

Greetings in Our Savior.

[1][1] All-Holy Sir, since it has been evident to me that Your Holiness
has received in a most favorable spirit what I had previously written, I
now take courage for this and dare to address Your Holiness again, hoping to receive the same indulgence. First of all, I am reverently and duly
grateful for this paternal kindness of Your Holiness. Furthermore, I am
sending you a little book that contains the main parts of our entire faith,
so that Your Holiness may see what our religion is, and whether we agree
with the teaching of the churches under the jurisdiction of Your
Holiness; or whether perhaps, there might be something that is not in
agreement (which I would not desire). I earnestly ask Your Holiness to
receive it with the same good favor with which you have accepted my
previous communications and, if it is not too much for your wise person,
to kindly express your most favorable judgment concerning these articles, if God would grant that we think alike in Christ. Farewell, most
Holy Father, together with the entire Church that is with you, for many
years. And look upon my Christ-respecting study with a fatherly disposition.

In Tübingen, the 16th of the month Maimakterion, which we call
September, in the year of salvation 1574.

> James Andreae, Professor of Theology, Provost of
> the Church at Tübingen, Chancellor of the local
> University.
>
> I, also, Martin Crusius, Professor of Latin and
> Greek in this place, have concurred.

*[B.] The Letter from the Tübingen Theologians to Patriarch Jeremiah [II] in Answer to the Patriarch's Letter after Receiving the Augsburg Confession*

To the All-Holy Ecumenical Patriarch, the Lord Jeremiah, Archbishop of Constantinople, New Rome, Most God-Beloved Sir,

Greetings in Christ.

[2] We have received the esteemed letter of Your Holiness, most God-Beloved Sir, at the beginning of the present year. It brought us all the more joy because we had been looking forward to it for a very long time with such eager longing. With all our heart we thank our true God and our Savior Christ, first of all, and then Your Esteemed Holiness. We thank the former because He has ordered matters in such a fatherly manner; and we thank Your Holiness because you have been, and continue to be, kindly disposed toward us. For, indeed, neither is the benevolence at all small, or is it a small honor that Your Holiness, with so exalted a degree of dignity, should have thought us, whose station is so much below that of Your Holiness, worthy of a reply. And what a reply it was! A wise and, indeed, a most pious one; one that has to do with the Good Shepherd and with the kingdom of heaven; paternal and one profoundly concerned about our salvation. Concerned, that is, that we always persevere without innovating and without cropping, in sound faith and in the salvific commandments, that which the Chief Shepherd, Christ, commanded through His inspired servants and thereafter attain the kingdom of heaven. Thus, wisely and so kindly has Your Holiness been disposed toward us. Let Your Holiness be assured that nothing more concerns us more than this. It is true that the highpriest of Rome accuses us of innovation because fifty years ago we here, and many others elsewhere in Germany, were more thoroughly instructed by Martin Luther, a divinely illumined man, who was distinguished by his zeal for the truth. As a result, they gave up the dogmas and traditions of the [3] Roman highpriest that were contradictory to the Holy Scriptures. Forty-four years ago our most pious princes and our theologians compiled a summary of the ancient faith that had come down to us from paradise. And they presented it to the Emperor Charles V, of blessed memory, who at the time was holding a synod at Augsburg (for this reason this summary is called the Augsburg Confession). Thus, they gave an account of their own orthodoxy, which we continue to hold to the present time. This celebrated confession of our blessed forebearers to which, through these many years up to the present, there have been thousands of witnesses and which we sent Your Holiness about five months before the arrival of your long awaited present letter. Although we might, perhaps, differ in some customs because very great geographical distances separate us, we, on our part, had hoped that we were in no way in-

novating on the main articles concerning salvation, since (as far as we know) we held and had kept the faith which had been handed down to us by the Holy Apostles and Prophets, by the God-bearing Fathers and Patriarchs, and by the seven Ecumenical Synods that were founded upon the God-given Scriptures. For that reason we did not regard it as necessary at the present time to burden Your Holiness with anything additional, especially because Your Holiness is busily shepherding the faithful of your own churches and is vigilantly solicitous about everything that promotes their salvation. However, we await your most wise and most pious judgment and reply with reference to the Confession which we have sent. And in all reverence and humility we ask Your Holiness with the paternal disposition of your soul to let this be effected at the opportune time (however, we do not wish to pressure Your Holiness). If the merciful Heavenly Father, through His beloved Son, the sole Savior of us all, would so direct us on both sides so that even though we are greatly separated as far as the places where we live are concerned, we become close to one another in our agreement on the correct teaching and the cities of Constantine and Tü-
[4] bingen become bound to each other by the bond of the same Christian faith and love, there is no event that we should desire more. Indeed, we intend, with God's help, by all means, to keep no other foundation of the faith (as Your Holiness most benevolently prays) than that which is laid [cf. 1 Cor 3:11], which is the immovable cornerstone, Christ [cf. Eph 2:20], i.e., the truth itself, without innovation and without subtraction. Farewell, most Holy Sir, together with your most august presbytery. May you successfully provide for your Christ-named flock for a long time to come. Count us worthy of your indulgence and receive us kindly into your paternal care.

Tübingen, the twentieth of the month of March, in the year of salvation, 1575.

> James Andreae, Professor of Theology, Provost of the Church at Tübingen, and the Chancellor of the local University.

> Martin Crusius, Professor of Latin and Greek Education at Tübingen.

## NOTES

1. The numbers enclosed in brackets in the left hand margin of the text correspond to the page numbers of the original text of the *Acta et Scripta*.

*Chapter 2*

# THE FIRST THEOLOGICAL EXCHANGE:

# CONSTANTINOPLE TO TÜBINGEN

*[A.] The Letter from Patriarch Jeremiah [II] of Constantinople Accompanying the First Answer to the Tübingen Theologians*

Jeremiah, by the grace of God, Archbishop of Constantinople, New Rome, and Ecumenical Patriarch to the wise and most learned men, the professors of Theology, Master Jacob the Chancellor and Master Martin Crucius. May you fare well.

[54]¹ Behold, with [the grace of] God, dear wise German men and spiritual sons of my humble self, the long awaited letters from us, which from the depths of your hearts you requested of us, have been completed and are sent to you with love and with commensurate spiritual joy and with the cheerfulness of a father to his children. We pray that God and His most blessed Mother will gladden you as much as for a two-fold person. And if it happens that in some doctrines of your piety you are not at first sight gladdened, we are, however, positive that being wise, well-educated, and prudent, nothing more would you prefer. That is [to say], neither innovating legislation, that would be in opposition to the evangelical philosophy of our Lord; nor time, which abused the doctrines in a different manner; nor illogical custom (all of us, being human, harbor unsafe suspicions according to the wise Solomon) of this truth, or rather of this very truth and this very philosophy of our Lord Jesus Christ with which His Divine Disciples and Apostles and their canonical and saving words, and with which the Ecumenical and local Synods of the Holy Fathers, and the theologically [oriented] preachers of the Church, manifestly agree, that salvation and the kingdom of heaven are attained by those who obey these writings. Just as eternal damnation and blame are for those who deny and transgress them . If, therefore, you desire and obey me (says the Lord), you shall eat of the goods of the earth. In like manner, my humble self, as the heir of Christ, by His mercy, exhort your love. Would that you might be of like mind with our Church of Christ, so that if truly and with all your hearts you do [good]

works, great joy will be in heaven and on earth, for the unity of each
others church, which we hope will be for the glory of Christ.

Jeremiah
Month of May, 4th Indiction.

### [B.] The First Answer of Patriarch Jeremiah [II] of Constantinople Concerning the Augsburg Confession Sent to Tübingen [May 15] 1576

[56][2] We received the letters which your love sent us and the booklet
which contains the articles of your faith. We accept your love, and in
compliance with your request we shall endeavor to clear the issues in
which we agree and those in which we disagree. The expression of love is
the fulfillment of the Law and Prophets [cf. Rom 13:10].[3] Indeed, it is
fulfilled, we may say, not only by mere words, but proven by the very
facts themselves and by deeds. Even as the most precious stones that
need no words of praise, yet they are looked upon with admiration
because of their own intrinsic worth by those who know their value. You
have displayed such a love, most wise German men, bereft of pride in
those matters which you have communicated to us.

In responding, then, we shall say nothing originating of ourselves, but
(what is pertinent) from the holy seven Ecumenical Synods with which,
as you write, you acquiesce and you accept. We shall further speak in accordance with the opinion of the divine teachers and exegetes of the
divinely inspired Scripture, whom the catholic Church of Christ has
received in common accord, for their words and miracles illuminated the
universe like another sun [cf. Mt 13:43]. Because the Holy Spirit
breathed on them and spoke through them. Indeed, their statements shall
remain unshaken forever because they are founded on the Word of the
Lord.

The Church of Christ, according to Saint Paul, is the "pillar and
bulwark of the truth" [1 Tim 3:15]. And according to the divine promise
of the Lord, the gates of Hades "shall not prevail against it"
[57] [Mt 16:18]. And although some are carried away by portentous
thoughts, nevertheless, this Church stands secure and steadfast, solidly
supported on the rock and on those other teachings on which the truth
has been established [cf. Eph 2:20]. For those who are of the Church of
Christ, are wholly of the truth; but those who are not wholly of the truth,
are also not of the Church of Christ. Therefore, we follow in the path of

truth and offer the sound word for the upbuilding of the true faith. And with this we beseech the prayers of those who love the Lord, so that our mind may be guided by His divine grace in the path of peace [cf. Lk 1:79].

## 1. [God]

So then we affirm that your first article, which cites the dogmatic definitions, or sacred symbol, of the holy Synod of Nicaea [c.325], concerning the one exceedingly holy essence and the three persons of the Godhead, is correct and has been piously proclaimed by you. However, this Synod of Nicaea and the others which agree with it declared that the Holy Spirit proceeds from the Father. The confession of the sound faith of Christians, this most sacred symbol (which was first drawn up by the 318 God-bearing Holy Fathers at Nicaea, and completed by the 150 Fathers in Constantinople, and ratified by the other five Ecumenical Synods, without adding or omitting anything, inasmuch as they agreed with it, as the holy men who blazed forth during the years between those holy Synods, and distinctly confessed, and as we by the grace of God confess with them), most clearly reveals that the Holy Spirit proceeds from the Father. This excellent confession reads as follows:

> I believe in one God, the Father Almighty, Maker of heaven and earth and of all things visible and invisible. And in one Lord Jesus Christ, the only-begotten Son of God, begotten of the Father before all ages, Light of Light, very God of very God [58], begotten not made, of one essence with the Father; through whom all things were made, who for us men and for our salvation came down from heaven, and was incarnate by the Holy Spirit and of the Virgin Mary, and became man. And was crucified also for us under Pontius Pilate. He suffered and was buried. And the third day He rose again according to the Scriptures. And ascended into heaven, and sits at the right hand of the Father. And He shall come again with the glory to judge the living and the dead; whose kingdom shall have no end. And in the Holy Spirit, the Lord, the giver of life, who proceeds from the Father, who with the Father and the Son together is worshipped and glorified, who spoke by the Prophets. In one holy, catholic and apostolic Church. I acknowledge one baptism for the remission of sins. I look for the resurrection of the dead; and the life of the ages to come. Amen.

This is the treasure of the true faith, which was sealed by the Holy Spirit, so that no one would omit anything nor introduce into it anything spurious. This divine, most sacred, and wholly perfect credo of our piety, the confession of all the Holy Fathers, the definition of Christianity, which we embrace and espouse, we boldly profess to preserve, unscathed and unadulterated to the end of time as the holy deposit [of faith] of the divinely inspired Holy Fathers. Thus, through the intercessions of those who formulated this [creed] and preserved it, we may offer up our sound profession of faith as a pure gift to the Trinity, so that we may be delivered from ever-lasting punishment, and we may enjoy the divine kingdom, which is eternal in Christ, which we hope to receive through the grace of Christ. Amen.

### 3.⁴ [Articles of Faith]

And now, coming to your third article concerning the articles of faith, we say the following: that the true and only divine faith of Christians, which is beyond mind and reason, the only existing true confession of the Triune God, which is contained in systematic form in these articles, is that which he who believes correctly must confess if he wishes to be saved.

[59] These articles, which are also called articles of faith because they are principles and foundations [of faith], are twelve in number, retaining the pattern of the twelve Holy Apostles of Christ. Thus, three of them deal with the blessed Trinity, six deal with the Incarnation of the Son and Logos, and three deal with the consummation [of the world].

The first of these articles [states]: that the Deity is by nature one, and not many, and also one in efficacy and rule and omnipotence and lordship.

Second, that this Deity is three, and not one person, even though it is one and undivided in the Godhead. The first [person] is unbegotten, the second [person] begotten and the third [person] proceeds. They are called and said to be by the theologians: Father, Son, and Spirit.

Third, that this Trinity is the creator of all things, who brought them forth out of nothingness and placed them in time, the intelligible and sensible, the visible and invisible.

Fourth, that through the providence of the Triune God, the good will of the Father and the synergism of the Spirit, the Logos, who remained unaltered and unchanged in divinity without suffering and not subject to corruption or change, became flesh for us by receiving the perfect human nature in one person.

Fifth, that He was born of a virgin, who had not known man, and who was preserved as a virgin by Him before His birth, during His birth, and after His birth.

Sixth, that He suffered in the flesh (human nature) for us and was crucified and died voluntarily, but not with respect to His divine nature, which is immune to suffering.

Seventh, that He did rise on the third day, by His own power, and appeared many times to His disciples.

Eighth, that on the fortieth day after His resurrection He ascended into heaven while the disciples were looking on, and He sat at the right of [60] the Father proving that His inseparable and deified body is glorified and worshipped with Him [the Father].

Ninth, that He will return again to earth from heaven in the glory of the Father, and He will grant His kingdom to His servants; and the impious He will condemn to suffering.

Tenth, He will resurrect our whole nature, uniting the souls with the pristine bodies in which they lived at one time for just retribution according to how they lived their lives, and they shall be immortal [cf. Eph 4:13].

[Eleventh], that He will judge the living and the dead. And He will punish the unfaithful ones, but He will glorify the pious and those who have lived according to the divine law.

[Twelfth], that the life hereafter will be eternal because nature will become incorruptible.

Thus, in these articles the following are included: In the first [article], that the Father together with the Son and the Spirit are one God and one Lord. For this article calls the Father, God; the Son, God of God; and the Holy Spirit, Lord. It says that the Trinity is of the same essence (ὁμοούσιον)[5]; that the Father, the Son, and the Spirit are glorified together. At the same time the Prophets declared that God [the Father], together with the Logos and the Spirit, are eternal, omnipotent, and Creator; while the angels sing of the one God in three consecrations [thrice-holy hymn].

In the second [article], that this, the only God, is a Trinity of persons and one in divinity: Father, Son, and Holy Spirit. That is, the Father is unbegotten and without cause, for He alone is the cause of those who are of Him. The Son, on the other hand, is begotten, God of God; while the Holy Spirit is Lord, the giver of life, who proceeds from the Father. And it further declares that this Trinity has, from time before all ages, one nature and glory and one power and worship. For the Holy Spirit is worshipped and glorified together with the Father and the Son.

[61] In the third [article] it is taught that the Trinity is the Creator, making all things out of nothingness. For that reason it declares the Father as maker of heaven and earth and all things; the Son, through whom all things were made; and the Spirit as the giver of life.

In the fourth [article] the details concerning the Incarnation proclaimed that the Logos was incarnate of the Holy Spirit and Mary the Theotokos [Mother of God].

In the fifth [article], that Mary remained the Ever-Virgin from whom the Logos took a living body, having a soul that is rational and a capacity for will (θελητική).[6] Being one, He became double for us, one consisting of two perfect natures.

In the sixth [article], that [the Logos] was crucified in the flesh for us, He suffered and was buried; that He rose and ascended and will come again from heaven to judge the living and the dead. And in the other six articles are included: that there will be a resurrection and punishment, and an everlasting kingdom [for all the living and the dead].

These articles or chapters which are included in the sacred symbol [creed] appear, in theory, to be the true philosophy according to Christ. But in practice they are the higher ethic which teaches us and leads us to salvation. For they state that our Lord came down for our salvation, so that we might emulate His life and be saved. He suffered and died for us. He rose again to give us hope. His coming in the future to judge the living and the dead prompts us to expectation and preparation. His promise of life eternal prompts us to hope to attain it, and to fear the punishment. Through these the three expressions of souls are cleansed: the power of reasoning by the pious confession of [faith in] the Holy Trinity, the spirited element by recalling the Incarnation, and the appetitive element by proclaiming the Resurrection. As we earnestly long for these things, let us speedily conduct our lives according to the commandment.

Just as the all-embracing virtues are seven in number: humility, modesty, poverty, fasting, chastity, patience, and forbearance, so also the opposite [vices] are seven in number: pride, ambition, greed, [62] gluttony, fornication, sloth, and anger. The most sacred symbol dissuades from the vices and urges one on to the virtues. Humility is aroused by the descent of God, the Logos, from the heavens; modesty, by the Incarnation; poverty, fasting, and purity, in that He was like that; patience and forbearance because He had all these, and finally endured the cross and death. The Savior abolished every iniquity. By humility, He abolished pride from which comes unbelief and blasphemy against God. By lowliness, He abolished ambition from which are engendered madness, envy and murder. By poverty, He abolished greed from which come stealing, deceit, lying, and treachery against God and fellowmen. By fasting, He abolished gluttony, the source of drunkenness, prodigality, disorder, and every evil passion. By virginity, He abolished fornication, the source of every defilement and departure from the holy God. By patience, He abolished sloth and meanness of spirit, the source of hopelessness, ingratitude, confusion of mind, and despair of soul. And finally, by forbearance, He destroyed anger and demonic madness against His fellowmen, the source of fury, wrath, hostility, hate, and murder, which refute the highest and chief virtues of hope, faith, and love. These three are in honor of the Trinity and completely unite the person who has them with the Triune God, and through grace they constitute God. Therefore, brethren, let us also cleanse our mind with the correct faith; and having purified ourselves by the virtues, primarily the general ones of courage, temperance, justice, and prudence, which also encompass the rest, let us become as far as possible impervious to evil. Let us live wholly according to Christ, conducting ourselves in the true faith in Christ and His life. Let us love Christ and fulfill His command- [63] ments. Let us become temples of Christ, a sweet-smelling savor, and His holy ones, so that we may attain eternal life and glory and the kingdom of Christ eternally through His grace, and not only by our works of righteousness, but according to His unfailing promise.

### [2. Original Sin]

Your second article contains the assertion that every man is guilty of original sin. We also affirm that this is, indeed, the truth. The psalmist says in the 50th Psalm [50:5]: "Behold, I was brought forth in iniquity, and in sin did my mother conceive me." And the Lord says in the Gospels concerning the purging away of such original sin: "Unless one is born of water and the Spirit, he cannot enter into the kingdom of heaven" [Jn 3:5].

However, in connection with that rebirth by holy baptism, which is included in the confession of the symbol that says, "I acknowledge one baptism for the remission of sins," we, on our part, are baptized by a triple immersion. The Latins, on the other hand, do not act correctly by baptizing with one immersion. For it is imperative to proclaim the three hypostases in the one Godhead, and by three immersions and emersions, pronounce aloud the [name of the] Father, and the Son, and the Holy Spirit, according to the ancient custom which has been handed down by the Church. At the same time, the three immersions and [the three] emersions signify the three-day burial and resurrection of the Lord who was crucified for us in the flesh and rose again.

One should immediately anoint with myrrh [oil of chrismation] the one who has been baptized. For this chrism is the seal and the mark of Christ. We receive grace from it. By virtue of the chrismation, we are called Christians and are the anointed ones of the Lord. For the Lord does not deem us unworthy to be named after Him because by grace He calls us sons of God and gods. And when the priest anoints the one baptized, he says: "The seal of the gift of the Holy Spirit, Amen." Therefore, it is reasonable that chrismation follows baptism and is not postponed for a time. It also follows, therefore, that the one baptized should be [64] given the Communion. For that is the end purpose of the entire mystery, that having been freed of error and the filth of sin, and having been cleansed anew and sealed by the holy myrrh, we may communion His body and His blood, and are united completely with Him. Then Christ will dwell in us, walk among us and be with us forever.

### [4. Justification]

The fourth [article] concerns the remission of sins. You contend that, as you believe, the remission of sins is granted mainly by faith alone. But the Church demands a living faith, which is made evident by good works; for as Paul says, faith without works is dead [Jas 2:17]. Furthermore, Basil the Great says:

The grace from above does not come to the one who is not striving. But both of them, the human endeavor and the assistance descending from above through faith, must be mixed together for the perfection of virtue...[7] Therefore, the authority of forgiveness has not been given unconditionally, but only if the repentant one is obedient and in harmony with what pertains to the care of his soul. It is written concerning these things: 'If two of you agree on earth about anything they ask, it will be done for them by my Father in heaven' [Mt 18:19]. One cannot ask about which sins this refers to, as if the New Testament has not declared any difference, for it promises absolution of every sin to those who have repented worthily.[8] He repents worthily who has adopted the intention of the one who said, 'I hate and abhor unrighteousness' [Ps 119:163], and who does those things which are said in the 6th Psalm and in others concerning works, and like Zacchaios does many virtuous deeds.[9]

In every respect, let us commend ourselves to God, [that we be] kept pure by Him in [our] works. Let us hold fast to the confession. The great High Priest demands these things from us. Let us believe that there is a resurrection, that there is retribution, that there are myriads of good things, that Christ is God, that the faith is correct. Let us confess these things. Let us hold fast to these things. Let us show our faith by works. [65] He does not ignore our deeds. Therefore, we should do good works according to our ability, and not plead the excuse of human weakness. For our High Priest first has undergone these things before us, and, therefore, He is well able to sympathize with us. If then, we have sinned in some thing, let us approach the Sinless One through sincere repentance and confession, and let us demonstrate complete abstinence from evil things. Let us openly come to repentance in order to receive mercy and anything else we ask. There is no sin which has overcome God's love for mankind. If we approach properly, the matter is one of divine honor, (and we shall receive) the royal gift. But when the consummation (of the world) takes place, then He shall rise to judge. Let us, therefore, approach repentance and the merciful Jesus with all openness, without an evil conscience, without any doubt at all. For he who doubts cannot approach with openness. Therefore, the Scriptures say: "In an acceptable time have I heard you, and in a day of salvation I have helped you" [Is 49:8]. But now, when we sin after baptism and find repentance, let us control our passions and attack them by repentance, and confession. Let us become kings greater than those who have the royal robe. Let us conquer our passions like bodyguards. There is no excuse at all for those who remain in sin, as it is written in many passages of the Holy Scriptures.

### [5. The Office of the Ministry]

The fifth is similar to the fourth [article], which concerns repentance and forgiveness of sins: that one is saved not because of any satisfactions, but only by faith and grace. The Church catholic perceives it in this manner: man receives remission of his sins when through true repentance he returns to God and has a living faith, which is displayed through good works, that is, as we said above and will never cease to say. For the Lord says: "Not every one who says to me, 'Lord, Lord,' shall enter the king-[66] dom of heaven, but he who does the will of my Father" [Mt 7:21]. And again: "For it is not the hearers of the law who are righteous before God, but the doers of the law will be justified" [Rom 2:13]. And again: "You are my friends if you do what I command you" [Jn 15:14]. As also Basil the Great, writing on the same subject, says:

> Let us be mindful of the kingdom of heaven. Our Lord Jesus Christ, when He ascended the mountain and started His teaching, said, 'Blessed are the poor in spirit' [Mt 5:3], and the rest of the beatitudes. And again at the time of retribution, in the parable of the shepherd, He says 'Come, O blessed of my Father' [Mt 25:34], and the following. And again: 'Sell your possessions, and give alms; provide yourselves with purses that do not grow old, with a treasure in the heavens' [Lk 12:33].[10]

Through these and similar acts one becomes worthy of the kingdom of heaven, and without them it is impossbile to enter the kingdom. In the Gospel according to Matthew, the Lord declares: "Unless your righteousness exceeds that of the Scribes and Pharisees, you will never enter the kingdom of heaven" [5:20]. And again: "Unless you turn and become like little children, you will never enter the kingdom of heaven" [Mt 18:3]. Also, in the Gospel according to John He says to Nikodemos: "Unless one is born anew, he cannot see the kingdom of God" [Jn 3:3], nor: "Unless one is born of water and the Spirit" [Jn 3:5]. According to all these there is only one verdict; the danger is the same in each case if a single condition is omitted. For if He says, "Not an iota, not a dot, will pass from the law until all is accomplished" [Mt 5:18], how much more is this true of the Gospel? The Lord himself says: "Heaven and earth will pass away, but my words shall not pass away" [Mt 24:35]. For that reason James also said: "Whoever keeps the whole law but fails in one point has become guilty of all of it" [2:10]. He learned to say it from that which the Lord threatened after [His] blessings and promises to Peter: "If I do not wash you, you have no part in me" [Jn 13:8]. Paul, speaking

[67] in Christ, testifies concerning those things because of which, indeed, one is deemed unworthy of the kingdom of heaven and comes under the judgment of death. At one time he definitely says, "those who do such things deserve to die" [Rom 1:32], and at another time, "the unrighteous will not inherit the kingdom of God" [1 Cor 6:9]. And the Lord says: "No one who puts his hand to the plow and looks back is fit for the kingdom of God" [Lk 9:62].

From these, then, and similar texts we are taught that those to whom the promise of the kingdom of heaven is proclaimed must fulfill all things perfectly and legitimately, and without them it shall be denied. However, whoever has kept these the commandments should expect to be deemed worthy of the promise. It is necessary that, in the struggle to be pleasing to God, one should not only be free from every evil, but also be unblemished and blameless in every word of God. For Paul, after contemplating the great and indescribable love of God and also of Christ himself for us, teaches: "We put no obstacle in anyone's way, so that no fault be found with our ministry" [2 Cor 6:3]. But in all things let us present ourselves as servants of God. For it is written: "That he might present the church to himself in splendor, without spot or wrinkle or any such thing, that she might be holy and without blemish" [Eph 5:27]. And the diligent student will find many more such references. As Paul when he teaches: "But thanks be to God, that you who were once slaves of sin have become obedient from the heart to the standard of teaching" [Rom 6:17]. So that just as the wax poured on the seal takes the exact shape of the form of the seal, so we, also, surrendering ourselves to the pattern of the teaching according to the Gospel, will be shaped according to the inner man, fulfilling that which is said by him [Paul]: "You have put off the old nature with its practices and have put on the new nature which is being renewed in knowledge after the image of its creator" [Col 3:9-10]. "As Christ was raised from the dead, we, too, might walk in newness of life" [Rom 6:46] so that, grace having anticipated us, we may contribute those things which we should, that in this way the purpose of God may [68] be made perfect in us. There is need for a struggle, and this struggle must be great and lawful so that we may not accept such a great grace of the love of God through Christ in vain.

We pray for help from above so that we may be led to virtue. Having walked this path, we need the divine influence. One ought not have confidence at all in our own righteousness, which in itself is worthless and incomplete, but we should trust in the divine righteousness and assistance in order to be led unerringly to heaven. The present life is a road which needs leading by the hand from above. When we wish to enter a city, we have need of someone who will show us the way. How much more, then, for our pilgrimage into heaven, do we need the guidance from above to show us the way, to support us, and to lead us by the hand! There are many narrow paths which lead us astray, and for this reason we grasp the right hand of God. The leading is God's work, but to be worthy to be held by His hand depends on our zealous effort. If we are unclean, that hand will not hold us. Good works and purity are necessary in order to acquire divine help.

But the divine Chrysostom, interpreting [a passage in] the Second Epistle to the Corinthians, "Working together with him, then, we entreat you not to accept the grace of God in vain" [2 Cor 6:1] says:

> The love of God constrains us, that is, presses hard on us, drives us, urges us... Thus, let us not lose the opportunity, but let us display a zeal worthy of grace. Let us not reject the gift... For reconciliation is not only believing, but also one must in earnest demonstrate a righteous life and strive after it. The one who had been freed from sins and became a friend [of God] but now wallows again in the former manner of life, is again returning to enmity and receives grace in vain. We reap no benefit from grace when we live impurely. But rather, we harm ourselves all the more; for in spite of such knowledge and such a gift, we return to our former vices. Therefore, as long as we are yet in the struggle, as long as we are working in the [69] vineyard, as long as the eleventh hour yet continues, let us draw nigh and exhibit a correct and virtuous life so that we may enjoy the everlasting benefits. If when we were laden with so many evils He received and freed us, shall He not all the more accept us when we have been delivered from all these evils and are carrying out our part?[11]

If we live in sin, sin will give birth to unbelief. Just as unbelief breeds an evil life, so the soul, when it has come to the abyss of evils, becomes disdainful; and having become disdainful, it does not tolerate belief. For it has been said: "The Lord shall not see, neither shall the God of Jacob understand" [Ps 93:7]. And again: "Our lips are our own; who is Lord over us?" [Ps 11:4]. And again: "the fool has said in his heart, 'There is no God' " [Ps 13:1]. And the Lord said: "For every one who does evil hates the light, and does not come to the light" [Jn 3:20]. As long as the time of the gift [of grace] continues, let no one despair. The time for despair shall be when the bridal chamber is closed, when those who will be worthy are received into the bosom of the Patriarch and shall enjoy the good things to come. But the time is not yet. The arena is still assembled; the contest is still imminent and the rewards are still held in abeyance. Let us pursue this further. One must run and run hard. Let us strive for perfection. Let us acquire an excellent life with true faith and have a correct life according to the commandment. If one has faith but does evil, he disgraces the teaching and evidently is childish.

One must not always dwell on the basic elements, nor merely lay a foundation, but one must also complete the rest of the building and even the roof [which is] the perfecting of good deeds. If one forever dwells on the basic elements, or about the foundation, there will be nothing more for him to do, neither will he complete the house, nor hold fast the foundation of wisdom, nor become wise. If, then, we love Christ as we ought to love Him, we will grow in virtue and will punish ourselves when we sin. We will not fear hell, but we will fear offending God who, when becoming angry, turns away. This latter is worse than the former. And so that you may know how much worse it is, consider the following. One [70] might see a bandit or criminal being punished, and the king himself give his beloved, only-begotten, and legitimate son, who was not like that, to be put to death, transferring the guilt from the wicked man to the son in order to save the condemned criminal and rid him from an evil reputation. If, then, after these things the son were raised up to great authority after he had saved [the offender], and then he was insulted in his unspeakable glory by the one on whose behalf he had been punished, would not the latter prefer to die a thousand deaths, if he had any intelligence, rather than to appear to be responsible for such great ingratitude? Let us now think about this and groan bitterly for those things [by which] we have provoked [our] Benefactor. Because He bears the insult with long-suffering, we should not be falsely confident; but, on the contrary, we should feel ourselves seriously wounded on that account.

It has happened among men that when someone who has been wounded on his right cheek and turns his left as well, he defends himself much better than if he were to retaliate ten thousand times over [cf. Mt 5:39]. Also, when one has been abused not only should he not abuse in return, but he should bless; for in this manner he has wounded [his abusers] more severely than if he were to rid them of the guilt by reproaching them ten thousand times. And if when we abuse human beings we are put to shame because we yet enjoy their forbearance, I fear that we should be much more ashamed when we continuously sin against God and yet nothing serious happens to us. For unspeakable punishment has been stored up over their head for evil. If we understand these things, let us, by all means, fear sin. This, indeed, is hell; this is *gehenna;* this is the ten thousand evils. We must not only be afraid, but we must flee from it and continuously endeavor to be pleasing to God. This truly is the kingdom; this is life; this is the ten thousand good things. And, thus, thenceforth we shall attain the kingdom and the good things to come, of which, may it be, all will receive by the grace and mercy of God.

Even though God implores and wills that all may be saved, we also beseech that we be reconciled with God. Let us not fall back to the same sins, but let us be forthright, lest it be said that we receive grace in vain. [71] Should we be idle because God has sent ambassadors? Should we not rather for this particular reason be anxious to please God and to acquire spiritual gain? Even if salvation is by grace, yet man himself, through whose achievements and the sweat of his brow attracts the grace of God, is also the cause. If one were to say, according to what has been said, that it seems that in the spiritual grace no offense was given, he would not miss the meaning. For those who have received the gift of tongues and have become arrogant [as a result] have been severely blamed. This also happens to one who has received a spiritual talent but has not used it in the proper manner. Let us become blameless in gifts, in toils, in time of vigilance, in times of fasting, and by purity [cf. 2 Cor 6:6]. And so long as we are still around, let us practice spiritual things by using our time on this earth in fear, living well and godly according to the commandment, in sincere love, in the word of truth and in the power of God. Let us commit all that is ours to God, taking into account all His beneficences.

## [6. The New Obedience]

The sixth [article] gives the assurance that it is necessary to do good works but not to be dependent on them according to the passage: "Enter not into judgment with thy servant" [Ps 143:2]. With regard to this we say that faith precedes, and then the works follow and are necessary according to the commandment of God. The one who fulfills them, as he must, receives reward and honor in everlasting life. Indeed, good works are not separate from, but necessary for, true faith. One should not trust in works nor be boastful in a Pharisaic manner. And even if we have fulfilled everything, according to the word of the Lord, "we are unworthy servants" [Lk 17:10]. All things should be referred to the righteousness of God because those things which have been offered by us are small or nothing at all. According to Chrysostom, it has been established that God does not lead those of us who are idle into His kingdom. The Lord "opposes the proud, but he gives grace to the humble" [1 Pet 5:5; see Jas 4:6; Pr 3:24]. One should not boast about works. But to do and fulfill them is most necessary. For without divine works it is impossible to be saved. If, then, we will be convinced by the Lord who says, "If you know these things, blessed are you if you do them" [Jn 13:17], it shall be to our benefit.

[72] It is necessary to join our good works together with the mercy from above. If we excuse ourselves because of our weakness or the goodness of God and do not add something of our own, there will be no benefit to us. How can we invoke mercy for the cure of our iniquities if in no way have we done anything to appease the Divine One? Let us hear how Chrysostom explained [the words of] Psalm 129, "Out of the depths I cry to thee, O Lord. Lord, hear my voice" [1-2]:

'From this we learn two things: that one cannot simply expect something from God if nothing from us is forthcoming,' because first it says, 'I cry,' and then follows, 'hear my voice.' Furthermore, lengthy prayer, full of tears, has more power to convince God to harken to that which has been asked. But so no one may say that, since he is a sinner and full of thousands of evils, 'I cannot come before and pray, and call upon God, 'He takes away all doubt by saying: 'If thou, O Lord, shouldst mark iniquities, Lord, who could stand?' [Ps 129:3]. Here the word 'who' should be replaced by the word 'no one,' because there is no one, no one who, according to a strict account of his works, could ever attain mercy and benevolence. If you withdraw mercy and God justly imposes the penalty of the sentence and metes out punishments for sins, who will be able to bear the judgment? Of necessity all would have to submit to destruction. And we say these things not to draw down souls into carelessness, but rather to console those who have fallen into despair. Because who can boast that he has a pure heart? Or who can proclaim that he is free from sins? And what can I say of others? For if I bring Saint Paul into our midst and wish to ask of him to give an accurate acount of what happened [in his case], he cannot hold his ground. For what can he say? He read the Prophets. He was a zealot with regard to the strictness of the law of the forefathers. He saw signs. Nevertheless, he had not yet ascended to that awesome sight which he enjoyed, nor had he heard that awesome voice. Before that he was, in all things, confused.

Furthermore, was not Peter, the chief [Apostle], who after thousands of miracles and such, reproved in council for his grievous fall? [73] If, then, He shall not judge by mercy and compassion but will pronounce an accurate judgment, then [the Lord] will find all of us guilty. Therefore, the Apostle Paul said: 'I am not aware of anything against myself, but I am not thereby acquitted. It is the Lord who judges me' [1 Cor 4:4]. And the Prophet said: 'If thou, O Lord, shouldst mark iniquities, Lord, who could stand?' [Ps 129:3]. And the doubling [of the word Lord,] is not simply said, but [the Prophet] was amazed at, and surprised by, the greatness of God's mercy, His boundless majesty, and the fathomless sea of His goodness. He knew, and knew clearly, that we are responsible to God for many debts, and that even the smallest of sins are deserving of great punishment. 'For with thee is forgiveness' [Ps 129:3]. This means that escape from eternal punishment does not depend on our achievements but on Thy goodness... If we do not enjoy Thy mercy, our achievements alone do not suffice to snatch us from the future wrath. But now You have mercy and justice united together, and You prefer to use the former rather than the latter. And the Lord has plainly said this through the Prophet: I am He who blots out your transgressions' [Is 43:25], that is, this is of me, it is of my goodness because those things which are yours, even though they are good, will never be sufficient to free you from punishment if the work of my mercy were not added. And [the Lord] also [said]: 'I will carry you' [Is 46:4]. Indeed atonement rightfully belongs to God, He who is truly merciful. Therefore, He examines sparingly. 'For Thy name's sake I have waited for Thee, O Lord' [Ps 129:5]. Because of Thy name, which is merciful, I have waited for salvation. When I was looking to matters of myself, I would again despair as in former times; but now, attending to Thy law and fulfilling Thy words, I have high expectations. Thou are He who said, 'as the heaven is distant from the earth' [Is 55:9], 'so my counsels are not as your counsels, nor are my ways as your ways' [Is 55:8]. And again: 'As the heaven is high above the earth, so the Lord has increased His mercy toward those who fear Him' [Ps 102:11]; that is, not only have I [God] saved those who accomplish [good] things, but I also have spared the sinners, and amid your iniquities I have demonstrated my guardianship.

In Ezekiel He says: 'I do not do this, except for the sake of my holy name, which you have profaned among the nations' [Ezek 36:22]. [This passage] says that we are not worthy to be saved, nor did we have any hope because of what we had done, but we look forward to [74] being saved for His name's sake. This is the hope of salvation and the sacred anchor which has been left for us, who repent in order to be granted His mercy. If we are obedient, we shall eat the good of the land [cf. Is 1:19] and we shall inherit the promise. It is necessary, therefore, to hope in God, even if myriads oppress us and drive us to despair and threaten [us with] death. For Him all things are easy; and for the impossible, He can find a way. For with Him is the fountain of redemption, the sea of salvation, the treasure of mercy which springs up eternally [see Ps 36:9-10; Mt 18:21f]. Where there is mercy, there also is redemption, and not only a little, but much, for the sea of mercy knows no bounds. If, then, we are bound up by our sins, it is not necessary to fall again, nor to be despondent. For wherever there is mercy and charity, there is no strict reckoning of iniquities by the one who judges. Because of His great mercy and inclination toward charity, many sins are overlooked. Being such a judge, God grants mercy without ceasing and grants pardon; He is compassionate and loves mankind and imparts salvation to all who have repented and who, according to their ability, perform the good. For truly He is good and abundantly pours forth everywhere the greatness of His mercy, and from Him is that which is truly mercy; it is very clear that He will save His own people, not punish them. Let us then offer those things we have done with all exactitude and wisdom, and let us cherish everything that is from Him, who possesses untold mercy.[12]

Wisdom comes first [to indicate] that a praiseworthy life is one that is cleansed by God rather than one that is deposed. The persons who are without remorse, walking in sin, inclining toward the baser things and are gluttonous, wallowing in the slime, never look to heaven, do not wish to be pitied; for they do not realize how greviously they suffer. It is better for someone to be polluted with unclean mud than with sins. Those who have fallen in the pit of sin will perish utterly unless they cleanse their [75] defilement not with water, but with great toil and time and sincere repentance, with tears, with wailings, and with the customary spiritual cleansing. These are the true satisfactions, and not those made through bribes, which arouse the anger of God against those who take them. And, thus, they are subject to myriads of evil things; and every misfortune sent by God comes to them. There is no forgiveness of sins possible for such persons because zeal is directed toward their own personal gain. External filth can be dusted off very rapidly, but that which is carried around within is not readily washed away. "For out of the heart come evil thoughts, fornication, adultery," [Mt 15:19] and the like. For this reason the Prophet also said: "Create in me a clean heart, O God" [Ps 50:10]. And another: "Cleanse your heart from wickedness, O Jerusalem" [Jer 4:14]. And do you see here what pertains to us and what pertains to God? And again: "Blessed are the pure in heart, for they shall see God" [Mt 5:8].

Let us become cleansed as far as our minds can comprehend and as much as we are capable of becoming. How can this be done? "Wash yourselves; make yourselves clean; remove your evils from your souls before my eyes" [Is 1:16]. He says: "Do not become like whitewashed tombs" [Mt 23:27], appearing to be guiltless; but, thus, remove [evils from your souls] as being seen by God. "Though your sins are like purple, I will make them white as snow" [Is 1:18]. Do you not see that we have to clean ourselves first, and then God will make us white as snow? For this reason no one, not even those who sink down to the lowest evil, should despair. Even if it becomes a habit for someone and he has almost arrived to the nature of evil in itself, let him not be afraid. For even colors which do not fade and have almost become one with the material, nevertheless, are transformed into the opposite condition and become white as snow. Thus, He grants us good hope. Let us seriously try as much as we can to become clean.

Let us pursue good works. Let us not seek the speck that is in the eye of another, but let us see the log that is in our own [cf. Mt 7:3]. And, thus, with the grace of God, we shall be able to attain worthily the good things to come. Therefore, the power of works is great; and even when they commit sins, God cleanses them through repentance. One should not boast of them nor depend on them, for that would be sinful; but as much [76] as you are able, fulfill the works which are the result of faith and are necessary. For if those who have cast out demons and who have prophecied are rejected, and have not lived a comparable life, how much more [shall we be rejected] if we are negligent and do not fulfill the commandments? Christ will say to such persons: "I never knew you" [Mt 7:23; cf. Lk 13:27].

We believe correctly to glorify Him and we live the good life to glorify Him, for there is no benefit of one without the other. And furthermore, when, perchance, we praise Him rightly but do not live properly according to the commandment, then we greatly insult Him. And although we give Him the title of Master and Teacher, we, nevertheless, scorn Him and do not fear His awesome judgment. The fact that the pagan Greeks lived an impure life is no surprise, nor are they deserving of such great condemnation. However, being Christians, who participate in so many sacraments, [and] who enjoy such glory yet live impurely is much worse and intolerable and beyond all compassion.

If, as the saying goes, we were to look earnestly toward the great and infinite compassion of God and His extraordinarily great gifts, and imagine that we will be saved by grace alone in the manner of the ingrates, we cannot hope to benefit. And besides, our own deeds, even if they may approach perfection, are nothing in comparison, except that they are supplementary and demonstrate our disposition—namely, that we are thankful, that we obey the commandments and perform good and virtuous deeds so that we may not be placed into paradise like insensible creatures, which absolutely is not done but, by our preference, through the grace of God. If we prefer to incline toward sin, we shall appear insensible as paying attention to nonexisting things. Indeed, we must avoid it [sin] and detest it since it places us far away from God. And when we intend to commit a sin, then we must conjecture and imagine the dread [77] and intolerable court of Christ in which the judge is sitting on a high and elevated throne to judge those who have lived. All creation is present and trembling at His glorious appearance.

### [7. The Church and Sacraments]

The seventh [article] says that you also have one holy catholic Church and perform correctly the sacraments and the ceremonies of the Church. To this we say the following: One is the holy, catholic, and apostolic Church of the Christians who correctly execute what has been legislated, defined, and determined by the canons, as given by the Holy Fathers and ratified by the Holy Spirit. The sacraments and ceremonies in this

Church catholic of the Orthodox Christians are seven as follows: baptism, chrismation with the holy unction, Holy Communion, ordination, marriage, penance, and holy oil. For the gifts of the Holy Spirit are seven, as Isaiah says [cf. Is 11:2]. Seven, also, are the sacraments of the Church which have been effected by the Spirit. And the fact that only these and not more are sacraments is proved by their division. For a sacrament either refers to the genesis of human beings, which is marriage in Christ, or to salvation, and is the order of holy actions effected through them and in them. Baptism, myrrh [chrismation], and Communion, are to be used by all. For those, however, who dedicate themselves to God, there is ordination, as there is marriage for laymen. For those who have committed sin after baptism there are penance and the anointing with holy oil, which grant remission of sins committed or cleanse the stains which lie in the soul. These are also called *mysteria*, because it is understood that the visible symbols have the completed action as well as the mystical effect. Furthermore, each one of these sacraments has been set down as law by the Scriptures with a definite matter and form, but also a definite productive or, rather, organic cause, such as in the use of baptism the water is the matter; and the words of the priest saying: "The servant of God (Name) is baptized in the name of the Father, and of the Son, and of the Holy Spirit" is the form. The priest is the organic cause. However, in a time of necessity the baptism performed even by a layman is not rejected. In the same way  the matter and form are to be found in [78] each of the other sacraments.

a. Baptism, therefore, is rebirth through the Spirit. Since we lost the first sinless birth and were conceived in iniquity, as David chants, and in sin each one of us was conceived by his mother [cf. Ps 51:5], baptism becomes a holy washing which cleanses such iniquities.

b. Chrismation imprints the first seal and the likeness [of God] and restores power to the soul which we lost because of disobedience [cf. Tit 3:5]. It also restores the grace which man had once received in the soul which the Divinity breathed [into his nostrils]. Therefore, anointing bears the power of the Spirit, is enriched by His [spiritual] fragrance, and is the mark and seal of Christ.

c. Holy Communion unites the one baptized and chrismated with the Lord himself, and we truly partake of His body and blood [cf Mk 10:16; Mt 9:18f; 2 Tim 1:6]. For since we are dead as the result of eating [the forbidden fruit] and have been separated from paradise and God, we again receive eternal life through the communion of the spiritual food, the body of the Lord [cf. Jn 1:12]. Thus, freed from corruption, we are united with the Immortal One, who through the flesh became liable to death for our salvation.

d. Ordination grants the authority and the power of the Maker [cf. Gen 1:28]. Since no being exists without Him, He came to lead us to the good life. Now that He has been taken away from us, He grants this possibility to us through His priesthood [cf. Mt 16:19; Jn 20:23]. By this sacrament [of priesthood], all ceremonies are wrought, and nothing is sanctified without the priest. Furthermore, as he appointed us from the beginning [of the world] as administrators of the visible creation, so in this present time He appoints us as greater administrators through the office of priesthood. He bestowed the keys of heaven upon the Apostles and to their ordained successors.

e. Marriage is a gift of condescension from God for procreation, so long as everything exists in this world of corruption [cf. Mt 22:24, 30]. For God did not intend an irrational, fluctuating, and sordid union to occur among us. But because we became subject to death by our own free will, He let the perpetuation of the species occur in the same manner as among the irrational animals so that we may know in what position we have placed ourselves. And this will continue to occur until the Incor-
[79] ruptible One, who died and rose for us, will resurrect nature and make it immortal. Therefore, He himself also blesses marriage so that the beginning of our life may not be without blessings.        ˏ

f. Penance works for our restoration again after we fall. And this great gift of penance has been granted because after baptism there is no other recovery, neither by grace or by gift, nor without struggle or pain, except through conversion and through tears, through confession of iniquities and an aversion for evil. And, indeed, there is here included the vow of monks to live in a manner which is a continuing pledge of repentance.

g. Holy unction has also been provided as a holy ceremony and as a type of divine mercy for the salvation and sanctification of those who turn away from sin. Therefore, this ceremony grants forgiveness of sins, and raises up from illness, and provides sanctification.

Jesus Christ our God has handed down all of these sacraments, and so have His holy Disciples through Him. For since we are of a dual nature, that of soul and of body, these sacraments likewise are given to us in twofold character, as, indeed, God himself became two-fold for us, true God and true man. On the one hand, He sanctifies our souls intelligibly through the grace of the Spirit, and on the other, through perceptible means of water, oil, bread, the cup, and the rest which have been sanctified by the Holy Spirit. With these He hallows our bodies also and grants full salvation. In this manner He will restore us to the perfection in which He had created us. He will resurrect us when we die, and we shall be rewarded according to what we have done. What each sacrament contributes to our salvation has been spelled out. We must now briefly state from whence each received its beginning.

[1.] Marriage has been legislated from the very beginning by the God of all, who himself joined together Adam and Eve. In the Gospels the Lord on one occasion honored marriage through a miracle [cf. Jn 2:1f], and on another, He was seen attacking the Mosaic Law which permitted the divorcing of women by submitting a statement of divorce [cf. Mt 19:8; Mk 10:5, 6, 8]. He emphasized that this rule was not in existence [80] from the beginning, but because of the hardness of heart of those who received the Law, this was allowed. And He adds: "What God has joined together, let no man put asunder" [Mt 19:6]. Furthermore, the Apostle [Paul] also declared that marriage is to be held in honor among all, and the marriage bed be undefiled [cf. Heb 13:4]. He calls marriage a mystery, saying: "Brethren, this is a great mystery, and I take it to mean Christ and the Church" [Eph 5:32]. In this manner, then, this sacrament has been given from above, and, as it has been said, was ratified by the New Testament.

[2.] Holy orders [ordination] was most obviously handed down by the God of all at the time of Moses and Aaron, and was appropriate for worship according to the Law [cf. Heb 10:1]. I am passing over the shadows of priesthood existing before the Law because of the obscurity attending these earlier appearances. The first ones, who under grace were honored with such an office, were chosen by the only-begotten Son, as the words testify that the Lord spoke to the Apostles: "You did not choose me, but I chose you...out of the world" [Jn 16:16, 19]. They were perfected at Pentecost when the Holy Spirit descended upon them; and they then handed down this gift to all who came after them.

[3.] Holy baptism, (and I am speaking about baptism according to us because now we have gone past the [various] types [of baptism]), has been handed down through word and action, by our Lord Jesus— through action, in that He accepted baptism from John in the Jordan; through word, in that He commanded His disciples: "Go and make disciples of all nations, baptizing them in the name of the Father and of the Son and of the Holy Spirit" [Mt 28:19].

[4.] The sacrament of holy myrrh [chrismation] is not mentioned in the Holy Scripture, but it was handed down by the disciples of the Logos. The most reverend Dionysios, who had been taught by Saint Paul, has recorded this in his sacred writings. He is a man whom the Church of God honors after the Apostles.

[5.] The sacrament of Holy Communion, the most sacred among the ceremonies, was foreshadowed typologically in the sacrifices of the Law [cf. Heb 10:1]. But in reality it was handed down by the Lord, who willed that His passion begin on that evening on which He ate with His initiated ones the Passover that the Law commanded. After eating of it, according to the traditional manner handed down by Moses, He instituted the new sacrifice, breaking the bread and distributing it to them, calling it His [81] own body, and offering to them the cup filled with a mixture of wine and water, which He called His very own blood. And He commanded them to do this in remembrance of Him, and to know that whenever they did this, they would be proclaiming the death of their Lord and Teacher [cf. Mt 26:26-28; Mk 14:22-24; Jn 19:34; Lk 22:19-20; 1 Cor 11:23-26].

[6.] The sacrament of penance was legislated in a typology by Moses, inasmuch as he commanded sacrifices for sins. But in complete reality it was instituted by the Lord himself. He gave this authority to the Disciples when He said: "If you forgive the sins of any, they are forgiven; if you retain the sins of any, they are retained" [Jn 20:23]. And He promised to give the keys of the kingdom to Peter himself specifically saying: "Whatever you bind on earth shall be bound in heaven, and whatever you loose on earth shall be loosed in heaven" [Mt 16:19]. And when Peter asked how many times he should forgive those who have committed sins and proposed seven times, Peter suggested with this thinking that he was doing something great [cf. Mt 18:21]. The Lord answered, "I do not say to you seven times, but seventy times seven" [Mt 18:22].

[7.] The anointing with oil [unction], perhaps, is spoken of by some other Apostles, but it is clearly handed down by Saint James the Apostle in his catholic Epistle where he says: brethren,

> Is any one among you suffering? Let him pray. Is any cheerful? Let him sing praise. Is any sick among you? Let him call for the elders [presbyters] of the church, and let them pray over him, anointing him with oil in the name of the Lord; and the prayer of faith will save the sick man, and the Lord will raise him up, and if he has commited sins, he will be forgiven [Jas 5:13-15].

These things, then, he handed down in this way, and from that time until now it has been so done. These, then, are the sacraments of the Church, their number, and the manner in which they were handed down. Through these the initiated receive the heavenly gift. One should not forget that the productive and original cause of all these sacraments is the revered and the most holy passion of our Lord from which, or through which, grace flows to those who participate in them. The reason for this is the subject and purpose of another discourse and not of this present treatise, which has its purpose in other matters.

### [8. What the Church Is]

The eighth [article] testifies that the Church is the gathering of believers and devout persons. And if the sacraments are administered by hypocrites and wicked men, those who are sanctified by them are not harmed in any way according to [Scripture]: "The Pharisees sit on Moses' [82] seat," etc. [Mt 23:2]. We ourselves also say that when the sacraments are administered by unworthy ones, they [the officiants] do not benefit, but rather are harmed. Yet the recipients are sanctified and benefit, for divine grace is efficacious even through unworthy servants because it [is grace that] perfects the sacraments. Those who administer the sacraments are to be honored, and the sincere ones are not to be scorned on the pretext that some may be hypocrites (even Judas was among the Apostles). For Saint Chrysostom, interpreting the Epistle to Timothy [2 Tim 1:12], says:

> Whoever honors the priest will honor God, and he who has learned to despise the priest will gradually proceed in time to insult God also. 'He who receives you receives me' [Mt 10:40]. And it is written: 'But hold His priests in honor' [Sir 7:31]. Hence, the Jews learned to despise God because they despised Moses and would have stoned him [cf. Ex 17:4]. And when someone acts reverently toward a priest, he will be much more reverent toward God. And even if a priest is wicked, God, who is watching, will bestow a reward on you because you have shown reverence to him who is unworthy of honor in order to honor Him. 'He who receives a prophet because he is a prophet shall receive a prophet's reward' [Mt 10:41], as it is written. 'And whosoever submits to and obeys the priest and honors him for the sake of the Lord will be blessed.' 'The scribes and Pharisees sit on Moses' seat, so practice and observe whatever they tell you, but not what they do; for they preach but do not practice' [Mt 23:2-3]. Do you know, they say, what a priest is? He is an angel of the Lord. Surely he does not say things that are his own. If you despise him, you are not despising him, but (you are despising) God who has ordained him. And from whence does it appear that God ordained him? If you do not have this faith and reverence, your hope is rendered vain. For if God does not [allow divine grace to] work through an unworthy celebrant, you have neither the washing [of baptism], nor do you participate in the sacraments, nor do you receive any blessings; and, therefore, you are not a Christian. For what reason then does God ordain all, even the unworthy ones? God does not ordain all, but He works through all, even though they may be unworthy, in order that the people may be saved. For if He spoke for the sake of His people through an ass, and through Balaam who was a wicked man [cf. Num 22:21], how much more does He speak through the priest.

> What, indeed, will not God do for our salvation? What does He not [83] utter? Through whom does He not act? If God worked through Judas and through the Prophets of whom He says: 'I never knew you; depart from me, you evildoers', [Mt 7:23]; and if such men have cast out even demons, will He not much more work through the priests. For if we were to try to examine the lives of such persons, we would be wishing to be the overseers of our teachers.

And then things would be turned upside down—the head down and the feet up. Hear Paul saying: 'But with me it is a very small thing that I should be judged by you or by any human court' [1 Cor 4:3]. And again: 'Why do you pass judgment on your brother?' [Rom 14:10]. If you should not judge your brother, much less should you judge your teacher? If God has commanded this, indeed, you do well, and you are committing sin if you are not doing this. But as for the opposite, do not dare to do it, and do not attempt to go beyond the limits. After worshipping the calf, those about Korah, Dathan, and Abiram rebelled against Aaron [cf. Num 16]. What then? Did they not perish? Then, let each one be concerned about himself.

And if someone holds a perverted doctrine, though he be an angel, do not be misled [cf. Gal 1:8]. But if he teaches the truth, pay attention not to his manner of life, but to his words. You have Paul, who by deeds and by words is instructing you toward what is proper. But they say that the priests are not giving to the poor, nor administering properly. Whence, then, is this made known to you? Before you have ascertained the truth, do not find fault. Be fearful of the responsibilities! Many judgments are formed by conjecture. Imitate your Master, and listen to Him saying: 'I will go down to see whether they have done altogether according to the outcry which has come to me; and if not, I will know' [Gen 18:21]. If you have ascertained and investigated, then wait for the judgment. Do not usurp the office of Christ. It is His responsibility to investigate these things, not yours. You are the least among servants and not the master. You are the lamb. Do not busy yourself with matters of the Shepherd, lest you have to give account of your accusations against Him. And how can He tell me to do that which He is not doing himself? It is not He that speaks to you. If it is Him you obey, you have no reward. Christ admonishes you about those things. But what am I saying? You should not obey even Paul if he tells you something of his own or something human, but obey that Apostle through whom Christ is speaking. Let us not judge the acts of others; but let each one judge his own acts.

Examine your own life carefully [cf. Lk 17:10]. But some say the priest should be better than I. Why? Because he is a priest? Isn't [84] he subject to more than you? Has he no hardships, no dangers, no agony, no difficulties? Does he steal and commit sacrilege? How do you know? Why do you edge your way to the abyss? These words are the result of madness. If someone says that a certain person has a purple robe, you cover up your ears [not to hear], even if you know it is so. But why in this case [of a priest] do you subject yourself to danger? These comments are not of responsibility. Hear what Christ says: 'I tell you, on the day of judgment men will account for every careless word they utter' [Mt 12:36]. Do you believe that you are totally better than another? Do you not lament? Do you not beat upon your chest, or bow down, or imitate the Publican? Even if you are better, have you not destroyed yourself? Are you better? Then be silent, so that you may remain better. If you say that you are (better), you have made everything of no avail...Examine your life! You are speaking about the priest: I am not sacrilegious like him [cf. Lk 18:11]. Do you not then make everything vain? He [Chrysostom] says: I am obliged to say so not because I am interested in them, but because I am afraid for you, lest you make your virtue ineffective through misuse.

Hear the exhortation of Paul: 'But let each one test his own work, and then his reason to boast will be in himself alone' [Gal 6:4]. Tell me, if you enter a hospital with a wound in order to have it cured, do you closely examine the physician to see whether or not he has an ulcer? Certainly not! If the priest is unworthy, there will be no relief whatsoever from punishment for him who discharges the office [of priesthood]. He will suffer the prescribed punishment, but you yourself will suffer the one appropriate to yourself. For what reason then, they say, does he officiate? Please, let us not speak evil against the priest, lest we grievously debase our own actions. Let us examine ourselves then, speaking evil of no one. Let us honor that day on which [the priest] illuminated us [in baptism].

If someone has a father, who even if he has done ten thousand terrible things, he, nevertheless, conceals everything. Even more so should we do this for our spiritual fathers. Reverence him because he ministers every day. He reads the Scriptures to you. He adorns the house of God for you. He keeps an all-night vigil for you. He prays. He pleads with God for you. You say to me that he is wicked. And what of it? For even he who is not wicked, does he himself bestow upon you these great benefits? Not at all! Everything works according to your faith. Not even the righteous [priest] can benefit you if you are unfaithful. Nor can the unrighteous [priest] harm you if you are faithful. When God willed to save His people with the ark [of the covenant], He made use of oxen [cf. 1 Sam 6:7]. Does [85] the life of the priest, or perhaps his virtue, contribute so much? What God gives in His grace does not come as a result of priestly virtue. Everything is from grace. The duty of a priest is to open his mouth [to speak], but everything [that comes forth] is of God. He only serves as a symbol. Consider the difference between John and Jesus, and hear John saying: 'I need to be baptized by you' [Mt 3:14]. Yet the Spirit descended. John did not have, neither did John cause [the Holy Spirit] to descend. What then does it mean? That you may learn that the priest serves as a sign, but God brings everything to completion. The oblation is the same, no matter what man offers it, whether it is Paul or if it is Peter: it is the same [offering] which Christ gave to the disciples and it is that which the priests now celebrate. This [sacrifice] is not inferior to that [of Christ] because it is not men that sanctify it, but God...And he who thinks that this is inferior to the other does not know that Christ is present even now, and even now works efficaciously. Moreover, you now know these things, and all these things have not been simply spoken by us [for the sake of saying something], but, rather, that we may correct your opinion and make certain you guard most carefully what has been spoken. For if we always listen but never act, nothing that has been spoken will be advantageous to us. Therefore, let us pay careful attention; let us attend with diligence to what has been spoken; let us erase from our hearts the evil reports; and let us have the good things engraved upon our consciences.[13]

Let us continually recall them to memory and execute them correctly according to the holy, written, and unwritten good tradition of the Fathers, ascribing glory to the blessed Trinity. Amen.

### [9. Baptism]

The ninth [article] says that infants should be baptized and that baptism should not be postponed. We, also, must act in this manner so that nothing may happen because of postponement. In part this has been explained in the reply to article two. Unless one is reborn of water and of the Spirit, he cannot enter into the kingdom of heaven [cf. Jn 3:5]. Moreover, as has been said, we give to them afterwards Holy Communion. According to Basil the Great, he who is born again needs spiritual food, also. And the Lord says: "Unless you eat the flesh [of the Son of Man] and drink [His] blood," you cannot enter into the kingdom of God [cf. Jn 6:53]. Consequently, both are necessary: baptism and Communion.

### [10. The Holy Supper of Our Lord]

[86] The tenth article concerns the Lord's Supper, yet not in depth and not too clearly. For we have heard many things about it from you which have not pleased us. The Church catholic is of the opinion that after the consecration the bread is changed by the Holy Spirit into the very body of Christ and the wine into [His] very blood. The bread must be leavened, that is, not unleavened. For the Lord, on the night when He was

betrayed, "took bread and gave thanks and broke it to the Disciples and said, 'Take, eat.' " He did not say: "This is unleavened bread, or a symbol of [my] body." But He said: "This is my body and my blood" [Mt 26:26, 28]. To be sure, the flesh of the Lord, which He bore, was not at that time given as food to the Apostles, nor His blood for drink, even as now the Lord's body does not descend from heaven in the Divine Liturgy, for it would be blasphemous to think that! But then and now, having been changed and altered by the *epiklesis* and grace of the all-powerful Spirit, the source of consecration, through the holy petitions and words of the priest, the bread is the very body of the Lord and the wine is the very blood of the Lord. He says: "And the bread which I shall give... is my flesh" [Jn 6:51], sanctifying all the unfaithful. For just as He, participating in our human nature, became God-man and shared our flesh and blood; thus we, also, having partaken of His body and blood, will be called gods by adoption and grace. The bread of the Lord's body, which has been sanctified by the priest, is not a mere type, nor is it unleavened; but it is leavened and is itself the body of the Lord, as He said concerning himself and as we have shown in detail. This matter, as well as that concerning the procession of the Spirit and the rest, will be clearly presented in greater length at the proper place. We shall discuss this in the place where you say that you agree with the Latins, and that the only disagreement between you and them concerns those matters which you call abuses.

## [11. Confession]

The eleventh article declares that the forgiveness of the sins of the one who confesses occurs through the steward of the sacraments [cf. 1 Cor 4:1], and that it is not necessary to say everything and to enumerate in [87] kind, according to the passage: "But who can discern his errors?" [Ps 19:12]. In answer we say, first, that this kind of steward should be a spiritual physician who is well versed in spiritual matters. Then the penitent must relate in particular as much as he is able and remembers and confess with a contrite and humble heart. In other words, He receives healing by doing the opposite of those sins which he committed. For instance, if he was arrogant, he should correct himself by humility. And if he was greedy for base of gain, he must restore even from his own [possessions] what he has unjustly received, and so on, according to the appropriate canon determined by the Fathers. This should be done in a way that will be pleasing to God and not for gain or compensation, which would be the worst, not satisfying but abhorred by God.

As for the confessors, who for their own gain exploit the divine things and let themselves be bribed with gifts and who possibly assume the sins of others in so doing, they are disgraceful and shall receive divine punishment and destruction. If such people are caught, we lay severe punishment on them, and condemn them to a retraction of their spiritual dignity. Spiritual values cannot be measured in silver or gifts or the like, for material things cannot be offered for atonement. But, as we said, only if the one who confesses has a contrite heart, does the opposite of sins committed, and completely abstains from evil [can his spiritual values be measured and his sins atoned for]. Moreover, with regard to those things which through forgetfulness or embarrassment are left unconfessed, we pray that the all-merciful and compassionate God will forgive him even these. And we are confident that God will forgive even these. As, indeed, Saint Basil, who was greatly versed in spiritual matters, says, every iniquity must be confessed to the confessor; for an evil which has been silenced is a festering sore in the soul. Let the cures be applied to the deeply afflicted in the manner of a physician. The confessor should not be angry with the spiritually sick but should combat the sickness and oppose the lusts, curing the disease of the soul by more effective methods as necessary. As, for instance, in [the case of] arrogance, by greater efforts to attain humility. In immoderate sleep, through keeping vigil in prayers. In laziness of the body, through toil. In unwarranted eating, through abstinence, etc. And let him who is being healed not regard the penances as tyranny because out of compassion consideration is brought to bear for the salvation of the [penitent's] soul. It is a shame, then, that while [88] those who are sick in their bodies trust the physicians so much that even when they perform painful surgery, when they cauterize and afflict them with bitter medicines, they consider them as benefactors; we on the other hand do not have the same disposition toward the healers of our souls when they are working for our salvation through a rigorous regimen. Furthermore, he who imposes penances should not impose the same penance on the sincerely pious as on the indifferent penitents, even when both are found to have committed the same sin.

For the sincerely pious person, being truly pious, strives eagerly to please God and in struggling may have, on occasion, accidentally failed and slipped. On the other hand, the indifferent person, who is unconcerned for himself or for God and who does not distinguish between sin and virtue, is already sick with great evils. For he either despises God, or he disbelieves in the existence of God. Indeed, these are the two causes of sin in the soul, as Scripture declares. On one occasion it declares that the lawless one who commits sin says to himself that "there is no fear of God" [Rom 3:18, quoting Ps 36:1]. And on another occasion: "The fool says in his heart, there is no God" [Ps 13:1; cf. Ps 52:1]. Thus, either he has despised [God], and because of this he commits sin; or he denies the existence of God, and for this reason he destroys himself in his futile pursuits, even though he appears to confess. For "they profess to know God, but they deny him by their deeds" [Tit 1:16]. Therefore, since these things are so, the method of imposing penalties should, of necessity, be different in each case. In addition to these things, it should further be known that it is necessary that the confessor who receives the grace of God freely should also give it freely, and not try to use it for his own lusts, according to the word of the Lord: "Heal the sick, raise the dead, cleanse lepers, cast out demons. You received without pay, give without pay" [Mt 10:8; cf. Acts 8:18f]. And Paul:

> For we never used either words of flattery, as you know, or a cloak for greed, as God is witness; nor did we seek glory from man whether from you or from others, though we might have made demands [89] as Apostles of Christ. But we were gentle among you, like a nurse taking care of her children. So being affectionately desirous of you, we were ready to share with you not only the gospel of God, but also our own selves because you had become very dear to us [1 Th 2:5-8].

### [12. Penance]

Your twelfth article states that the sinners receive forgiveness of sins after baptism when they return and show repentance by contrition of heart and sound faith. We reply to this by saying: This is certainly true. for the Lord himself says that sins are to be forgiven not up to seven, but up to seventy times seven [cf. Mt 18:22]. In so saying, the Lord used a definite number to stand for an indefinite number. And again: "And he who comes to me I will not cast out" [Jn 6:37]. Nevertheless, with reference to your complete and altogether rejection of the canonical satisfactions, we say: If they are imposed as medicines by the spiritual men, that is, gratis and without exploitation, let us say, against the arrogant or miserly, or gluttons, or immoral persons, or those who envy, the wrathful, or those who are lazy, or those guilty of other sins, the canonical penances are contritive and helpful, as the Holy Fathers set down for those who return and repent. But if the penance should be for the gain or profit of those who impose them and not for the correct and spiritually beneficial purpose, nor as they were formulated and prescribed for the cure of each sin, then we, too, reject them; and we say and we maintain that they have been imposed evilly and in vain — this is totally incontestable. Yet we pronounce absolution in connection with penances for many sound reasons.

First, because by this voluntary affliction, the penitent will be free from the involuntary punishment in the life to come, for God is not conciliated by anything as much as by affliction. Hence, Gregory also has said: "Mercy is the compensation for tears."

Second, so the lust of the flesh, which is the cause for sin, should be uprooted. For the things which are contrary [to God's law] are corrected by their opposites, as we learned.

Third, since penance is a kind of fetter and a bridle of the soul, so that the penitent should not attempt the same or even worse evils.

Fourth, that one become accustomed to labor because virtue is gained by great effort.

[90] Fifth, that our faith should be strengthened if we completely abhor sin. But we should overlook all of these [considerations] for those who are already departing this life. In this case, it is sufficient for the religious leaders to grant forgiveness of sins upon the genuine intention and the return of the repentent person. We absolve these sins on the authority of Him who has said: "If you forgive the sins of any...etc." [Jn 20:23]; and, thus, we believe that the punishment is also absolved. And to assure them of this fact we give them the divine gift of the Eucharist. For genuine repentance depends on the intention of the sinner, but the punishment which has not been fulfilled is reserved for God's judgment. And for this reason absolution is granted in the manner of a king out of mercy alone, as in the case of the thief who merely asked to be remembered in [Christ's] kingdom [cf. Lk 23:42]. If someone gives food to the hungry, and gives drink to the thirsty, and performs the rest of the works of charity which God acknowledges in the judgment and mentions in the Gospels [cf. Mt 25:35-40], he will surely obtain absolution and will be delivered from Hades. For charity is the most necessary of the virtues. He who has taught [people], they say [cf. Mt 5:19], to give alms to others will himself receive an hundredfold from this virtuous exhortation. What has been given to the needy shall be equally restored to the one who gave it. For their beneficial value we set down these thoughts: "Boiled meat without salt, a word without truth, works without faith, a beginning without an end, and virtue without charity are dead."

As no animal can walk on one leg, and no bird can fly with one wing and no ships can sail with one side, thus, none of those who would be saved will be saved if he does not yoke love together with the virtue he already has. For when love has been neglected, it leads to punishment because it is lacking; but when it is practiced, it saves because it is a plus. Therefore, when one has God as a friend, he will have everyone as a friend, and, consequently, the saints also. In like manner, everyone who has the virtue of love has all the other virtues also, but not so the reverse. And no one should at this point project those who have sought perfection on mountains and in caves, as if without love [charity] they have supposedly satisfied the Lord. For they had previously distributed all [91] their belongings to the needy, and, thus, they left behind those who lived amid the noise of the world.

Moreover, bring these benefits and let us look at them through everyday examples and [discover] how easy and advantageous the rejection of property is. Tell me, if you owed one thousand pounds of gold and through the kindness of your creditor it would be possible to be released from all this debt immediately in return for everything you have, and suppose that you possessed nothing more than three coins, would you not willingly turn them over to him? Another example: If you were taken captive by an alien people, and you had to labor in extreme misery, heavily chained, and then it was made known to you that you could be free for the rest of your life, on the condition that you would give to the needy only those things which are unnecessary for your needs, would you not give away even those things which are necessary to you? If the inhabited part of the earth were for sale at a price equal to the value of your properties, would you not willingly give up everything in order to be the possessor of it? And would you not consider it a great loss, if you had failed to take advantage of such an enterprise for such gain? If you were very old and expected to die in great poverty, and then suddenly you were told that without toil or pain, you would become young and healthy, immortal and very wealthy, if you would freely give only one of your properties to your fellow slaves, would you not give it immediately and willingly?

If indeed you were the most destitute of all men, and a king would promise you that if you kept only one of his commandments, he would shortly make you an immortal king, would you not willingly keep this one precept? If one of the rulers of the world would give you ten thousand of his goods for your pleasure, and demand only a thousandth part from you in return, and this again for your own sake and for your own prosperity, would you not willingly give that which was demanded? If for your many sins a judge would sentence you to die in a most shameful fashion today, unless you gave the government and the nation a smallest part of your possessions, would you not gladly give even half of your possessions? If someone would show you in an instant all pleasures as well as all punishments, and would promise to release you from the punishments and grant you the enjoyment of the pleasures, but demanded from you a small gift on that account, would you not gladly give him all that you possess?

[92] But do not marvel that alms alone can do everything. For he who gives alms and who loves the poor for the Lord's sake is set free from the debt of infinite sins as well as from dreadful captivity among the demons. He purchases for a small price the whole world, and is renewed at once, and remains immortal and he rules the heavenly kingdom. And as a righteous servant he will inherit everything from the Lord, and when He calls out to him: "Come, O blessed of my Father" [Mt 25:34], he will truly be worthy to become rich. He is set free from every punishment and enjoys everything good uninterruptedly. Indeed, it is my opinion that you should not wait for your life to end, but while you live, give daily of your table, of your bread, of your profits, of your clothes, of your income to the needy. For "he who gives alms to the poor lends to God" [Pr 19:17]. Above all, lay up treasures in heaven, and gather them in the

heavenly storerooms. Do you treasure your body [cf. Mt 6:20]? Treasure also [your] soul. Do you provide for your needs? Take care of your neighbor, also. Do you enjoy your present possessions? Provide for the future as well. The ox that works lives a long time because it toils along with us. The pig lives a short time because it lives only for itself. The bee is useful because it gathers [honey] for us, but the beetle is useless because it is concerned only with its own affairs. Recognize God and give thanks to Him that you may become not one of those who beg, but of those who give; not one of the strangers and of the poor, but one of the wealthy and one of the native sons; not one of those who are slaves and are oppressed, but one of those who are happy and free; not one of those who are sick and debtors, but one of those who are healthy and creditors.

Think how much you must give in order to be righteous, so that you do not hear from the Lord those horrendous words: "Depart from me" [Mt 7:23]; "You wicked and slothful servant [Mt 25:26]; "So take the talent from him" [Mt 25:28]; "Bind him hand and foot" [Mt 22:13]; "I never knew you; depart from me, you evildoers" [Mt 7:23]. Oh how much of his fortune would someone give willingly to hear these words: "Come, O blessed of my Father" [Mt 25:34]; "Well done, good and faithful servant; you have been faithful over a little, I will set you over much" [Mt 25:21]. And: "Enter into the joy of your master [Mt 25:21]. And: "Sit at table [93] with Abraham and Isaac and Jacob in the kingdom of heaven" [Mt 8:11]. Everyone who thinks seriously about these and similar ways of beneficial giving will be praised to the end of his life because of his noble generosity, and he will be honored and saved by God.

We understand alms-giving not as giving alms to one person only once, but as always giving alms in every way to everyone [in need]. To the one, as your relative; to the other, as your friend; to that one, as your neighbor; and to this one, as your acquaintance, and to still another as a fellow-man out of compassion for human beings. Give to this one by preference, to that one out of habit, to the next one by a [kind] word, to the other by a deed, to this one something tangible. To this one, food; to that one, drink; to the next one, clothes; and to the other, shelter. To the one, [show] friendliness, and to another by honoring him, and simply, in every way that you are able. You have with you one who accompanies you gladly and guides you in all of this, namely, Christ. Since He does not cease doing good to you, do not stop imitating Him in doing good, so that you will be worthy of His kingdom. Therefore, one who continues in almsgiving and does good works through almsgiving, who uses almsgiving as a remedy, and accepts penances for sins in a godly and spiritual manner and not in an adulterous spirit, obtains pardon for his wrong-doings and receives true healing. Moreover, his good deeds and all his God-pleasing works benefit not only the living, but also those who departed [this life] after having made their confession.

While the fear of God is great, His goodness is much greater. And although His threats are terrible, yet His mercy is incomparable. His sentences are dreadful, but the ocean of His mercies is ineffable. For that reason the well-known Dionysios says:

> Prayer implores the divine goodness to absolve the departed of all the iniquities that he committed through human weakness, and to bring him into the place of the living, into the bosoms of Abraham, Isaac, and Jacob... that through the goodness of the divine majesty the blemishes of weakness might be overlooked because, as the Gospel says, no one is clean from defilement [cf. Rom 3:23; Job 14:4].

Furthermore, Gregory [of Nazianzos], in his eulogy on Caesarios, points out that good works are of benefit even after death. He says:

> [94] 'A proclamation has been heard, worthy of hearing by all. The grief of a mother has found expression in the good and pious promise, to give everything on behalf of her son, his wealth as a gift for his burial'. And again: 'Such is our offering: part we have already given, and part we will give by offering the annual honors and memorials, that is to say, the services which are offered and performed for the dead'.[14] Further, Chrysostom also, in his commentary on Philippians says: 'If the Greeks [pagans] cremate with the departed ones their possessions, how much more is it necessary for you, the believer, to send along with the faithful departed his belongings, not so that they may become ashes, as they [the pagan Greeks] did, but that you may invest him with more glory. And if the departed one was a sinner, [in doing so] that you may free him from iniquities. But if he was just, so that it may be an increase of reward and recompense.[15]

And again [Chrysostom says]:

> Let us have in mind the welfare of those who have departed. Let us give them the proper help; compassion, I say, and oblation. For it brings to them a great comfort and gain and benefit; and he who performs these things confers great benefits upon his own soul as well as upon that of his neighbor.[16]

And again, in another place:

> Had you not, while you lived, arranged everything for your soul? At the end of your life, command your people to send your belongings on to you after your death and to give you help by means of good works, through alms I say, and offering. In this way you will conciliate the Redeemer; for, these things are acceptable to Him and fruitful. In the formulation [of your will] include the Master as co-heir along with children and relatives. Let your testament [last

will] contain the name of the Judge. Let your remembrance of the poor not fail; I am a guarantor of these things.[17]

Nevertheless, by saying these things we do not wish to supply a motive and excuse for not giving alms to the living; for that would be wrong. But as it is said, to give alms after death is most excellent. Also, the prayers of the righteous ones are efficacious [cf. Jas 5:16]. Also, Gregory the Dialogos concerning whom it is said that when he celebrated the Liturgy, a heavenly and divine angel concelebrated with him, saved Trajan through his prayers. Thekla, the first [woman] martyr, saved Falconilla. And similar things are recorded in the ecclesiastical histories. Furthermore, he who wishes to know more, let him peruse the discourse of Saint Damascene, *Concerning Those Who Have Fallen Asleep in Faith,*[18] and [95] he will learn that the liturgies which were offered for them, as well as good works, benefited them.

### [13. The Use of the Sacraments]

Your thirteenth [article], which says that the use of the divine sacraments was instituted not only in order that they might be some type of symbols or marks, or tokens to distinguish Christians from the outsiders [non-Christians], but much more, that they be signs and witnesses of the kindness and grace of God toward us. We also confirm this and have the same opinion concerning them.

When our Lord Jesus Christ had completed the entire work of salvation for us on earth, before He ascended to His own Father, He left to us the Divine Liturgy and the holy sacraments in remembrance of His magnificant condescension for us. He ordained James, the brother of the Lord, to be the first hierarch (as he is called). Now, if the prayers of the saints have effect for the present life and especially after death for the believers, as Dionysios, who is greatly versed in spiritual matters says, so much the more will the holy sacraments and the sacred ceremonies benefit us. What their value is and how these awesome ceremonies conciliate God on account of our iniquities, God himself showed explicitly in the past with great force. For Noah, the just one, after the cessation of the flood, offered sacrifice to God in order to plead with God to be forgiving and serene toward those who were in weakness. As the great Cyril has declared that a judgment would not again fall upon all, and the human race undergo a second flood. Whereupon "the Lord God, having considered, said, I will not anymore curse the earth because of the works of man, because the imagination of man is intently bent upon evil things from his youth" [Gen 8:21]. If then, the sacrifice which was offered by Noah, although it was only a typology, predisposed God [kindly toward the human race], much more so will the only-begotten Son of God, who was sacrificed for us, reconcile us to the Father when we come with faith to the holy ceremonies.

Thus we, too, condemn those who think that without faith they have
[96] the forgiveness of sins and benefit from the sacred ceremonies. For
whatever does not proceed from faith is sin [cf. Rom 14:23]. Therefore,
we call blessed those whose work it is to celebrate the sacred ceremony of
the holy sacraments, the change of the gifts into the holy body and
blood. And they do this so that those who believe may be sanctified by
them, receive the forgiveness of sins, the inheritance of the kingdom, and
similar [blessings].

Moreover, the preparation for, and the fulfillment of, that function
should be the prayers, the singing of hymns, the readings of Holy Scripture and, in general, all that is reverently done and said before and after
the sanctification of the Gifts. Although God bestows all the holy things
freely and we contribute nothing to them, and while they are simply
favors, He of necessity requires us to be worthy to receive and preserve
them. Even He would not bestow sanctification on those who are not
properly disposed to receive it. Thus He baptizes; thus He anoints; thus
He receives us and imparts of the awesome Table to us. And this He
made known in the parable of the seed. He said that the sower went out
not to plow the land, but to sow, and left the plowing and all the preparation which is needed to be done by us [cf. Mk 4:3]. Moreover, since it is
so imperative for the partaking of the sacraments to be well-prepared to
meet Him, this also must be and is required in the order of the sacred
ceremony. Indeed, the prayers and hymns and whatever else transpires
and is said reverently [in the ceremony] make it possible to do this for us.
For they sanctify and prepare us to receive sanctification worthily, to
preserve it and to continue to retain it.

Therefore, they sanctify in a two-fold manner. The first way is that we
derive benefit from the prayers and the hymns and the [Gospel] readings
themselves. For the supplications return to God and cause the
forgiveness of sins; while the singing of hymns similarly propitiates Him
and makes Him well-disposed toward us, for He says: "Offer to God the
sacrifice of praise...I will deliver thee, and thou shall glorify me" [Ps
50:14]. Furthermore, the readings of Holy Scripture herald the goodness
and benevolence of God, as well as His justice and judgement. They [the
Scriptures] put the fear of Him into our souls and enkindle our love for
[97] Him, and thus they inspire great willingness to keep His commandments. All the above activate within the priest and the people a better and
holier soul and make them both more susceptible for the reception and
retention of the divine gifts, which, indeed, is the purpose of the sacred
rites. They especially prepare the priest to celebrate the [holy] Sacrifice
worthily which, indeed, as has been said, is the work of the sacred
ceremony. Moreover, this very purpose is found in many places in the
prayers. The priest prays that he may not be looked on as unworthy for

the service, but that he may celebrate the sacrament [of the holy Eucharist] with clean hands and soul and tongue. And thus we are benefited from this power of the words that are spoken and sung in the service [of the Divine Liturgy].

We are sanctified in yet another way by these and all else which takes place in the sacred ceremony [of the Liturgy]. For we see Christ typified in them, along with His works [of atonement] and sufferings for us. Thus the work of redemption of the Savior is signified in the hymns and in the [Gospel] readings and in all the [symbolic] acts which are performed throughout the entire Divine Liturgy by the priest. The first acts of this [our Lord's] work of redemption are signified by those [symbolic] acts which are declared in the first part of the Divine Liturgy. The further acts of this work [of redemption] are signified by the [symbolic] acts of the second part in the Divine Liturgy. And the final acts [of redemption] which took place later, are signified by the [symbolic] acts in the final part of the Divine Liturgy. Thus, it is possible for those who closely observe the above parts [of the Liturgy] to have the whole work of redemption before their very eyes. For the sanctification of the gifts, which itself is the sacrifice, proclaims His death [cf. 1 Cor 11:26], His resurrection, His ascension; it changes these precious gifts into the Lord's body itself, which underwent all these things: the crucifixion, the resurrection, and the ascension into the heavens. That which takes place before the sacrifice signifies those events which took place before His death, His coming, His self-disclosure, His complete manifestation. And that which takes place after the sacrifice signifies the promise of the Father, as He himself said, the descent of the Holy Spirit upon the Apostles, and through them the conversion and inclusion of the pagan world into the community [cf. Ac 1:8]. The entire sacred ceremony, as a picture of one body portrays, before one's vision, the life of the Savior, bringing into view all of its parts from the beginning to the end, each in order and in harmony with the other.[19]

[98] For one thing, the hymns that are sung at the introit and even before that, the symbolic acts and spoken words of the oblation of the gifts, signify the first years of the dispensation of Christ. That which follows afterwards, the readings of Holy Scriptures, exhort us to anoint ourselves towards [the acquisition of] virtue, so that we may find mercy in God's sights and hearken to those things which are implied in the dispensation of Christ. These lessons contain hymns to God which exhort the singers to virtuous living and sanctify them. The lessons that the Church has chosen and so ordered, are sufficient to indicate the coming of Christ and His life on earth. And everything that transpires in the Divine Liturgy, as the printed form of order indicates and includes, addresses itself to the present need, and also signifies some of the works, or deeds, or sufferings of Christ. Take, for example, the 'minor entrance' of

the Gospel and the 'great entrance' of the gifts into the sanctuary. They are both necessary. The former so the Gospel can be read. And the latter so that the sacrifice can be consummated. Yet, both signify the manifestation and appearance of the Savior. The former signifies the yet dim and incomplete manifestation [of Christ], while the latter signifies the total and final manifestation.

Finally, all that transpires in the Liturgy of the [holy] gifts, as James, the brother of the Lord, taught by the Savior first ordered it, as well as is found in the sacred canons of the Holy Fathers and in the ecclesiastical histories, and as truth has it, is also held by us. And after him [James], Basil the Great [also held thus], as is clear from the form of the liturgy and the sacred prayers which he formulated. Later Chrysostom also related all things [in his liturgy] to the dispensation of the Savior, so that the vision of it might be before our eyes, to sanctify our souls, and thus make us worthy of the Sacred Gifts. And just as the work of salvation, [99] when it occurred, renewed the inhabited world, so always after whenever it is beheld it cultivates the holiness of the soul. Moreover, [the work of salvation] would not benefit us if it had not been witnessed and believed. And for this reason it was preached.

And again, in order that it might be believed, God laid innumerable plans. For it [the work of salvation] cannot fulfill its purpose and save human beings if the people who are to be saved did not know of it. For when [the work of salvation] was first preached, it created reverence, faith, and the love of Christ in the souls of the grateful hearers. On the other hand, when it is devoutly witnessed by those who are already believers, the blessed passion [of our Lord] is not introduced to them, but since they are already there, it preserves and renews and increases them. It makes them more firm in faith, and perfects them more ardently in piety and love. Inasmuch as it [the work of salvation] caused those things which did not exist to come into being, how much more easily can it protect, preserve and renew those things which already exist. But this piety, faith and warm love, are with what one must necessarily approach the holy things, and without them even looking on is absolutely unholy.

And for this, to visualize that which brings about such emotions in us had to be signified in the sacred assembly so that we should not only think about it in our minds, but also see with our eyes the great poverty of Him who is rich, the confinement of Him who possesses every land, the pains of the blessed One, the sufferings of the one not subject to suffering, how the more He was hated, the more He loved; how He, being great, yet humiliated himself, and however else He suffered and whatever else He did to prepare for us such a table [cf. Ps 23:5]. And thus, marvelling at the newness of salvation and being awed by the multitude of His mercies, let us venerate Him who had such pity on us and thus saved us. Let us entrust our souls to Him, let us commend our lives to Him and let us enkindle our hearts with the flame of His love. And when we become like this, we will communicate with the flame of the sacraments truly and in a proper manner [cf. Heb 12:18; 10:19]. For it is not enough to intend to become this kind of person and to learn of Christ. But it is necessary that we actually see, we must affix the eye of the mind there, we must reject all rationalizing if we would cultivate our soul to become worthy of the sanctification of which I have spoken. [100] Piety should be discerned not by words alone, but also by works. The divine service brings everything before our view, so to speak, and also implants what is seen in the soul. The imagination is more clearly impressed through the eye, so that we cannot forget such a table [the Eucharist] [cf. Jn 1:16]. And thus, being full of holy thoughts, we partake of the holy sacraments adding sanctification to sanctification, and going from glory to glory. This then is, the gist of, the meaning of the entire sacred ceremony. The prayers have purpose and harmony; that is, the sacred ceremony itself, namely, the sanctification of the living and the dead, and above all the Savior's dispensation, which is manifest throughout the entire service.

What parts of the service are signified? And by whom are they signified in the sacred ceremony? And why are the gifts not placed in the sanctuary from the beginning? Because the slaying of animals and the golden and silver vessels were offered to God by the ancients. The body of Christ clearly includes both. For He was slain for the glory of the Father. He was consecrated to God from the beginning [cf. Col 1:15]. He was an offering to Him because He is the only-begotten, and because the bread is changed into the very body of Christ. Therefore it is separated from other loaves of a similar nature, and only a part of the bread is offered, and not the entire loaf. This typifies the passion of Christ. And as long as it [the bread] lies on the table of oblation, it is mere bread, which was merely offered to God. Later however, it is truly changed and becomes the true bread [cf. Jn 6:33]. But if we were to try to describe and explain this happening by way of reason and in practical terms, it would require ten thousand mouths and yet they would not satisfactorily accomplish this.

Therefore, the Lord, himself, commanded us to do this in remembrance of Him, so that we would not be ungrateful [cf. 1 Cor 11:24]. Benefactors receive a kind of return from those who have received a favor from them, when they remember them and their works, through which they have benefited [cf. 1 Th 1:2]. For such remembrances men have contrived many means: graves, statues, columns, feasts, games. These contrivances have one purpose, to keep the excellent among men from being delivered over into the abyss of oblivion. And just as we inscribe on columns the hero's victories by which we have been saved, in [101] the same manner by these divine gifts we memorialize the death of the Lord, by which we have been saved, and in which a total victory has been gained over the Evil One. We do not have a picture, but through [our] intercession, thanksgiving, doxology, confession, and petition to God we have the very body of the hero.

First of all, we make petition for the peace and the salvation of our souls. The benefit of peace is very great. Rather, we constantly need this virtue in every facet of our lives, because it is impossible for a troubled mind to be united with God. For just as peace makes a multitude appear to be one, so confusion makes the one appear to be many. We also make petition for the salvation of our souls, as Christ commanded us to do, to pray first for the kingdom of God, which is salvation, "and all other things shall be added unto you" [Mt 6:33]. In the sacraments, the Church becomes known not as in symbols, but as the members in the example of the heart, and as the branches of the plant in the example of the root, as the Lord said: as the branches of the plant in the illustration of the vine [cf. Jn 15:5]. For here is not a communion in name only or a similarity by analogy, but an actual identity. For the sacraments are truly the body and blood of Christ. They are not changed into a human body, but we are changed into them, because the greater ones are victorious. For when iron comes together with fire, the iron itself becomes fire, but it does not allow the fire to become iron. And just as in burning iron we do not see iron, but simply fire, because the attributes of iron completely disappear in the fire, so it is with the Church of Christ. If one would be able to see it in itself, how it is united with Him and is a part of His flesh, one would see nothing else than the Lord's body itself. For this reason, the Apostle Paul writes: "Now you are the body of Christ, and individually members of it" [1 Cor 12:27]. For when he wrote about Christ's providence and about His teaching and exhortation and about our submission to Him, and when he said that Christ is the head and we are the body [cf. Eph 5:23; 1 Cor 11:3], he did not mean it as we do when, by way of exaggeration, we call relatives or friends members of us. Rather, he meant precisely this, as He expessed it: that he knew through this blood, that the faithful who live their life in Christ, are truly dependent on Him as the head, and belong to His body.

[102] In this sacred ceremony [Eucharist], the commemoration of the saints takes place, during the offering of the gifts, and during the sacrifice [cf. Rom 12:1]. For this gift is a votive offering and a spiritual [reasonable, living] sacrifice. We remember foremost what [our Lord] underwent for us: the Cross and everything else which Christ suffered for us. We commemorate and glorify the all-holy [Virgin Mary]. We ask for the intercession of all the saints. We entreat the mercy of God and we offer supplications for the living and the dead. As we offer our spiritual [reasonable-living] worship to Him from those things which are from Him, we praise and bless Him. During the oblation which follows, the

sacrifice and the change of the elements into the very body and blood of the Lord take place invisibly, while the divine grace consecrates mystically through the prayers of the ceremony [cf. Rom 12:2].

This ceremony and spiritual [reasonable-living] worship is called the Eucharist because it offers the oblation to God through the efficacious words alone and consummates the change of the divine body and blood. And [the Eucharist] is so named from that which it accomplishes [cf. Rom 8:32; 1 Cor 4:7-8], as it affords more causes for thanksgiving than supplication, and we receive more than we have asked for. Indeed, we have received everything that is of God; and there is nothing given which He has not given [cf. Rom 12:2]. But the time has not yet come for us to attain some things: incorruption and the kingdom of heaven. But what we have received have not been withheld: the remission of sins and the other gifts which are granted to us through the sacraments. The source of the divine initiation into the sacred mysteries is the great High Priest, Jesus Christ our Lord and God. The immediate beneficiaries were His eyewitnesses and followers. They became like rivers flowing from a fountain, gladdening the City of God. Indeed, in the words of our Lord: that which they have heard with their ears they have proclaimed up on the housetops [cf. Mt 10:27]. That which David prophetically foretold in psalms has been fulfilled: "There are no speeches or works in which their voices are not heard" [Ps 19:3]. Therefore, the things that have to do with the sacred ceremonies are built on ecclesiastical and priestly foun-
[103] dations, according to Apostle James, the brother of the Lord and bishop of Jerusalem, as the 32nd canon of the Synod in Trullo [A.D. 692] has testified:

> For also James, the brother, according to the flesh, of Christ our God to whom the throne of the Church of Jerusalem first was entrusted, and Basil the Archbishop of the Church of Caesarea, whose glory has spread through all the world, when they delivered to us direction for the mystical sacrifice in writing, declared that the holy chalice is consecrated in the Divine Liturgy with water and wine.[20]

There are also some other indications to be found interspersed in the documents of the church to the effect that Saint Mark the Evangelist had also composed liturgical writings which pertain to that holy and mystical sacrifice. Yet it is not accurately clear whether the writings of both Apostles were corrupted, like the later Clementine Decrees, or whether, because of their lengthy text, they might have been compiled in a shorter and well-ordered form by our father Basil the Great and later more concisely by Chrysostom. This much we know certainly, that of old, two volumes according to which we celebrate the Liturgy have been handed down to us and have been acknowledged and brought to light, ie., the Liturgy of Basil the Great himself, and that of the holy father John Chrysostom. Both men are [inspired] by the same Holy Spirit and are of the same tradition. However, Basil is more verbose while Chrysostom speaks more concisely. For these two sacred volumes, we celebrate the unaltered mystical sacrifice. During the Sundays of the great forty-day Fast before Easter and on other prescribed days the Liturgy of Basil the Great is celebrated, and thereby the sacrament of the Holy Sacrifice is consummated. On all other days, the Liturgy of Chrysostom is celebrated.

Our Holy Church of God is the fatherland of all churches, and by the grace of God is sovereign in knowledge. It is preeminent in the purity and brilliance of its apostolic and patristic teachings. New Rome [i.e., Constantinople] has received the primacy, and has been designated the head church of Orthodoxy. It is necessary that every [104] Christian church celebrate the liturgies in this same manner. If, however, it is necessary to respect local and long-standing custom and to celebrate the Liturgy of Saint James or, on occasion, that of Saint Mark, the principal parts [of the service] must piously be preserved and the Liturgy must be celebrated to the glory of God with tranquil spirit and careful observance. Thus, before all else, that sanctification may be bestowed upon us through the partaking of the divine gifts, which first enter into the very care of the soul through the body. This is indicated by the Apostle Paul who said: "He who is united to the Lord becomes one spirit with him" [1 Cor 6:17], since this union and joining is principally brought about in the soul. Here is where a human being truly exists. Here is where sanctification takes place through the practice of virtue and human effort. Here also is where the sinful which needs healing makes petition through the gifts. Everything that happens to the body happens through the soul. And just as [the body] is defiled by evil thoughts which come from the heart [cf. Mt 15:19], in like manner sanctification comes from the same source. And just as sanctification is derived from virtue, so also it is derived from the sacraments, but much more, much better and more perfectly.

It appears that this divine and sacred Liturgy sanctifies in a two-fold manner. One way is by intercession: when the gifts are offered, the offering itself sanctifies those who offer as well as those for whom the gifts are offered, for God becomes merciful to them also. The other way is by communing. For to us it is food and drink, according to the Lord's word [cf. Jn 6:55]. Of the above two ways, the first is common to the living and the dead, for the sacrifice is offered for both. The second belongs only to the living, for the dead cannot eat or drink. What then? Are the dead then not sanctified by this sanctification from the communion? And do the dead in this case then have less than the living? No, not at all. For Christ gives of himself to them in a way which

is known to Him alone. Furthermore, in order that this may become
clear to you, observe this and similar matters in the interpretation of the
liturgy.

### [14. Holy Orders in the Church]

The fourteenth article declares that the Gospel should be publicly read
[105], and proclaimed and the sacraments should be distributed by no
one except those who have been legally designated for this ministry. We
say this is properly stated; for the Church catholic, as ecclesiastical tradition demands, permits only the canonically confirmed and called and
ordained persons, who hold no evil heresy to preach and to celebrate the
Liturgy. Therefore, the Church declares that they are mistaken who
regard lightly the matter of the celebration of the divine and sacred
sacraments by laymen who might have been ordained by clergymen who
may themselves be canonically ordained or not.

Ordinations take place in compliance with the canons. And concerning
the bishop, the 1st canon of the Holy Apostles says: "A bishop must be
ordained by two or three other bishops," but "let a presbyter, deacon,
and the rest of the clergy [be ordained] by one bishop."[21] The Acts of the
Apostles state:

> Now in the church at Antioch there were prophets and teachers,
> Barnabas, Symeon who was called Niger, Lucius of Cyrene, Ma-
> naen the tetrarch and Saul. While they were worshipping the Lord
> and fasting, the Holy Spirit said, 'Set apart for me Barnabas and
> Saul for the work to which I have called them.' Then after fast-
> ing and praying, they laid their hands on them and sent them off
> [Acts 13:1-3].

Of five people mentioned, the three ordained the two who had been set
apart.

Secular rulers are forbidden to elect bishops or the laying on of hands,
as was practiced according to the ancient custom. That this practice has
now already been banned by the holy Synods, let us be assured by the
30th canon of the Holy Apostles, which says: "If any bishop obtains
possession of a church with the aid of the temporal powers, let him and
all who communicate with him be deposed and excommunicated."[22] The
25th canon of the Holy Apostles[23] says that one should not be punished
twice for the same offense, but for excessive wickedness and notorious
accursed sin it prescribes double punishment. And election of this kind is
null and void. The ones who forced it and are responsible are punished,
[106] and such men are called and are unholy. For the one who is to be
promoted to the bishopric should be elected by bishops, as the Holy
Fathers of Nicaea determined in the canon which says:

> It is by all means proper that a bishop should be appointed by all the

bishops in the province. But should this be difficult either on account of urgent necessity, or because of distance to be traveled, at least three [bishops] should meet together, and by their votes, together with those of the ones absent, given and communicated in writing, the ordination should then take place. But as for the ratification of what is done, it should be entrusted in each province to the metropolitan.[24]

Those words are from the 4th canon of the holy First Ecumenical Synod in Nicaea [A.D. 325]. In addition, the 12th canon of the Synod of Laodicea [A.D. 343-381] declares:

Bishops are to be appointed to ecclesiastical office by the judgment of the metropolitans and neighboring bishops, provided that they have been tried and tested for a long time, both in respect to the matter of faith and in point of behavior and conduct in right living.[25]

That is to say, they are to be correct and sound in the faith and way of life. The 13th canon of the same Synod [Laodicea] says something similar "concerning the necessity of not permitting the multitude to conduct the election of candidates for the priesthood."[26] In the interpretation of the canons it is explicitly stated that the multitude of laymen was not only prevented from electing bishops, but also that they were not allowed to elect priests. Thus the canon cited indicates that in ancient times, not only bishops, but priests also were elected by the multitude. This latter practice has not been entirely forbidden as being inexpedient. Again, the 19th canon of the Synod of Antioch [A.D. 341] orders:

A bishop shall not be ordained without a synod and the presence of the metropolitan of the province. He must be present in any case, and it is by all means better that all his brethren in the ministry of the province should assemble together with him; accordingly, the bishops in the metropolis should be invited by letter. And it were better that all should meet; but if this be found difficult, at least a majority of them ought in any case to be present or to take part in the election by letter, and thus let the appointment be granted by a majority of votes of those present or joining by letter. If any ordination has been obtained otherwise than has been defined and prescribed, let it be of no effect. But if an appointment has been [107] granted in accordance with the prescribed canon, and if some persons should object to it on account of a personal quarrel, the decision of the majority vote shall prevail.[27]

The interpretation of Zonaras says:

In the past the inhabitants of the cities elected the bishops. But since this gave rise to riots, the voting on the election of the bishops was transferred to the bishops of each vicinity.' Moreover, the bishops—and not the laymen—not only elected and consecrated the bishops and priests, as we have said, but the canons also refer to the ordination, i.e., the consecration of him who has been elected to become a clergyman by means of a ritual of prayer and by the liturgical invocation of the Holy Spirit. Because the bishop by the imposition of his hand blesses the person being ordained.

In the past the election was also called *cheirotonia* [laying on of hands]. For when the urban populace was still allowed to select the bishops, the multitudes would gather together, and then some would elect the one, while others would elect another. In order, however, that the vote of the majority would prevail, those who were doing the choosing were told to raise their hands, and by this method the votes would be counted. And he who was elected by the majority would become the candidate for the office of bishop. And thus, from this custom the designation *cheirotonia* [or imposition of hands] was evolved. The Fathers of the Synods also are found to have applied this truth when they called the election *cheirotonia*. Thus the Synod of Laodicea says in the 5th canon: 'Ordinations must not be performed in the presence of hearers.' [28] Therefore they called the election *cheirotonia*. But in the consecration of the bishop it was the custom for many to congregate together. During the time of election, when some accusations against the men voted upon might be introduced, it was forbidden for laymen to be present and listen to the proceedings. Moreover, this canon decrees that a bishop must be ordained by two bishops. The 4th canon of the First Ecumenical Synod[29] decrees that a bishop should be elected by the bishops of his diocese, or by at least three, while the others consent in writing.[30]

[108] It is apparent from the canons and from the Apostolic decrees that the bishops should be ordained after careful examination and on the proof of correct belief and moral life, but that the unworthy should be rejected. Saint Gregory the Theologian in his great apology,[31] inveighing against the unworthy, the impure and evil candidates for priesthood, but also underscoring and declaring what the candidates for the priesthood must be, explicitly and boldly states among other things the following:

Who has tested himself by the rules and standards which Paul laid down for bishops and presbyters—that they are to be temperate, soberminded, and the rest, blameless in all things, and inaccessible to fornicators—and could not find considerable deflection from the forthrightness of the rules? [cf. 1 Tim 3:1-2; Tit 1:5].

And again:

> First one must himself be cleansed, and then cleanse others; himself
> become wise, and then make others wise; himself be illuminated,
> and then illuminate others; draw near to God, and then so lead
> others to Him; himself be sanctified, and then sanctify others.[32]

And again, crying out against those who by chance were not ordained according to the demand of the canons, he says: "Who can mold, as clay figures are molded, in a single day the officient of the Divine Liturgy, who is to take his stand with angels, and give glory with the archangels, and is their co-celebrant?"

And again:

> Those who have brought nothing to the priesthood, both disciples
> as well as teachers, before they themselves have become cleansed
> they cleanse [others]. Yesterday they were outside the holy province
> and today [they are] priests and ministers of the mysteries, grown
> with regard to iniquity, all but pious. Their work is of human
> effort, but not by the grace of the Spirit.[33]

Thus, it is clearly evident that he [Gregory] attacks the unworthy and the evil ones, and describes what the true liturgical servants of the Lord must be. In addition, it is necessary to avoid and reject those who embrace any heresy. Canon 46, along with other [Apostolic canons], declares:

> We ordain that a bishop or presbyter who has acknowledged the
> baptism or sacrifice of heretics is to be deposed. For what concord
> has Christ with Belial? Or what part does a believer have with an
> infidel?[34] [cf. 1 Cor 6:15].

### [15. Church Usages]

[109] With regard to the fifteenth article, which says that the ministers should be innocent and blameless and of a good life, and that prayers and offerings and celebrations which are performed for the purpose of receiving money for grace, as well as receiving money or anything else for the remission of sins are of no avail, we are of the following opinion. On the one hand, persons ministering the divine things are not elevated to office unless they are, as much as possible, blameless and exempt from reproach. They are obligated to remain pure and void of offense, living and conducting themselves in all prudence and propriety. On the other hand, we affirm that the prayers, and the liturgies, and the offerings, and the celebrations which are performed in a manner pleasing to God and out of love for God to the glory of God; and in commemoration of those who were well pleasing to Him, and offered for the rousing up and imitation of the divine and good works, are rightly done and for the benefit of

souls. For the Scriptures say: "The prayer of a righteous man has great powers in its effect" [Jn 5:16] for the benefit of the faithful and of those who are worthy of the divine grace. Also Saint Chrysostom, commenting on the Epistle to the Hebrews, says: "Just men frequently accomplish everything through a single petition."[35] And also, commenting on the Epistle to the Philippians, he says:

> Let us devise some assistance for the departed. Small though it be, still let us help them. How and in what way? By praying and by entreating others to make supplications for them, and by giving alms continually to the poor in their name. This gesture provides some consolation. Listen to God saying: 'I will defend this city for mine own sake, and for my servant David's sake' [2 Kg 19:34]. If only the remembrance of a just man has such great power, how much more power is exerted when works are done in his behalf! It was not in vain that the Apostles decreed that remembrance should be made of the departed during the awesome sacraments. They knew that there is great gain and great benefit [for the departed] in this. For when an entire people stands with uplifted hands, a priestly assembly and that awesome Sacrifice is celebrated, how could we not propitiate the Lord for them?[36]

That honors are due to the saints by us, and that it is accepted by them, [110] and to offer it in churches, is just as the God-man clearly expressed it: "He who receives you receives me" [Mt 10:40]. And Chrysostom also says:

> Just as the army that stands and fights deserves to be paid by those who are living in peace and not fighting—for on their behalf the army is standing [and fighting]—so also it is justified that one should think in this way with regard to the saints. For is it not absurd that we provide everything for one who serves as a soldier under an earthly king [but fail to do so], for those who are serving as soldiers under the heavenly King? They are drawn up for battle against a much more formidable enemy. They entreat God for us. We pray to them and beseech them for things beneficial to us. How great is our ingratitude if we fail to appear generous, as far as our circumstances will permit, toward their shrines and toward the priestly men who are vigilantly engaged [in conducting worship in these shrines] and toward those who are thereby nourished by our alms?[37]

Moreover, it is beneficial for us to pray; it is most necessary and indispensable for Christians. This is evident from what our Lord taught: "When you pray, say, Our Father" [Lk 11:2], and "This kind cannot be driven out by anything, but by prayer and fasting" [Mk 9:29], and many other similar sayings. Furthermore, Paul in his Epistle to Timothy exhorts:

> First of all, then, I urge that supplications, prayers, intercessions, and thanksgiving, be made for all men...This good, and it is acceptable in the sight of God, who desires all men to be saved and to come to the knowledge of the truth [1 Tim 2:1, 3-4].[38]

It is, indeed, right to also honor the priests. Let us again hear from the divine John [Chrysostom]:

> The priest is the common father, as it were, of all the world. Therefore, it is proper to honor him before all others. He offers worship to God for the world; he offers supplication for kings, and for all who are in high positions that they may attain salvation and that we may lead a quiet and peaceable life [cf. 1 Tim 2:2]...For God ordained the authorities for the public good. It would be improper for us not to offer prayers for those who fight for us.[39]

And again: "Have you not read in the Scripture that Job was offering sacrifices for his children to rid them of sins; lest at sometime, he said, [111] they think evil in their heart?" [cf. Job 1:5].[40] And again [Chrysostom continues]:

> You know, as disciples of Christ, that we pray for peace and for the well being of the whole world and for its stability. We seek after the kingdom of God, and we knock at the door, so that God in His compassion will open it and lead us back again to our original blessedness. And it is good to enjoy the prayers of the saints, as long as we ourselves are also practicing [Christians]; otherwise it would be of no benefit. For we know what happened to Jeremiah. Three times he approached God and for the third time he heard Him say: 'Pray not, for I will not harken to you' [Jer 7:16; cf. 11:14]. Even if Noah, Jacob, and Daniel would intercede, the people will not be delivered, because their iniquity has prevailed' [cf. Ezek 14:14]. But, someone might say, what is the advantage of prayers offered by others, when I myself am well pleasing to God? Never say that, man! There is much need. There is need for prayer. Hear what God says: 'He will pray for you and your sins will be forgiven' [cf. Job 42:8].

There are many similar passages that someone who is searching will find. The Divine Scriptures are filled with them.[41]

In the same way sacrifices that are offered to God are gladly accepted. He says; "Pray, and pay your vows," as when Hannah dedicated Samuel to God. There are a myriad such [examples] similar to that [cf. Ps 49:14; 75:11; 1 Kg 1:24; i.e., 1 Sam 1:24, RSV].

We celebrate the feast days in the same manner, and honor the saints as friends of God according to the words of the sainted David: "But thy friends, O God, have been greatly honored by me" [Ps 139:17]. If we would not offer prayers, celebrate liturgies, feast days and the like—of course without petty gain, but in the fear of God, which are divine works and are the results of faith—we would appear to have neither the fear of God nor a living faith, which of course precede everything else. For if we in any way whatsoever negate the latter, then the former will also appear to be negated.

According to Basil the Great, it is necessary for the preacher of the word [of God] to seek with prudence and with great care to please God in all that he does and says. He should be both tested and approved by those who have been entrusted to him, according to: [Saint Paul saying to the Thessalonians]: "You are witnesses, and God also, how holy and righteous and blameless was our behavior to you believers" [2:10]. If the ones who are serving chance to be unworthy, it is the grace of God that still is efficacious, as the whole company of theologians testifies.

## [16. Civil Government]

[112] The sixteenth article says that it is not forbidden for Christians to govern others, to administer justice according to the laws, and to take part in other government affairs. We say in reference to this that we should obey every rule and every authority, not only the good, but also the unjust rulers [cf. 1 Pet 2:18], and without fail to keep the ordinances that they enact. In general, however, "we must obey God rather than men" [Acts 5:29]. In another place we read: "He who resists the authorities resists what God has appointed, and those who resist will incur judgment" [Rom 13:2]. And also, they who disobey the ones who have been sent by the Lord dishonor not only them, but also the One who sent them. They bring a condemnation on themselves worse than that of Sodom and Gomorrah [cf. Mt 10:15]. For Scripture says: "He who receives you receives me" [Mt 10:40]. "He who receives any one whom I send receives me" [Jn 13:20]. "He who hears you hears me" [Lk 10:16]. "And if anyone will not receive you or listen to your words, shake off the dust from your feet as you leave that house or town" [Mt 10:14]. And the Apostle [Paul] says: "Therefore whoever disregards this, disregards not man but God, who gives his Holy Spirit to us" [1 Th 4:8; cf Tit 3:1]. Thus it is necessary that one should obey not only rulers, but also the apostles of God and the teachers and the Spirit-bearing exegetes of the Scriptures, and one would not oppose them, because of the threats [that God pronounces].

But we do not accept your views when you condemn those who sell their property and forsake the world and the things that are in the world for the sake of their salvation [cf. 1 Jn 2:15]. And [we do not accept it] when you so understand the evangelical word that you say that the Gospel is not concerned about those transitory things, but about the things that are eternal, and that it speaks [only] about an everlasting righteousness of the heart.

We, on our part, follow the interpretation of the doctors of the Church of Christ and declare that the evangelical word explicitly says: "Sell what you possess, and give to the poor, and you will have treasure in heaven, and come, follow me" [Mt 19:21]. We do not understand this allegorically or figuratively, but literally, and in a [113] pragmatic manner. For the one who posed the question, thought that Jesus would advise him according to his question and show him a way by which he might live eternally and at the same time retain his possessions. But when the Lord said that the giving away of possessions brings about eternal life, the poser of the question went away lamenting his question and the answer of Jesus [cf. Mt 19:22]. Note that the one who posed the question said: "All these I have observed from my youth" [Lk 18:21]. The Lord then places on him the highest demand of all, that of poverty, by saying: "Sell all that you have"—for if even one thing remains, he remains its slave— "and distribute to the poor, and come, and follow me" [Lk 18:22]. That is to say, be my disciple in everything else, and follow me always. Do not be my disciple in such a way that you perhaps fulfill all the commandments today, but tomorrow you do not.

The great luminary of the universe, John [Chrysostom], said that the young man indeed desired eternal life, and yearned for it, but that he was possessed by a greater passion, that of avarice [cf. Mt 19:21]. He who wishes to be perfect does not err if he sells all his belongings for the sake of eternal life, but he will live eternally according to the promise. Neither we, nor the laws, nor the canons declare that it is lawful for bishops to punish criminals according to the laws, to execute them, to wage wars or to lead an army.

[17. The Second Coming of Christ for Judgment-Parousia]

As for the seventeenth [article]: that Christ will come at the consummation of the age, that He will judge the living and the dead, and that He will grant to the pious everlasting life and endless bliss, while the impious will receive everlasting punishment, we also avowedly say this and hold it to be true. But they speak nonsense who say that there will be an end to the blessings or the punishments, or who introduce the Judaistic opinions, or rather mythologies, saying that the saints and the pious will reign over the world before the time of the resurrection of the dead. Hence we shun them, and we condemn them as fabricators of fables and contrivers of evil imaginings [cf. Rev 20:4-6].

[18. Freedom of the Will]

The eighteenth [article] deals with free will. This is how we understand it. You are correct concerning how it is among us. Concerning the [statement] that no one can be saved without the help of God, we also know that before all else we need divine help and grace, according to the word of the Lord: "For apart from me you can do nothing" [Jn 15:5]. Yet we hear also the sayings of the holy teachers and exegetes of the divine words of the Lord. These men did not speak from their own purpose, but [114] were moved by the Holy Spirit, and instructed and taught us with the clearness of light. Saint Chrysostom says "that grace, even though it is grace, saves those who are willing." In his interpretation of the Epistle to the Hebrews, he also says concerning morals:

> Wherefore we ought always to guard ourselves lest at any time we should fall asleep. 'Behold, he that keeps Israel [is the one that] shall not slumber nor sleep' [Ps 120:4]. And again: 'Let not thy foot be moved' [Ps 120:3]. He did not say, 'Do not move', but only, 'Let not [your foot] be moved.' Consequently it depends on ourselves, and not on any other, to allow it to happen. For if we will stand steadfast and unmovable, we shall not be shaken [1 Cor 25:58]! What then? Does nothing depend upon God? Indeed, everything depends on God, but not so that our free will is violated [cf. Rom 9:16]. If, they say, everything depends upon God, why does he blame us [cf. Rom 11:32]? For that reason I said: 'So that our free will is not violated.' It then depends upon us as well as on Him.

> For we must first choose the good; and then He leads us to His part. He does not anticipate our choice, lest our free will be destroyed. When we have made our choice, then He brings to us great assistance, as Paul says: 'So it depends not upon man's will or exertion, but upon God's mercy' [Rom 9:16; 11:32]. First of all, he [Paul] did not introduce this as his own opinion, but inferred it from the context and from what had preceded. For when he says, 'It is written, I will have mercy on whom I will have mercy, and will have pity on whom I will have pity' [Ex 33:19; cf. Rom 9:15-19], [Paul] says [by way of interpretation], 'So it depends not upon man's will or exertion' [Rom 9:16]. 'You will say to me then, why does he still find fault' [Rom 9:19]?

> Secondly, this too is to be said that [Paul] speaks of all as His, whose the greater part is. For it is ours to choose and to wish, but God's to complete and to bring to an end. Since, therefore, the greater part is of Him [Paul says], all is of Him speaking, according to the custom of man. We ourselves also do the same. For example, when we see a well-built house we say that everything has been

made by the architect. Yet certainly it is not all his work alone, but also that of the laborers and of the master of the house who supplied the materials, and of many others; but, nevertheless, because [the architect] has contributed the greatest share, we say that [115] everything is his work. So also in this case! Again, for example, when we speak of a crowd of many people, we say that all are there. But when there are only a few, we say that no one is there. Thus Paul also says: 'Not upon man's will or exertion' [Rom 9:16]. He [Paul] establishes herein two great truths. One, that we not become arrogant. He says: even if you run, even if you are in dead earnest, do not think that the achievement is yours. For if you did not receive power from above, everything is in vain. The second, that you will attain what you zealously pursue is very evident; as long as you run, and as long as you are resolute in your desire. For he [Paul] did not assert this, that we run in vain, but that if we think that everything depends on us and do not attribute the greater part to God, we are running in vain. For God did not will that everything depend on Him, lest He should appear to be crowning us without cause. Nor did he will that it depend wholly on us, lest we fall into arrogance. For if we have a high opinion of ourselves when the least part depends on us, what would happen if we were really lords over the whole? For God has done the great share in order to cut off our arrogance...But again some say: 'Why is this?' 'Of what use is this?'...If we attain even some small success, we raise ourselves all the way to heaven itself in our thinking.[42]

Again, in his Epistle to the Philippians, [Paul] says:

For when we perform some good work,...then do we rejoice; 'for God is at work in you' [Phil 2:13]. Let us take care not to spend ourselves in vain pursuits. If this be the case, God will work all things...If, then, He is working, it is necessary for us, being of resolute mind, to remain always bound together and not split apart from Him...If He is working willingness in us, how does he [Paul] exhort us? For if He himself is working the will to obey, then His command to us would be in vain. For then we would not be obeying. If everything is from God, then he [Paul] refers in vain to fear and trembling [cf. Phil 2:12]. But it was not for this reason that [Paul] said: '[God] is the One who is working both to will and to work' [Phil 2:13], but because he wanted to relieve us from anxiety. If you will, He will 'work in you to will',...and He will also grant you the desire to do the work. If we have the will, then He will increase our will. For instance, if I desire to do some good, He has already wrought the good work itself, and by means of it, He has also wrought the will to do it...Thus when [Paul]

[116] calls these gifts, he does not exclude the free will, but accords to us free will. When he says 'to work in us the will', he does not deprive us of free will, but rather he shows that by actually doing something good we greatly increase our inclination to will.

For even as doing comes from not doing, so non-doing comes from not doing. Have you given alms? By this you are more inclined to keep on giving. Have you refused to give alms? You have become the more disinclined to be generous. Have you been temperate for one day? Then you have an incitement to be temperate on the next day, as well. Were you careless? Thereby, you have fostered carelessness. It is said that, 'when an ungodly man comes into a depth of evils, he despises them' [Prov 18:3]. Thus when a just person comes into a depth of goodness, he quickens his exertions. For just as the former person becomes more careless in his desperation, so also the just person, realizing the multitude of good deeds, exerts himself the more in the fear that he might lose everything. Paul says 'according to [God's] good pleasure,' that is, for the sake of love, because it pleases Him, so that what is acceptable to Him may take place, that things may happen, according to His will. Behold, He does everything!...For it is His will that we live as He desires we should. And if He desires it, He himself works in us to this end, and will certainly accomplish it. For it is His will that we live rightly. Do you see how He does not deprive us of free will? He says: 'do all things without grumbling or questioning' [Phil 2:14]. Whenever the devil finds that he cannot dissuade us from doing good, he tries to deprive us of our reward by other means. Either he seduces us into arrogance or into laziness or, if neither of these, then into murmuring, or, if not this, then into disputes about the virtue or vice of customs and doctrines... Punishment is reserved for the last-named.[43]

We should keep the ancient customs and obey the interpreters of the Scriptures. Paul spoke in the Holy Spirit. So did Peter and the rest, as well as the hierarchs, Basil the Great, Gregory the Theologian, John Chrysostom, and the remainder of the chorus of teachers. They appear as luminaries in the world, who clearly stated the word of life, proclaiming the things of our God and most adequately clarifying all of those things for us.

The same Chrysostom commenting on the Epistle to Timothy says:

If anyone purges himself from what is ignoble, then he will be [117] a vessel sanctified for noble use [cf. 2 Tim 2:21]. Do you see that to be a vessel of gold or of clay is not of nature or of some material necessity? It is a matter of our own choice. For otherwise the clay could not become gold, nor could the reverse happen. But in this case there is a great change. Paul was an earthen vessel; however, he became a golden vessel [cf. 2 Cor 4:7]. Judas was a golden vessel, but he became an earthen vessel.[44]

On the Epistle to the Ephesians [Chrysostom in his commentary], interpreting the passage "by grace you have been saved," [Eph 2:8] says:

In order then that the greatness of the benefits bestowed may not too greatly elate you, observe how he restrains you [by adding] 'through faith' [Eph 2:8]. Again, in order not to impair free will, he added that we must do on our part. But again, [he adds that] even this does not derive from us. Neither is faith, he says, of ourselves. For if [God] did not call us, how could we believe?... It is a gift from God [cf. Rom 10:14; Eph 2:8]. Paul says that faith is not sufficient for salvation. In order to save us, being neither fruitless nor idle, God has required faith through works... This itself is a gift from God, so that no one should boast [cf. Eph 2:9]...No one, he [Paul] says, has been justified by works, in order that the grace and the loving kindness of God may be revealed [cf. Tit 3:4]. He did not reject us because of our works, but in the fear that we might be betrayed by works He saved us by grace. Furthermore, lest it should happen that someone having heard that everything is achieved not because of good works, but because of faith, becomes lazy [cf. Eph 2:9], observe how he continues: 'For we are his workmanship, created in Christ Jesus for good works, which God prepared beforehand that we should walk in them' [Eph 2:10]...for the necessity of virtue should continuously increase in our awareness...Otherwise, the whole matter has been of no avail to us...For it is necessary to keep those things which Christ has commanded, and we must not relax even one of the least of the commandments [cf. Mt 5:19] so that the true faith may be proved through the good works of virtue.[45]

[19. The Cause of Sin]

The nineteenth [article] asserts that the cause of sin is ourselves and evil is of our will and choosing, and that God is absolutely not the cause of evil. This is correct and true. Indeed, Chrysostom, interpreting the Epistle to Timothy, said:

Know that God dispenses all things and provides all...Some things He works; others He permits. He wills nothing evil to be done. Everything good is of us, and of His influence, since nothing is concealed from Him. On the other hand, all evil comes from our [118] will...The just are afflicted so that they may be crowned. The sinners are afflicted so that they may pay the punishment of their sins [cf. Rev 2:10]. Indeed, not all the sinners pay the punishment here, lest many doubt the resurrection. Not all the just ones are afflicted, so that we do not think that the evil is approved... If we are mindful for these things, nothing will be able to make us fearful. If we would hear the Scriptures continuously, we would find those thoughts which can make us wise unto salvation.[46]

Continuing, [Chrysostom] says:

It rests with us either to profit or to be injured by afflictions. It depends not upon the nature of the affliction, but upon the disposition of our own minds [cf. 2 Tim 3:15]. Job was afflicted, yet he suffered with thankfulness; and he was justified...But another who had been afflicted by much less, bore it impatiently, was angry, and was indignant toward God. He is accused and condemned... Therefore, strength of soul is necessary, and nothing will appear grievous to us. But if our soul is weak, everything will appear troublesome.[47] Perchance someone wishes to hear in what manner the evil one works, when he finds the mind not inspired by God, or when he finds a soul that is not prudent. Indeed, when one does not have in mind the commandments of God, nor keep His ordinances, then taking him captive, he [the devil] departs. For if Adam had been mindful of the commandment which says, 'Thou mayest freely eat;' if he had kept the law which said, 'You shall not eat, but in whatsoever day ye eat of it ye shall die by death' [Gen 2:16, 17], he would not have suffered by those things which he suffered.[48]

Therefore, it is not right for one to accuse God. For disbelief does not take place because of the One who is calling, but because of those who are turning away. Some say that the unwilling also should be forced back. By no means! For He does not use force, neither does He compel. For who invites people to honors and crowns and feasts and celebrations who are unwilling and brings them bound up? There is no such one! For this would be a mockery. God sends the unwilling to Gehenna. But he invites the willing ones into the kingdom. And why are all not elected? Because of their own weakness. But why does He not shatter the illness? Did He not make the creation that teaches His benevolence and power? Did He not send prophets? Did He not call all? Did He not perform miracles? Did He not threaten with Gehenna? Did He not promise the kingdom? Does He not raise the sun everyday?

Some say: I would rather be good by force, and be absolutely deprived of all rewards than to be evil by my own choice and be accused and pun-[119] ished. There is no time when force is good. If, on the one hand, you are ignorant of what should be done, say so, and we will say whatever needs to be said. If, on the other hand, you know what is forbidden, why do you not flee from evil? "I cannot do that," someone says. But others who have overcome greater difficulties admonish you and completely silence you. Someone may say that, perhaps, you do not practice moderation even though you have a wife. On the other hand, another person retains purity even without a wife. What excuse do you then have for not maintaining the standard? But, someone says, I am not like that by nature. Then it is so because you do not want to be like that, not because you are not able to be like that.

I declare that everyone is capable of virtue. For whatever a person is not able to do, he is not able to do even if forced. But if a person is able when forced to do what he is not doing, then it is by his own choice that he is not doing it. For example, to fly upward and to lift oneself up toward the sky is completely impossible for one who has a heavy body. What would happen if a king would command that this be done and would threaten it by death, saying: "I command that men who are not trying to fly be beheaded or burned or suffer some similar punishment." Could someone, perchance, then be able to fly? Not at all, for nature does not permit it. But if [the king] issued an ordinance commanding temperance, would not many obey this command? No, you say, because there are those who are violating the rules. But if I must either do as commanded or be shut up in prison, I would take care not to suffer this unpleasant experience. It is not by nature that one person is good, nor is it by nature that another is bad. For if it were, one could not be changed, as we have clearly seen.

### [20. Faith and Good Works]

The twentieth [article] says that you do not forbid good works. Yet you characterize feasts, ceremonies, fixed fasts, brotherhoods, monastic life, and other similar works as useless. This is not good, nor does it agree with the Holy Fathers. For if you love all good works, as you say you do, you should love these also because they are good works. To begin with, Basil the Great says:

An ascetical life has one aim, the salvation of the soul. Everything that can contribute to this purpose must be observed as a divine commandment in the fear of God. The commandments of God themselves have no other aim than the salvation of him who obeys [120] them. Therefore, just as those who enter the bath must strip themselves of all clothing, so also those who are entering the ascetic life should strip themselves of all worldly things and enter upon a way of life according to the philosophy of Christ. The first thing is to get rid of evil passions, and the next is to get rid of all the worldly, material possessions... When people enter life in community, these, before all else, must prevail among them that they must be of one heart, of one will, and of one desire, as the Apostle ordained

[cf. Eph 4:4-5]. They must become one body consisting of various
members [cf. 1 Cor 12:12], achieving the fullness of the company of
brethren who possess nothing for themselves, but have everything in
common [cf. 1 Cor 9:27].[49]

Therefore, one must praise such monks who, pierced by the desire for
heaven, strive to understand the good and to honor Christ the
bridegroom. They have concerned themselves with differing ideas in the
church of what is good. Some sang hymns in praise of virginity, and
others sang the praise of those who mortified their bodies by fastings and
by sleeping on pallets of rushes. Others marvelled at the generosity of
those who sold all their possessions for the Lord's sake. They go on with
these lengthy praises not with the intention that everyone should do the
same, but because they think that such praise alone suffices to promote
that which is good, and reprove that which is not. Just as in the instance
of persons who have been called by someone! If the purpose of the one
who calls involves gathering crops, those called prepare themselves for
that purpose. If, on the other hand, his purpose is to build, they ready
themselves for building. In like manner, those who have been gathered in
the name of the Lord would, by all means, know the purpose of Him
who gathers them and prepare themselves for it so that they may not fail,
but may find the grace of His good pleasure and may not fall into condemnation because of wickedness or negligence.

They also should be mindful of the Apostle's saying: "I, therefore, a
prisoner for the Lord, beg you to lead a life worthy of the calling to
which you have been called" [Eph 4:1]. Moreover, the Lord makes
everything clearer for us through the promise that He directed to [Jude,
not Iscariot]: "If a man loves me, he will keep my word, and my Father
[121] will love him, and we will come to him and make our home with
him" [Jn 14:23]. Just as living with Him is achieved by keeping the commandments; thus also, He is in the midst of two or three [cf. Mt 18:20], if
they prepare themselves for His will. But if they are not worthy of their
calling and are not gathered together according to the will of the Lord,
but only think that they are gathered in His name, they hear Him say:
"Why do you call me 'Lord, Lord,' and do not do what I tell you?" [Lk
6:46].

Therefore, he who wishes to become a participant in the divine glory
and, as in a clear mirror, to see the face of Christ, in the first place he
must seek to lay hold of the things of God to the fullest extent of which he
is capable with insatiable affection and boundless intent with all his heart
and might, by night and by day. He will be unable to participate in this
unless he first withdraws from the pleasures of the world, from its passions, and the powerful adversary [that is, Satan] who is foreign to the
light and opposed to the good powers, who is, indeed, totally alienated

from them.

Furthermore, if you desire to learn why men were created [by God] and placed in paradise, and lately have been compared to the foolish beasts and have become like them, having fallen from the undefiled glory, know that this has happened because of disobedience, that we have become, by our lusts, slaves of the flesh [cf. 1 Jn 2:17]. We have transplanted ourselves from the life of bliss, from the land of the living; and having been taken captives [cf. Lk 15:13], we still sit by the rivers of Babylon [cf. Ps 137:1]. And because we are still captives in Egypt, we have not yet inherited the promised land which flows with honey and milk [cf. Ex 3:8]. Our hearts have not yet been sprinkled by the blood of the Lamb of God. The trap of Hades and the hook of evil are still imbedded in them. We have not yet received the joy of the Savior Christ, for we are still pierced by the sting of death. We have not yet put on the new man, who is created, according to God, in holiness and righteousness [cf. Eph 4:24]. We have not yet given up the old man, who is corrupt according to the deceitful lusts [cf. Eph 4:22]. We have not yet put on the heavenly image and become conformed to His glory [cf. 1 Cor 15:49], for we are still wearing the image of the earthly [cf. Phil 3:21]. We have not yet worshipped in the spirit and in the truth of God [cf. Jn 4:23], for [122] sin is still reigning in our mortal bodies [cf. Rom 6:12]. We have not yet seen the glory of the incorruptible God [cf. Rom 1:23], for we are still separated [from Him] by darkness. We have not yet put on the armor of light [cf. Rom 13:12], since we have not yet taken off the armor and the works of darkness. We have not yet been transformed by the renewal of our mind [cf. Rom 12:2], for we are still conformed to this age in vanity of mind [cf. Eph 4:17]. We are still [mired] in passions of the flesh and immoral desires. We have not yet become heirs of God and co-heirs of Christ [cf. Rom 8:17].

The spirit of slavery still exists in us, and not that of sonship [cf. Rom 8:15]. We have not yet become the temple of God and the dwelling place of the Holy Spirit [cf. 1 Cor 3:16], for we are still a temple of idols and the vessel of evil spirits, because of our inclination to lustful passions. Verily, yea in truth, we have not yet come into the purity of behavior and the brightness of mind. We have not yet become worthy of the pure milk of reason, nor have we become worthy of spiritual growth. The day has not yet arrived for us, nor has the morning star dawned in our hearts. We have not yet become united with the sun of righteousness [cf. Mal 3:20], nor have we begun to shine together with its dawning rays. We have not yet received the likeness of the Lord [cf. 1 Jn 3:2; Gen 1:26], neither have we become partakers of the divine nature [cf. 2 Pet 1:4]. We have not yet become the spotless purple royal robe, nor the unadulterated divine image. We have not yet been wounded by the divine *eros*, nor have we been smitten by the spiritual love of the bridegroom. We have not yet known the invisible and mystic communion. In summary, we have not yet become "a chosen race, a royal priesthood, a holy nation" [1 Pet 2:9], for we are serpents, the offspring of vipers [cf. Mt 23:33].

How are we not serpents, we who crawl on the earth and think the things of earth and do not have our commonwealth in heaven? [cf. Phil 3:19-20]. And how are we not the offspring of vipers, we who are not to be found in the obedience of God, but rather in disobedience and in our own self desires? How can I not cry out aloud with tears to Him who is able to remove the deceit which is around and in me? How shall I destroy the passions which are in me and become a partaker of the glory of God? I will strive earnestly to become a blameless child of God and enter into that dwelling which Jesus Christ entered as our forefunner [cf. Heb 4:1; 6:20]. I will shed tears like streams. I will flood my bed every night with tears [cf. Ps 6:6], so that I, because of my contrition and distress of [123] heart, may receive mercy and so that I, who have chosen the good portion like Mary [cf. Lk 10:42], will be heard and deemed worthy of the heavenly bread.

> Someone may ask, if some benefit accrues to the multitudes of Christians who have not kept all the commandments but have nevertheless kept some of them? Here it is good to recall blessed Peter, who after so many achievements and after being pronounced blessed so often, hears [Christ say to him] on account of only one [word that he had spoken]: 'If I do not wash you, you have no part in me' [Jn 13:8]. Let me say that [the word Peter has spoken] indicated neither indifference nor contempt, but was an expression of honor and reverence. But, someone may say, it is written: 'that whoever calls on the name of the Lord shall be saved' [Acts 2:21]. Does this mean that the mere invocation of the Lord is sufficient to save the one who invokes [Him]? But then listen to the Apostle saying: 'How are men to call upon him in whom they have not believed?' [Rom 10:14]. If you believe, hearken to the Lord: 'Not every one who says to me, 'Lord, Lord,' shall enter into the kingdom of heaven but he who does the will of my Father' [Mt 7:21]. Therefore, whenever a person does the will of the Lord, but not as God wills, that is, if he does not do it out of love for God, the zeal with which he does the work is to no purpose. According to the voice of God: 'They do all their deeds to be seen by men' [Mt 23:5]; 'truly, I say to you, they have their reward' [Mt 6:2]. Therefore, Paul also was taught to say: 'If I give away all I have, and if I deliver my body to be burned, but have not love, I gain nothing' [1 Cor 13:3].[50]

How then can we, who have preferred a life of lust rather than a life of obedience to the commandments, take for granted that we shall share in the blessed life and the commonwealth of the saints and the rejoicing of the angels in the presence of Christ? [cf. Eph 2:19].

> Indeed, such wishful thinking belongs to a childish mind! I have not accepted the common faith with thankfulness; how can I be with Job? I have not been mercifully disposed toward my enemy; how can I be with David? I have not sought God with continuous self-control and diligent prayer; how can I be with Daniel? I have not walked in the footsteps of the other saints; how can I be with them? Who would be such an unjust judge as to bestow the same equal [124] wreaths of reward on both the victor and on the one who has never competed for the prize? What general sends forth the spoils of war in equal portions, both to those who have conquered and to those who were not even present at the battle? God is good, but He is also just...Let us not then know God only in part...Let us not accept His mercy in a way that it becomes a pretext for laziness. There is thunder and there is lightning, so that goodness should not be slighted. The One who causes the sun to rise [cf. Mt 5:45] also strikes men with blindness [cf. 2 Kg 6:18]. He who sends the rain [cf. Zech 10:1], also causes the rain of fire [cf. Gen 19:24]. By the former He manifests His goodness. By the latter He shows His severity. We should love [God] because of the former, and we should be afraid [of Him] because of the latter, so that it will not be said of us also; 'Or do you presume upon the riches of his kindness and forbearance and patience? Do you not know that God's kindness is meant to lead you to repentance? But by your hard and impenitent heart you are storing up wrath for yourself on the day of wrath' [Rom 2:4-5].

Therefore, it is not possible to be saved without doing works according to the commandment of God, nor is it safe to neglect some of the things which have been commanded. It would be grossly arrogant on our part if we wished to set ourselves up as critics of the Lawgiver. Let us, therefore, honor the keeping of the evangelical doctrines according to the true faith, and let us make it our common concern and resolve to be zealous that we avoid none of those things which have been commanded. If the man of God is to be perfect [cf. 2 Tim 3:17], he must be perfected by every commandment, according to the measure of the stature of the fullness of Christ [cf. Eph 4:13]. For just as the 'necessity is laid upon me, woe to me if I do not preach the Gospel' [1 Cor 9:16]; you also must exert an equal struggle either to abandon the inquiry, or lazily and carelessly to keep what has been handed down and fulfill it through works. For the Lord says: 'The word I have spoken will be his judge on the last day' [Jn 12:48]. A servant who did not know, (the will of the Lord) but who did things that 'deserved a beating' [Lk 12:48], shall be beaten with few stripes. Another, who knew, and did not, but neither prepared himself according to his [Master's] will, he shall be beaten with many stripes [cf. Lk 12:47]. Let the dispensation of the word [of God] take place in such a way that I am without re-[125] proach and that it be fruitful for you. For we know that the words of the inspired Scripture will be set up to confront us at the judgement seat of Christ. For He says: 'I will reprove you and I will lay the sin before your face' [Ps 50:21]. Let us then in all sobriety carefully attend to what has been said and hasten to put the divine doctrines into practice, for we know not the day nor the hour when our Lord will come [cf. Mt 24:42; Eph 2:19].[51]

Intimacy with God is not a matter of kinship according to the flesh, but it is achieved through zeal for the will of God [cf. Mk 3:35]. "He who is of God hears the word of God" [Jn 8:47]. Also, the Epistle to the Romans says: "All who are led by the Spirit of God are sons of God" [Rom 8:14]. Chrysostom, interpreting this verse, says:

> To keep them from placing their confidence in the gift of [bap-tismal] cleansing and then neglecting the manner of life in the city [of God]....He did not say 'they received,' but 'they are led.' [52]

That is to say, as many as live right throughout their lives are the sons of God. In Saint John we read: "You are my friends, if you do what I com-mand you" [Jn 15:14]. It is impossible to be deemed worthy of the kingdom of heaven, if one does not have the righteousness according to the Gospel, which is greater than that of the Law. [Scripture] says: "Unless your righteousness exceeds that of the Scribes and Pharisees, you will never enter into the kingdom of heaven" [Mt 5:20]. The Apostle [Paul] also says:

> Indeed I count every thing as loss because of the surpassing worth of knowing Christ Jesus my Lord. For his sake I have suffered the loss of all things, and count them as refuse, in order that I may gain Christ, and be found in him, not having a righteousness of my own based on law, but that which is through faith in Christ, the righ-teousness from God [Phil 3:8-9], for whatever does not proceed from faith is sin [Rom 14:23].

Therefore, we must be led by the Holy Spirit and by a correct faith if we are to be deemed worthy of the kingdom of God. Moreover, it is necessary to know and confess that the grace needed for every good deed, and patience in our sufferings for Christ come from God. For Saint John says: "No one can receive anything except what is given him from heaven" [Jn 3:27]. "What have you that you did not receive?" [1 Cor 4:7]. "For by grace you have been saved through faith; and this is not your own doing; it is the gift of God, not because of works, lest any man should boast" [Eph 2:8-9]. This also is from God: "For it has been [126] granted to you that for the sake of Christ you should not only believe in him, but also suffer for his sake, engaged in the same conflict" [Phil 1:29-30].

Moreover, a person must not be arrogant in himself, because of his achievements, and look with contempt upon others. Saint Luke says: "He also told this parable to some who trusted in themselves that they were righteous and despised others: 'Two men went up into the temple to pray' " [Lk 18:9-10]. When a person ascribes his achievements to himself and not to God, what else is that but a rejection of God and rebellion against Him? Those who trust in themselves and do not ascribe everything to God, but rather hold others in contempt, show that—although righteousness is otherwise admirable and brings a man near to God—when a righteous person becomes arrogant, it casts him into the lowest state and makes a demon out of him, who before had been endowed with the likeness of God. Men must for that reason not rely on themselves, nor may they boast, as Basil said,[53] that the blessing of the preaching [of the Gospel] is the result of their individual devising, but they must entrust everything to God. Paul says: "Such is the confidence that we have through Christ toward God. Not that we are sufficient of ourselves to claim anything as coming from us: our sufficiency is from God, who has qualified us to be ministers of a new covenant" [2 Cor 3:4-6]. And elsewhere: "But we have this treasure in earthen vessels, to show that the transcendent power belongs to God, and not to us" [2 Cor 4:7]. Again our Lord says: "If you love me, you will keep my commandments" [Jn 14:15]. As long as we are not keeping all the commandments of the Lord, we are not the kind of person concerning whom He can testify: "You are not of this world" [Jn 15:9]. Nor can [in that case] we expect the gifts of the Holy Spirit.

It is right not only to obey the commandments but also the virtues, the customs and the feasts are not to be scorned, in compliance with canon 53 of the Apostles[54] which says: "On feast days one who does not partake of meat...[let him be deposed]". Concerning fasting, canon 69 says: "If anyone...fails to fast through the forty days of Holy Lent, or on [127] Wednesdays and Fridays, let him be deposed from office", and so on.[55] Fasting was instituted by God through Moses, as it is written. One passage says explicitly that a soul which has not been humbled by fasting before the feast shall be excommunicated [cf. Ex 12:15, 19]. Let us hasten, then, to do what salvation calls for through fasting and prayer. But when we are fasting, let us not fast by way of judgment of contention, nor strike the humble and the proselytes [cf. Is 58:4]. Let us loose

every bond of wickedness, and let us destroy the documents of forced
negotiations. Let us share our bread with those who are hungry. Let us
open our homes to those who are poor and homeless, according to the
commandments of the prophet [cf. Is 58:6-7]. Having fasted bodily, let
us also fast spiritually, continually abstaining from evil. "Then shall
your light break forth like the dawn" as it is written [Is 58:8]. God will
hear our cry; do not be sad, for while we are still speaking He will say:
"Here I am" [Is 58:9].


### [21. The Cult of the Saints]

The twenty-first and final [article] contains as its subject the cultus of
the saints; and we say that the remembrance of the saints is profitable
for the strengthening of our faith, bearing in mind that they attained
grace and help from God through faith. We say that *epiklesis* or invocation in the strict sense belongs to God alone, and that primarily and particularly it is directed to Him. Invoking the saints, however, is not in a
strict sense invocation, but merely, as it were, invocation by chance and
by grace. For Peter or Paul will not hearken to those who are invoking
them, but the grace which they have received does that, as the Lord
says: "I am with you always, to the close of the age" [Mt 28:20].

And concerning the invocation of God, Paul the Divine, writing to
the Romans, says: "But how are men to call upon him in whom they
have not believed?" [Rom 10:14]. This proves that we must invoke only
Him in whom we have believed, that is, God. We, too, address invocation in the strict sense to God alone. Thus, we cry out during the Divine
Liturgy: "Deem us worthy, O Master, with boldness and without condemnation to dare to call upon Thee, the heavenly God, as Father, and
to say: 'Our Father, who are in heaven' " [Mt 6:9]. And elsewhere
[128] our rites say: "O Lord of hosts, be with us, for beside Thee we
have no other helper in adversity." Again, "Beside Thee we know not
another God" [Great Compline]. We make mediators of all the saints,
especially the Mother of the Lord, and along with her the choir of
angels and saints, whom we venerate in a relative manner, but not in the
manner of divine worship with temples, votive offerings, invocations,
and holy icons. We know, indeed, that we must worship God exclusively
and know no other than Him, nor do we worship any other god [cf. Mt
4:10; Ps 81:10]. We do not wish to be too greatly involved in relation
with the saints, fearing, perhaps, lest we unwittingly fall into divine worship. God forbid! For it is sinful for the Church of Christ and for her
children to worship, except in a relative manner [i.e., venerate], the holy
icons, the honor of which passes over to the prototype [therein
depicted], as Basil says.[56]

Furthermore, we regard all the saints as our mediators and in-
tercessors. We say that not only in the present age, but also in the age to

come there will be a mediation of angels and of saints, and by no means the least of whom will be the Lady of the World [Virgin Mary], who will entreat the Lord for some. However, they will not intercede simply for all, nor for those who died in sin—not at all, for God once and for all has cut off his mercy to such [persons]. God has pronounced this judgment against them: even if Noah and Job and Daniel were to stand up on their behalf, they could not set free their own sons and daughters [cf. Ezek 14:14]. All [the saints and angels] pray only for those for whom their supplications are acceptable, that is to say, for those who have left this life in repentance, but have not yet been able to cleanse away the spots of sins so long as the judgment continues. But after the dissolution of this court, when each [offender] will have been taken to the place of punishment which has been determined for him, there can and will be no further intercession. This supplication now occurs and is preached in the Church. We cry aloud to the saints and to our Lady and to the holy angels.

To our Lady [we say]: "Oh, all-holy sovereign Lady, Mother of God, intercede for us sinners." To the holy angels [we say]: "Oh, all ye heavenly hosts, angels, and archangels, intercede for us." We also ask the [129] Prophet-Forerunner and Baptizer of the Lord, the glorified Apostles, the Prophets, the Martyrs, the Hallowed Ones, the Spiritual Shepherds, the Ecumenical Teachers, the other categories of saints, and the choir of Holy Women to intercede for us sinners. That by the grace of God and by the unconquerable and divine and incomprehensible power of the cross, He would be merciful to us sinners, who worship Him and who persist steadfastly in confession and repentance. We ask that the eyes of our souls may be illumined [cf. Eph 1:18], lest, while sinning, we sleep in death, and the enemy may have power against us. Thus, through the supplication of all those whom we have mentioned, we entreat God to be our protector, and to deliver us from the snares of the Evil One.

Now, replying to those so-called abuses, we say:

### [22. Both Kinds in the Sacrament]
First, you say that it is necessary for a person to receive both kinds. You speak correctly. We also administer both kinds, to those who are worthy to receive the awesome sacraments. We do not, however, use unleavened, but leavened, bread as one kind.

### [23. The Married Life of Priests]
Second, you say that it is better to marry than to be aflame with passion [cf. 1 Cor 7:9], according to Saint Paul's command about "the husband of one wife..." [1 Tim 3:2; cf. Tit 1:6]. We too permit those priests who are unable to remain celibate to marry before ordination. God has

ordained marriage, and we are not ignorant that severe disorders take place among those in the clergy who have been prevented from being married. If he [a priest] has decided to remain celibate, let him practice celibacy. But we do not grant permission to marry after one has made the promise of celibacy. [Jesus says]: "No one who puts his hand to the plow and looks back is fit for the kingdom of God" [Lk 9:62]. If someone commits a human failing, we chasten him through penance and confession and other corrective measures, and cleanse him by restraining him from [further] evil deeds. And the mercy of God will not reject him.

### [24. The Divine Liturgy]

Third, you emphasize that the Divine Liturgy is celebrated by you in a more pious manner than by your opponents. Some [among the latter] perform it for gain, resulting in an increase in the number of private [130] liturgies. You celebrate one liturgy, in contrast to the custom of the Church of Rome. A person who celebrates the Liturgy for gain acts wickedly. This is also certainly admitted by all of us, and it is true. And in addition, you say that the passion of Christ has set us free not only from original sin, but from all sin. To this we say that we are obligated to keep the whole law [cf. Jas 2:10]. And as He has lived, who died and rose for us, so we, also, as we are able, should live mindful of what the Apostles wrote: "The love of Christ controls us, because we are convinced that one died for all; therefore, all have died. And he died for all, that those who live might live no longer for themselves but for him who for their sake died and was raised" [2 Cor 5:14-15]. If he who has been circumcised is under obligation to keep the whole law, how much more is he who has been circumcised with the circumcision in Christ [cf. Gal 5:3; Col 2:11]. That is, by taking off the whole body of sins of the flesh, he is obliged to fulfill that which the Apostle has said: "I am crucified unto the world and the world unto me" [Gal 2:20; 6:14]. "For to me to live is Christ, and to die is gain" [Phil 1:21]. Thus, it is necessary that we must be dead to sin [cf. Rom 6:11], and not a slave of it, and to follow the Lord, which, indeed, is to live totally in God [cf. Rom 6:10]. If we sin without repenting, the passion of Christ will not benefit us in the least.

### [25. Confession]

Fourth, you write concerning confession and forgiveness of sins. To this we say, following Basil the Great, that each Christian who desires to show significant progress and to lead a manner of life that conforms to the commandments of our Lord must keep no discomposure of his soul hidden within himself, nor express a word without first examining it, but must disclose the hidden things of the heart. He is to do this [confess] not to just anyone, but to those who are able to heal him. And elsewhere, he

[Basil] says that one must confess one's sins to those who are entrusted with the dispensation of the sacraments of God. This is what the penitent Christians among the saints of ancient times were found to be doing. Concerning the authority to forgive, he says that it was not given in an [131] absolute sense, but on the agreement between the penitent person who is obedient and sincere and the one who cares for his soul. Indeed, to repent means not to do the same deeds again. The one who attempts to do the same deeds again is like "the dog which turns back to his own vomit" [2 Pet 2:22]. Therefore, one must abstain in deed and in thought from what has been committed, and apply to the wounds the remedies which prevent sins.

### [26. The Distinction of Foods]

Fifth, concerning feast offerings, fasts, and traditions, you say that we should believe that Christ forgives our sins freely, and not on account of our own righteousness. You also say that it is impossible to keep all the traditions, and that as a result pious consciences are greatly distressed. Concerning these matters let us hear what Saint Basil says: "We must guard ourselves so that we do not on the pretext of one commandment appear to abolish another one." Therefore, in commenting on the subject of food, he says that the Apostle did not merely direct [his readers to] "make no provision for the flesh," but that [the Apostle also added,] "to gratify its desires" [Rom 13:14]. Thus on the one hand, one must through ascetic practices cut off the covetous and lustful desires of the flesh, and, on the other hand, one must take care to preserve that which promotes the good. He says: "Food will not commend us to God" [1 Cor 8:8]. "The kingdom of God does not mean food and drink but righteousness and peace and joy in the Holy Spirit" [Rom 14:17]. For this reason a rational abstinence from foods is also allowed. When one examines this matter of abstinence from food in itself, "we are no worse off if we do not eat, and no better off if we do" [1 Cor 8:8]. The ones who do not eat are not more . virtuous than the ones who do eat merely because they do not eat; nor are those who eat inferior to those who do not eat simply because they eat, as long as their inner virtue is equal. Of course, in considering the virtue in the soul, one must also include the things that concern the body. Things that are not good in themselves become good through the good grace of the goods that adorn them.

All the traditions that have been handed down by the Holy Fathers, must be preserved and accepted as referring to the same purpose. For [the Apostle] says that whoever disregards this disregards God [cf. 1 Th 4:8]. For that reason one must not tear to shreds such traditions, even though some persons misuse them in spite of their pious intent. One must [132] rebuke such persons and admonish them, to demonstrate correct judgement. We see Basil the Great doing this in many cases, especially when he asks if the work that the law commands is acceptable to God even though it has not been carried out according to the commandment of God. Nothing can make us such imitators of Christ, as the concern for our neighbor. It is not fitting for the faithful to say anything that burdens consciences. "Whatever is born of God overcomes the world" [1 Jn 5:4]. Therefore, the same [Basil] says:

> Who can be so insensitive and so unbelieving as to be satisfied with what has already been done or to refuse something as too burdensome or wearisome?

> For this reason not one of the faithful has dared to ridicule monastic life, which has been instituted for a divine purpose. Although many perhaps have undertaken to begin this [way of life], there have been few who have worthily achieved it. Assuredly, the achievement does not exist simply in the intention, but the gain is in the achievement for those who laboriously apply the effort. Certainly everyone admires and praises this kind [of life] in which a competent person admonishes the young and the uninstructed in a manner prescribed and ordered elsewhere. You, follower of the monastic life, faithful man, does of pious works, learn and be instructed in the evangelical manner of life, and so on.[57]

Again, when [Basil] sets forth what trials must precede the reception of novices, he says that one must allow them to dedicate themselves to God even at a youthful age. He who does so shows genuine love toward God and may be assured of a certain reward from the Lord.

With regard to the verses of Paul that you [theologians] offer concerning tradition, the solution is obvious from what has already been said. For the Apostle in those verses is not discussing pious customs and traditions, but heretical ones and others. For that reason Chrysostom says, in commenting on the statements in the 4th chapter of the Epistle to Timothy, that it refers to Manicheans, Encratites, and Marcionites [cf. 1 Tim 4:1-5].[58]

Just as those who hold the faith are safely moored by the anchor, so those who have fallen from [the faith] cannot stand upright anywhere. After they have been misled, they wander up and down, and at the end they descent to the depths of destruction. Furthermore, he [Chrysostom] says that what was written in the 2nd chapter of Colossians [cf. 2:20-23][59] was intended to overturn the Greek and Judaistic superstitious observances, so that these verses [133] refer to those who do not hold fast to Christ. This, he says, is also true of [Paul's] statements in the 5th chapter of the Epistle to the Galatians [cf. 5:1-15].[60] And in the 1st chapter of the Epistle to Titus [cf. 1:10-16].[61] Basil also says:

> If the righteousness according to the Law that some pursue who have dedicated themselves in baptism to God and promised to 'live no longer for themselves but for him who for their sake died and was raised' [2 Cor 5:15] leads to a verdict of adultery according to the Apostle, what would one have to say with regard to human traditions? [cf. Rom 7:2-4].[62]

Concerning justification by faith, we say, as Chrysostom[63] does, that knowledge comes through faith, and that without faith there is no way to know Christ. Behold, no reasoning can prove the resurrection and the birth [of Christ]; only faith can do so. These things create righteousness. You will observe that not simply faith is necessary, but faith through works. For that person most certainly believes that Christ is risen who exposes himself boldly to danger and who shares in His suffering, and so on. For this reason the Apostle says:

> [That I might] be found in him, not having a righteousness of my own, based on law, but that which is through faith in Christ, the righteousness from God that depends on faith; that I may know him and the power of his resurrection, and may share his sufferings, becoming like him in his death [Phil 3:9-11].

And again: "God is faithful" [1 Cor 1:9]. He who has promised to save will surely save just as He has promised. But how has He promised? If we are willing and if we will obey Him. But not simply this — not if we are idle like sticks and stones. He has properly added: "We trust," that is, we must believe in His kindness and depend totally upon Him [cf. 1 Tim 4:10]. We must cast everything in with Him. But at the same time, we ourselves should labor that virtue will be present in us until our final breath. Therefore, let us not merely hold fast to Christ, but also follow Him. For if we stand apart [from Him], we perish. For they who separate themselves from Christ are lost. But let us be joined to Him through works [cf. 1 Cor 6:17]. He says: "All who keep my commandments abide in me" [1 Jn 3:24]. He shows us our union with Him by means of many metaphors. Consider: He is the head [cf. Eph 4:15], and we the body. [134] He is the cornerstone [cf. Eph 2:20], we the building. He is the vine, we the branches [cf. Jn 15:5]. All these indicate our union with Him. He allows no empty space to come between us and Him, not even the least. He who remains a small distance away, even though he proceeds greatly forward, will be left behind. If the vine is cut off only slightly from its root, it is useless. Thus, the very least is not small, but it is almost the whole. Therefore, when we commit small iniquities or are a little remiss, let us not overlook this very little thing since, once overlooked, it quickly becomes great.

### [27. Monastic Vows]

Moreover, on the [sixth] subject concerning monks, we say with Basil the Great that:

> The merciful God solicitous for our salvation ordained two states of life for men, marriage and virginity. He who is not able to endure the hardships of virginity, may enter into union with a wife, knowing that he will be required to give an account of his sobriety

and holiness, and his resemblance to the saints, who lived in the marriage bond and who reared children.[64] A reckoning will be required of everyone concerning the fruits of his love of God and of his neighbor and concerning his transgressions of the commandments and of the established order, as the Lord declares in the Gospel when He says:'He that loves father or mother more than me is not worthy of me' [Mt 10:37]....Therefore, do not relax, you who have chosen the marriage relationship with a wife, as if you had authority to embrace worldliness. You have need of greater labors and vigilance if you are to gain salvation. And you, the lover of the celestial polity, and an active participant in the angelical life, who seeks to become a fellow-soldier with the holy disciples of Christ, brace yourself to endure tribulations and courageously proceed to the assemblage of the monks. Be a zealous imitator of those who live upright lives and inscribe their deeds upon your heart. Pray to be among the few, for the good is rare. Wherefore they who enter the kingdom are few in number...If you desire to seize [the kingdom], seize it by force [cf. Mt 11:12]. Submit your neck to the yoke of Christ. Bind the yoke tightly about your throat. Let it pinch your neck. Rub it thin by labor to acquire virtue, in fast-[135] ings [cf. 2 Cor 6:5], in vigils, in obedience, in silence, in psalms, in prayers, in tears, in manual labor, and in enduring all tribulations which befall you from demons and from men.[65] In this serious task virginity is an ally of those who use this gift according to reason. The gift of virginity, however, does not solely consist in abstaining from the procreation of children, but our whole life, conduct, and ethos, should be virginal. The whole life-style of the unmarried person must demonstrate freedom from corruption...Therefore, if we desire to adorn the character of our soul by freedom from passion after the likeness of God [cf. Gen 1:26], so that thereby we may attain eternal life, let us pay attention to ourselves lest we do something unworthy of our promise and thus incur the judgment pronounced upon Ananias [cf. Acts 5:1-5].

Initially Ananias did not have to promise his property to God. But since, with a view to human glory, he dedicated his property to God through his promises in order to be admired by men for his munificence, and then kept back part of the sum of money, he provoked the Lord to such wrath—of which Peter was the minister— that he was not able to find the gate to repentance.

Accordingly, before a person commits himself to the praiseworthy [monastic] life, he is free, if he desires, within permitted and lawful limits, to follow the way of the world and give himself to the yoke of wedlock. However, when he has already become subject to a prior claim, through his own commitment, it is fitting that he reserve himself for God, as a kind of sacred offering, lest he involve himself in a verdict of sacrilege by defiling again in an ordinary way of life, the body which he had consecrated to God by his vow. And I say this not only with one kind of passion in mind — as some think, who would reserve the integrity of virginity by guarding the body alone — but with reference to every manifestation of passionate inclination. The person who determines to reserve himself for God may not be defiled by any worldly passion...For everything which occurs as a result of passion somehow mars the purity of the soul and hinders the divine life. For that reason the person who renounces the world must look to those things so that he does not defile himself, the vessel of God, in any way by the employment of any passion. It is particularly necessary that a person who has chosen the way of the angels remember that he has gone past and [136] beyond the limits of human nature and has devoted himself to a spiritual manner of life. For it is characteristic of the angelic nature to be free from the marriage yoke [cf. Mt 18:10], and not to be distracted by any other kind of beauty, but ceaselessly to intently gaze at the divine countenance.[66]

Whoever would truly follow God must sever the bonds of attachment to life. This can be achieved through complete separation from and forgetfulness of old habits. For if we do not separate ourselves from fleshly ties and worldly society and, as it were, be transported to another world according to him who said that 'our commonwealth is in heaven' [Phil 3:20], we shall be left helpless to achieve our goal of pleasing God. The Lord has said specifically: 'So therefore, whoever of you does not renounce all that he has cannot be my disciple' [Lk 14:33]. And when we have done this, it is essential to keep guard over our heart [cf. Pr 4:23] so that we neither banish the thought of God nor sully the memory of His wonders by vain and idle imaginations; but through a continuous and pure recollection of divine things, stamped upon our souls as by an indelible seal, carry about the holy thought of God. In this way the love of God prevails over us, and at the same time it alerts us to observe the commandments of the Lord. By these, in turn, our love is preserved in perfect continuation. The Lord indicates this when He says: 'If you love me, you keep my commandments' [Jn 14:15]. And at another time: 'If you keep my comandments, you will abide in my love' [Jn 15:10]. Elsewhere the Lord calls such people perfect [cf. Mt 5:48; 19:21].[67]

For that reason one need not marvel if the manner of life of those monks who are living uprightly is called perfect. Chrysostom[68] says that:

> through the washing of regeneration all previous sins have been forgiven; after this forgiveness and baptism, the Lord again gives the sinner help through repentance. 'Though your sins be as purple, I will make them white as snow' [Is 1:18]; and I [God] will change [137] it to the opposite condition. For that reason it is not so bad to fall as it is to remain lying in a fallen condition.

This is the reason why one must praise the life of the monks and not disparage it. For he who honors such virtuous men will also honor God. But he who has learned to scorn them, proceeding in that direction, will also at some time insult God. "He who receives you," He says, "receives me" [Mt 10:40], and "he who rejects you rejects me" [Lk 10:16]. Let us also therefore imitate them, and let us glorify God everywhere by a conscientious life. No one can say that it is impossible to become that kind of person today, because the love for God is not taught. The law is the gardener and cultivator of the powers that are spermatically inherent in us [cf. Gal 3:24].

Since we have been commanded to love our neighbor as ourselves, let us learn if we have the power from God to carry out this commandment. Who then does not know that human beings are civilized and social creatures, and not an isolated or wild animal? For nothing is thus more peculiar to our nature than to be in one another's company, to need each other and to love those of the same race. From the seeds which the Lord himself has given us, He later seeks the fruits, saying: "A new commandment I give to you, that you love one another" [Jn 13:34]. The Lord desires to arouse our soul with such a commandment. He did not demand that His disciples prove themselves by signs and marvelous powers, although God had granted them the power to perform them through the Holy Spirit. But what does He say? "By this all men will know that you are my disciples, if you have love for one another" [Jn 13:35]. Thus, in every instance He joins these commandments together so that He transfers to himself the kindness that we do toward our neighbor. He says: "I was hungry and you gave me food" [Mt 25:35]. He then adds: "As you did it to one of the least of these my brethren, you did it to me" [Mt 25:40]. Indeed, through the first, the second is achieved and through the second, in turn, the first is accomplished.

If we love the Lord, it follows that also we love our neighbor. He said: "If a man loves me he will keep my commandments" [Jn 14:23]. "This is my commandment, that you love one another as I have loved you" [Jn 15:12]. The person who loves his neighbor fulfills the commandments to [138] love God, and receives the grace back to himself. For this reason the faithful servant of God, Moses, showed such great love toward his brothers, that he preferred himself be taken out of the book of God, in which his name was written [cf. Ex 32:32], so that the sin of the people might be forgiven. If we have this love, it is not right to mock that which was commanded by the Fathers.

### [28. The Power of the Bishops]

[With reference to the seventh section,] Basil says: "The differences among those who govern should not hinder the obedience of subordinates."[69] Moses did not disobey the good advice of Jethro [cf. Ex 18:24]. But there is no small difference among the commandments. Some [man-made laws] contradict the commandment of the Lord, either by starting to corrupt it, or by greatly defiling it by blending it with that which has been prohibited. On the other hand, there are [man-made laws] which coincide with the [divine] commandment, and still others which, although they do not obviously coincide, nevertheless contribute to and reinforce the [divine] commandment.

In view of this, it is necessary to recall the words of the Apostle: "Do not despise prophesying but test everything; hold fast what is good, abstain from every form of evil" [1 Th 5:20-22]. And further: "We destroy arguments and every proud obstacle to the knowledge of God, and take every thought captive to obey Christ" [2 Cor 10:5]. So if a [man-made law] coincides with the commandment of the Lord or reinforces it, we must accept it most earnestly and carefully as the will of God, and so fulfill the saying: "Forbearing one another in the love" [Eph 4:2] of Christ. If on the contrary, we are ordered by someone to do something [against] the commandment of the Lord which either corrupts or defiles it, then it is time to say: "We must obey God rather than men" [Acts 5:29], and to remember the Lord saying, "A stranger they will not follow, but they will flee from him, for they do not know the voice of strangers" [Jn 10:5].

[We must also remember] the words of the Apostle who dared for our safety to reproach even the angels, of whom he says: "Even if we, or an angel from heaven, should preach to you a gospel contrary to that which we preach to you, let him be accursed" [Gal 1:8]. From these passages we are taught that even if a very celebrated and highly honored person forbids that which is commanded by the Lord, or urges us to do things which are forbidden by Him, such a person should be avoided and detested by everyone who loves the Lord.

[139] Therefore, no one can make excuses concerning those things which have been said. All the faithful must accept those matters which have been decided synodically as being in accord with the inspired Scripture. Therefore, even up to today we do not eat anything that has been strangled [cf. Acts 15:20], rather we abhor it, abiding by that which the Fathers and the Apostles have proclaimed. For it is written: "Abstain

from what has been sacrificed to idols and from blood and from what is strangled" [Acts 15:29]. Likewise, the 63rd Apostolic canon[70] and the 67th canon of the Sixth Ecumenical Synod say: "If anyone attempts to eat the blood of any animal...let him be excommunicated." [71] Basil also, in legislating concerning these things, says:

> I find further in taking up the Holy Scriptures, that in the Old and New Testament, disobedience toward God is explicitly condemned, not in the great number, nor by the gravity of sins, but only in the violation of whatsoever ordinance, and that there is a common judgment against every disobedience to God.[72]

And again:

> From this, as well as from similar evidence, I thought it to be obvious that, in general, wicked lusts derive from ignorance concerning God or false knowledge, especially the disagreement of many with each other through which we make ourselves unworthy to receive God's guidance. Further, I have given consideration to such a life, if ever it had to come, but I was unable to assess the magnitude of such foolishness or senselessness or madness, whether it came out of an excess of malice or from some cause about which I am not able to speak. For if among the irrational creatures we find such agreement achieved among one another through obedience toward a leader, what ought we to say when we [human beings] find ourselves in such disagreement with each other and in such an opposition against the commandments of the Lord? Or do we not think that God appointed all those things to teach us and to make us humble; and that on the great and awesome day of judgment those who have refused to be chastened will be brought forth in disgrace and contempt by the One who has said that 'the ox knows his owner, and the ass, his master's crib, but Israel does [140] not know [me], and my people do not understand [me]' [Is 1:3]. And many similar things.

> In a similar vein the Apostle says: 'If one member suffers, all suffer together' [1 Cor 12:26]. Likewise: 'That there may be no discord in the body, that the members may have the same care for one another' [1 Cor 12:25], that is to say, animated by one soul, which dwells in all of them. For what purpose has it been ordained thus? In my opinion the purpose is so that consistency and discipline may be preserved. Much more so is this in the case of the Church of God, concerning which it is said: 'Now you are the body of Christ and individually members of it' [1 Cor 12:27], that is to say: the Church holds and unites each member to the other, and in harmony with the one and only true head, which is

Christ. Among those where this harmony has not been achieved, the bond of peace is not preserved. Then the Church is not guarded in the spirit of meekness; instead dissension, and strife and rivalry are found. It would be very presumptuous to call such people 'members of Christ,' or to say that they are governed by Him. Moreover, one would be simple-minded not to say openly that in this case the spirit of the flesh conquers and reigns, as the Apostle definitively declares: 'If you yield yourselves to any one as obedient slaves, you are slaves of the one whom you obey' [Rom 6:16].

The same Apostle clearly shows the characteristics of just such an attitude when he says: 'For while there is jealousy and strife [and division] among you, are you not of the flesh?' [1 Cor 3:3; cf. Rom 8:6]. He [Paul] makes explicitly clear both the tragic end of such people and how irreconcilable their attitude is with godliness. For that reason he says: 'the mind that is set on the flesh is hostile to God' [Rom 8:7]. For the mind that is set on the flesh does not submit itself to the law of God, nor can it. Therefore, the Lord says: 'No servant can serve two masters' [Lk 16:13; cf. Mt 6:24]. That which is said in the Acts [of the Apostles], that 'now the company of those who believed were of one heart and soul', [Acts 4:32], is not realized by such people. There, no one person stood above the rest, but all sought together as one through the Holy Spirit, the will of the one Lord Jesus Christ, Who had said: 'I have come down from heaven not to do my own will, but the will of him who sent me' [Jn 6:38].[73]

[141] Let us proceed according to the rule of the saints, as having been "built upon the foundation of the apostles and prophets, Christ Jesus himself being the cornerstone in whom the whole structure is joined together and grows into a holy temple in the Lord" [Eph 3:20-21]. "May the God of peace himself sanctify you wholly; and may your spirit and soul and body be kept sound and blameless at the coming of our Lord Jesus Christ" [1 Th 5:23]. Indeed, God is trustworthy, who calls both you [the Lutherans] and us [the Eastern Orthodox] and who desires all to be saved [cf. 1 Tim 2:4]. He will save us, if we keep His commandments — which indeed is the crown in the salvation of all, without which it is impossible to be saved — through the grace of Christ in the Holy Spirit, as has been made clear and explained, part by part.

Let us not know God only in part, then, or make His compassion and kindness a pretext for negligence. Instead, let us soberly cling to that which has been said, and let us strive zealously to realize the divine commandments in practice, directing our attention nowhere else than toward Him who has said, "I came to cast fire" [Lk 12:49]. What else would I want than that it already is lit! Blessed David, who likewise sought power of this fire, said: "Prove me, O Lord, and try me; purify with fire my reins and my heart" [Ps 26:2]. This fire, burning the log which is in the eye [cf. Mt 7:3], purifies it so that with its natural clear-sightedness restored, it sees, without ceasing, the wonders of God, as the [Psalmist] said: "Unveil thou mine eyes, and I shall perceive wondrous things out of thy law" [Ps 118:18].

This fire puts the demons to flight and burns up iniquities. It is the power of the resurrection and the energy of immortality [cf. Eph 1:20], the illumination of holy souls and that which holds together the powers of reasoning. Let us pray that this fire may reach us also, so that we may always walk in the light of good works [cf. Phil 2:15-16], not stumbling even a little, but shining as luminaries in the world. Let us always hold fast to the word of life so that, having a part in all the things of God with our Lord Jesus Christ, we may come to rest in [everlasting] life, after we have fulfilled in a saintly manner the commandments and the virtues and everything holy and necessary for salvation. If we dwell thus throughout the time of our existence on earth, we shall reach the true fatherland. May we be deemed worthy thereof by the grace of Christ! Amen.

### [29. An Invitation To Follow the Holy Synods]

[142] All these things which we have spoken, beloved, are founded, as you very well know, upon the inspired Scriptures, according to the interpretation and the sound teaching and explanation of our wise and holy theologians [the Fathers of the Church]. For we may not rely upon our own interpretation and understand and interpret any of the words of the inspired Scripture except in accord with the theologizing Fathers who have been approved by the Holy Synods, [inspired] by the Holy Spirit for a pious purpose, lest our thought, like that of Proteus move around here and there, deviating from the correct evangelical teaching, from true wisdom and from prudence. But someone will say, how can these things be corrected? In this way: with the help of God.

Let no one undertake or think anything contrary to the decisions of the Holy Apostles and the Holy Synods. He who uprightly keeps this principle will be a partner with us in our rejoicing, a member of our community and one who holds the same faith. But what communion would one have with us, who rejects the aforementioned canons and opposes the Apostles and shamelessly turns himself against the Holy Apostles? What part could he have with us? Somewhere one of the teachers [of the Church] says to those who strive to be pious: "One who speaks contrary to the things which have been decided—even though he is trustworthy [cf. 1 Cor 4:2; 9:1], lives as a virgin, does wonders, and prophesies—is a wolf in sheep's clothing, who causes the ruin of the sheep." Another teacher says: "It shakes loose something that seemed good to the God-bearing Fathers, that cannot be called administration, but violation and betrayal of the dogma." Still another teacher [Saint Basil] says:

> One who has the judgment of Christ before his eyes, who has seen the great danger that threatens those who dare to subtract from or add to those things which have been handed down by the Spirit, must not be ambitious to innovate, but must content himself with those things which have been proclaimed by the saints.[74]

Therefore, since so many and such important of our theologizing Fathers forbid thinking otherwise, there is only one correction: conform to the Holy Synod and follow the canons of the Apostles and, thus, follow Christ in all things.

### [30. Closing Salutations]

[143] O most wise German men and beloved children of our humble self, since, as sensible men, you wish with your whole heart to enter our most Holy Church, we, as affectionate fathers, willingly accept your love and friendliness, if you will follow the Apostolic and Synodal decrees in harmony with us and will submit to them. For then you will indeed be in communion with us, and having openly submitted to our holy and catholic church of Christ, you will be praised by all prudent men. In this way the two churches will become one by the grace of God, we shall live together hereafter and we will exist together in a God-pleasing way until we attain the heavenly kingdom. May all of us attain it in Christ Jesus, to whom belongs glory unto the ages. Amen.

Written with the help of God, in Constantinople, in the year of the Incarnation of our Lord Jesus Christ 1576, 15 May, at the venerable Patriarchal Monastery of the Pammakaristos [All-Blessed Ever-Virgin Mary].

Jeremiah, by the mercy of God, Archbishop of
Constantinople, New Rome, and Ecumenical Patriarch

### NOTES

1. Pages 3-53 contain the text of the Augsburg Confession which is not presented here.

2. Page 55 contains the Latin translation of Patriarch Jeremiah's letter found in Greek on page 54 of the *Acta et Scripta*.

3. Unless otherwise noted, the quotations from the Old Testament are from the Septuagint, while those of the New Testament are from the Revised Standard Version.

4. Although numbered three in the original text, this should be number two, while number two below should be marked number three.

5. Ὁμοούσιον *(homoousion)*, "of the same essence" rather than 'consubstantial,' since the word 'substance' implies a 'material' entity.

6. Θελητικόν *(theletikon)*, "capacity for will." John of Damascus, *Exposition of the*

*Orthodox Faith*; Philip Schaff (ed.), *Nicene and Post Nicene Fathers of the Christian Church*. Ser. 2 (Grand Rapids, Michigan, 1969), 9, p. 39. Hereafter cited as NPNF.

7. *Ascetic Rules*, PG 31.1377C.

8. *Short Rules*, PG 31.1092.

9. Ibid. 31.1085.

10. *Concerning Baptism*, bk. 1, PG 31.1528; cf. St. Basil, Ascetical Works. Trans. M. Monica Wagner. *The Fathers of the Church* (Washington, D.C., 1962), 9, p. 349. Hereafter cited as FC.

11. *Commentary on 2nd Epistle to the Corinthians, Homily 10*, PG 61.481-82; cf. NPNF Ser. 1, vol. 12, pp. 336-37.

12. St. John Chrysostom, *Homily on Psalm 129*, PG 55.373-77.

13. St. John Chrysostom. *Commentary on 2nd Timothy, Homily 2*, PG 62.605-13; cf. NPNF Ser. 1, vol. 13, 481.

14. St. Gregory of Nazianzos, *Panegyric on His Brother Caesarios*, PG 35.785; cf. NPNF Ser. 2, vol. 7, 235-36.

15. This quotation from John of Damascus is wrongly attributed to Chrysostom's *Commentary on Philippians*, but is actually from Chrysostom's *Commentary on the Gospel of St. Matthew, Homily 31*, PG 57.375; cf. NPNF Ser. 1, vol. 10, 209.

16. St. John Chrysostom, *Commentary on Gospel of St. Matthew, Homily 17*, PG 57.261; cf. NPNF Ser. 1, vol. 10, 115-23.

17. St. John of Damascus, *Concerning Those Who Have Fallen Asleep in Faith*, PG 95.268-69.

18. Ibid. PG. 95.247-61.

19. "In the Orthodox Liturgy we see Christ symbolized and His works and passion for us." Nicholas Kabasilas: *A Commentary on the Divine Liturgy*, PG 150.369.

20. *Decrees and Canons of the Seven Ecumenical Councils, canon 32 of the Council of Trullo*, PG 137.624; cf. NPNF Ser. 2, vol. 14, 380.

21. *Apostolic Canons*, canon 1, PG 137.35; cf. NPNF Ser. 2, vol. 14, 594.

22. Ibid. canon 30, PG 137.93; cf. NPNF Ser. 2, vol. 14, 595.

23. Ibid. canon 25, PG 137.109; cf. NPNF Ser. 2, vol. 14, 595.

24. *Synod of Nicaea*, canon 4, PG 137.233; cf. NPNF Ser. 2, vol. 14, 11; Rallis-Potlis, 2, 122.

25. *Synod of Laodicea*, canon 12, PG. 137.1357; cf. NPNF Ser. 2, vol. 14, 131; Rallis-Potlis, 3, 182.

26. Ibid. canon 13, PG 137.1360; cf. NPNF Ser. 2, vol. 14, 131; Rallis-Potlis, 3, 183.

27. *Synod of Antioch*, canon 19, PG 137.1328; cf. NPNF Ser. 2, vol. 14, 117. Rallis-Potlis, 3, 160.

28. *Synod of Laodicea*, canon 5, PG 137.1348; cf. NPNF Ser. 2, vol. 14, 126.

29. *Synod of Nicaea*, canon 4, PG 137.233; cf. NPNF Ser. 2, vol. 14, 126.

30. *Synod of Antioch, Interpretation of Canon 19* by John Zonaras, PG 137.1328; cf. Rallis-Potlis, 2, 2.

31. St. Gregory Nazianzos the Theologian, *In Defense of His Flight to Pontus*, PG 35.407; cf. NPNF Ser. 2, vol. 7, 219.

32. Ibid. PG 35.407; cf. NPNF Ser. 2, vol. 7, 219.

33. Ibid. cf. NPNF Ser. 2, vol. 7, 220.

34. *Apostolic Canons*, canon 46, PG 137.129; cf. NPNF Ser. 2, vol. 14, 597.

35. St. John Chrysostom, *Commentary on Epistle to the Hebrew Homily 8*, PG 63.134-37; cf. NPNF Ser. 1, vol. 14, 452.

36. St. John Chrysostom, *Commentary on Epistle to the Philippians Homily 3*, PG 62.204; cf. NPNF Ser. 1, vol. 13, 197.

37. St. John Chrysostom, *Homily 9*, PG 62.242; cf. NPNF Ser. 1, vol. 13, 226.

38. St. John Chrysostom, *Commentary on 1st Epistle to Timothy, (1 Tim 2:1, 3-4) Homily 6*, PG 62.529-33; cf. NPNF Ser. 1, vol. 13, 426.

39. St. John Chrysostom, PG 62.529; cf. NPNF Ser. 1, vol. 13, 426.

40. St. John Chrysostom, *Commentary on Epistle to Philippians, Homily 3*, PG 62.204; cf. NPNF Ser. 1, vol. 13, 197.

41. St. John Chrysostom, *Commentary on 2nd Epistle to Thessalonians, Homily 3*, PG 62.397; cf. NPNF Ser. 1, vol. 13, 326.

42. St. John Chrysostom, *Commentary on Epistle to Hebrews, Homily 12*, PG 63.100; cf. NPNF Ser. 1, vol. 14, 425.

43. St. John Chrysostom, *Commentary on Epistle to the Philippians, Homily 8*, PG 62.239-40; cf. NPNF Ser. 1, vol. 12, 219-220.

44. St. John Chrysostom, *Commentary on 2nd Epistle to Timothy, Homily 6*, PG 62.624-631; cf. NPNF Ser. 1, vol. 13, 496.

45. St. John Chrysostom, *Commentary on Epistle to the Ephesians, (2.8) Homily 4*, PG 62.33; cf. NPNF Ser. 1, vol. 13, 67-8.

46. St. John Chrysostom, *Commentary on 2nd Epistle to Timothy, Homily 8*, PG 62.647-48; cf. NPNF Ser. 1, vol. 13, 507-08.

47. Ibid. *Homily 9*, PG 62.654; cf. NPNF Ser. 1, vol. 13, 512.

48. St. John Chrysostom, *Commentary on 2nd Epistle to Corinthians Homily 2*, PG 61.392-404; cf. NPNF Ser. 1, vol. 12, 284.

49. St. Basil, *The Long Rules*. PG 31.881; cf. FC vol. 9, 217.

50. Ibid. PG 31.893; cf. FC vol, 9, 226-27.

51. Ibid. PG 31.893; cf. FC vol. 9, 229-31.

52. St. John Chrysostom, *Commentary on the Epistle to the Romans Homily 14*, PG 69.525; cf. NPNF Ser. 1, vol. 2, 440-41.

53. St. Basil, *The Long Rules*, PG 31.893; cf. FC vol. 9, 233.

54. *Apostolic Canons*, canon 53, PG 137.145; cf. NPNF Ser. 2, vol. 14, 597.

55. Ibid. canon 69, PG 137.176-77; cf. NPNF Ser. 2, vol. 14, 598.

56. St. Basil quoted by St. John of Damascus in *Concerning Images*, PG 94.1261.

57. "On the Renunciation of Ascetical Works," in *Ascetical Works*, PG 31.620ff.

58. St. John Chrysostom, *Commentary on 1st Epistle to Timothy, Homily 12*, PG 62.557-58; cf. NPNF Ser. 1, vol. 13, 444.

59. St. John Chrysostom, *Commentary on Epistle to the Colossians Homily 7*, PG 62.344-52; cf. NPNF Ser. 1, vol. 13, 288-93.

60. St. John Chrysostom, *Commentary on Epistle to the Galatians*, PG 61.665-74; cf. NPNF Ser. 1, vol. 13, 36-42.

61. St. John Chrysostom, *Commentary on Epistle to Titus, Homily 3*, PG 62.677-78; cf. NPNF Ser. 1, vol, 13, 528.

62. St. Basil, *Concerning Baptism*, Book 1 Sermon 2, PG 31.1557; cf. FC vol. 9, 374-75.

63. St. John Chrysostom, *Commentary on Epistle to the Philippians, Homily 11*, PG 62.263-69; cf. NPNF Ser. 1, vol. 13, 235.

64. St. Basil "On the Renunciation of the World," in *Ascetical Works*, PG 31.628-29; cf. FC vol. 9, 16-29.

65. Ibid. 31.645-48; cf. FC vol. 9, 30.

66. Ibid. PG 31.876-73; cf. FC vol, 9, 207-09.

67. St. Basil, *The Long Rules*, PG 31.921; cf. FC vol 9, 242-43

68. St. John Chrysostom, *Instruction to Catechumen*, PG 49.223-27; cf. NPNF Ser. 1, vol. 9, 161-62.

69. St. Basil, *Commentary on Isaiah the Prophet*, chapter 1, PG 30.221.

70. *Apostolic Canons*, canon 63, PG 137.164; cf. NPNF Ser. 2, vol. 14, 598.

71. *Sixth Ecumenical Synod*, canon 67, PG 137.748; cf. NPNF Ser. 2, vol. 14, 395.

72. St. Basil, "On the Judgment of God," *Ascetical Works*, PG 31.653-76; cf. FC vol. 9, 43.

73. Ibid. PG 31.653-76; cf. FC vol. 9, 40-42.

74. St. Basil, *Against Eunomius 2*, PG 29.573-652.

## Chapter 3

## THE FIRST THEOLOGICAL EXCHANGE:
## TÜBINGEN TO CONSTANTINOPLE

*[A.] The Letter to Patriarch Jeremiah [II] Accompanying the First
Reply of the Tübingen Theologians*

[144] We received, All-holy Sir Patriarch, the honorable letter of Your
Holiness which is most courteous, or rather [we should say] of Christian
love, together with the most valuable book of Your Holiness on the 18th
of the month of June of last year. Nothing could have been more joyful,
nor desirable, than that written by the excellent man, holding the highest
degree of office, Father and most reverend Bishop.

If there is true love, there is nothing more amiable (if there is a common bond, the people grow together into one body under the
head — Christ); and when it has the common witness of the recommendation of such an enlightened person, it causes greater love in our souls.
However, not only because of this did we receive it [letter] with great joy,
but also because, which, it should be added, is greater, we are exhorted
by Your Holiness to embrace the true, and by all means, the absolute
perfect philosophy, which again the wise men of ancient Greece
miraculously came to know, the very wisdom of our Savior and Lord,
Jesus Christ, whom we have as our leader from which [wisdom] if one
strays, we consider it the chief of all sins, and with what final danger
their body and soul have united. Who will show us a better way to the
kingdom above, than that which is the way, and the truth, and the life?
This (which is the last and holy anchor of our salvation), the unchangeable and most sure truth, expounded in the writings of the Proph-
[145] ets, and the Apostles, and known by those who wish. This we do
not doubt.

Not the untrue and unstable, but the truly excellent recommended to
us by Your Holiness, the philosophy of our Lord and Savior, which
human writings, or synods try to explain, or the diaconate of those who
the Lord himself by His will, was pleased to make interpreters to the
human race. Every human mind is subject to making errors. Even if one

is most careful; yet from such, indeed, one learns who they are, as Saint Basil very beautifully wrote: "They are the pen of the Holy Spirit".

Again the Apostle anathematizes even an angel from heaven, if he should preach something other than the confessed truth. And the Savior said that every growing thing that was not planted by the Heavenly Father shall be up-rooted. For these reasons, we accept not only the teachings of the Holy Synods, but also justify those teachings, which are by the will of the people, the canons, which are interpreted and written according to the Holy Scriptures.

Lately we have great hope that Your Holiness would not disapprove if, we, being convinced, did not accept the aforesaid causes. Since, indeed, men of high office expressed moderately but wisely opinions concerning this self same truth that prove that our book, which is brief, yet is founded on the rock of the Holy Scriptures. It contains nothing that is subjectively understood, nor has it taken anything from the philosophy according to the flesh (which obviously, doubly, so to speak, errs from the truth). Our book contains only that which is the philosophy, which indeed, Your Holiness courteously and paternally recommended to us. We, therefore, hope that not only by Your Holiness will it be approved, but also by Christ, who admonishes us to search the Scriptures, and by the Psalmist who said in his own words that it is "a lamp unto our feet".

However, we do not believe that the true Church can be led astray, as long as her foundation and columns remain edified and unbroken. Furthermore our souls agree with the Divine Scriptures and we believe that it [146] has been granted to the holy angels, who, just as is every will of the Lord, are His unhesitant servers. Thus by the manifestation of the canonical Scriptures, indeed they hope, that the will of God be done.

We earnestly beseech Christ, our only Savior, with all our hearts, that we ourselves sometime in this blessed congregation become witnesses, and with the all-blessed spirits, eternally and unceasingly praise Him.

In closing, we humbly expect that Your Holiness does not find anything that we have written to be difficult, but continue to have a paternal spirit [opinion] toward us. Please accept the gift which we send, whatever it is (even if the value of the honor of your Holiness is greater) with spiritual affection. We hope that you will accept it as a wise, diligently pious, and truthful, gentle work.

Farewell, Your Holiness, Most Reverend Bishop, together with all the reverend and pious complement of the Lord.

From Tübingen the 18th of the month of June, year of salvation 1577.

> Lucas Osiander, Professor of Theology in the Wittenberg University, Magistrate of the Ecclesiastical Court, and Ecclesiastic of the Synod meeting in Stuttgart, in behalf of Jacob Andreae, Provost and

Chancellor of Tübingen, who is abroad in Saxony, I have signed.

Martin Crusius, Professor and Teacher of Greek and Latin Languages in Tübingen. I have signed.

## [B.] The First Reply of the Tübingen Theologians to the First Answer of Patriarch Jeremiah [II][1]

[147] Sir All-holy Patriarch, last year Your Holiness gave us an answer to the articles of our religion. It was overflowing with benevolence and Christian love and delighted us greatly. We owe Your Holiness the greatest gratitude, that in spite of the burdensome tasks that the overseeing of the churches everywhere imposes on Your Holiness, nevertheless Your Holiness thought the said articles worthy not only to be read but of an answer, and what is more, of an answer written with a sincere heart, and without any reservation or any sarcasm. We should have prepared long ago a reply to the critical evaluation and decision of Your Holiness, except for the fact that I, Kob Andreae, was summoned for the correction of the churches in Saxony by the most illustrious ruler of that country (one of the seven leading princes, whom we call electors), and that I was sent upon that mission by my most illustrious master, Louis, Duke of Wittenberg. During this entire time I have undertaken many and great tasks, so that I was unable to send anything to Your Holiness. But since we know the desire with which Your Holiness is awaiting our reply, both Martin Crusius and I have overcome the very great distractions, and we have tried to present our opinion clearly to the judgment of Your Holiness.

With due respect, we ask Your Holiness to accept our reply with a glad countenance and a gentle spirit, to read it attentively and carefully, to conduct an investigation and to scrutinize it commensurate with your own piety and wisdom in these great matters. For these are not something we dreamed up, but the true exposition and interpretation of the words received from the Holy Scriptures which with God's help we will present so as to defend our opinion. And [we will present] this as briefly as possible because a concise exposition, yet not lacking proper [148] clarity, may be acceptable to Your Holiness, who is involved in many weighty matters. And we are well convinced that it will be evident to you, that no innovation has been introduced by us, but out of love for the heavenly truth, we believe these truths, which we have learned from the inspired Scriptures through the illumination of the Holy Spirit.

First of all then, we will state all those things in which both Your Holiness and we agree. But in the other articles in which we disagree, it is necessary, to set down a rule, by which those subjects which are disputed may be investigated and judged. In short, we shall indicate which rule is the most certain and the most sure, by which all dogmas may be ascertained and determined. After that, we will piously and peacefully discuss the articles in dispute; we will produce firm and unshakeable proofs of our opinion, which compel our conscience to think in this manner concerning the articles of faith.

We are very glad indeed (how think you?) that between Your Holiness and us there is agreement on many of the subjects in question. Among these are the following: God is one in essence as well as tri-hypostatic persons, and that the three hypostases are co-eternal. That the holy Apostolic Symbol is received with joy, as an accurate epitome of the Christian faith. That God is not the cause of sin, but the devil and human will. That Christ has paid sufficient ransom for all sins, not only for original sin, but also for personal sins. That there is forgiveness of all sins for those who will repent them. That virtue is acquired through the practice of good works is to be diligently discussed. That the ecclesiastical ministry (which you call the priesthood) is indispensable for the edification of the Church. That servers in the Church are to be held in honor on account of the work with which they have been entrusted, even though their manner of life may be afflicted by human weakness. Yet, if they should teach falsely, they must not be tolerated.

The efficacy and the power of the minister does not depend upon his worthiness or his moral excellence, only insofar as he does not teach false doctrine. It is not right for the ministers of the Word, to express opinions on political matters and civil affairs or to participate in wars. It is not generally forbidden for the ministers of the Church to be married. No one, if not officially called, is permitted to teach in the church, or to administer the holy sacraments. Yet, in time of emergency it is also lawful for the laymen to baptize.

[149] Baptism is the washing of regeneration. Infants should be baptized, and not postponed to the age of maturity. Through the Communion, that is, the Lord's Supper we are bound together and are united with the Lord, since in it we are truly receiving His body and blood under both kinds. The liturgies privately celebrated for profit, as in the church of Old Rome, are to be rejected. Moreover, also, that the opinion of those who think that at some time in the future there will be an end to the punishment for those who are wicked, is to be rejected. For we believe that both the reward for the good and the punishment of the wicked will be everlasting following this present life. In all these things mentioned above, by God's grace, we acknowledge agreement.

On the other hand there are some statements in your discourse which differ from our opinion. Come let us consider, which rule is the most accurate and most unmovable, by which every dogma may be investigated and ascertained, so that truth may be discerned from falsehood, and human inventions may be separated from what is known from Divine Revelation.

### [1.] The Standard Rule for All Dogmas

There is, indeed, no more sure, nor truer, nor better standard rule for judging all dogmas, all institutes, and usages of faith and human traditions and works, than the Word of the Almighty God of all; the Word, which has been revealed to the human race by the Prophets and Christ and the Apostles and written in the Old and New Testaments for the benefit and the salvation of the entire Church. For in the same manner that we search to find the truth of a civil matter which is in dispute, from the ancient writings and documents, whose [authenticity] has been confirmed by seals; so also, when in matters of religion a controversy arises, it is to be answered by both the Old and the New Testaments, as heavenly documents and schools, both of which have been guaranteed and made sure by admirable signs and wonders—with seals, as it were. Consequently, on the one hand, everything which can be established by one of these two documents, or by both, should be believed without any doubt whatever; on the other hand, whatever disagrees [with Scripture], must be dismissed by those who introduce them. For this reason, also, the [150] Prophet Isaiah, called people of God back to the law and to the testimony, that is, to the divine oracles, so that from them they might learn the will of God and the truth. And he continues: "Surely for this word which they speak there is no dawn" [Is 8:20, RSV]. Thus is this word from the Hebrew truth [O.T.], interpreted by us: explicitly declaring that they who do not follow in the light of the revealed Word of God, fall into dreadful darkness and ignorance of religion. Furthermore, the writer of the Psalms chants: "Thy law is the lamp unto my feet, and light to my paths" [Ps 119:105]; by which he means not opinion and human traditions, but the heavenly, revealed Word of God. This shows us what is necessary to believe, and by which way we are to proceed toward salvation. And, just as one, who finds it necessary to travel on a dark night, very easily stumbles and falls down if he disregards the lamp preceding him, and turns in another direction; in the same way he, who does not fix his eyes solely upon the Word of God and follows [it] steadfastly, he cannot escape the deceptions and trickeries of the ruler of darkness of this world. Hence, also blessed Peter, exhorting us to follow in this light, says: "And we have the prophetic word made more sure. You will do well to pay attention to this as to a lamp shining in a dark place" [2 Pet 1:19]. Yes, indeed!

It is altogether evident, that none of the prophetic and apostolic Scriptures have been intermixed with error; no deceit has come out of them for anyone. Since they have been written under the inspiration of and brought to mind by the Holy Spirit (who is the Spirit of Truth) [cf. Jn 15:26], as the same Apostle Peter bears witness. He says: "no prophecy of the scripture ever came by the impulse of man, but men moved by the Holy Spirit spoke from God" [2 Pet 1:20-21]. And who would not gladly investigate and define accurately all the dogmas according to this criterion, which is the most exact, and contains nothing perverse nor distorted? For this purpose the Lord, also has summoned His own people back, to the precepts of his revealed Word, not only concerning those things which have to do with this common life, but primarily concerning the matters pertaining to religion, and rejected all other worship which was not established on His Word. For he says: "You shall not do...every man doing whatever is right in his own eyes" [Dt 12:8], "Everything that I command you [today] you shall be careful to do; you shall not add to it [151] or take from it" [Dt 12:32]. And elsewhere: "This book of the law shall not depart out of your mouth, but you shall meditate on it day and night, that you may be careful to do according to all that is written in it; for then you shall make your way prosperous, and then you shall have good success. Turn not from the words of this law to the right hand or to the left, that you may have good success wherever you go [Jos 1:7-8].

These things have been legislated not only, indeed, for the Israelites, but for us also. So that if we should believe correctly, and also, live with piety, we would not allow ourselves to be led astray from that one and most correct rule and standard of the Word of God, by any one whosoever it may be (whatever honor and name he may have now in holiness, or education). But we should make use of this criterion in all the controversies concerning the faith, and all matters concerning worship, and all matters concerning [religious] practices. For this is also something from the excellence of the will of the unattainable wisdom of God; that the teaching of the Prophets and of Christ and of the Apostles which was given, was recorded in writing; so that, with the passing of time the memory of men would not diminish, nor the divine words be rashly adulterated by human folly. Since this is the highest beneficence of God, it is fitting that it be gladly accepted: this is the touchstone by which all things should be examined, as the holy Prophet of God did in ancient times. For, whenever a difference concerning divine things would occur among the people of Israel, did they not bring forth that law of Moses? Did they not also put the people to shame who were sinning by their own innovations, and arbitrary ceremonial worship, contrary to the commandments and the inscribed notice of the God-given Word? Moreover, did not Christ himself, repeatedly quote those words of the prophets, in support and confirmation of what He was teaching? [He did this] even though He is worthy of belief without any external witness. For indeed, the Heavenly Father said concerning Him: "This is my beloved Son, with whom I am well pleased; listen to him" [Mt 17:5].

Furthermore, whenever they preached the Gospel (as the book of Acts bears witness), did not the Apostles confirm that which would be taught through the Holy Scripture? They did not advance some oral tradition for the illumination and defense of the Gospel teaching; but being armed with the divinely inspired writings they fought against the unbelief of the [152] Jews. It is true that the God-bearing Fathers, the most brilliant luminaries of the Church, while they witnessed to the continuous consensus of the Church, yet they banished the madness of the heretics with the written sacred witnesses. Moreover, those Synods which smote the leaders of heresies by pious decisions and canons, did not overcome those heresies either by private opinion or by the witness of ancestors or (for such weapons would not be effective in such a struggle), but having carefully considered the witness of the Holy Scriptures, they exposed and refuted the impiety of the heretics. For the dogmas should be judged solely by the God-inspired Scriptures if we are earnestly concerned to discover the truth. Concerning this let us listen to what Saint Chrysostom says:

> For this reason at this time (as the Latin translation in our posses-
> sion reads, for there is no Greek text at our disposal), all Chris-
> tians should now use the Scriptures, because at the present time,
> when heresy has captured those churches, there is no defense of
> true Christianity, nor other refuge for Christians who wish to know
> the true content of the faith save the divine Scriptures.[2]

Also, Origen says (according to the Latin text): "It is necessary for us, to call in the Holy Scriptures for witness, for without these witnesses our opinions and expositions are not credible."[3] Also, Basil the Great writing to the physician Eustathios says:

> I do not consider it fair that the custom which prevails among
> them should be regarded as a law and canon of orthodox opinion.
> If custom is to be taken in proof of what is correct, then it is
> certainly lawful for me to follow it in all things...Therefore, let the
> God-inspired Scriptures decide between us; and on whichever
> side the dogmas be found to be in harmony with the Word of God,
> in favor of that side will be cast vote of truth.[4]

He [Basil] writing to the Western bishops concerning Apollinarios also says: "There are his theological works which are not founded on Scriptural proofs, but have their basis on human origin."[5]

Therefore, it is also the judgment of the Fathers (that in disputed questions of religion) only those things are to be accepted which are based on [153] the witness of the Holy Scriptures. But as for the others, which are not witnessed in the Scriptures, we are not bound to believe or receive them, no matter what the dignity or honor of the one who wrote or decreed them may have been.

Therefore, (one might ask us) do you hold in contempt what the Holy Fathers and the Synods canonically assembled in the Holy Spirit wrote? By no means do we! We thank the merciful Lord of all for the exceptional writings by the Fathers which lead to salvation, and in which they have interpreted the Holy Scriptures, and bravely opposed those who introduced heresies. We also accept and hold in respect all those conciliar decrees which are in harmony with the Holy Scriptures (such as the decrees of the First Synod of Nicaea). But we cannot indiscriminently accept everything and whatever either has been written by the Fathers, or decreed by the Synods. For without doubt a difference must exist be-- tween the Prophets and Christ and the Apostles on the one hand, and the Fathers and Synods on the other. For, indeed, whatever the Prophets and Christ and the Apostles taught should, without any exception, be received as divine words and decrees. On the other hand, those which were written by the Holy Fathers, and which were decreed by the Synods, should not be held in equal honor as the above mentioned. For then it would be necessary to place the writings of the Fathers as well as the decrees of the Synods in the same category as the prophetic and apostolic Scriptures, which neither the Fathers themselves, nor any of the Holy Synods have ever claimed. For example, Saint Theodoretos, commenting on Genesis after teaching that the angels were not created before the creation of the world, proceeds:

> But I do not say these things by way of official utterance (for it is bold to speak decisively about those things of which Holy Scripture does not explicitly speak), but I have said that which I perceived to be in agreement with pious reasoning.[6]

Also, Basil the Great says: "If I would say something of my own, do not accept it; if I would say something of the Lord, accept it."[7] And again Chrysostom says:

> Let us not, therefore, carry about the notions of the many, but examine the facts. For how is it not absurd that with respect to money, indeed, we do not trust to others, but refer this to figures and calculations; but in calculating upon facts we are lightly drawn aside by the notions of others, and that, too, though we possess an exact balance and standard and canon for all things the [154] declaration of the divine laws? Wherefore I exhort and entreat you all: disregard what this man and that man thinks about these things, and inquire from the Scriptures all these things.[8]

And these things they have said, and with good reason. For it is just as the water from a bubbling fountain as it passes through a channel of red or muddy earth becomes wholly colored by it, or takes on some sediment so that it no longer flows as purely as it did when it gushed out; thus, in the same manner there exist blemishes in the writings of the Fathers and in the decrees of the Synods which were drawn from the notions of their time, which are not in harmony with that purity, which belong to the Sacred Scriptures as the distinct springing fountain. It is for that reason, indeed, that we do well to defend ourselves if we are giving the preference to the fountain, rather than an emanation; and besides this, the fountain is accessible to all pious people. And again, it is not to be thought that the holy and inspired Scriptures are mutilated and imperfect, and that they do not contain all those things which are necessary for our salvation. For we have not only one or two prophetic and apostolic books, but many. And those things which are omitted in one book are explicitly read in another. For [Paul says]: "all scripture is inspired by God and profitable for teaching, for reproof, for correction, and for training in righteousness, that the man of God may be complete, equipped for every good work" [2 Tim 3:16-17]. Saint Chrysostom, also, mentioned this verse in the 8th paragraph of his *Concerning the Priesthood.*[9] And on the [2nd] Epistle to Timothy, he briefly comments thus:

> He [Paul] says, 'for doctrine.' For thence we shall know whether we ought to learn or to be ignorant of anything. And thence we may disprove what is false, thence we may be corrected and brought to a right mind, may be comforted, and consoled; and if anything is deficient we may have it added to us...so that the man of God may be rendered perfect by it; without this, therefore, he cannot be perfect. He says, 'You have the Scriptures in place of me. If you would learn anything you may learn it from them.'[10]

If, indeed, the Holy Scriptures are able to make the pious man perfect (that is, reach a perfection, which can be attained in the present life), then, indeed, to attain completeness and perfection, there is no need of tradition. The Holy Scriptures, indeed, are sufficient for it, as the same Chrysostom himself testifies in his commentary on the Epistle to Titus saying:

> [155] [God]...'hath in due times manifested His word through preaching, which is committed unto me' [Tit 1:3 KJV]. That is, the preaching is committed unto me. For this, the Gospel, included everything, things present and things future: life, and godliness, and faith, and all things at once.[11]

And without these things, this also is worthy of mention, it is dangerous to the Church to accept something, or to believe in it, or to act if it is not explicitly witnessed by the Scriptures. For, how easy is the possibility of falling into error if we attempt to believe also those things which are in no way indicated by the Scriptures, the lamp of truth? Would it be without risk (in religious matters) to strongly assert something as being true and pious, which the mouth of the Lord, however, has not spoken? And that which has not been ordered anywhere by God? And which nowhere has it been accepted by Him? And if we ought to do everything in faith (for everything which is not from faith is sin), how then can we do in faith those things which have not been established by the Word of God [cf. Rom 14]? For surely the faith has to be established not on our opinion, but only on the Word of God. Thus, we run the risk that wherever the Word of God is absent, faith is also absent; and the work which is not from faith, but from human opinion, does not please God.

Perhaps, someone again will say that on the one hand, the Scriptures are absolutely free from error; but on the other hand, they have been concealed by much obscurity, so that without the interpretation of the Spirit-bearing Fathers they could not be clearly understood. It is necessary, then, to follow their interpretation, or at least not depart from them. We say with regard to this: we do not at all deny that there are some passages that are difficult to understand in the writings of the Prophets and the Apostles, which the ignorant and unstable persons twist (as Peter says concerning those things which Paul wrote), as they do the rest of the Scriptures and to their own destruction. But meanwhile this, too, is very true that what has been said in a scarcely perceptible manner in some places in the Scriptures, these same things have been stated in another place in them explicitly and most clearly so that even the most simple person can understand them. If, however, some of them happen to be cloudy and remain as such, their illumination, the dissolution of clouds, as it were, has been stored up safely for us in the life to come. Therefore, no better way could ever be found to interpret the [156] Scriptures, other than that Scripture be interpreted by Scripture, that is to say, through itself. For the entire Scripture has been dictated by the one and the same Spirit, who best understands His own will and is best able to state His own meaning.

Indeed, this is also a customary practice in civil matters, just as if by carelessness, when a difference has occurred concerning the provisions of a will to the heirs, which has been understood in one manner by some and differently by others, new provisions are not sought from another source. Rather, they themselves, concerning which their meaning is disputed, will be carefully studied and will be self-scrutinized by placing them side by side with each other. When many have been compared with each other and with concrete statements (often only from the style and reference of what has been written), the meaning of the author is understood. For if this man was good and prudent, he certainly did not intend to write contradictory things about which the heirs would contend. Indeed, the same thing takes place also when we wish to interpret the Holy Scriptures (whose skilled artisan is the Holy Spirit). We are right to do that, that is, to compare the passages with each other; and from this comparison to trace out the true meaning, having before all else invoked the help of the Spirit to open the eyes of our understanding, and to guide us into all truth (according to the promise of the Lord) [cf. Jn 16:13].

Basil the Great also agrees with these things for he writes:

Now then if a commandment be given to us and the manner of carrying it is not added, let us obey the Lord who says: 'Search the Scriptures' [Jn 5:39]. Let us follow the example of the Apostles, who questioned the Lord himself as to the interpretation of His words, and learn the true and saving course from His words in another place.[12]

And so much for that. Here, we should greatly thank the Almighty and most merciful God, who in these last days has granted the knowledge of the chief languages in the whole area of Germany, and has awakened many people to study the area of liberal arts, so that the study of Hebrew and Greek languages flourishes. In unfolding on the one hand, the Old Testament, and on the other, the New Testament, we are able to have [157] recourse to the sources of the Hebrew and the Greek languages whenever it is necessary, and draw from them the true meaning of the Scriptures. In this regard, our times do not seem to be inferior to ancient times. Here we must not hesitate, but rather openly state the following (which we respectfully request you will kindly accept) that among the ecclesiastical writers—the Greek, as well as the Latin—who are greatly respected among us, some were unacquainted with the Hebrew language, while others were unacquainted with the Greek language. Hence those who were ignorant of the Hebrew language happened to be weak in the interpretation of the Old Testament, and those who were ignorant of the Greek were not always able to skillfully interpret the writings of the Apostles. And although, in truth, we hold in high regard the labors of the Fathers to interpret the Scriptures and not a few times have we been want to use them.

It should, however, not be supposed that they are so indispensable as to imagine that without their explanations and commentaries, it would be impossible to find out, with the guidance of the Holy Spirit, the true and genuine meaning and power of the Scriptures. For the sacred writings of the Holy Fathers which have come down to us and have been preserved (we speak of the chief and most celebrated expositors) were made and written long enough after the Apostles, so that hundreds of years elapsed in the meantime. Therefore, in the same manner the

Christians, who lived before the above-mentioned Fathers, read and interpreted the Scriptures of the Prophets and of the Apostles without any risk to their own salvation, even though they did not have recourse to their times and writings. The same applies to us also. Through God our sovereign and with the help of the aids which we have mentioned, we are convinced that the Holy Scriptures are understood correctly and, indeed, by those, who in a way befittng the pious and in fear of God, study them without the interpretations of the Fathers. And just as those who lived before those seven Synods (which you sometimes mentioned in your [158] book) had been summoned, they nevertheless had learned, at that time, the true religion concerning God from the holy writers. Therefore, in the same manner those who lived after the assembly of those Synods drew the true and heavenly teaching of piety from the Holy Scriptures with the help of the Holy Spirit without the above-mentioned Synods. Since this is the case, if some persons find the Divine Scriptures sufficient, and believe those things, and strive to do those things which the Scriptures teach them to believe and do, they are by no means to be held in the category of heretics, even though they do not accept all things which have been said by the Holy Fathers, or which were formulated by the Synods.

When we say that only those things by necessity should be believed and done which have been proposed by the Sacred Scriptures, we do not demand that those very same words and syllables be read in the Scriptures, but that we gladly retain everything which can be logically deduced from the Scriptures, even when these words cannot be found in them. Thus, concerning the Son of God, we gladly accept the word 'homoousion,' even though this word is not found in the Sacred Books. Moreover, we accept it not because it is found or ratified by the Synod in Nicaea, but because the sense [or meaning] of this word is expressed in many places in the Scriptures wherever there is a reference to the eternal divinity of the Son, much as this same Synod, being motivated by the Holy Scriptures, held the Arians in check with this adopted term.

Having defined and established the truth and steadfastness of this rule, let us now deal with the articles which are in dispute.

### [2.] The Procession of the Holy Spirit

[159] It did not escape us that the Greek churches reject that which we positively assert, [i.e.], that the Holy Spirit, proceeds not only from the Father, but from the Son also. Indeed, that which is against us is the symbol of the Synod of Nicaea in which it is said that the Holy Spirit proceeds from the Father, but has failed to mention that He also proceeds from the Son. Nevertheless, looking carefully at the decree of the said Synod, we have to say truthfully and faultlessly that the Synod consisting of 318 God-bearing Fathers assembled at the time of the most

pious Constantine the Great, did not at all formulate a doctrine concerning the procession of the Spirit. Why? Because at that time there was no controversy concerning the divinity of the Spirit or His procession; but rather there was a dispute concerning the eternal divinity of the Son of God. We will present, therefore, the decree of the Synod of Nicaea word for word as it is in the *Ecclesiastical History* of Socrates:

> We believe in one God, the Father Almighty, Maker of all things visible and invisible. And in one Lord Jesus Christ, the Son of God, begotten of the Father. The only begotten, that is, of the essence of the Father: God of God, Light of Light, True God of True God; begotten not made, of the same essence with the Father, through whom all things were made, those which are in heaven and those on earth, who for the sake of us men, and for our salvation, descended, became incarnate, and became man, suffered, and rose again the third day; and He ascended into the heavens, and will come to judge the living and the dead. [We believe] also in the Holy Spirit. But those who say that 'there was a time when He was not,' or 'He did not exist before He was begotten,' or 'He is of another substance, or essence than the Father,' that 'the Son of God is created, or mutable, or susceptible to change,' the catholic and apostolic Church of God anathematizes.[13]

Yet this decree of the Synod at Nicaea does not conflict with our faith in which we believe that the Holy Spirit proceeds both from the Father and from the Son. However, only in this does it result: that it will alienate from the Church of Christ those who deny the true and eternal [160] and of the same essence divinity of the Son of God. Nevertheless, for this article we firmly stand on the testimony of the Scriptures. For the Son of God spoke thus: "When the Counselor comes, whom I shall send to you from the Father, even the Spirit of truth who proceeds from the Father, He will bear witness to me" [Jn 15:26], for "He [Holy Spirit] will take what is mine and declare it unto you" [Jn 16:14]. If indeed the Son sends the Paraclete [the Holy Spirit], and the Paraclete is sent by the Son, how does He not then proceed from the Son by whom He is sent? And, if that Spirit is the Spirit of truth, then truly the Spirit proceeds from the Son as from the Father.

Indeed, it would be dangerous if the revelation of the truth from heaven were given only by the Father and not by the Son also, although the Son has said that "no one knows the Father except the Son and anyone to whom the Son chooses to reveal him" [Mt 11:27]. Moreover, the Son reveals the Father to us not only by the audible preaching of the word, but also by sending the Holy Spirit into our hearts, "the Spirit himself bearing witness with our spirit that we are children of God" [Rom 8:16]. In addition, in the letter to Romans Paul calls the Holy

Spirit "the Spirit of holiness" [Rom 1:4], that is, the One who sanctifies. But who will dare to say that our sanctification is from the Father only, and not also from the Son, Who redeemed us? Paul says, indeed, concerning the Son of God: "Christ loved the Church and gave himself up for her that he might sanctify her" [Eph 5:25-26]. For He sanctified His Church not only by cleansing it from sins by His own blood, but also by regenerating it through water and the Spirit. Furthermore, why has the Holy Spirit so frequently been called the Spirit of Christ by the Apostle Paul and Peter in their epistles? It is not only for this reason [i.e.] that He is in Christ, but is it not also because He is sent by Christ into the hearts of those who believe? This, indeed, is irrefutable. Then, if the Holy Spirit is sent by the Son, most assuredly He proceeds from Christ, the Son of God. And for this reason by both [the above] Apostles He is called the Spirit of Christ, because He proceeds from the Son of God.

Moreover, the Spirit is also called the finger of God by Christ. For He [161] says: "But it is by the finger of God that I cast out demons, then the kingdom of God has come upon you" [Lk 11:20]. The finger of God is not something carnal, as the anthropomorphites have dreamed in the past, but that efficacious virtue and infinite power of God. Nonetheless, He either comes forth and proceeds no less without doubt from the Son than from the Father. For just as John testifies that the Spirit had not been given to Him by measure [cf. Jn 3:34], in like manner the Son manifested the same power and strength in casting out the demons, in raising the dead, and in performing other miracles and wonders. And if the Holy Spirit is that most efficacious power and almightiness of God, through whom everything has been created, then it is absolutely necessary that He proceeds from the Son, also. For it is said concerning the Son of God, the Logos, "all things were made through him, and without him was not anything made that was made" [Jn 1:3]. For how was the Son able to make and create everything with the Father if this eternal power and strength which brought forth everything into existence did not also proceed from Him? If this were not so, one could only attribute to the Son such wisdom as would fall short of almighty power. And yet, if indeed we believe in the equality of the Son to the Father (to which the Scriptures and the totality of the truly Christian community in unanimity bear witness), consequently this also will be believed: that the procession of the Holy Spirit is no less from Him [the Son] than from the Father, so that we in no respect make the Son of God (in regard to His Godhead) less than the Father. For if Christ speaks the truth when He says: "I and the Father are one" [Jn 10:30], then the following will also be true: that the Holy Spirit proceeds from both (from the Father and from the Son), as they are one.

If someone [however] thinks that the Holy Spirit is from the Father alone and through the Son but does not proceed from the Son, he thinks the impossible for these things clearly oppose each other and contradict one another. For when one says "through the Son," this means that the Holy Spirit proceeds indirectly; and if one says "from the Father alone," then the Holy Spirit proceeds directly. Wherefore we know that what is taught in the Latin churches is correct: that the Holy Spirit, [162] proceeds from the Father and from the Son. And besides Saint Cyril [of Alexandria] agrees with us, when in regard to the passage, "and [God] breathed into his nostrils" [Gen 2:7], he comments in this manner:

> Does the Holy Spirit, therefore, become a soul in man? And would it not be altogether absurd to think that? For then the soul would be immutable, not subject to change, and would always remain the same. But the soul is subject to [mutable] change. The Spirit, however, is in no way mutable [subject to change]. Or if, indeed, could He suffer change, would the disgrace retroactively revert to the divine nature, which is of God the Father and certainly also the Son? In other words [it would revert] to that which is the essence of both, that is, that the Spirit comes forth from the Father through the Son. In conclusion, it is then sheer ignorance to think that the Spirit can be changed into a soul and pass into the nature of man. But that which was formed [i.e., man] was given a soul by an unutterable power, and it was immediately adorned with the gift of the Spirit.[14]

Thus has Cyril spoken! Concerning the words 'through' (διά) and 'from' (ἐκ), they are here to be understood in the same way as in the statement: "yet we know that a man is not justified by works of the law but 'through' faith in Jesus Christ, even we have believed in Christ Jesus in order to be justified by faith in Christ, and not 'from' works of the law" [Gal 2:16]. Therefore, Athanasios the Great, agreeing that the Spirit proceeds from the Son, also, in his Confession of Faith of which the beginning is as follows: "Whosoever will be saved, before all things it is necessary that he hold the catholic faith," says: "the Holy Spirit is of the Father and of the Son, neither made nor created, nor begotten, but proceeding."[15]

Furthermore, Saint Epiphanios [315-403 A.D.] says in his treatise titled the *Ancoratos* [i.e., *The Firmly Anchored Man*]: "The Holy Spirit, has no brother, neither is he a brother of the Father, but He is from the same essence of the Father and the Son." [16] Truly, the only begotten [Son] himself says: "the Spirit of the Father,"[17] and "He who proceeds from the Father" and "that He will take what is mine" [Jn 16:14], in order that He [the Spirit] would "not be thought of another kind than the Father, or of the Son."[18] Furthermore, the Holy Spirit by the words "from the Father, and from the Son" "is named third." And again: "wherefore the Father is eternal"[19] and the Spirit blows from the Father and the Son [cf. Jn 3:8].

### [3.] Concerning Free Will

And now we will also briefly express what is held by us: whether man has free will and what kind of free will (in spiritual matters and those matters which contribute to the eternal salvaton of the soul) when he is [163] either not yet reborn, or again when he is spiritually dead because of sins and has drowned in the abyss of wickedness. And, indeed, one must do this without neglecting to take into account how great the power of regenerated man is (according to spiritual matters).

Consequently, we are speaking about the pristine generation, not that it was that they first chose the good and then God supplemented what was from Him. But we say that God both starts and completes the good in us. And this is how we choose the good: when by the Lord we are either reborn or raised from the death of sin, for the Lord says: "no one can come to us unless the Father who sent me draws him" [Jn 6:44]. The Father, therefore, draws men toward Christ through the preaching of the Word of God, together with which the Holy Spirit works to give the increase to the heavenly field [cf. 1 Cor 3:9]. And it is no wonder that if a man is not drawn, he does not approach God, nor does he choose the good, nor do it, since he has been completely depraved by original sin. "For God saw"...(according to what has been said by Moses) "that every imagination of the heart turns intently toward evil continually" [Gen 6:5]. And the Lord himself said: "The imagination of man is evil from his youth" [Gen 8:21]. Hence (Christ says): "For out of the heart come evil thoughts, murders, adulteries, fornications, thefts, false witness, blasphemies" [Mt 15:19]. Why? Because of the malice of our heart. [David says]: "I was brought forth in iniquity, and in sin did my mother conceive me" [Ps 50:5]. It is for that reason that a man who has not been reborn is flesh, that is to say, his entire being is concerned with the things of the flesh. As the Savior says: "that which is born of the flesh is flesh" [Jn 3:6]. And (according to the Apostle [Paul]) "the mind that is set on the flesh is hostile to God; it does not submit to God's law, indeed it cannot" [Rom 8:7]. Therefore, the carnal man, who is not reborn, can do nothing by his own power in regard to spiritual matters except to oppose God and His law. Indeed, then he will never choose the good first, so that in the second place God would then bring in His personal assistance. [164] And how could such men select the good when the Apostle calls such men dead through trespasses [cf. Eph 2:5]? Or, also, when he [Paul] declares that the widows who are self-indulgent (that is, the [widows] who are slaves to the belly and of wicked sensual pleasures) are dead even while they live [cf. 1 Tim 5:6]? But a dead body neither wills anything, nor does it do anything; it only gives off a most ill-smelling odor. In like manner, the spiritually dead person cannot choose anything good (unless he is awakened by God). Therefore, to a greater degree, whatever comes from him [the spiritually dead] is considered an abomination by good

men, the holy angels, and God. It is for that reason then, that the one
who has not been reborn, or again he is spiritually dead, does not have
enough strength in order to choose the good. But even those who have
been regenerated and resurrected from the death of sin can choose and
do only such good as God inspires in them: "for apart from me" (He
says) "you can do nothing" [Jn 15:5]. No, indeed, we cannot choose
anything good without Him. The Apostle (Paul) says: "For God is at
work in you, both to will and to work for his good pleasure" [Phil
2:13]. It is then obvious that it is the work of God in us not only to
complete the good works, but also to will them. Hence, the Apostle
says: "for all who are led by the Spirit of God are sons of God" [Rom
8:14]. We have need then of awakening by, as well as guidance of, the
Spirit to choose and to do good works. And there remains in us, also
(even if we happen to be reborn), much weakness of the flesh and lack
of perfection, so that we do not always obey the urging spirit, but also
(at the instigation of the old Adam) do those things which we do not
want to do. So, therefore, Paul also concerning himself (a man who
certainly was reborn) says: "I do not do what I want, but I do the very
thing I hate" [Rom 7:15]. And furthermore: "For I know that nothing
good dwells within me, that is, in my flesh" [Rom 7:18]. And again: "I
of myself serve the law of God with my mind, but with my flesh I serve
the law of sin" [Rom 7:25]. And elsewhere he says: "For the desires of
the flesh are against the Spirit; and the desires of the Spirit are against
the flesh; for these are opposed to each other, to prevent you from doing what you would" [Gal 5:17]. Therefore, we strongly believe that
even among the regenerated persons there remain a multitude of
sicknesses, even though they will and do as much good as God works in
them. Moreover, those who have no part in the regeneration, or again
those who are spiritually dead, do not possess power of themselves to
choose the good much less to do it.

[165] In addition, Basil the Great, being of like mind, says:

> Tell me, why do you exalt yourself in your goods as if they were
> your own, instead of giving thanks for these gifts to Him who is
> the Giver? 'What have you that you have not received? If then
> you have received, why do you boast as if you had not received it'
> [1 Cor 4:7]? You have not known God by reason of your righteous-
> ness, but God has known you by reason of His goodness. He [the
> Apostle] says, 'but now that you have come to know God, or rather
> to be known by God' [Gal 4:9]. You have not apprehended Christ
> because of your virtues; but Christ has apprehended you by His
> coming, etc.[20]

Also, [Saint Chrysostom] on the passage [1 Cor 8:6, says]: "Yet for us
there is one God, the Father, from whom are all things;" [further on] he

says: "We are from Him in two ways: by being through creation, when we did not exist, and by being made believers."[21] Also, [Chrysostom] on the passage says: "not that we are competent of ourselves to claim anything as coming from us" [2 Cor 3:5; Sermon 6]. "That is I said not 'that we are competent,' as though part were ours and part God's; but I refer and ascribe the whole to Him" [cf. 2 Cor 3:4].[22] And again [he says]: "Did we not act in the same Spirit [2 Cor 12:18]? What is meant by 'in the same Spirit'? He ascribes the whole to grace and shows that the whole of this praise is the good result not of our labours, but of the gift of the Spirit and of grace." [23] This is what we have from the above [Fathers].

This doctrine, therefore, received from the Word of God, does not refute the urgency concerning good works on the part of the elect. Nor again does it justify the impiety and desperaton of those rejected. But it restrains us, who consider our weakness and wretchedness, in true humility toward God and our neighbor. It [this doctrine] also combines the wondrous goodness of God concerning us, who resurrects us who are dead because of sins and who have not even asked for His blessings, and who endures our great weaknesses with paternal affection.

[4.] Concerning Justification by Faith and Good Works

Whensoever we say that one is justified before God by faith alone in Christ, we wish to make this clear: that through faith alone we receive our Savior Christ in order that we might receive forgiveness of sins and [166] life eternal through His most perfect act. For we take faith alone in Christ to be that hand, whereby we received whatever our redeemer Christ has wrought for us. We do not even debate whether we should do good works or not, or whether good works follow true faith or not. For according to the Baptizer, we teach: "every tree, therefore, that does not bear good fruit is cut down and thrown into the fire" [Mt 3:10]. Nor do we say that dead faith, which is merely knowledge of history and which, according to James, even the demons have [cf. Jas 2:26] produced righteousness; but, [we are speaking of] that faith about which Paul speaks: "faith working through love" [Gal 5:6]. Neither do we claim that those who have not repented are justified, that is, that they obtain forgiveness of sins and life everlasting. Obviously, these are condemned. And thus, this is sufficient for what is mentioned above. Nevertheless, we are not saying that our good works should be included in the article of justification by God where the following is involved: through whom and by what means are we reconciled to God and are numbered among the children and heirs of God. Why? Because by as much as is ascribed in this matter to our works and righteousness, by that much do we judge that the worth of Christ's work is diminished.

The Holy Scriptures ascribe righteousness before God and everlasting salvation not to our virtues and works, but alone to the superior merit of Christ, which we can acquire only through faith. Paul says: "Since all have sinned and fall short of the glory of God, they are justified by His grace as a gift through the redemption which is in Christ Jesus, whom God put forward as an expiation by His blood to be received by faith" [Rom 3:23-25]. And shortly thereafter the same Apostle says: "For we hold that a man is justified by faith apart from works of law" [Rom 3:28]. Here the blessed Apostle excludes our works from justification. And by excluding the works of the Law, he means not only the ceremonial or civil works, but also the Decalogue, that most exalted part of the Law, the Ten Commandments. For the Ten Commandments seek the most excellent and most holy works of all. Since then no one in [167] this mortal life is able to keep these perfectly, for this reason the Apostle discards justification before God through the works of the Law. For whatever is to stand before the just and honest court of God, it is necessary that it be completely perfect. This then leaves nothing else to be found except the completely perfect work of Christ, which work is reckoned as their own to those who believe through faith in Him. And even our good works are excluded in such a matter of justification, so that we are by no means justified by them (we here use this word in this sense, that is, in the instance in which the sinner appears before the judgment seat of God), but our entire justification takes place freely and by grace alone.

That the word 'grace,' when it is used in connection with our salvation, excludes all our works becomes obvious from what the Apostle Paul himself says: "but if it is by grace, it is no longer on the basis of works; otherwise grace would no longer be grace" [Rom 11:6]. And elsewhere: "now to one who works, his wages are not reckoned as a gift, but as his due. And to one who does not work but trusts him who justifies the ungodly, his faith is reckoned as righteousness" [Rom 4:4-5]. In some manuscripts there is added: "according to the intention of the grace of God." You certainly see that when the Apostle speaks concerning justification, he not only does not include our works, but on the contrary, he sets them over against grace which justifies and saves us, and in this case he even sets faith over against our worthiness. Therefore, he also refers our salvation to the eternal election and predestination of God in Christ by excluding all our works when he says: "Even as he chose us in him before the foundation of the world" [Eph 1:4].

And in the Epistle to the Romans: "though they were not yet born and had done nothing either good or bad in order that God's purpose of election might continue, not because of works, but because of his call, she was told, 'the elder will serve the younger' " [Rom 9:11-12]. And again the same Apostle: "For by grace you have been saved through faith; and this is not your own doing, it is the gift of God—not because of works, lest any man should boast" [Eph 2:8-9]. Here, as you see, works have been excluded, so that they should not in any way be understood either as [168] the cause, or the joint cause of our eternal salvation. For the Lord desires to keep this glory inviolate for himself alone that He saves us by grace and not by our good works. Therefore, in highly praising this mercy toward the human race, Paul says: "but when the goodness and loving kindness of God our Savior appeared, he saved us not because of deeds done by us in righteousness, but in virtue of his own mercy" [Tit 3:4-5]. It is, therefore, by mercy and not by our goodness and worthiness that we are saved by obtaining forgiveness of our sins. Consequently, faith alone is that which gives us a share in this divine mercy. Hence, also, Saint Peter says, in speaking concerning Christ: "to him all the prophets bear witness that everyone who believes in him receives forgiveness of sins through His name" [Acts 14:43]. Therefore, we receive forgiveness of sins by faith, but not by deeds. The Savior also says: "as Moses lifted up the serpent in the wilderness, so must the Son of man be lifted up, that whoever believes in him should not perish, but have eternal life" [Jn 3:14-15]. For those who had been bitten by the serpents, desiring to be healed, were saved not by doing something, but only by looking up to that bronze serpent [cf. Num 21:6]. Thus, we obtain the healing and the everlasting salvation not by doing something, but by looking through the eyes of faith unto Christ crucified.

Indeed, by being reconciled to God through faith, we will also do good works, and that for many and great reasons, which we will recount later on in the proper place, as much as we shall be able. Moreover, blessedness depends not on deeds, but on the forgiveness of sins freely given, as the Apostle Paul teaches, saying: "So also David pronounces a blessing upon the man to whom God reckons righteousness apart from works: 'Blessed are those whose iniquities are forgiven, and whose sins are covered; blessed is the man against whom the Lord will not reckon his sin' " [Rom 4:6-8]. Because of Christ, sins are forgiven in that He has completely obeyed the law of God and has fulfilled it. He has borne all our sins and made atonement through His suffering. Therefore, the [169] Apostle Paul writes: "for as by one man's disobedience many were made sinners, so by one man's obedience many will be made righteous" [Rom 5:19]. Also Isaiah: "And the Lord has laid on him the iniquity of us all" [Is 53:6] (although this is rendered by the Septuagint: "And the Lord gave him up for our sins"). Therefore, he who has embraced Christ through faith is outside of eternal destruction. For it is just as if one not knowing how to swim were to fall into a very swift and deep river would certainly drown unless someone else, who was better able to swim and stronger and accustomed to struggling succesfully against all kinds of terrible waves, would have pity upon him who was in danger of perishing and go into the river to the rescue; and he, tenaciously holding with his hands the one who has the ability to swim, would undoubtedly be saved by him. Thus, in this same manner, whoever has taken hold of our mediator and Savior Christ through faith and firmly embraced Him, is together with Him carried back and drawn up from the whirlpool and tides of the divine wrath of the curse and of hades; and he will enter into the blessedness of heaven and endless rejoicing. Therefore, either the Heavenly Father will not accept the work of Christ, which is impossible, or he cannot reject the one who in true faith rests on the excellence of Christ.

If, however, contrary to what has been said above, it seems to someone that our works are indispensable for justification and salvation, this person will make all the promises of God, concerning the forgiveness of sins and everlasting life, unintelligible and uncertain. If our virtues are indispensable for justification, who will inform us whether we have sufficient works or lack some of them, and how much we must still pay in full? But it is necessary that the divine promise be most clear and certain, so that faith may firmly depend upon it. For were the assurance and steadfastness of the promise shaken, then faith would collapse. And if faith is overturned, then our justification and salvation will vanish. Therefore, the Apostle Paul positively asserted that righteousness be maintained: "that is why it depends on faith, in order that the promise may rest on grace" [Rom 4:16]. For of old the promises of the Law were not absolute, but depended on this: that the Law be fulfilled. However, [170] the promises of the Gospel do not demand anything more from us but to believe. For if they were not steadfast and sure, unless the Law were to be completely fulfilled, then this New Testament would not differ from the Old one. Indeed, it is for this reason that we see that the sins of the thief on the cross were forgiven, and participation in the heavenly inheritance was given as a gift, although he obviously could not boast of any merit of works. Nevertheless, Christ said: "today you will be with me in Paradise" [Lk 23:43]. And furthermore, the history of the ancient Church testifies that while the most severe persecutions were taking place, many pagans (being astounded by the unconquerable spirit of the holy martyrs) suddenly turned to belief in Christ and were immediately seized by the tyrants and punished. They received absolution from all iniquities through nothing else save only by faith in Christ, and they attained life everlasting. Indeed, we have learned from the Scriptures and we believe that man is justified and saved before God by faith alone without the merit of his own works. Moreover, in additon to what has been said, we also have Saint Epiphanios in agreement with us writing thus:

> While I was sick in the flesh, the Savior was sent to me in the likeness of sinful flesh, fulfilling such a dispensation, to redeem me from slavery, from corruption, and from death. And He became to me righteousness, and sanctification, and salvation. Righteousness,

by setting me free from sin through faith in Him. Sanctification, in having set me free through water and the Spirit and His word. And salvation, His blood being the ransom of the true Lamb, having given Himself up for my behalf. An expiatory sacrifice for the cleansing of the world, for the reconciliation of all things in heaven as well as on earth, the mystery hidden before the ages and generations, fulfilled at the ordained time.[24]

Furthermore, Basil the Great says: "Indeed, this is the perfect and complete glorification in God, when one does not exult in his own righteousness, but recognizing oneself as lacking true righteousness to be justified by faith alone in Christ." And the Apostle Paul also boasts of [171] despising his own righteousness and in seeking the righteousness of God, says:

'through faith in Christ, the righteousness from God that depends on faith, that I may know Him and the power of His resurrection, and may share His sufferings, becoming like Him in His death, that if possible I may attain the resurrection from the dead' [Phil 3:9-11]. Herewith topples the whole lofty pinacle of arrogant pride.[25]

Saint Chrysostom also says: "They said that he who adhered to faith alone was cursed; but he, Paul, shows that he who adhered to faith alone is blessed." [26] Also, elsewhere Chrysostom continues: "For you believe the faith; why then do you add other things, as if faith were not sufficient to justify? You make yourself captive, and you subject yourself to the law."[27] Furthermore, Gregory the Theologian also says:

What is more brief than this wealth? What is more easily received than this gift? Confess Jesus Christ, and believe that He is risen from the dead, and you will be saved. For, indeed, righteousness is only to be believed; but a complete salvation is also to be confessed, and knowledge to be added to confidence.[28]

So be it. Moreover, we do not exhort our hearers simply in an incidental way to do those good works which God has commanded. For it is proper that those who are nourished in piety obey the Lord, according to that which the Apostle Paul writes: "So then, brethren, we are debtors not to the flesh, to live according to the flesh" [Rom 8:12]. The same Apostle elsewhere says: "And He [Christ] died for all, that those who live might live no longer for themselves, but for Him who for their sake died and was raised" [2 Cor 5:15]. Naturally! Nothing is more shameful than an ungrateful man, especially one who is ungrateful to God and for such great blessings, which surpass the power of any human tongue and praise. And it is greatly necessary to be on guard when one has been reconciled to God, not to offend Him again and thus fall away from His grace. Paul says: "For if you live according to the flesh, you will die; but if by the Spirit you put to death the deeds of the body, you will live" [Rom 8:13]. For those who have wounded their own consciences by committing sin and iniquities, they bring to themselves anew the divine wrath and censure, and cast themselves into eternal perdition, unless through true repentance they are brought back into the path by the Lord. [172] Moreover, for this reason too, we must abstain from sin so that we will not bring down upon ourselves physical afflictions. Therefore, the Lord said to him whom He had healed: "See, you are well! Sin no more, that nothing worse befall you" [Jn 5:14]. One must also bear in mind the glory of God, so that His name may not be disgraced because of our sins. The Lord, in some instances, finds fault with the people saying: "The name of God is blasphemed among the Gentiles because of you" [Rom 2:24]. But on the contrary, because of our pious way of living, the name of the Lord is praised, according to what has been said by Christ: "Let your light so shine before men, that they may see your good works and give glory to your Father who is in heaven" [Mt 5:16]. And in addition it is proper to endeavor to encourage good works for the sake of rewards in this and in the age to come. Therefore, the Apostle writing to Timothy says: "Godliness is of value in every way, as it holds promise for the present life and also for the life to come"[1 Tim 4:8; cf. Mt 25:31]. The Son of God has frequently promised an abundant reward on His glorious parousia [second coming], indeed, for those good things we do. For the Scriptures testify that there is such a great abundance of kindness in Him, that He wishes to reward the works, which He himself is working in us, although He owes us absolutely nothing. Until then it is always necessary to confess this: that they who do good works would already previously be sons of God and pre-justified by faith, "for a bad tree cannot bear good fruit" [Mt 7:18].

This then is sufficient to be said concerning justification by faith. And now, let us turn to the discussion of the holy sacraments.

### [5]. Concerning the Sacraments

The Greek churches number the sacraments and [sacred] ceremonies as seven; we name properly only two. For if we wished to name all the holy mysteries, which are beyond our understanding, to those which we now call sacraments and sacred ceremonies, there would be not only the seven sacraments, but many more. And if we also were to name with the word, *mysterion,* all those things by which the Lord wished to lightly sketch out heavenly and spiritual matters, it would be impossible for the number [173] seven alone to include them all. We, however, call sacraments those ceremonies which were ordained by God; which according to the word of the divine promise (concerning the forgiveness of sins and the benevolence of God to us), have bound up with them some perceptible symbol by which total action our faith in the forgiveness of sins is strengthened, and lay up for us heavenly benefactions. Thus, indeed, we know that holy baptism was ordered so that we may be cleansed from our sins, and born by water and the Spirit. Wherefore Paul has said: "Rise and be baptized, and wash away your sins" [Acts 22:16]. And Peter says: "Repent, and be baptized every one of you in the name of Jesus Christ for the forgiveness of your sins; and you shall receive the gift of the Holy Spirit" [Acts 2:38]. And again Paul says: "he saved us...in virtue of his own mercy, by the washing of regeneration" [Tit 3:5]. And the Savior: "unless one is born of water and the Spirit, he cannot enter the kingdom of God" [Jn 3:5]. Thus, we also know that the Lord's Supper was instituted by Christ, so that by eating and drinking His body and His blood, we may be reminded and fully assured that we were saved through Christ; and that we have the forgiveness of our sins (which He acquired for us with His passion and death), and the inheritance of the heavenly kingdom. Indeed, we are furthermore nourished and given to drink of such a precious and saving food, so that we may increase more and more in newness of life, that the deadly corruption of the old Adam may be restrained by this most healthy antidote and little by little cleared away.

This is what we hold, in general, concerning the holy sacraments. And now we shall also deal briefly with each of them in particular.

### [6.] Concerning Baptism

In baptizing, you make use of three immersions, and you assert that it must be done this way and not in any other way. We do not use immersion, but triple pouring. We do this in the name of God the Father, God the Son, and God the Holy Spirit. Since Christ and the Apostles have [174] declared nothing specifically in relation to these, we think baptism to be valid and efficacious wherever, by the pouring of water, one is baptized in the name of the Father, and of the Son, and of the Holy Spirit, without altering the words of institution of this action. For the element, that is, the matter, and the word comprise the essence of the sacrament. We teach our hearers often and diligently that baptism is useful and has great power.

### [7.] Concerning Chrismation

You are convinced that the external chrismating of the body with fragrant myrrh was instituted by Christ. In this you follow the tradition of Dionysios the Areopagite (as it is supposed), whose books, as we know well, are held in high esteem by some. But we do not accept this. For neither Christ nor the Apostles make mention of that chrismation, no, not in the least. Nor do the writings of Dionysios bear any resemblance to the Apostolic spirit. We are amazed at that Dionysios, and not without reason! For he endeavored to write such things in his treaties *Concerning the Celestial Hierarchy*, which not even Paul, who having ascended to the third heaven and was in paradise, dared to express or hand down in writing. And do not be surprised if this Dionysios does not appear to be credible in those matters to those who investigate the events of the ancient times, when he somewhere quotes Clement of Alexandria, although Clement lived over one hundred years after Dionysios the Areopagite. Furthermore, since this chrismation is not founded on the Word of God, that is, on a commandment and a promise in addition to it, we cannot see how anyone could say with certainty that there is a power of the Holy Spirit in it. So we omit the use of it as something superfluous. Instead of it we prefer, as a more genuine anointing, pious prayers and zealous catechizing and educating the children to attain godliness. For the external anointing is neither confirmed by command of God, nor by apostolic example. Now Phillip baptized an Ethiopian eunuch, the treasurer of the Candace, Queen of the Ethiopians; but [175] absolutely nothing at all is mentioned there of chrismation [cf. Acts 8:38].

Approximately 3000 people were baptized after Peter finished preaching on the day of Pentecost [cf. Acts 2:41]; but there is no mention of chrismation. Also many others were baptized, as mentioned in the Acts of the Apostles, but chrismation continues to remain unmentioned. Paul baptized Crispus and Gaius and also the household of Stephanas [cf. 1 Cor 1:14]. Nor is there any word concerning chrismation here, not one! Naturally. For just as Christ was not named [Christ] because of external anointing with oil, but because of the anointing with the Holy Spirit (the so-called "oil of gladness") [cf. Ps 45:8], so we also are called Christians because of the anointing with the Holy Spirit (which has been given to us in measure). For we are the spiritual members of Christ, the Anointed King. For this reason there is no danger to our souls even if we are not anointed by the material oil.

### [8.] Concerning Ordination or Priesthood

We do not appoint the priest (whom by custom we call ministers of the church) to offer in the liturgy the body and blood of Christ (concerning which we will speak later in the proper place), but to preach Christ; to baptize and to administer the Holy Communion publicly in the sanctuary, and privately in homes to those who desire it and to those who are nearing death. We apply to them the name of ministers of the church, so that they will see that they are not the masters but servants of the Church of God, according to what was said by Peter to the elders: "not as domineering over those in your charge but being examples to the flock" [1 Pet 5:3]. Moreover, those among us who shall minister in the church are, from an early age first, not only reared toward piety, but are also educated in the important languages (namely Latin, Greek and Hebrew). They also study the liberal arts and sciences. But above all, they are taught holy theology, and it is presented to them accurately, according to the Holy Scriptures by the teachers of theology. And when the time comes, following their schooling, to enter into the ministry of the church, they are called by the theologians and counselors, who have been appointed for this purpose by our most illustrious and most pious prince. [176] They bring from their teachers written testimonies of their conduct of life. Then they are carefully examined whether they understand the pure content of the Christian faith and whether they possess the necessary gifts to teach the multitudes. When they are judged worthy, if they will be engaged [as ministers], they pledge under oath to teach the church piously and correctly, and to lead a blameless life so that to no one is given occasion for scandal [cf. Rom 14:13]. Following this they are sent to the church which they are to be assigned, where in one or two sermons they give a sample of those gifts which they have received from God. When they are approved by the church, then in a full assembly of the people (after a sermon has been preached and a number of prayers said relating to this matter), they are ordained by the superintendent[29] of the locality in the presence of one or more ministers. And from then on, he takes care of the church which has been entrusted to him. Moreover, twice annually, each of the superintendents travels around to visit the churches which have been entrusted to them. He examines their manner of life and the teaching of the pastor, and at the same time, concerning the people, with what zeal they listen to the sermons, and how they comply with their superiors and their subordinates. The superintendent corrects those things which need correction. But he refers the more serious matters to an ecclesiastical synod. In this synod a consultation takes place, and the minister who has committed a light offence is earnestly admonished to conduct himself in a way conformable to his position. If someone has done something more serious, he is defrocked and another replaces him. Moreover, other offences of the listeners are in turn dealt with according to the regulation of our pious prince, who himself diligently supervises the condition of the churches. With his personal theologians and counselors he provides the remedial measures.

Moreover, we permit marriage to the ministers of the church, who wish to marry, even after ordination, and also, to take another in marriage if his previous wife had died. For we know that the Apostle where he wills to the bishops to be "the husband of one wife" [1 Tim 3:2], does not forbid a second marriage, but polygamy. At that time it was still being practiced by some (according to the custom of the Jews). For to have two wives simultaneously was contrary to the institution of marriage [177] from the beginning, and was a sign of incontinence. We believe that inasmuch as Paul wills that the younger widows be married again, it is also allowed for the ministers of the church to do the same [cf. 1 Tim 5:14]. For the Lord says concerning the gift of continence: that "not all men can receive this precept, but only those to whom it is given" [Mt 19:11]. Therefore, we say with Paul: "but if they cannot exercise self-control, they should marry. For it is better to marry than to be aflame with passion" [1 Cor 7:9]. However, we force no one to be married.

### [9.] Concerning Penance

There is no doubt that it is necessary to repent. Furthermore, for true repentance, it is necessary to recognize that we ourselves are sinners, to grieve from our soul for our sins, and to place all of our confidence in the Son of God, who has redeemed us. In addition, we must have a genuine and firm intent to amend our lives. We place all of this beyond any disputation.

Nevertheless, we do not believe that it is necessary for a true and redemptive repentance to enumerate all those sins we perceive ourselves to have committed. For the Scriptures, indeed, teach that if we confess our sins to the Lord our God, we shall receive forgiveness of them. Thus, for example, David says: "I said, I will confess my transgression to the Lord 'then thou didst forgive the guilt of my sin' " [Ps 32:5]. Also, John: "if we confess our sins, he is faithful and just, and will forgive our sins and cleanse us from all unrighteousness" [1 Jn 1:9]. To enumerate all our sins before man, namely before the ministers of the church, has nowhere been ordered in the Holy Scriptures. We by no means impose on the flock, which has been given to our care, such burdens as the Lord himself has not imposed on them. That tax collector, who confessed his sins in the temple, did not confess privately, but in general, saying: "God, be merciful to me a sinner" [Lk 18:13]. Nevertheless, "this man went down to his house justified." [Lk 18:14]. The thief who was crucified with Him [Christ] did not enumerate the murders which he had committed, nor [178] how often he had robbed others, but he said: "and we, indeed, justly; for we are receiving the due reward of our deeds," and "Lord remember me when you come in your kingdom" [Lk 23:41-42]. And he hears from Christ: "truly, I say to you, today you will be with me in Paradise" [Lk 23:43]. Therefore, the general confession of sins is sufficient. While the other, the particular confession, is not without danger, and this in many ways, to those stricken in conscience. For, indeed, those who conceal sins because of a shame, and yet are convinced that it is necessary to enumerate them, fall into doubt or even despair, for they are not convinced that their sins are forgiven since they have not confessed all of them. Furthermore, the enumeration of all iniquities is impossible, as David says: "for my iniquities have gone over my head; they weigh like a burden too heavy for me" [Ps 38:4]. And elsewhere: "but who can discern his errors? Cleanse thou me from hidden faults" [Ps 19:12].

Wherefore, the prophet acknowledges, that his sins are so many that they cannot all be known or remembered. In addition, you are not ignorant of the case in which the famed Nektarios, the Bishop of Constantinople, well known for his learning and holiness, annulled long ago in the case of Constantine such a confession of sins as we now discuss. This is written by Socrates in the *Ecclesiastical History*.[30] And Saint Chrysostom himself does not urge such confessions as we are discussing, but contents himself with the confession which is made before God:[31] For he writes likewise (according to the edition in the Latin language):

> Acknowledge your sins, that you may wipe them away; if you feel ashamed to say wherein you have sinned then say them everyday in your souls. I do not command you to confess to your fellow-servant, who would insult you with abusive language; say them to God Who heals them.[32]

And elsewhere, he says: "Let the examination of your iniquities be made in your thought; let the judgment be without witness; let God alone see your confession."[33] And again elsewhere:

> I do not lead you to become a spectacle before your fellow-servants; neither do I force you to reveal your iniquities to the people; lay open and unfold your conscience before God. Show your wounds to [179] the Lord who is the best physician, and receive the remedies from Him; show Him, who does not blame you for anything, but who cures you with the greatest compassion.[34]

And again elsewhere: "Beware, do not tell any man, lest he blame you. Even it is not to be confessed to a fellow-servant, who would divulge it, but before the Lord, who cares for you, etc."

Therefore, we remain contented with the general confession of sins, lest we plunge our consciences into doubt as to whether our sins have been forgiven or not. For if that consolation has been added, that God, who is merciful, will forgive the sins which either have escaped the memory, or have been kept secret out of shame, then there is the fear that they will be omitted when the enumeration of all iniquities is demanded, and those terrified consciences will retain unceasing trouble and agony, if out of shame or fear, they have concealed some of them in silence, as we said above. Just as we do not think it is necessary to confess all transgressions, in like manner we cannot accept such satisfaction as some demand.

We are not speaking at the present time concerning the following: whether or not one who has injured either the honor or property of his neighbor is obliged to give satisfaction. For we hold this to be incontestable. Because we do not believe that a person repents, who although he is able to return the things which belong to another, knowingly keeps them, or refuses to make amends to his neighbor, since this must absolutely be done. Again, we are not ignorant of the fact that it was the custom in the early Church to impose satisfactions on those who had committed sins publicly, and had seriously scandalized the Church. Nevertheless, we do not find this being done at the time of the Apostles. Insofar as we are able to ascertain from the histories and the circumstances of the times, we think such satisfactions were imposed on sinners not that they might thereby absolve themselves from sins committed against God, nor that they might be protected against punishment hereafter, but that they might be tested as to whether they had truly repented of their trespasses. For such persons sustained with humility the [180] burden of the punishment. Penances were imposed upon them so that they would be more cautious after that, and conduct themselves more carefully throughout their entire life. And this was an example to admonish others not to act in similar wicked ways. This was also done so that the Church, which was scandalized by them, might in some way or another be satisfied. From this practice the word 'satisfaction,' perhaps, had its beginning. And in addition, the stumbling block which had occurred was corrected, so that those who were outside of the Church, that is, the pagans, would not think that the Christians allowed themselves permission to do such wicked things with impunity. For during those years, most of those in authority were still thinking in terms of the pagans, and did not pay much attention to the things of the Christians. Therefore, such a discipline was not only tolerable at that time, but altogether necessary. If, however, one would introduce such a satisfaction to appease God for our sins, we cannot see how this would concur with the Holy Scriptures, since they ascribe to Christ the most perfect satisfaction for the sins of the whole world. If this is true (for it is true, and, indeed, most true), satisfactions from us are not required: for the satisfaction by Christ is, indeed, sufficient. The Apostle [Paul] says: "for by a single offering he has perfected for all times those who are sanctified" [Heb 10:14]. And John: "he is the expiation for our sins, and not for ours only but also for the sins of the whole world" [1 Jn 2:2]. And "the blood of Jesus Christ the Son of God cleanses us from all sins" [1 Jn 1:7]. Therefore, we cannot see how it is possible that satisfactions for our sins against God can stand without destroying the entire satisfaction which our Redeemer Jesus Christ has made. In addition to that, the Apostles' Creed denies such satisfactions. If we believe in the remission of sins, how can we believe in a satisfaction? We are speaking about satisfactions by us. For if the remission of sins has been accomplished through the satisfaction by Christ, then with respect to us, it does not occur because of satisfaction by us (as it might appear), for then it would not be remission. For remission and satisfaction contradict each other. Furthermore, the teaching concerning satisfaction contradicts the

[181] teaching of Paul that righteousness is given freely. For if we are freely justified, satisfaction through works can have no place, as is written above in the article concerning justification. For Christ distinctly teaches in the parable concerning the servant who owed him ten thousand talents, that the remission of our sins occurs in such a manner that nothing at all is paid by us. For He says: "out of pity for him the lord of that servant released him and forgave him the debt" [Mt 18:27]. Therefore, our satisfactions have no power to set us free from the sins committed against God. Neither, again, are satisfactions necessary in order that we may avoid punishments after this life, which some think are imposed on those who some day will be saved. For the Holy Scriptures positively assert nothing of the kind, but know of only two places which men inherit after this life, one for the blessed, and one for the condemned. Christ said: "he who believes and is baptized will be saved; but he who does not believe will be condemned" [Mk 16:16]. And elsewhere: "he who believes in the Son has eternal life; he who does not obey the Son shall not see life, but the wrath of God rests upon him" [Jn 3:36]. Also, the penitent thief on the cross hears that without any satisfactions he will certainly be in Paradise with Christ on that same day. Although God is just, nevertheless, He also is greatly abundant with mercy. Since He is satisfied with the satisfaction of His only-begotten Son, He does not demand any compensation on our part for our sins. For even after the forgiveness of sin, He, nevertheless, inflicts blows in this life (such as David and many great ones sustained). This does not occur by way of satisfaction for sins, but that we might abstain from sin and thereafter more diligently guard against sin, and prevent others from sinning.

## [10. Prayers for the Dead—Memorials]

For the same reason we do not approve of prayers and alms offered for the dead. If they have truly believed in Christ, we do not doubt that they do live with Christ enjoying the gladness in heaven, since their souls [182] have now been separated from their bodies. For Christ says: "truly, truly, I say to you, he who hears my word and believes him who sent me, has eternal life; he does not come into judgment, but has passed from death to life" [Jn 5:24]. But if they departed without true and living faith, they cannot be helped neither by prayers nor by alms. Paul, also, writing to the Thessalonians concerning the condition of those who have fallen asleep in Christ, makes no mention of punishments which those who believed in Christ would suffer after their departure from this life [cf. 1 Th 4:14ff]. Not even with one word does he declare whether or how it is possible to help such souls. But certainly such a great Apostle would not omit this, if the souls of the pious were to suffer in the hereafter. For, indeed, he had such fervent love, as to wish to be anathema from Christ for the sake of unbelievers among his own people [cf. Rom 9:1-3], if by his condemnation he might redeem their condemnation. Indeed, how greatly inhumane it would be, or rather cruel, if the Apostles, having forseen the future sufferings of souls and their therapy and healing, and yet never, neither to a greater nor lesser extent, made mention of such an important matter in so many letters? Who could write and make mention of it better or more truthfully than Paul, who while he was yet living among mortals, saw what occurred in the next life [cf. 2 Cor 12:1-4]; [or] who else better and with greater certainty than John, who was loved by Christ over the other Apostles, and whose epistle is entirely full of love [cf. Jn 12:23ff]? But even if someone would wish to concede this: that the souls of those who lived piously, but have not made satisfaction in the present life, will suffer in the future life; yet there is Chrysostom himself who strongly denies the possibility of those who are in danger to receive assistance after this life. For he says the following:

> If you have seized something by force from someone, restore it and say with Zacchaios: 'if I have defrauded any one of anything, I restore it fourfold' [Lk 19:8]. If you became hostile to someone, be reconciled before you come to the judgment. Be reconciled in everything here, so that you may see that judgment seat without sorrow.[35]

[183] As long as we are here, we have good hopes. But as soon as we depart to that place, we can no longer repent nor cleanse ourselves from our iniquities.

### [11. Fasting]

In addition to what has been said, fasting, also (by no means the least of the satisfactions), is greatly stressed. And we are not ignorant that there existed in the Old Testament the rule of fasting during specified times, especially before the day of Atonement [cf. Num 29]. But this discipline was peculiar to the Old Testament. The Apostles also sometimes kept the custom of fasting, yet not as something indispensable, but that they might not provide a scandal to the Jews, and because they were thus accustomed, and also for the purpose of burying Moses and his ceremonies by gracefully abrogating them. Indeed, concerning the keeping of days of fasting and distinction of foods they handed down no commandment, but they very strongly commanded us to be vigilant as well as to exercise self-control. Although these things are so, we do not prevent any one from fasting according to his own will whenever he senses the need for fasting as a restraint to the flesh. But we do not formulate a general rule which would force all Christians to practice it. For the difference is great among persons in temperament, occupations, and hardships through which the pious are troubled. Therefore, even Saint

Chrysostom does not sternly demand fasting. For he writes somewhere in this way: "If you are unable to fast, you can, however, abstain from iniquities. This is no small thing, nor far removed from fasting; this, too, is suitable for suppressing the fury of the devil."[36]

For this reason we continually admonish our hearers to lead a temperate life. We do not entreat them to keep a fixed time of fasting, nor to abstain from certain foods. We exhort them, following the example of the holy Apostle, not to make use of Christian freedom to fulfill the desire of the flesh [cf. Gal 5:15].

### [12. Almsgiving]

It is beyond doubt that the gesture of giving alms is ordered by God and worthy of a Christian person (for the indication of love). We urge [184] our people to practice it [almsgiving] not sparingly, nor in a petty manner, but with generosity in proportion to their possessions. He [Paul] says: "he who sows sparingly will also reap sparingly" [2 Cor 9:6]. In addition, alms have divine promises that they will be rewarded by God in this life, according to what has been said in the Psalm: "Blessed is he who considers the poor and the destitute. The Lord delivers him in the day of trouble; the Lord protects him and keeps him alive; he is called blessed in the land; Thou dost not give him up to the will of his enemies. The Lord sustains him on his sick bed; in his illness Thou healest all his infirmities" [Ps 41:1-3]. Indeed, He promised these things as an earthly reward for those who, having been moved by true love, treat their neighbor well with alms.

Moreover, the Savior also promised a reward will be ours in the future life, if we treat the needy well, in which He assures us that what we would do "to one of the least of these my brethren" [Mt 25:40] for the sake of the Lord, He will reckon as if it had been done to Him. So be it. However, we do not think it appropriate to praise almsgiving too excessively, as to attribute to such works of love such power to help us, which belongs only to the work of Christ. For that which was said by Christ to the rich young man: "if you would be perfect, go, sell what you possess and give to the poor, and you will have treasure in heaven; and come, follow me" [Mt 19:21], should not be understood as if the Lord wished to place perfection in the following: that a man should sell everything in his possession and give everything to the poor. For what the Apostle has written does not agree with this interpretation. For who would doubt that the Apostles intended to further this purpose with their writings: that men strive as much as possible toward true perfection? Yet, at the same time, they nowhere ordered the Christians to sell all their possessions and give them in alms. Paul, for instance, asking the Corinthians to assist in relieving the poverty and extreme want of the brethren in Judea by alms, does not command them to distribute all of their possessions to the

[185] needy, but to give of their abundance to those in want in proportion to their possessions [cf. 2 Cor 8:14]. He [Paul] says: "for if the readiness is there, it is acceptable according to what a man has, not according to what he has not. I do not mean that others should be eased and you burdened, but that as a matter of equality your abundance at the present time should supply their want" [2 Cor 8:12-13]. Also, in his First Epistle to the Corinthians, he writes thus about alms: "Concerning the contributions for the saints, as I directed the churches of Galatia, so you, also, are to do. On the first day of every week, each of you is to put something aside and store it up, as he may prosper, so that contributions need not be made when I come" [16:1-2]. Hence, it is obvious that this was commanded by Paul: each week, each of them was to put aside something, whatever seemed right to him, from his own possessions for the needs of the poor. For nothing in this command would indicate that it is necessary to sell all things and distribute them among the poor.

Again, neither could it be said that the Apostle wished by this command to lead the Corinthians away from perfection. The Lord had something else in mind, namely this: He saw that the young man had not yet recognized the disease of avarice in himself [cf. Mt 19:16]. For he thought that he had already kept all the commandments of God, nevertheless, he was suffering from avarice and loved wealth far beyond what is proper. Therefore, when Christ wanted to bring this condition of soul to light, He ordered him to sell his possessions and give them to the poor so that it would become obvious that he still loved wealth and was not ready to obey God to the degree which he had boasted only a short time before. For in the same manner, as when God said to Abraham that he should offer up his only son Isaac as a burnt-offering [Gen 22:2], He did not seriously wish that the child be sacrificed, but rather wished that the obedience of Abraham become known to all. So, in this same manner, the Lord ordered this young man to sell his possessions so that his disobedience, his love of money and his boasting would become known so that he might, perhaps, come to a better understanding, perceive his own sins, and gain salvation.

In the same manner, the word of Daniel to the king of Babylon should [186] be correctly understood: "Therefore, O king, let my counsel please thee, and atone for thy sins by alms, and thine iniquities by compassion on the poor: it may be God will be long-suffering to thy trespasses" [4:24]. Here Daniel did not wish that the king should make atonement before God for sins by giving alms (for what need would there then be of the Messiah, and His exceeding benevolence?). Nor did he wish the king to doubt whether or not his sins had been forgiven before God when he said: "It may be that God will be long-suffering over against thy trespasses," (for that is characteristic of unbelief, for according to what has been written in Romans 4 [18ff], doubt cannot stand together with faith). But Daniel intended to say this:

> You, O king, in your administration have been bold to do many
> things in arrogance, avarice, and cruelty. You have deprived many
> people of possessions, of life, and of kingdom. Therefore, the Lord
> will indeed chastise you in this present life with heavy punishment
> so that you may be an example to the people. Come then, repent;
> and because you are not able to give back life and possessions to
> those from whom you have already taken them, show then a true
> repentance by doing good and by distributing alms to the poor.
> Perhaps, then, you might thus persuade God from a sense of shame,
> and He would spare you by taking away the impending punishment,
> so that the miseries which had been announced previously in the
> dream will not happen to you.

That the prophet does not speak about the reward of good works (which
undoubtedly follow them), is obvious from the word, *perhaps*. For the
reward for good works is certain, but the prevention of bodily
punishments and penalties is conditional. This understanding of the
prophet, then, agrees with all the inspired Scriptures, and, indeed, with
the Christian faith (concerning the expiation of sins through the mediation of Christ). We gladly agree with the words in praise of alms provided that the precious work of Christ remains unharmed.

And now we will also say something concerning the invocation of the
saints.

### [13. The Invocation of the Saints]

Indeed, it should not be doubted that it is necessary to think and speak
with honor concerning the saints. Therefore, we exhort our people, when
we have the opportunity, to imitate their faith, their forbearance, their
patience, their piety and the other virtues for which they have been
distinguished.

Truly, this is good. We do not hold that it is necessary to invoke them
[187] in order that they may be our mediators and intercede with God
either for ourselves or for those who already are dead. Nor do we approve of worshipping either the saints or their icons, nor of honoring
them with churches and votive offerings. For we do not transfer to
creatures the honor which is owed only to God. For this same reason we
do not worship the holy angels. Why? For even if a scholarly distinction
is sought between worship, which is wed to God, and the state and servitude, which would be assigned to the saints, nevertheless, in reality, we
see the same thing attributed to the saints which belongs to God alone.
For when the invocation of the saints occurs, this is ascribed to them:
that they perceive and hear the thoughts, sorrows, lamentations of man.
But this belongs to God alone. And, indeed, the Prophet Isaiah shows

that the saints do not know specifically what is done here on earth, for he says: "For thou art our Father, though Abraham does not know us and Israel does not acknowledge us" [Is 63:16]. And Elijah, before he was taken up into heaven, said to Elisha: "ask what I shall do for you before I am taken from you" [2 Kg 2:9], thus implying that it is not possible in the future life for him to know what Elisha would ask for. And if the God-loving patriarchs and prophets were, thus, ignorant then of the situation of things on earth, consequently, neither do they know today how things are with us, nor do they hear for what we are praying. For although, in general, they are well disposed toward the Church of God, and they intercede with Him (in accordance to the conditions of that time) so that the Lord will take care of His Church, it does not follow from this, however, that we are to worship or pray to them so that they will take care of each one of us or pray to the Lord for us. Therefore, we have no right to call them mediators.

Paul says: "For there is one mediator between God and man— the man, Christ Jesus" [1 Tim 2:5]. This mediator suffices for us, for the Holy Scriptures nowhere exhorts us to invoke saints or angels, nor to worship them and their images. For even the angels would not allow themselves to be worshipped, saying that they are our fellow servants. And Peter refused to be worshipped by Cornelius [cf. Acts 10:26]. Similarly, Saint Epiphanios [of Salamis 315-403] abrogates the worship of the saints. He writes word for word:

> [188] But neither was Elijah worshipped, even though he was among the living. Neither was John worshipped, although by his own prayers he attained a wondrous death, and received grace from God. Not even Thecla,[37] nor any of the saints was worshipped. For the ancient error will not conquer us: to abandon the living and to worship those who have been made by Him. For they worshipped and served the creature rather than the Creator, and became fools [cf. Rom 1:25]. For if He does not want the angels to be worshipped, how much more does He not want her who was born from Anna, who was given by Joachim to Anna, to be worshipped?[38]

Continuing, he says:

> Let Mary be held in honor, but let the Father and the Son and the Holy Spirit be worshipped; let no one worship Mary. This mystery is due God, not to women, neither to man. Nor does such a doxology belong to the angels. Let those things be erased which have been wrongly written in the heart of those who have been deceived. Let the lust of the idol be extinguished from the eyes. (Epiphanios refers here to the icons which are worshipped.) Let the creature return again to the Master. Let Eve with Adam return

to honor God alone. Let no one be led by the voice of the serpent. Let him abide by the command of God.[39]

And earlier [he wrote]:

Yes, certainly, the body of Mary was holy, but she was not God. Yes, indeed, the Virgin was a virgin, and honorable, but she was not given to us to worship. She worshipped Him to whom she gave birth from her flesh; the one who is from heaven and from the Father's bosom. And for this reason the Gospel reassures us of this, the Lord himself declaring that: 'O woman, what have you to do with me? My hour has not yet come' [Jn 2:4]. And so that no one would think from the words, 'O woman, what have you to do with me,' that the holy Virgin is superior, He calls her 'woman.'[40]

This much from Epiphanios. And Saint Basil writes:

For neither do you seek a brother for salvation, but Him who excels you in nature; nor a mere man, but the man who is God, Jesus Christ, who alone can offer expiation to God for all of us, 'whom God put forward as an expiation by his blood to be received by faith' [Rom 3:25; cf. Heb 4:16]. Moses was brother of Israel, [189] but could not save him. How can an ordinary man save you?[41]

Saint Chrysostom also writes in the same vein of thought:

See the wisdom of the woman [Canaanite woman; cf. Mt 15:21ff]. She does not ask James; she does not beg John; neither does she go to Peter; nor does she look to the group of the Apostles. She was not looking for a mediator. But instead of all of these she took repentance to accompany her, which fulfilled the task of an advocate. Thus, she went up to the highest source. He says, 'For this reason, He descended; for this reason He took flesh and became man, that even I may be encouraged to speak to Him. Now on high in the heavens the Cherubim tremble before Him, the Seraphim fear Him, etc. O what a miracle! On high, trembling: and down here, confidence. Have mercy on me (I have no need of a mediator), have mercy on me.'[42] These things have been said by those mentioned above.

Neither do we find anywhere a promise in the Scriptures that such invocation or worship would be profitable to us. Nor is there in the Scriptures an example of any pious man who invoked some saint. Nor do we have need of any mediator, who might reconcile Christ to us, if in truth the Son of God became man for this very reason: to recncile us, as His brethren, to the Father. He, too, is so kindly disposed toward us as to say: "come to me, all who labor and are heavy laden, and I will give you rest" [Mt 11:28]. And elsewhere He says: "and him who comes to me I will not cast out" [Jn 6:37].

Christ is the Mediator not only in the matter of our salvation as some claim, but also in the purpose of intercession, according to Paul: "[Jesus Christ] who is at the right hand of God, who, indeed, intercedes for us" [Rom 8:34]. Christ commands us, who are going to pray, to approach God simply and directly, saying: "pray, then, like this: our Father who art in heaven" [Mt 6:10]. And He promises that we shall be heard. For He says: "truly, truly, I say to you, if you ask anything of the Father, he will give it to you in my name" [Jn 16:23]. For no one need think that there are any saints or angels that have such great concern and love as God has for us. "For God so loved the world that he gave his only Son, [190] that whoever believes in him should not perish but have eternal life" [Jn 3:16]. And Paul says: "what then shall we say to this? If God is for us, who is against us" [Rom 8:31]? He who did not spare His own Son, but offered Him up for all of us, how will He not also together with Him freely give us all things? Why, then, is there need for more mediators, when the Father himself loves us very much? Therefore, we worship Him who loves us much more ardently than all the saints. He does not only love, but He also knows what we need, even before we pray to Him [cf. Mt 6:8]. He wishes to be invoked by us, and He is willing to listen. And according to Paul, He "is able to do far more abundantly than all that we ask or think" [Eph 3:20]. And although we find in the histories some who invoked the saint and received not inconsiderable help, yet such signs (if they can be called signs) are justly suspected by us. For Scripture does not simply accept every sort of signs, but is as Moses in Deuteronomy 13 [v. 12], and Paul in 2 Thessalonians [2:9], and the Savior himself in Matthew 24 [v. 4] dissuade us, in a most friendly manner, not to be deceived by false signs and wonders.

If, indeed, any signs could be sufficient to confirm a religion, then, certainly, much would be found in the profane and credible histories to confirm the self-chosen pagan superstitions. Consequently, only those signs ought to be accepted and made much of, which do not oppose the sound teaching of the divine word. Saint Chrysostom, also, testifies that not even a trace is left of that power (that is, the power of the Apostles) of performing miracles which existed at the time of the Apostles.[43] Therefore, we invoke, worship, and praise only God, and are fully persuaded that we are offering Him truly a very pleasing worship, according to the Psalm: "Call upon me in the day of trouble; I will deliver you, and you shall glorify me" [Ps 50:15]. And the Apostle [Paul] also says: "through him, then, let us continually offer up a sacrifice of praise of God, that is, the fruit of lips that acknowledge his name" [Heb 13:15].

But in discussing satisfactions and true repentance, we have digressed in these discussions; let us now come to the other of our two

[191] sacraments (the Lord's Supper). We will discuss it briefly, and with the reverence and respect with which we have conversed with Your Holiness up till now.

### [14.] Concerning the Lord's Supper

We often exhort our people who have repented to partake frequently of the Lord's Supper. However, we do not commune the infants, for Paul says: "Let a man examine himself, and so eat of the bread and drink of the cup. For any one who eats and drinks without discerning the Lord's body, eats and drinks judgment upon himself" [1 Cor 11:28-29]. And since the children are not able to examine themselves and, thus, cannot discern the Lord's body, we think that the ceremony of the baptism is sufficient for their salvation, and also the hidden faith with which the Lord has bestowed them. For through this faith they spiritually eat the flesh of Christ, even if they do not, in the communion of the supper, physically eat It. That spiritual eating, which Christ speaks of in Saint John's Gospel, is always necessary; but the other, the mystical one [the Lord's Supper], is not always necessary.

We do not call the Supper of the Lord a sacrifice through which either the living or the dead are reconciled to God. For the Evangelists and the Apostle Paul, writing concerning its institution, say with one accord: that Christ commands us to eat His own body and to drink the blood in His remembrance [cf. Mt 26:26; Mk 14:22; Lk 22:19; 1 Cor 11:23]. Indeed, no word of His is found anywhere saying that it is necessary to sacrifice His body and His blood in that Supper. For Christ was the sacrifice on the cross, but He is food and drink for us in the Supper. For what reason? To have remembrance and conviction that we are saved only by His offering and sacrifice. Hence, the Apostle says: "by his own blood he entered once and for all into the Holy Place...thus, securing an eternal redemption" [Heb 9:12]. For we know that since Christ (who is the body, as the Apostle says) has come, the shadows have ceased [cf. Col 2:17]. Nor is that great sacrifice, which has been once accomplished on the cross, to be portrayed again by new representations in the Church. [192] And in addition, since it occurs for the remembrance of Christ, it is a remembrance of a sacrifice, but not a sacrifice. Precisely for this reason we never sacrifice anew the body and blood of Christ, but we eat and drink these divine and venerable gifts with devout disposition of the soul and with thanksgiving. While we believe that the body and blood of the Lord are truly present in the Lord's Supper, we do not take this to mean that the bread is changed into the body of Christ. For the great Paul calls that mystic bread no less bread when he says: "let a man examine himself, and so eat of the bread" [1 Cor 11:28]. And elsewhere he says: "the bread which we break, is it not a participation in the body of Christ?" [1 Cor 10:16]. For as when one offers a glass of wine to some-

one he correctly says, "behold the wine," although the glass has not been
changed into wine, but that which is offered with the glass. Consequently, it is correctly said of the bread "this is my body," for the body of
Christ is given to us with that bread. Neither do we mix water with the
wine in the Holy Communion, for the Lord said at its institution: "I shall
not drink again of this fruit of the vine" [Mt 26:29], mentioning nothing
at all of water being mixed with it. Consequently, we do not think such a
mixture is necessary. And should it take place, we do not think that it
makes any difference.

Furthermore, we do not use leavened bread, but unleavened.
However, we do not think that there is a great difference should the Supper be celebrated with either leavened or unleavened bread, because we
celebrate the Passover of the New Testament. For just as in ancient times
in the Old Testament (which was a type of the New) all the leaven had to
be removed in the celebration of the Paschal Feast; similarly, there is in
our churches an admonition to eat unleavened bread: "let us eat" (according to Paul) "not with the old leaven, the leaven of malice and evil,
but with the unleavened bread of sincerity and truth" [1 Cor 5:8].

The All-Holy Communion is celebrated among us today with a
minimum of ceremonial. The church assembles at an appointed time.
[193] Hymns are sung. Sermons are preached concerning the benefits of
Christ for mankind. Again, hymns are sung. An awesome exhortation is
read, which in part explains the words of institution of the Most-Holy
Supper, and in part demands that each person should prepare for a worthy communion. A general but sincere confession of sins is made.
Forgiveness is publicly pronounced. With devout prayers we ask the
Lord to make us partakers of the heavenly gifts and benefits. The words
of institution of the sacrament are read, after which the congregation ap-
proaches with reverence and receives (offered by the holy minister) the
body and the blood of Christ. Again we give thanks to God in prescribed
words for the heavenly gifts. Finally, the holy minister of God says the
blessing over the assembled congregation, and all are dismissed to go to
their homes. We think that these rites are sufficient, because a multitude
of distracting customs, beyond those which are necessary, prevent the
people from properly paying attention to the important and necessary
ones. Certainly, we do not contend with anyone about customs so long as
they do not include anything which contradicts the Word of God, or
(contrary to Christian freedom) is insisted upon as necessary for salvation.

We judge that this use of the Lord's Supper by us agrees with the command of Christ and serves the Church in the work of salvation.

[15.] Concerning the Anointing of the Sick
We are not unaware that for a period of time in the primitive Church

of Christ, the anointing of the sick was practiced. For when the preaching of the Gospel was newly established, it needed to be confirmed through signs and miracles. For it is written concerning the Apostles: "so they went out and preached that men should repent. And they cast out many demons, and anointed with oil many that were sick and healed them" [Mk 6:12-13]. We believe that this gift of healing the sick through miracles remained in the Church for a time, just as the gift of the tongues and that of prophesying. Hence, we admit that anointing was still in use [194] at the time of James. For he writes: "Is any among you sick? Let him call for the elders of the church, and let them pray over him, anointing him with oil in the name of the Lord; and the prayer of faith will save the sick man, and the Lord will raise him up; and if he has committed sins, he will be forgiven" [Jas 5:14-15]. This passage of James indicates that the anointing took place so that the sick person would regain his former health, and that forgiveness of sins (through the faith of prayers) would be accomplished. But since the preaching of the Gospel has already been sufficiently confirmed through signs and wonders, and since experience itself testifies today that those who are anointed by such an oil are no better off in body than before, we believe that the gift of the performing miracles has ceased. For if the Lord deemed anointing to be a perpetual sacrament and ceremony in the Church, He undoubtedly would have explicitly ordered it, just as he instituted baptism and Holy Communion. It is for this reason that we have given up that anointing. We visit the sick, urge them to repent; we comfort them, we help them as much as we are able, we pray to the Lord for them, we strengthen their faith by giving them the Lord's Supper. In the agony of death we arm them with the counsel from the Scriptures (concerning divine mercy and the gift of everlasting life). Thus, we commend them into the hands of the Lord, not doubting that they depart from this life in a good and blessed way.

## [16.] Concerning Vows and the Monastic Life

We know that it is necessary to keep the pious vows which are within our capabilities. It is written concerning them: "Make your vows to the Lord your God, and perform them" [Ps 76:11]. And: "pay your vows to the Most High" [Ps 50:14]. But because there are times when men rush headlong before they think, and without thinking make vows which they either cannot accomplish or which they might better omit, the Lord himself permitted some vows to be cancelled and abrogated through either the parents or spouses, and this without sin on the part of the one [195] who has made this vow. Moses himself, who was such a severe taskmaster of the divine laws, bears witness to this [cf. Num 30:3]. We think that the following belongs to this kind of vow: when someone takes a vow of perpetual chastity or celibacy without a sufficient examination of his own gifts or especially when this is done at an age when he still has not had the experience of the desires of the flesh. For the results of those vows, which have failed, show that the majority of persons who at first promised to abstain from marriage, afterwards, because they lacked the gift of continence, stained their souls and bodies, and at the same time became a great stumbling block to the church and also plunged their own soul into danger. So we do not doubt that the Apostles themselves, if they were living in our times, would refute such vows. For burdens are not to be placed on consciences, as Paul teaches [cf. 1 Cor 7:35]. It is better for those who have thoughtlessly taken vows to exercise a kind of relaxation of the vow, rather than to tempt God by undertaking the impossible. "Again it is written, 'you shall not tempt the Lord your God' " [Mt 4:7]. But the Lord does not judge that the vow of chastity is kept in the case of one who does not outwardly commit sin but who inwardly is aflame with very shameful thoughts. For these reasons we free such people from such rashly made vows, so that they may live purely in wedlock, rather than by incontinence in the unmarried state. In this we are following the law of Christian love, which is the noblest rule of all [cf. Rom 13:10], and because Paul has declared, "for it is better to marry than to be aflame with passion" [1 Cor 7:9].

Concerning that which belongs to the monastic manner of life, we do not disapprove of the fact that God-fearing men came together in the past under one who was distinguished in learning and virtue (the so-called archimandrites whom we call abbots) to devote themselves to the daily study of the Holy Scriptures. For some renowned men have come forth from them, who have presided faithfully and usefully over the churches of God (according to the understanding of those years). Such orders and societies might be very worthy of praise and would bring [196] salvation to the Church, if with their blessing they were free from the vows concerning perpetual celibacy. Thus, for example, here in this territory of Wittenberg, the honorable Louis, our most renowned duke and pious prince, maintains approximately four hundred young men in monasteries and in schools, that is to say, in private schools as well as in the university. All of these are being prepared for the ministry in the churches, but not one of them is bound by a vow of celibacy. Nor would we disapprove if some persons living a private life and independently would come together in the same place, and by their own work would provide a livelihood for themselves.

It is evident that many such cenobia [monasteries] existed in ancient times. But to bind oneself permanently by a vow and a particular confession to such a manner of living and necessity from which no one can subsequently free himself without wounding his conscience; this, indeed, does not seem advisable to us. For since no one has been born for himself alone but for God and for his neighbor, and since the Lord calls now this one and then that one to this or that life: it is not safe for anyone to impose bonds on himself from which he cannot later free himself. And yet, human nature has been constituted to be subject to many changes, and the will of man does not always remain the same to the time of one's death. It happens to many, who thoughtlessly throw themselves into such a life, that later in life they do everything unwillingly and discontentedly. They murmur within themselves against God and those by whose words they were willingly but thoughtlessly beguiled to be enclosed in such prisons. And did not Basil, the one who so greatly praised the monastic life, say how dangerous it is to choose the celibate life without the special gift of God? For he writes thus: "If you are youthful, either in body or in mind, flee from living together with peers of the same age; and run away from them as from a flame. For the Enemy has set many aflame, and has consigned them to eternal fire, etc." [44]

Moreover, it is necessary above all to remember that the ascetic life has in no way been commanded by God, nor has it been indicated in the Holy [197] Scriptures. Neither the example of John the Baptist, nor of the Prophet Elijah, nor that of Jesus Christ our Savior, has any power to authenticate and confirm the monastic life. For though they had spent their time in the wilderness, they later came into the midst and lived and associated with the people. They taught, but they did not urge anyone to live in solitude. No, indeed, even the fiercest preacher of repentance, the holy Forerunner, did not command anyone to withdraw into the wilderness. He did not prescribe monastic exercises for anyone, but he ordered each to abide to his own calling, and to live in piety. He did this to such an extent that he neither exhorted the tax collectors nor the soldiers to adopt another kind of life [cf. Lk 3:13ff]. He only encouraged them to do no more than what is appropriate for good and pious men to do.

The holy zeal of the Apostle Paul, and no less that of Peter, is known to all. Would they not have urged men to live the monastic life if they had thought it of great importance? They made all kinds of exhortations in their epistles concerning the affairs of church, of the state and of domestic life; but they did not mention the monastic life. Moreover, there is no small danger, that while one is following the angelic manner of living (as some love to call the monastic life), he may fall into those labyrinths, which the Apostle warns against. He says: "Let no one dis-qualify you, insisting on self-abasement and worship of angels, taking his stand on visions, puffed up without reason by his sensuous mind" [Col 2:18]. No one could say that Paul warned only against the self-chosen worship familiar to the Jews. He also warned about the innova-tions which he saw would be brought into the Church in the future, lest the Christians bind themselves unguardedly and fall in them. For the human mind is easily dimmed by the splendors of a self-chosen religion and piety, so that the known and daily services of piety are not greatly honored [cf. 1 Sol 10:7], while the newly innovated ones are excessively admired. And those people who choose such a life, which removes them from ordinary acquaintance and from pious men, drastically [198] change and easily fall into pharisaism, disdain others, and think themselves perfect, saying with the Pharisee: "God, I thank Thee that I am not like other men, extortioners, unjust, adulterers, or even like this tax collector. I fast twice a week, I give tithes of all that I get" [Lk 18:11-12]. Since each in his own station can live piously before God, we do not see how the monastic manner of life could be in some way preferable, since it has not been confirmed either by a divine order, or as an example pleasing to God in the Holy Scriptures. And let us remember what the wise Paul held concerning those physical exercises which, indeed, were later ardently practiced. (He said:) "train yourself in godliness" [1 Tim 4:7]. For physical exercise is slightly profitable but piety is profitable for all things, having the promise of this life and of the future life. Not without reason have these things come forth from the mouth of the Apostle. For this great man foresaw in spirit that there would be a time in which some people would value those exercises of the body (that is, fasting, low hard beds, and many other such [practices]), more than those which are required of us by the commandments of the Lord, and for which temporal and eternal rewards are surely set before us. Therefore, we ask our people to exercise themselves in obedience to the commandments of God. For since this exercise is sufficient to keep men occupied, there is very little or no time left for other things. And one could show no time in which he who is striving after piety might not worship God and do good to his neighbor.

### [17. Epilogue]

These, then, Most-Holy Master, are those things which we have thought it appropriate to state in reply to Your Holiness. We have done this with pure hearts, with courteous devotion, and sincere love. They are few in comparison to the size and importance of the subject matter, but, on the other hand, they happen to be considerable in view of the multitude of matters which occupy Your Holiness. Nevertheless, we humbly and kindly ask that if we spoke to Your Holiness too openly, in paternal kindness you will not be angry. We are greatly convinced that our love of the truth and our candor will not displease Your Holiness, [199] since we judge Your Holiness' attitude with our own. Moreover, we believe that in what we have written, we are not following our own, that is, human reasoning, but are obeying the holy and divinely inspired Scriptures which, we are convinced, speak concerning the subjects dealt with in the previous pages as we have analyzed them. We abound by the grace of God in a tranquil and peaceful conscience, because it is reinforced by the Word of God, the most solid foundation. And we desire from the bottom of our hearts to preserve a God-pleasing peace with all who love the Gospel of Christ, who hold the right interpretation of Christ, the unique teacher (who speaks to us through the words of the Old as well as the New [Testaments]). We do not innovate in any matters of faith, but we believe and teach those things which are written and contained in the books of the Prophets and Apostles. Nothing, indeed, is more ancient, more truthful, more plain, or more steadfast than this teaching. May the heavenly and most benevolent Lord grant grace that this statement which we have prepared of the teaching which has been sent by God may be acceptable and appear adequate to Your Holiness. In the meantime, let us offer fervent prayers to the Lord for each other, that He govern our souls by His Holy Spirit so that all things which have been said, and written, and done by us, may contribute to the glory of His name and to the edification of the Church.

> Lucas Osiander, Teacher of Theology, in the Ducal Ecclesiastical Court of Wittenberg and the Associate Ecclesiastical Chaplain in the Stuttgart Consistorium in behalf of Mr. Jacob Andreae, Prepositor and Chancellor of Tübingen, presently travelling in Saxony, I affix my signature.

> I, Martin Crusius, Teacher of the Greek and Latin Languages and Education in Tübingen have affixed my signature.

## NOTES

1. This first *Reply* from Tübingen to the First *Answer* of His Holiness, Patriarch Jeremiah II, was written in German and translated into Greek by Martin Crucius; it was sent to Constantinople 18 June 1577.

2. St. John Chrysostom, *The Gospel of Matthew, Homily 47*, PG 57.446f; cf. NPNF Ser. 1, vol. 10, 294.

3. Origen, *On Jeremiah, Homily 1*, PG 13.261.

4. St. Basil, *Letter* 189, PG 32.688; cf. NPNF Ser. 2, vol. 8, 229.

5. St. Basil, *Letter* 263, PG 32.980 ff; cf. NPNF Ser. 2, vol. 8, 302.

6. St. Theodoretos, *Commentary on Genesis*, PG 80.84.

7. St. Basil, *Hexaemeron, Homily 6.1*, PG 29, cf. NPNF Ser. 2, vol. 8, 81.

8. St. John Chrysostom, *Second Corinthians, Homily 13*, PG 61.496f; cf. NPNF Ser. 1, vol. 12, 346.

9. St. John Chrysostom, *On the Priesthood*, 4.8; cf. PG 48.669; cf. NPNF Ser. 1, vol. 9, 68.

10. St. John Chrysostom, *Second Epistle to Timothy, Homily 9*, PG 62.649; cf. NPNF Ser. 1, vol. 13, 510.

11. St. John Chrysostom, *Epistle to Titus, Homily 1*, PG 62.664; cf. NPNF Ser. 1, vol.

13, 552.

12. St. Basil, *On Baptism,* 2.4, PG 31.1589; cf. St. Basil, *Ascetical Works,* vol. 9, 399.

13. Socrates, *Ecclesiastical History,* 1.8. NPNF Ser. 2, vol. 2, 11 (with corrections).

14. St. Cyril of Alexandria, *The Adoration and Worship of God in Spirit and in Truth, Homily 1,* PG 68.148.

15. *Athanasian Creed.* Schaff, *The Creeds of Christendom,* 2, pp. 68, 23.

16. St. Epiphanios, *Against Heresies,* 3.1, 74, PG 42.493.

17. Ibid. 3.1, 11, PG 42.500.

18. Ibid. 3.1, 12, PG 42.496.

19. Ibid. 3.1, 12, PG 42.497.

20. St. Basil, "Homily on Humility," *Ascetical Works,* PG 31.532; cf. FC vol. 9, 480 (with corrections).

21. St. John Chrysostom, *First Corinthians, Homily 20,* PG 61.164; cf. NPNF Ser. 1, vol. 12, 114.

22. St. John Chrysostom, *Second Corinthians (3.5), Homily 6,* PG 61; cf. NPNF Ser. 1, vol. 12, 307.

23. Ibid. *Homily (28),* PG 61.590; cf. NPNF Ser. 1, vol. 12, 408.

24. St. Epiphanios, *Against Heresies,* 3.1, 2, PG 42.477.

25. St. Basil, "Homily on Humility," *Ascetical Works,* PG 31.529; cf. FC vol 9, 479 (with corrections).

26. St. John Chrysostom, *Epistle to Galatians (3.9f),* PG 51.651; cf. NPNF Ser. 1, vol. 13, 26.

27. St. John Chrysostom, *Epistle to Titus, Homily 3,* PG 62.651; cf. NPNF Ser. 1, vol. 13, 529.

28. St. Gregory the Theologian (Nazianzos), *On Moderation and Purpose in Controversies, Homily 32, 25,* PG 36.204.

29. The Lutheran Church did not have bishops but superintendents; see *Documents Der Orthodoxen Kirchen zur Ökumenischen Frage,* vol. 2, *Wort Und Mysterium* (Witten, 1958), p. 157.

30. Socrates, *Ecclesiastical History,* 5.19, PG 67.616; cf. NPNF Ser. 2, vol. 2, 128.

31. St. John Chrysostom, *Sermon on Psalm 51, Homily 2,* PG 55.581.

32. St. John Chrysostom, *Sermon on Repentance and Confession, Homily 1,* PG 49.277ff.

33. St. John Chrysostom, *Sermon on the Incomprehensibility of the Nature of God, Homily 1,* PG 48.702ff.

34. St. John Chrysostom, *Sermon on Lazarus, Homily 4,* PG 48.1012. The Latin translation from which the Lutheran Theologians of Tübingen translated into Greek differs slightly from the original Greek text.

35. Ibid. *Homily 2,* PG 48.985. (The original Greek is slightly different).

36. St. John Chrysostom, *On Genesis,* Chapter 2, PG 53.83.

37. *Legends of the Ancient Christian Martyrs,* O.S. 85, A. 84.

38. St. Epiphanios, *Against Heresies,* 3.2, 5, PG 42.748.

39. Ibid. 3.2, 7, PG 42.752.

40. Ibid. 3.2, 4, PG 42.745.

41. St. Basil, *Homily on Psalm 48,* PG 29.440.

42. St. John Chrysostom, "Concerning the Canaanite Woman," *The Gospel of Matthew,* PG 52.452; cf. NPNF Ser. 1.

43. St. John Chrysostom, *On the Priesthood,* 4.3, PG 48.665; cf. NPNF Ser. 1, vol. 9.64.

44. St. Basil, *On the Renunciation of the World,* PG 31.637; cf. FC vol. 9, 23.

*Chapter 4*

# THE SECOND THEOLOGICAL EXCHANGE:

# CONSTANTINOPLE TO TÜBINGEN

*The Second Answer of Patriarch Jeremiah [II] of Constantinople
to Tübingen, 1579, Sent to the Most Wise Theologians,
Residents of the Famous City of Tübingen*

Jeremiah, by the mercy of God, Archbishop of Constantinople, New
Rome, and Ecumenical Patriarch.

[200] Our Humble Self[1] received your sagacious second letters which
you have sent concerning the procession of the Holy Spirit and other
theological questions. We might have answered earlier had we not been
traveling in the West and the Peloponnesos. We, therefore, thank God,
the giver of all good things, and rejoice over the many other benefits, not
the least of which is that you, for the most part, agree with our Church.
So may it be also in the matters in which we disagree, that we may piously agree, by the will of God, who perfects all things for what is most
beneficial.

## [A.] CONCERNING THE PROCESSION OF THE HOLY SPIRIT

The first matter, then, in which we disagree is the procession of the
Holy Spirit. Wherefore, my beloved [spiritual] sons, although this matter
was brought to the fore many times, and accurately examined by every
related canon of the Church, and by every spiritual Lydian stone, it was
obviously analyzed and clarified so much so that it has no further need of
research.

And yet, even though we are preoccupied with many and continuing
responsibilities, we are condescending to you in [Christian] love, no less
than a father would, and abundantly as in the myth of [armed] Athena,[2]
[201] who will deliberate still further with you for your edification, sup-
porting our position with holy testimonies as the God-inspired Fathers
received them.

For it is a stipulation of the holy and Sixth Ecumenical Synod directing
that the Holy Scriptures be understood as the tried and proved teachers

151

of the Church have interpreted them and not as those who, by their own sophistry, wish to interpret such matters superfluously. Read also the stipulation of the 19th canon:

> And if any controversy in regard to Scripture shall have been raised, let them not interpret it otherwise than as the luminaries and doctors of the Church have expounded it. And in these let them glory rather than in composing things out of their own heads lest, through their lack of skill, they may depart from what is fitting.[3]

[1. Distinction between Procession and Sending]

Let us hearken, I entreat you, to what will be said with good will and in the fear of God. The procession of the Holy Spirit is one thing, while the sending is another. For on the one hand, the procession is the natural existence of the Holy Spirit, directly alone from the Father, who is the cause. On the other hand, the sending is a sending forth on a mission in time in which the Son also sends the Spirit, as is the case here, and the Spirit also sends the Son, as it is said, "the Spirit of the Lord is upon me, because the Lord hath anointed me; he has sent me to preach glad tidings to the poor" [Is 61:1; cf. Lk 4:18]. How then and why do you innovate and say that the Holy Spirit proceeds from the Father and from the Son? If the Spirit did not proceed from the Father alone, then the Lord would have said concerning the Paraclete, whom I and the Father sent forth just as He frequently said "whom I shall send" [Jn 15:26]. To begin with, then, the undeceiving mouth of Christ declares that the Holy Spirit proceeds from the Father [cf. Jn 15:26]. Second, even Paul himself in the Epistle to Titus reiterates: "Not because of deeds done by us in righteousness, but in virtue of his own mercy, by the washing of regeneration and renewal in the Holy Spirit, which he poured out upon us richly through Jesus Christ our Savior" [3:5-6]. What is more explicit than this? The Lord has said, "Behold, I send the promise of my Father upon you" [Lk 24:49; cf. Acts 2:1-4; Jn 14:26; 20:21-23]. Paul subsequently asserts: "which he poured out upon us richly" [Tit 3:6].

[2. Apostles and Fathers on Procession and Sending]

[202] Also, the most eminent Peter has suggested this same thing, saying: "[This Jesus] being, therefore, exalted at the right hand of God, and having received from the Father the promise of the Holy Spirit, he has poured out this which you see and hear" [Acts 2:33]. So, the most eminent of the Apostles are speaking in this way, and it is not fitting to contradict them. Concerning them and even concerning the God-filled Fathers gathered in the Holy Synods, Cyril the Great says: "It was not they who spoke [Apostles and Fathers], but the Spirit of God the Father, who [Spirit] proceeds ineffably from the Father, and yet is not different from the Son in essence." [4]

Moreover, Athanasios the Divine in his writing to Serapion says: "If they had believed correctly concerning the Son, then they would also have believed correctly concerning the Spirit, who proceeds from the Father; and it is a characteristic of the Son that, through Him, He [the Spirit] is given to the Disciples."[5]

Some suppose that these sayings of ours do not apply, nor do they imply such thoughts, as if they also attribute to the Son the procession of the Spirit. They do not say that the Spirit proceeds from the Son, also, but that He is given, and that He is of the same essence, which are, indeed, admissable.

[3. Two Streams from One Source or Two Illustrations from Nature]
Furthermore, Gregory the great Theologian in his discourse addressed to Evagrios says:

> Just as two streams spring forth from one source and are sent on their separate courses but yet are not cut-off from their source, in like manner, one should also think concerning divine nature: the Father is called the source, the Son and the Spirit are called the two rivers, which are poured forth directly from the one cause, the Father; or like two buds sprouting from one root, simultaneously growing, which cannot possibly be the cause of the existence of each other.[6]

[4. Difference between 'Ek' and 'Dia']
In addition to that, O wise and beloved men, if you state for your justification that the great Athanasios used the [Greek] preposition 'ek' [from] in those places where he speaks about the Holy Spirit against the Arians, saying that the Holy Spirit is given to all from the Son himself, and that the Father creates, activates, and gives all things through the Logos in the Spirit—if you allege this, then listen and consider two things. One, that the Saint [Athanasios] writing against the Arians,[7] because they (as you well know) called the Son a creature and, by saying this, that the Son is a creature and not a creator, nor a co-[203] creator with the Father, they were forced to call the Holy Spirit a creature, also. Simply because of this alone did the great Athanasios, in attempting to prove that the Holy Spirit is *homoousion* [of the same essence] and not of another essence than the Father and the Son, thus and for this very reason he made timely and proper use of the preposition 'ek.' Another thing that you should consider is: that nowhere else in his writings does this Saint say that the Holy Spirit proceeds from the Son, also, but is given and granted to the created world[8]

Moreover, we have previously mentioned that here is a very great difference between the sending to the created world and the procession which is timeless and eternal, in which He alone directly proceeds from the Father, as we said, and as we will more fully explain with the help of God in the course of our exposition. Consequently, the great Athanasios, whom you presented as your advocate, does not help you. Instead, he argues against you for he allies himself with the Lord and with all the God-filled and wise theologians of the Church. Therefore, he ridicules those of contrary opinion, that is, against these pneumatomachs[9] [adversaries of the Spirit], by directing this jest at them: "If the Holy Spirit is not a creature, then He is a son; thus, there will be found to be two sons and brothers, or rather, the Logos will be a son, the Spirit will be a grandson, and the Father will be a grandfather."[10] These are their nonsensical prattlings, and that is why he ridicules them.

[5. The Interpretation by the Theologians of 'Ek' and 'Dia' Is Incorrect]
In spite of these things, our humble self is greatly astonished at your sagacity. When you write in your second reply, and we quote: "If there is one who believes that the Holy Spirit alone is from the Father, and through the Son, but does not proceed from the Son, let him know that he believes the impossible; for these are contradictory to each other, and cancel one the other." However, those things which we profess are not impossible, nor do they contradict each other, nor do they cancel one the other, as you say. For the truth never conflicts with the truth. And although not fully treated, this much is sufficient for the present concerning these matters. However, I diligently researched the matter and found but two main differences between us on the subject. First, that you understand the sending and the procession to be one and the same things. [204] And for this reason you say incorrectly: "If the Spirit is sent by the Son, then it follows that He also proceeds from him." [11]

[6. The Difference between Essence and Divine Operation in God]
Second, that you understand that the essence and divine operation of God are one and the same thing, which, indeed, they are not. That the essence and divine operation of God are not the same, but different, give heed to God. If there is no provision for the members of the body in God, then those things concerning Him, which are often spoken of in Scripture as members, are references to the divine operations which descend upon us, while the essence remains inaccessible, as the theologians verify. That is to say, the same should be accepted in a way worthy of God. For if it is said that the divine operation proceeds, as well as derives, from the essence eternally. Then by no means may one dare to say, concerning the created beings, that the divine operation is not a creature, and that neither is the essence. If, indeed, these divine operations are God, it is said that He possesses them, that He is life and has life, and [He] is wisdom and has wisdom, etc. If, then, these [things] are God, they can by no means be distinguished from Him, for they are essential and natural to God.

However, if He [God] has these divine operations, they also descend upon us as distinct from Him; and they, by increasing singly and inseparably, are distinguished from the one essence. If "ever since the creation of the world His invisible nature, namely, His eternal power and deity has been clearly perceived in the things that have been made" [Rom 1:20], then we become part and parcel of the created world – not from the essence, but from the divine operation. Therefore, the essence of God is one thing, while still another is His power and Godhead which are clearly perceived and understood by the created beings. And these [power and divinity] also happen to be eternal. If the essence of God is not spoken of in many ways, it is because His essence is one. However, the divine operations of God are spoken of in many and various ways because His divine operations are many. Therefore, His essence is one thing, and His divine operation is something else. If every power is spoken of as something else, since this is given as a possibility, as Thomas Aquinas has believed, then the essence of God is [205] one thing and His divine operations are another, unless one says that the essence refers to something else. But let us listen to something that the Latins once said, but who were refuted by our teachers of that time.

### [a. The Relation between Father and Son]

The Father and the Son are the same, for the Lord himself said: "I and my Father are one" [Jn 10:30]. For all things that are the same are also the cause of the same things.[2] It follows, then, since the Father is the cause of the Holy Spirit, the Son is also the cause. Which of the two do you choose if both refer to the same matter? Or, more specifically, because of the ambiguity do you reason falsely by choosing, in one instance, the major premise and in another instance, the minor one? For this is necessarily so if, indeed, both statements are true. For the Father and the Son are the same in kind and in essence. Indeed, it is true; things that are the same are causes of the same things when they are the same as to number and word. Or when in one instance or another, you choose the same thing, the figure [of speech] is not logical since it has no middle term by which to connect the two parts in order to draw the necessary conclusion. Or in the same instance [if you choose the first], the second of the two statements will of necessity be false. For if you take the same number of statements [of the premise], the minor statements cannot be true. For the Father and the Son are not one according to number, which is in fact the teaching of the Sabellians. If, however, you hear that they are not the same, but the same in kind and essence, then the major [statement] is false. For it is not necessary that those things which are the same in kind also be the cause of the same number of things.

[b. The Relation between the Holy Spirit and the Son]

Whatever belongs to the Father also belongs to the Son, for the Lord says: "All mine are thine, and thine are mine" [Jn 17:10]. Thus, to be the emitter of the Holy Spirit [a divine operation] also belongs to the Son. But this is an absurd statement. Because what belongs to the Father is not something that is simply said. For either it is said as belonging to His person as a characteristic and description, such as incomprehensible and unbegotten, or it is said as belonging to that which is common to the entire Divinity [Godhead], such as without beginning and the eternal. Now, if you take as the middle term the characteristic that belongs [to the Father], then the minor [statement] will be true, but the major [statement] will be false. For the Father and the Son are not one in number. And it will happen that the unbegotten will become begotten while the [206] begotten will become unbegotten. Consequently, the saying: "All mine are thine, and thine are mine" [Jn 17:10] has been said not concerning the personal [hypostatic] attributes, but concerning everything that was said about the Godhead. And if it should be said about both [the Father and Son], then Sabellios was not saying anything irrational when he limited the Holy Trinity to one person.

[c. The Sending of Grace to the Disciples (Not the Spirit) by the Son]

Unless the Spirit proceeded from the Son also, He would not give it to the disciples by breathing on them. Surely you may be saying many things in order to cast a shadow over the truth. According to Saint Chrysostom and other theologians, He [the Son] granted the gift of forgiving sins to them, but not the Spirit itself. Now suppose that even this was granted them, that He granted to the Disciples the person of the Holy Spirit, which is absurd. What then? Does it necessarily follow that by this [the Spirit] proceeded from Him also? Not at all. The procession and the giving are not the same thing, for even if the one is eternal and the other temporal, so be it then, they are the same thing. For that which, indeed, is the begetting for the Son is the procession for the Spirit. But the Son is also given by the Father, as is stated in many places in the Holy Scriptures. Therefore, the giving should be the same as the begetting. Now, the begetting and the proceeding are the same as the giving. Then the one is the same as the other two [which are the same] and [all three] are the same as each other. And then the begetting and the proceeding are the same, which, indeed, is absurd. On the other hand, if the Holy Spirit not only is given by the Son, but also gives, as is obvious from those passages in which the Lord says "when the Counselor comes" [Jn 15:26], and the [Word] "will come," and "that the Holy Spirit has come upon you" [Acts 1:8], then, it will be the same [Holy Spirit] which eminates and has existence from himself. Or do you not profess this also, that He gives himself? The Son and the Spirit, therefore, do not have the same authority; for if the Son has authority to give himself, as well as the Spirit, but the Holy Spirit gives neither himself nor the Son, then their authority is divided. Yet truly the authority of the Trinity is the same, as the faithful are assured.

[d. The Difference between Sending and Existing]

"He will take what is mine" [Jn 16:14]. The Gospels are replete with many assurances such as: "I will send" and many other similar ones. It is not necessary that the sender be the cause of the existence in any way [207] whatsoever of the one sent. Not only does the Son, as is said in the Scriptures, send the Spirit, but, also, the Spirit sends the Son. And the scriptural phrase, "He will take what is mine" [Jn 16:14], means "what is mine" from the Father. Furthermore, if one would concede to them that the Lord said "from me" it still would not be necessary for them to claim that the Spirit proceeds from Him. For to receive is one thing, and another thing from whom he receives; and still another thing is that which is received. The Spirit, then, is the one who receives; and the Son is He from whom He [the Spirit] receives, as they claim that which has been received is different from both. For He adds: "and [He will] declare it to you" [Jn 16:14]; that is to say, that which you shall receive from me, this He has declared to you. So that, perhaps, that which has been received proceeds necessarily from Him, but not from the receiver; or, that the receiver and the one which is received are the same, in which case, the receiver receives himself. Therefore, the indivisible is divisible and the simple is complex; and then it will happen that the receiver and that which is received will be the same. On the other hand, if it were to receive its own self, how is it that it has not yet received its being? Therefore, this seems to be the most unsolvable of all the captious arguments, for it contains great difficulties for those who would try to solve it.

[e. The Son's Spirit Is Not a Fourth Person]

The Holy Spirit is avowedly said to be of the Father and of the Son. Holy Scripture is replete with such references, e.g., it says: "Anyone who does not have the Spirit of Christ does not belong to him" [Rom 8:9], and "God has sent the Spirit of His Son" [Gal 4:6]. And then when we pray to the Son, we ask Him to send us His Spirit. Therefore, either what is said of the Son pertains to one Spirit and that which is said of the Father pertains to another, or they are both the same Spirit. But of a truth, it is not another spirit. For then the Trinity would be a foursome or quartet.

If, however, it is the same Spirit, in what way is He said to be the Spirit of both? Which of the two is it? As being related to both of them or as having no relation at all? But, indeed, how could it have been said of them, if He was not related to them? If He is called Spirit because He is related to both, then the name is indicative of His relation to them. (Just as the name "Father" and the name "Son" indicate a relationship), in the same manner, "He" must have the same relationship to both the others. For just as the other names [Father and Son] indicate a relationship to one specific thing (this is as to a myriad of things), the [name] Spirit has one and the same relation to both the others. For the major premise, even though it may be said of many, nevertheless, it is said of the lesser [208] of all; furthermore, equality that is attributed to the many is also attributed to all as equal. And in the same manner as to the others, this thus applies to them, also.

[7. The Holy Spirit in Relation to the Father and the Son]
If the Spirit is said to indicate the relationship which exists with them, it must have the same relationship to both of them. And yet the indication of His [Spirit's] relationship to them is made manifest by His being called by many names, such as Almighty Paraclete, All-seeing and many more. But He [the Spirit] is not called Almighty of the Father and of the Son, nor All-seeing [of the Father and of the Son], nor Paraclete [of the Father and of the Son], nor any other name, but He is simply called Spirit of both the Father and Son, as this name is indicative of His relationship to them. Is it necessary then for them also to revert back into the Spirit? For such is the case of the others in regard to one specific thing. How then can one save from reverting back? For it is absurd to say that the Father and the Son are from the Spirit. For, thus, the Father and Son will then be the same, and the Spirit will be the Son of the Father, and He will also be the Father of the Son. But further, we understand that which has been said reverses the relationship of the Father to the Spirit; for it is said that the Father is the cause, emitter, origin, and source of the Spirit. Consequently, the same will also be said concerning the Son, e.g., His relationship with the Spirit is reversed. And then He [the Son] will be the emitter and the origin and the cause and the source of the Spirit, for the Spirit has the same relationship to the Son, also. It is just as if something is said to be greater than Peter and Paul; or if it is not said of Peter that he is greater than him [Paul], but inferior, then Paul also will be said to be inferior to him. And this is the case here. Since it is said that the Spirit is both of the Father and of the Son, while it is not said that the Father is the Father of the Spirit, but rather that He [the Father] is the cause and the emitter then, consequently, the Son will also be said to be His cause and emitter. However, if someone would say that, indeed, where the Spirit is mentioned, it is the Spirit of the Father, but it is not the Spirit of the Son. But yet further say that as *homoousios*, i.e., of the same essence, it consequently is *homoousios* with Him [the Son]. This would be absurd. For there is nothing to prevent one from saying that the Son is also the Father of the Spirit since both are *homoousia*, i.e., of the same essence.

And besides, one is not considered to be *homoousios,* i.e., of the same essence with another unless the *homoousios* is a reality. Peter is said to be *homoousios* with Paul; but Paul is not *homoousios* with Peter unless he actually is of the same essence with him. Consequently [in that case], the Holy Spirit would proceed from both the Father and the Son. However, it is easy to perceive that this is the result of false reasoning. For it is not true to say "the Spirit" explains the relationship which it has with the Father. Also, this is evident to say: that the Father is the cause and emitter and origin and source, particularly of the Spirit.

[8. The Spirit Is Not Emission, Cause, Source, or Origin]

[209] Neither is the Spirit said to be merely the Spirit of emission or of cause, or of source, or of origin. Nor, again, the Spirit of them. If it is an emitter, it is by no means called the emitter of the Spirit. Or if it is a cause, it is by no means called the cause of the Spirit. The same is true concerning the terms 'origin' and 'source.' But the term 'emitter' refers to an emission, while the term 'cause' refers to that which is caused, and the term 'source' refers to that which springs forth, and the term 'origin' refers to that which derives from it. Therefore, if you name it [Spirit] and emission, or that which is caused, or that which is derived, or that which received its origin, you have mentioned the names which define the relationship with which it is related to the Father, as the emitter, the cause, the origin, and the source. In no way do you define the relationship which it has with the Father if you should call it Spirit. For it is called Spirit by virtue of its characteristic of an airy spirit which is transparent, non-material and pervades all things. Why then is it necessary that the Son be an emitter and cause and origin and source of the Holy Spirit, if this is said of the Spirit, also? For if it should be said that the Spirit is an emission and that which is caused by the Son, also, as it is said of the Father, it would then be necessary that the Son, also, be an emitter and cause of the Spirit. And surely the Spirit is not called an emission nor that which is caused by the Son, also, but is merely called Spirit [of the Son]. Consequently, it is not necessary for the Spirit to be an emitter and a cause. The fallacy, then, arises from coincidence. For since it is said that the self same thing is the Spirit and an emission and that which is caused, but yet He has a relationship with the Father as the emitter and the cause, and inasmuch as he [the Spirit] is an emission and that which is caused, they who tried to hide the emission and that which is caused perpetrated a wrong view of the fact, that is, said that the Spirit has a relationship and that they considered the Father as the emitter and the cause. And, thus, they seemed to reason that since the Spirit is said to be the Spirit of the Son, also (and this explains His relationship to the emitter and the cause), consequently, the Son is the emitter and the cause of the Spirit.

However, if it is said that the Spirit is the Spirit of the Father and of the Son, there is no need to be troubled. For not all things which are said to be related to others are necessarily related to any particular thing in the same way. Therefore, it is necessary for you to be convinced by those who have systematically treated them by way of explanation. Thus, on the one hand, it is said that the Spirit of the Father is from Him [the Father] and He [the Spirit] has His existence from Him [Father], and to distinguish Him from the other spirits, while on the other hand, it is said that the Spirit of the Son being with Him [the Son] is produced from the same source, as Cyril [of Alexandria] says in his homily concerning the Spirit.[13]

[9. Son and Spirit from the Father, Single and Not Dual]

[210] For the Holy Spirit, also, just as [He] is in essence the Spirit of God the Father, so also is He [Spirit] in essence the Spirit of the Son. Also, as He [Spirit] was born in essence with the Son, He proceeds ineffably from the Father. Therefore, following the Holy Scripture and the truth, we bring duality under the monad by placing the monad as the origin and the cause of the duality. But the Latins placed the duality as the origin and the cause of the monad. For if the three hypostases by reason of essence and identification are one or a monad, but yet each of the three by reason of the hypostases is a monad in itself, and, further, the two are a duality, then the three are also a trinity. Therefore, those who say that the Spirit is from the Father and Son are placing the duality as the origin of the monad which, of course, is absurd. Furthermore, it was handed down to us by the Holy Fathers that the three hypostases are of the same essence and dignity proceeding through one another without any confusion and comingling. That is to say, just as the Father in His entirety is entirely in the Son and in the Holy Spirit, and the Son in His entirety is entirely in the Father and in the Holy Spirit, so also the Holy Spirit in His entirety is entirely in the Father and in the Son; but they are inifinite [the hypostases and their advancing *perichoresis* ( =co-inherence)]. Hence, when all of the above statements are taken into account, it is obvious that their position will prove to be absurd. For if the Holy Spirit has His existence from the Father through the Son but not directly from the Father, then it [the Spirit] would be separate apart from the Father. For there can be nothing in between those things which are undivided [by nature]. But those for which there is something in between are absolutely separate from one another. For that which unites them with each other is that which separates them. Thus [concluding, according to the above reasoning], the Trinity is not undivided. And this conclusion, indeed, was not proposed by us.

Again, inasmuch as the three persons are of the same essence and equal among themselves, they also are infinite, proceeding through each other, and by no means is it possible that one of them come between the other two. So, by that one the other two are united to each other. For everything that is caused by something is also caused through it; and it is determined by it, either by place or by nature. Therefore, without an intermediary, the Holy Spirit proceeds from the Father. Again, how do the Father and the Son exist in entirety in the Holy Spirit? Which is the case—do both of them exist without an intermediary or does the Son alone exist without an intermediary and, through Him, the Father? The Holy Spirit, then, is more closely related to the Son than to the Father.

### [10. The One without an Intermediary Is Nearer]

[211] For that which exists without an intermediary is nearer, and that which is nearer is more closely related to the whole. If, however, this is absurd and the Father exists directly [without an intermediary] and is entirely in the Spirit, it is obvious that this reverses the conclusion so that the Spirit in its entirety exists without an intermediary entirely in the Father. Therefore, He [the Spirit] would surely not have His existence indirectly from Him [Father], and especially if someone would investigate it as being inconsistent with the arguments which some, who wish to introduce their own personal concept, may advance. For as they say, they do not project the Spirit as proceeding from the Son for any other reason than to prove that the Son is equal to the Father, understanding that He is not equal to the Father unless the Paraclete [Spirit] proceeds from Him [the Son], also. Indeed, it was necessary for Him to proceed in the same way from both either without an intermediary [i.e., directly] or indirectly and not alone indirectly, but henceforth without an intermediary [directly] if they truly wished to equalize the Son to the Father by this method of thinking. But now this incorrect doctrine has crept in, and the inequality has remained as before. Again, if it is necessary for the Son also to be the cause, if truly He is *homoousios* with the Father, it is necessary also for this Holy Spirit to be, thus, *homoousios*. If, indeed, both of them [Father and Son] are of the same essence and not in one way here and in another way there, but in the very same way, the three themselves are the cause. So, inasmuch as the Father is the cause of the Son and of the Holy Spirit, the cause of the former [Son] should be by way of begetting; and the cause of the latter [Spirit] should be by way of proceeding. It is necessary, then, that both the Son and the Spirit also be the causes of the same; however, this is impossible.

### [11. The Interpretation of Gregory the Theologian]

In some places Gregory the Theologian speaks of the Son and the Spirit as a double flowing grace and a twin ray coming from the one source, the Father. In other places, where he says that both [the Son and Spirit] are caused, he is referring to the Father who is the one cause. First it is said that there is one first origin from which all things derive and then, according to what has been said, that the Son is of the same essence as the Father. He, the Son, is in everything exactly the same as the Father. And in like manner the Holy Spirit, also, is the same since He [Spirit] is of the same essence with both [the Father and the Son].

### [12. The Dilemma of the Procession]

Moreover, whatever one of the three hypostases does not have the same as the Father, the other one does have. This is a characteristic of an hypostasis. Then, one proceeds directly [without and intermediary] from [212] the two, either entirely as from one source, which is one in number, or as from two sources. If, then, the Spirit proceeds as from one source, which is one in number from the Father and from the Son, that which is emitted will be one in number. So, the Father and the Son will be one in number as emitter and cause of the Holy Spirit. Consequently, the Father and Son will be one hypostasis and the Trinity will be eliminated by being condensed into a duality. For to be emitter and cause is a characteristic of the hypostasis if, indeed, it is not also of the Spirit. If, however, He [the Spirit] proceeds from two sources which are two in number and both of the first rank, there will be two first origins without subjecting the one to the other. For insofar as origin is concerned, it does not happen that the Son is subject to the Father, which, indeed, is the case among those who teach that the Spirit is emitted through Him [the Son] from the Father. But if, indeed, this happened, since He is the Son, then there is not one first origin of all things.[14]

### [13. Irrational Results from the Filioque]

See how many absurd conclusions from every side trail those who say that the Spirit proceeds both from the Father and the Son! Do not desire to think incorrectly concerning the Lord. For if the Latins, that is, the Church of Rome, and others can produce witnesses who are acceptable such as Augustine, Ambrose, Jerome, and some others, we also can produce many more and even more trustworthy Fathers to speak up for the truth. Who are they? They are the God-bearing Fathers who distinguished themselves in the holy Synods, who deified the earth, and who through miracles and good works shined brighter than the sun and declared that the Holy Spirit proceeds from the Father alone. They ordered heavy penalties against those who might think otherwise following the anathema of the Apostle Paul who explicitly declared: "If any one is preaching to you a gospel contrary to that which you received, let him be accursed" [Gal 1:9].

### [14. The Ecumenical Synods Would Not Remain Silent]

If the Son was the emitter and the cause of the Spirit, how could the

Ecumenical Synods have remained silent concerning such a most necessary dogma? It is very clear, therefore, from this that some persons gave way to their own wills and affixed this addition after the holy Synods had made their definition. For if this had not happened, there would not have been a concensus of all present, since the most reverend primates of Rome were present in the seven holy Synods.[15]

### [15. Scriptural Proofs and Not Human Wisdom]

[213] Even though those who spoke before us had devised some manner in which to overthrow sophisms, as we said, by resounding a wooden peg on wooden pegs, nevertheless, we cannot order our own thinking by persuasion of human wisdom. But rather we would hold to the consistency of scriptural proofs. For Paul says: "Let no one make a prey of you by philosophy and empty deceit" [Col 2:8]. From this truly divine saying we are taught that true philosophy never contradicts theology. For truth can never contradict truth. This is obvious from the following: "and empty deceit" [Col 2:8]. Consequently, the wisdom which is not empty serves, rather than opposes, theology. And you, then, O my beloved children in Christ, by the grace of God, having no empty wisdom, are constrained to advocate a theology whose leader is not an angel nor a man but totally the Lord himself. And, as a consequence, [leaders are] the divine shepherds and teachers of the Church who are in agreement with Him [the Lord]. Of these [Fathers], among others, the Fathers, also, of the holy Seventh Ecumenical Synod have declared this, too: "we anathematize those who add or eliminate anything."[16]

Again, neither should this be overlooked, beloved, that from the time of the Seventh Ecumenical Synod seventy-five years had passed when, during the sovereignty of Basil the Macedonian, a local synod had convened in Constantinople. The reason this holy synod was summoned at that particular time was, for which everything was wrought by the will of the pope and the urging of the emperor: [1] to install the most holy Photios on the throne of the Queen City [of Constantinople], and [2] to banish those who under some kind of guile dared to claim that the Holy Spirit proceeds from the Son, also. At least, then, in this synod the most holy Pope John, through a bishop and cardinal named Peter, and also Paul and Eugene, his bishops and locum tenens [authorized representatives] mutually agreed and pronounced anathema on those who would dare in the future to add to or delete [anything from the Creed]. But further, this same Pope John, following this, sent a letter to Photios himself saying:

> Again I make this clear to Your Reverence in reference to this article, concerning which the scandals took place among the churches of Christ; be on notice from us that we do not simply say this, but we also say that those who originally took courage by their own folly

to do this, we pronounce as being transgressors of the divine words [214] and perverters of the theology of the Master Christ and of the Holy Fathers, and we rank them together with Judas." [17]

Furthermore, we are reassured by the fact that from that time up to the time of Christopher, 130 years have passed during which all the most reverend primates of Rome have agreed with us.

### [16. The Utterances of the Ecumenical Synods]
But why would anyone repeat these things if the concept of the truth which is sought concerning the Spirit is made admirably clearer: [1] by the utterances of the holy Seven Ecumenical Synods in which the Holy Fathers, who numbered about two thousand, struggled which is more than sufficient evidence; and [2] by the utterances of the Lord himself. Indeed, it is right to respect the doctrines and the laws of those saints, to marvel at and cleave unto them. For no less were they [the Fathers] renowned for their illustrious lives or the power of their preaching than as shining stars who enkindled the piety not only of one nation, but, indeed, of as many nations as the visible sun entirely illuminates.

### [17. First Ecumenical Synod Decreed the Father as Godhead]
Therefore, the radiant Holy Fathers, gathered together in the First Synod at Nicaea, said to the doubting philosopher, among other things, the following:

Accept the one Godhead of the Father, who begat the Son ineffably, the one divinity of the Son who was begotten of Him, and the one divinity of the Holy Spirit, who proceeds from the Father himself, and is also the Son's, as the Divine Apostle says: 'anyone who does not have the spirit of Christ does not belong to Him' [Rom 8:9]. [18]

It is worth noting that what has been said concerning the Holy Spirit, who proceeds from the Father himself, was not said in vain by that divine gathering [First Ecumenical Synod]. It is not because we were accustomed to express these thoughts in this manner, but because they [the Fathers], shortly after they spoke of the Son, saying that they accept also the same divinity of the Son who was born of Him [the Father], added afterwards the divinity, also, of the Holy Spirit who proceeds from Him [the Father]. The blessed Fathers fearing lest at some time there may appear some who might say that the phrase "from Him" refers to the Son, added the phrase "from the Father" to the phrase "from Him" so that no one area might be omitted on such a pretext. If, however, they definitely knew that the Holy Spirit proceeds from the Son, the addition would have been peculiar but true. They knew how to use the word and thus derive and separate it. To attribute the emission to the Father and to say concerning the Son that it is characteristic of Him, which, indeed, it is characteristic to display a natural relationship of the Spirit to the [215] Son, is true. And this proves that the Spirit is His, although not proceeding from Him, but as Paul says: "anyone who does not have the Spirit of Christ does not belong to Him" [Rom 8:9]. And Basil says: "He is moreover styled 'Spirit of Christ' as being by nature closely related to Him." [19]

And Chrysostom says: "Spirit of God" and "Spirit who proceeds from God." It is one thing to say "of God," and another to say "proceeds from God." It is, then, most necessary to clarify that it is one thing to say the Spirit *of* the Son, and another thing to say that the Spirit is *from* the Son. And again, this blessed group says that the nature, indeed, is one, but the three persons may be called as follows: source, river, water. However, no one calls the river the source or the source the river. Therefore, in this context the source of the Godhead is the Father, who begets the Son and emits the Spirit. And [the term] 'source' denies [the term] 'from the Son.' As Chrysostom, in interpreting the ninety-sixth Psalm, [20] makes it clear by saying: "From whence is the living water? Let us seek its source... The source of the living water is the Father; the river deriving from it is the Son...its water is the Holy Spirit, deriving from the source, who is God and Father." [21]

[18. The Decree of the Second Ecumenical Synod on the Spirit]
Moreover, the Fathers of the Second Ecumenical Synod [Constantinople A.D. 381], speaking in accord on the subject in question, theologized about God as follows: "and we believe in the Holy Spirit, the Lord, the giver of life, who proceedeth from the Father, who with the Father and the Son together is worshipped and glorified." [22]

Wherefore, the assembly of this Second Synod, as you know, which had been summoned during the reign of Theodosios the Great, convened to refute Macedonios the Pneumatomachos [i.e., adversary of the Spirit]. Therefore, as the First [Ecumenical] Synod formulated the doctrine of the *homoousion*, when the stark mad Arius had blasphemed declaring that the Son is a creature, thus, also, the Second [Ecumenical] Synod had as its prime purpose the formulation of the doctrine concerning the Holy Spirit. Consequently, it also clarified the matter of the procession of the Spirit.

[19. The Third and Fourth Ecumenical Synods in Harmony
with the First in Nicaea]
Also, the Third and, likewise, the Fourth Ecumenical Synods agree with them. The former decreed that "it is unlawful for any man to bring forward, or to write, or to compose a different Faith...than that established in Nicaea." [23] The latter [the Fourth Synod, canon 1] decreed

that: "We have judged it right that the canons of the Holy Fathers made in every synod even until now should remain in force," [24] indicating that by no means would they endure agitating the faith which has been determined. As it appears, the doctrine of the First and the Second Synods concerning the Spirit is that He [Spirit] proceeds from the Father. The teaching of those two synods concerning the Son is also the same. Do you see how they [synods] relate to each other and how the one ratifies the other?

[20. The Fifth Ecumenical Synod Agrees with the First Four]

[216] It is apparent that the Fathers of the Fifth Ecumenical Synod [Constantinople, A.D. 553] also spoke concerning Him [the Holy Spirit], as well as about other theological subjects. In reference to these matters they explicitly stated that: "there were many followers of Origen who did not speak out of piety on account of whom the synod was summoned, and which condemned them to perdition." [25] [The purpose of this synod was to deal with the doctrines of Origen and to condemn him.] It appears also that the Synod [of Ephesos] against the Messalians had decided the same thing. For it says in their definitions explicitly that: "When it was proposed to consider in common the case of those [the Messalians, that is, the Euchetes or Enthusiasts] who were blaspheming in all things, the synod, of course, denounced them." [26] It was not the custom of the ecumenical synods to make decisions concerning those matters for which they were intended alone, but they, also, decreed on all related matters which had developed as a result of them, as it becomes obvious from the First, Second, Third, Fourth, Fifth, and the other synods. Furthermore, the Fathers of the synods did not limit their willingness to formulate dogmas alone, but they endeavored to order other ecclesiastical disciplines by issuing canons for the correct policy within the Church. They did not consider it sufficient for the worshippers of the Living God to merely hold correctly formulated doctrines and be lacking in works. They considered such a faith to be dead and not worthy of the Living God.

[21. The Sixth Ecumenical Synod's First Canon against Innovations]

In addition, the Sixth Synod [Constantinople, A.D. 680-81] in its first canon, being in agreement with previous Synods and being inspired by the Holy Spirit, says:

> We decree that the faith which has been handed down to us shall stand firm and remain without innovation and inviolate as set forth by the Holy Apostles and the 318 holy and blessed Fathers assembled at Nicaea and the other holy Synods and by all those who have beatified and adorned the Church of God and who became luminaries in the world, having embraced the Word of Life... etc. [27]

[22. The Seventh Ecumenical Synod Extols the Steadfastness
of the First Six Synods]
In addition, also, the Seventh [Synod, Nicaea, A.D. 787], weaving this
chain with golden threads and drawing them together in the one Holy
Spirit, in its dogmatic utterance declared [canon 1]: "We in following the
ancient legislations of the Church catholic, we in holding fast all the or-
[217] dinances of the Fathers, we anathematize those who add to or omit
anything from the teaching of the Church." [28] And, thus, the general concensus of the seven holy ecumenical synods has been declared in brief.

[23. The Holy Fathers in Agreement Concerning the Procession
of the Holy Spirit]
Let us consider, if you deem it proper, the related sayings in the personal writings of the chief leaders and ecumenical teachers, i.e., what
each one of them said concerning the Holy Spirit and dogmatizing in
reference to the matter of procession.

[24. Saint Silvester I, Pope (A.D. 314-335)]
First, we shall consider what Saint Silvester, Bishop of Old Rome, said
in his curse against that sorcerer [Arius], since he was an exarch in the
First Synod [not present but represented by two presbyters]: "There exists
one true God, the Father, having begotten from himself [Father] the true
Son, having proceeded from himself [Father] the true Holy Spirit." [29]

[25. Saint Athanasios the Great (A.D. 295-373)]
And certainly the great preacher of truth, the blessed Athanasios, says
many things [concerning the Holy Spirit] in his writings, but expecially in
his epistle to Serapion:

> Therefore, while thinking falsely of the Holy Spirit, they do not
> think correctly even of the Son. For if they thought correctly of the
> Logos, they would think soundly of the Holy Spirit also, who pro-
> ceeds from the Father and, belonging to the Son, is from Him [Son]
> given to the disciples and to all who believe in Him. [30]

And he says the same, as well, in this discourse dealing with the Holy
Spirit, [31] and also in his discourse, *On the Holy Trinity,* [32] and in his
discourse which begins with "We believe in one God" [Athanasios, *Symbol of Faith*]; and in many other of his discourses he elucidates the doctrine of the procession [of the Holy Spirit] from the Father.

[26. Saint Cyril of Jerusalem (A.D. 315-386)]
Also, Cyril, famous for his wisdom, in his discourse, *On the Holy
Trinity,* says: "The powers which are worshipped are known and believed
to be: the Father who is without beginning, without cause and unbegot-

ten; the only begotten Son, born ineffably from the Father; and the Holy Spirit who proceeds from the Father, not begotten as the Son, that there are not two sons in the Trinity, but proceeding from the Father alone, as from a mouth, speaking clearly through the Son to all the saints..." [33] Furthermore, He [Cyril] declares the procession [of the Holy Spirit] by interpreting the passage in the Gospel according to Luke [1:35-41] [34] and, also, in his polemic discourse, *On the Holy Spirit,* and in infinite other places.

### [27. Pope Damasus (A.D. 366-384)]

[218] Moreover, Damasus, the Pope of Rome, the exarch [not present but represented] in the Second Synod (as Cyril was in the Third), writing to Paulinus says: "whosoever would not truly and forcibly say that the Holy Spirit is from the Father, even as is the Son, who is of the divine essence of God, the God Logos, let him be anathema. [35]

### [28. Pope Agathon (A.D. 678-681)]

And as Pope Agathon, writing to [Constantios] the emperor [and Herodius and Tiberius the Augustae] of the Roman Empire, says: [We believe] "and in the Holy Spirit, the Lord, the giver of life, who proceedeth from the Father, who with the Father and the Son together is worshipped and glorified." [36] And he begins, thus: "This is our absolute notification that we should guard the definitions of faith of the Church catholic, believing in one God...etc."[37]

### [29. Saint Basil the Great (A.D. 330-379)]

And the above-mentioned hierarchs of the Romans, the three Eastern luminaries, agree with Basil on the one hand in his discourse, *Against the Anomoeans,* the beginning words of which are: "Judaism opposes Hellenism," when he says: "generally [it is said that] the Son is from God and the Spirit is from God, since the Son came forth from the Father and the Spirit proceeds from the Father. But the Son, on the one hand, is from the Father because He is begotten while, on the other hand, the Spirit is ineffably from God." [38] Furthermore, in his epistle to his brother Gregory he preaches on this subject, as also in other writings.

### [30. Saint Gregory the Theologian (A.D. 330-389)]

And Gregory [the Theologian] in his third theological oration, [39] *On the Son,* says: "therefore, let us confine ourselves within our limits and speak of the unbegotten and the begotten and that which proceeds from the Father, as somewhere God the Logos himself says." [40] Furthermore, in his discourse, *On the Holy Spirit,* he [Gregory] theologizes about the procession from the Father as he does in others of his writings. [41]

[31. Saint John Chrysostom (A.D. 344-407)]

Saint Chrysostom, also, in his discourse, *On the Holy Spirit,* says: "if you hear that I will send to you the Holy Spirit, do not take it to mean the Godhead, for the Godhead is not sent. These are merely names which signify the action [operation of the Godhead]. Therefore, when He says: 'I will send to you the Holy Spirit,' He means 'the gift of the Spirit.' Indeed, the Savior solves this by saying: 'but in the city [of Jerusalem] until you are clothed with power from on high'[42] [Lk 24:29]."

[32. Gregory of Nyssa (A.D. 335-394)]

Furthermore, Gregory of Nyssa in his discourse, *On Common Notions,*[43] says: "For one and the same person, of the Father, from whom the Son is begotten and from whom the Holy Spirit proceeds, etc." [44]

[33. Saint Dionysios the (Pseudo) Areopagite and Other Fathers]

[219] Furthermore, Dionysios, the sublime Areopagite, in his discourse, *On the Divine Names* [Theonymiac],[45] in chapter 2, "On the United and Distinguished Theology," discoursing on theology agrees with the above: "the Father is the only source of the super substantial deity," [46] etc.

Furthermore, Saint Augustine in the epistle to Maximinus,[47] Gregory the Thaumaturgos [Wonder-worker] in the statement of his own faith,[48] and Saint Jerome in his epistle to Damasos, also agree.[49]

Saint Nilos in his discourse, *On the Holy Trinity*, says: "The Holy and Catholic Church, indeed, sets forth as dogma that the Father is unbegotten, that the Son is begotten from the Father, and that the Holy Spirit proceeds from the Father alone and not from the Son." [50]

[34. Saint John Damascene (A.D. 675-749)]

And after all of the above is Saint John the Damascene, the most excellent among the leaders, a teacher and most accurate lecturer on the correct dogma, who removed every possible doubt with spiritual power and who recapitulates and harmoniously and superbly interprets the doctrines of the saintly Fathers before him.

In the reign of Emperor Leo III, the Isaurian [A.D. 717-741], who had violently opposed the holy icons, John of Damascus took the lead in the religious struggle by imitating the zeal of Elijah and the censure of the one who has the same name [John the Baptizer]. This John of Damascus, by epistolary dissertations, defended the revered icons and exposed and publicly stigmatized the impiety of the iconoclasts. In the interim between the Sixth and Seventh Ecumenical Synods he also joined forces with the Church catholic and fought against heresy. He wrote an exposition of the true faith [title: *Exposition of the Orthodox Faith*] and other outstanding theological treatises, as well as three discourses, *On the Holy Icons*. They are to be found in the treatises on theology at Verona and in the discourses in the city of Basle in Switzerland which I request that you read that you might be correctly informed on the subjects of icons, of supplication of the saints, and many others, as well. For the most holy John does not promulgate his own ideas, but derives the witnesses from the Scriptures as is reasonable and as requested by you. This, then, Saint John the Damascene, theologizing in his discourse, *On the Holy Trinity*, in the 8th chapter says:

> Further, it should be understood that we do not speak of the Father as derived from anyone, but we speak of Him as the Father of the Son. And we do not speak of the Son as cause or Father, but we speak of Him as from the Father and as the Son of the Father. And, likewise, we speak of the Holy Spirit as from the [220] Father and call Him the Spirit of the Father. Nor do we speak of the Spirit as proceeding from the Son, but yet we call Him the Spirit of the Son. 'Anyone who does not have the Spirit of Christ,' says the divine Apostle, 'does not belong to Him' [Rom 8:9]. And we confess that the Spirit is manifested and imparted to us through the Son. For he says: 'He [the Son] breathed on them and said to His Disciples, receive the Holy Spirit' [Jn 20:22]. It is just the same as in the case of the sun from which come both the ray and the radiance; for the sun itself is the source of both the ray and the radiance, and it is through the ray that the radiance is imparted to us. And it is the radiance itself by which we are illumined and in which we participate. Further, we do not speak of the Son of the Spirit.[51]

Who could say it more clearly than do these admirable words of the holy soul of John?

[35. The Procession of the Spirit in the Form of a Dove]

But it would be too lengthy to further select the comments of all who specifically declare that the Holy Spirit proceeds from the Father or who say more from which we draw this same conclusion. And, consequently, it would be absurd to say that the Holy Spirit proceeds from the Son, also. And how could we understand John's declaration when Jesus was baptized: "I saw the Spirit descend as a dove from heaven, and it remained on Him" [Jn 1:32]. For if you say that the Spirit proceeded not from the Father alone, but also from the Son, you destroy the one Christ by dividing Him into two, as did Nestorios, in order that you might say that the Spirit descended from the Son of God to the Son of man. Hence, it follows that the truth is that the Spirit, who proceeds from the Father, remains and rests in the Son. But those who do not wish to proceed willingly along the royal and untrammeled road surely stray into hopeless byways and forsake the one and fixed path of true and straightforward opinion. How can we say that the Holy Spirit proceeds from the Son, also? If, on the one hand, the Spirit proceeds from the Son as a cause, we then have two causes and two sources—Father and Son, i.e., we have a diarchy rather than a monarchy in which we believe. And we cannot account for the many absurdities that would ensue. But on the other hand, if the Spirit proceeds as being mutually linked to the Son (because of the mutual concession of the Spirit and the Son to each other) and the Spirit [221] being as simply sent, then the mind comes to a halt, but sin arises from another reason. Because of this, then, they first incorrectly inserted in the article of faith, which had been ratified by the seven synods, the word "Son"; and then they added the preposition *kai* [and], making it appear that the procession is equally from the Father *and* the Son, even though the Latins understand it otherwise. It is necessary, however, not only to understand correctly, but also not to scandalize others. For if he who scandalizes one person is condemned by the Gospels to a horrible hell, what punishment will those receive who from the beginning first scandalized the world by adding false teachings into the Creed?

### [36. Profound Men on Filioque]
However, some use the pretext that they did not happen to be the first who said it (and thus were able to understand the scandal which had been altered), but that Ambrose and Augustine and Jerome, men who are holy and trustworthy, had previously said it in their own discourses. The above defend their use of pretexts for falsely alleged motives either by having falsified the writings of the above Fathers, or perhaps saying that Athanasios, while arguing against the Arians, was speaking by dispensation, as did Basil, as well as others among the holy men. However, when the above Fathers answered thus, they did it for the sake of argument and out of necessity. And even when they spoke with accuracy, as human beings, they could have fallen into error. "For the thoughts of mortal men are miserable and our devices are but uncertain" [Wis of Sol 9:14].

Indeed, how many of the great religious leaders, among whom are Bishop Dionysios of Alexandria, Bishop Methodios of Patara, Pierios, Pamphilos, Theognostos, Bishop Irenaios of Lyon, his pupil Hippolytos, and others, have suffered as a result of such pretexts. For we do not accept some of their utterances although we greatly admire some of their writings. Now, let it be said and let it be forgiven whatever these three said as the Romans claim. However, who knows against whom they were writing and what they wished to uproot when they fell among such thorns and lost control of their minds, being drawn forward against the Pneumatomachians [i.e., the 'adversaries of the Spirit'], or perhaps against some 'adversaries of the Son,' or against those who introduced a very evil and even worse opinion.

### [37. Filioque Not Decreed by Synods]

[222] This, however, is a fact, as we have said, that the two thousand participants of the seven [Ecumenical] Synods did not formulate the opinion that the Holy Spirit proceeds from the Son, also. Among these, indeed, were the primates and luminaries of the Roman Church, who without contradiction voted in support of the definition of the faith [i.e., that the Holy Spirit proceeds from the Father alone]. And I believe that the three, whom we mentioned above, had also truly acquiesced. But, also, a mutual doctrinaire agreement was adopted by them to neither eliminate from the definitions of the faith, nor, indeed, to add to them. And this definition, that is, the Creed proclaims: [I believe] "and in the Holy Ghost, the Lord, the giver of life, who proceedeth from the Father," etc.

### [38. Pope Gregory the Great Author of the
### *Dialogues* as Pope (A.D. 590-604)]

Also, Saint Gregory [the Great], the Dialogos [A.D. 540-604], who lived not long after the Sixth [Ecumenical] Synod, theologized in the Latin language and in writings that the Holy Spirit proceeds alone from the Father.

### [39. Pope Zacharias (A.D. 741-752) Stressed the
### Procession from the Father]

Also, Pope Zacharias one hundred fifteen years later, translating this Gregory's writings into the Greek language, says: "the Paraclete Spirit proceeds from the Father and abides in the Son," having learned this from [John] the Forefunner, who [at the time of our Lord's baptism] saw the Spirit descend as a dove and rest on Him.

### [40. Popes Leo III (A.D. 795-816) and Benedict III (A.D. 855-858)
### Decreed That Creed Should Be Recited in Greek—without the Filioque]

Moreover, Leo and Benedict, who later became great hierarchs of Rome, decreed that the Symbol of Faith should be recited in Greek during the Divine Liturgy in Rome and in other churches under their jurisdiction, so that the limitations of dialect, as it is claimed, furnishes no pretext for error. Indeed, it was the creed of the Second Ecumenical Synod [A.D. 381] in which this belief was clarified by the Holy Fathers:

> And [I believe] in the Holy Spirit, the Lord, the giver of life, who proceedeth from the Father, who with the Father and the Son together is worshipped and glorified, who spake by the prophets; in one holy catholic and apostolic Church;... I look for the resurrection of the dead and the life of the ages to come. Amen.[52]

Moreover, this same [Pope] Leo opened the treasury of the apostolic church of the Romans and drew forth two plaques which were stored in the treasury together with the sacred treasures. These plaques have inscribed on them the holy edition of faith [Creed] in Greek letters and words. Pope Leo sanctioned them to be recited before the Roman multitude.

[41. Newly Elected Popes Reaffirm Creed without Filioque]
[223] Moreover, up to the time of the pious Sergios I, Patriarch of Constantinople [A.D. 610-638], the hierarchs of Rome, upon assuming their hierarchical ministry when they sent forth enthronement letters of introduction expressing their own religious beliefs to all the patriarchs, also included in them the Symbol of Faith [Creed] without any change in its original form. Is it necessary to further say more?

The Son and Master, Christ, rules and mystically ordains that the Holy Spirit will proceed from the Father, but absolutely not from himself [Son]. I deem it worthy that no one, then, will seek another more excellent teacher unless he desires to offend and to pursue the argument to no useful purpose; for he will never come to a definite conclusion even if he will invent many other subtleties expressing, perhaps, these and similar sayings from the Holy Gospels, such as: "but when the Counselor comes" [Jn 15:26], "he will take what is mine" [Jn 16:14]; "He breathed on them, and said to them" [Jn 20:22]; "God has sent the Spirit of his Son" [Gal 4:6]; and "The Spirit of the Lord is upon me" [Lk 4:18]. For they are far from attaining such an aim, having been interpreted differently by the great and divine Ecumenical Teachers, as we have witnesses and have been informed. And all these, to state it briefly, express association and relationships, but are not manifestations of procession. Therefore, it follows that the unity and the equality among the three hypostases is proven.

[42. Plea to Theologians To Keep the Truths of the Creed Undefiled]
Therefore, for the sake of God let it be; cease to utter words about that which are remote from the truth, and accept the holy doctrine, as we have made clear knowing full well that the Spirit proceeds from the Father. And, thus, concerning this subject, let us continue to be friends and brothers in Christ, abiding in Orthodoxy together, keeping the Confession of Faith unfragmented, unshakable, and steadfast, respecting the Holy Fathers and [keeping] in respectful awe of Christ himself, who has, thus, specifically dogmatized concerning the Holy Spirit, as we have said. Do not, for the sake of human glory, perhaps as pious persons, betray piety and your salvation after being taught by the preaching of so many and great saints concerning the truth of this doctrine. Indeed, we have reminded your esteemed selves of these matters not in the spirit of argument and not with ambiguity, but in a devout manner with the help of God. Indeed, may the Paraclete himself, the Spirit who proceeds from

the Father, strengthen the thoughts according to His will in hope and in faith for the fulfilment of the commandments of Christ, and lead us to think correctly about this matter of procession of the Holy Spirit and [224] about all other matters. Thus, by pleasing the Trinity, the cause of all things, through upright thinking and good deeds, you may achieve the blessedness which is reserved for the Orthodox faithful by the grace of Christ to whom belong all glory, power and majesty forever and ever, amen.

### [B.] CONCERNING FREE WILL

#### [1. Chrysostom on Ephesians and Romans]

Concerning human will or, rather, free will among the spiritual matters which you have questioned in your second inquiry, we shall call again upon the golden-mouthed John [Chrysostom] who makes very clear the subjects in which he examines theologically. He interprets the passage of Saint Paul which reads: "and you he made alive when you were dead through the trespasses and sins in which you once walked" [Eph 2:1], etc. up to "the spirit that is at work in the sons of disobedience" [Eph 2:2]. Here is how, indeed, Chrysostom makes it explicit by saying and interpreting:

> You observe that it is neither by force nor by compulsion, but by persuasion he wins us over 'when you were dead.' Indeed, then, there is corporal and there is also a spiritual dying. The former is a matter of nature, not of deliberate choice, whereas the spiritual dying, being a matter of deliberate choice, has criminality and has no termination.[53]

One wills and chooses to do not by force, but of his own free will whatsoever he would do, either the good or evil. Therefore, Paul says in the second chapter of his Letter to the Romans: "but by your hard and impenitent heart you are storing up wrath for yourself" [Rom 2:5]. This, too, Chrysostom himself interprets saying:

> Not he who judges, but he who is condemned who is the cause of storing up wrath for yourself and not God for you. For God did all whatsoever things were fitting and created you with a power to discern between the good and what was not so and showed long-suffering over you and called you to repentance. But if you should continue unyielding, you store up wrath for yourself.[54]

And as Paul continues: "and do not obey the truth, but obey wickedness" [Rom 2:8]; Chrysostom interprets thus:

> Here is again another accusation. For what defense has he who flees from the light and chooses the dark? And he [Paul] did not

say who are 'compelled by,' but he who 'obeys wickedness' to [225] teach us that it is a mattter of free choice; the crime is not of necessity.[55]

### [2. Saint Basil the Great Agrees]
On this subject Basil the Great also agrees and says:

'When we were dead through our trespasses, God made us alive together with Christ' [Eph 2:5]. Nonetheless, everything is by grace in so far as it comes from grace; for without grace we can do nothing whatsoever. Therefore, on the one hand, it is said that grace comes first because of the weakness inherent in the creature; on the other hand, it is said that our choice is to follow, while grace leads, not in order to force choice, but to help us use our free will just like one who holds a light for those who wish to see it. Hence, he says, also, 'through faith' [Eph 2:8] so that the free will is not outraged.[56]

And let us use an illustration so that the subject matter may be clear to us.

### [3. Comparison of John the Baptist and Herod]
John, on the other hand, chooses that which is better, and Herod, on the other hand, that which is worse. Thus, if Herod did as well as choose that which was worse, would not John in this case receive that which was better? Furthermore, if John did not do that which was better, would not Herod achieve that which was worse? Therefore, neither was John good for Herod, except for his own purpose, nor was Herod evil for John, except for himself. However, he [Herod] would have been good because of John if, indeed, he had chosen the good. Man's disobedience to the divine commandments was not in itself desirable to him; for he could not be disobedient without the presupposition of a disturbed will.

### [4. Saint Augustine]
And this is what Augustine says to Orosius [A.D. 415], that man acted according to something which already existed. First, whatever he [man] desired was the result of a disturbed will, for evil is inherent and not generated; it is something that happens as a result of certain conditions. Just as the brilliant sun, depending either on the density or the lightness of the air, sends forth its rays to us, thus, also, the spiritual soul displays its own characteristics depending on the choice made by the person in which it exists. Thus it is that we see a foolish person and a wise person, a sleepy and an alert person, a mean person, and a meek person, a brave and a cowardly person, and many other such types of persons.

[5. Saint Anastasios of Mount Sinai (7th Century)]

No one should claim that what we have said is fictitious, for there is Saint Anastasios of Mount Sinai who says that:

[226] God is not the cause of those things, but rather nature itself and the influence upon it and the working together of the four elements [i.e., fire, earth, air, water]. For if there is an abundance of the element of heat at the time of the conception of an infant, the child which will be born will be of warm temperament. However, if the cold element should prevail, then the child will tend to be of a colder disposition. From this, then, develop the mean and the meek, the brave and the cowardly persons. Observe the swine and the deer. The former is ready for war because of the *element* of warmth. The latter avoids the battle because of its cowardice which is the result of the cold element. And if the element of warmth prevails, it gives birth to a sober and alert person.[57]

[6. Heraklitos of Ephesos (544-484 B.C.)]

Consequently, the wise Heraklitos also said, "the drier the soul is, the wiser," [58] calling the soul here the essence of the mind. And if the moist element prevails, it makes one lazy and sluggish. Accordingly, then, a person's meekness and prudence, as well as the soundness of his mind, are not considered to be virtues, according to the Holy Fathers, but rather native abilities.

[7. Saint Basil the Great]

Also, give heed to Basil the Great as he says: "I have known many men who by nature hate to sleep with women; do we, therefore, call them prudent? Not at all." It follows, then, that the crime results from the intent and natural tendency of a person. Let us further listen to Basil who interprets the scriptural verse: "let us make man in our image after our likeness" [Gen 1:26]: "This means," he says, "let us give him abundance of reason." [59] For man received his "image" from God, namely his rational being, but the "likeness" is a potential which God left for us to develop ourselves. If I had received this likeness from Him completed, what merit would be mine? Therefore, I attain the "likeness" [of God], whensoever I myself become Christ-like. We have been baptized in His death, that is to say, when we are baptized, we must die according to every evil and wickedness which we must abolish by living virtuously. For Christ has cured those things which are not caused by us. But the cure of the others depends on our own initiative. For the benevolence of God does not cause dreadful evils in us, rather it is our indifference and the inclination of our thoughts toward evil. But nothing prevents man [227] from doing whatever he likes to do, for he has free will. For God would not forbid when He saw man turning away from the straight road that He would force him back. Where, then, would be that endowment which remains in him and which is considered to be rational and self-determining? Where, then, is virtue? What good are the wreathes, then, which were given in reward for virtue? Therefore, Basil also said: "It did not become necessary for evil to be abolished also through baptism in order that rational man should not be counted among the irrational, as if he did not possess the grace of free will." Furthermore, the same Basil elsewhere again professes: "Why did God not create us to be sinless? For no other reason save that one prefers either the irrational nature or the rational, and the idle and sluggish, or the willing and active, since freedom of choice is to be found in a particular act.[60]

[8. Saint John of Damascus on Free Will]
"Moreover, it is necessary to know this also," as Saint John the Damascene says in chapter 46 where he discusses matters concerning [divine] providence theologically. He refers in related chapters to the subjects of self-will and predestination. He who will read them will learn much:

...the choice of what is to be done depends on us, but the final result, when our actions are good, depends on the synergy [co-operation] of God, who in His justice assists, according to His foreknowledge, those who choose the good with a right conscience. However, when our actions are evil, it depends on the desertion of God, who again in His justice stands aloof, according to His foreknowledge. There are two kinds of desertions: there is one desertion by dispensation and for instruction, and there is a complete and hopeless desertion. Desertion by dispensation, as well as for instruction, occurs for the correction and glory of the sufferer, either for arousing the zeal and imitation in others, or for the glory of God. The complete desertion takes place when man remains obdurate and incurable of his own accord after God has done all that was possible to save him. And then man is given over to total destruction like Judas [cf. Mt 26:24].[61]

[9. Saint John of Damascus on Free Will and Responsibilities]

May God be gracious to us and deliver us from such desertion... Moreover, it is necessary to know that all the assaults of dark and evil fortune contribute to the salvation of those who accept them with thanksgiving and are definitely made ambassadors of help. It is necessary, also, to know this, that God antecedently wills that all [228] should be saved and attain His Kingdom [1 Tim 2:4]. For He did not form us for punishment, but because He is good, that we might share in His goodness. But inasmuch as He is just, His will is that sinners should suffer punishment. The first, then, is called *antecedent will* and *favor*, which springs from himself [God]. The second is called *consequent will* and *permission* and has its origin in us. This latter is two-fold: that which is by dispensation for our instruction and salvation, and that which is abandonment to absolute punishment, as we have said. These, however, refer to those things which do not depend upon us. However, those things which do depend upon us, the good ones, God wills antecedently and approves; whereas the wicked ones, which are truly evil, He neither wills antecedently nor consequently, but permits and concedes them to the free will. For that which is done under compulsion is not rational nor is it an act of virtue. God makes provision for all creation, and through all creation He does good, and instructs, and frequently even uses the demons themselves, as in the case of Job [cf. Job 1:12] and in that of the swine [cf. Mk 5:13]. For it is necessary to know this, also, that while God knows all things beforehand, yet He does not predestine them all.[62] Truly He knows beforehand those things which depend upon us; but He does not predestine them because He does not will evil to be done, nor does He force virtue.[63] Thus, predestination is the work of the divine command based on foreknowledge.[64]

[See] the rest which the divine Damascene says in the 30th chapter.[65]

## [C.] CONCERNING JUSTIFICATION AND GOOD WORKS

[1. The Distinction between Law and Spiritual Law]
Following is the third section concerning justification by faith and good works, which shall be further explained. We do not merely say that those who obey the law shall be justified, but those who obey the spiritual law, which is understood spiritually and according to the inner man. Indeed, by "fulfilling the law of the spirit as much as we are able, we will be justified and we will not fall from grace because the cleansing Word has passed into the depths of the soul. However, those who serve [229] the law according to its outward expression fall totally from divine grace, for they do not know" that the completion by grace of the spiritual law cleanses the mind from every spot; nor do they know the end of the law, which is Christ. He, as the maker of all, is also the maker of the law of nature, and as He who preconceived the law, is giver both of that which is written in the letter and also of that which is in spirit or in grace. "For Christ is the end of the law" [Rom 10:4], that is to say, of the written law understood spiritually. Therefore, in Christ the Creator, who preconceived the law as lawgiver and redeemer, the law of na-

ture, the written law, and that of grace are drawn together. The Apostle [Paul] speaks the truth when he says: "according to my gospel, God judges the secrets of men" [Rom 2:16]. That is to say, just as he preached through Jesus Christ in all laws, he rebuked some and accepted others in a fitting way, giving to each his due. If, then, one is judged according to the law, he will be judged in Christ; or if he is judged outside the law, again he will be judged in Him [Christ]. The Logos, as creator, is the beginning and the mediator and the end of all that exists. Having been begotten without sin, He had stripped himself of all rule and authority [cf. Col 2:10] even though in some way He also put them on. For He, the Logos of God, who became perfect man without sin, had the characteristics of the first Adam, as at the beginning, being free from corruption and sin. For when Adam transgressed the commandment, he was condemned to give birth through suffering and in sin from which [transgression] no one is [born] without sin. And since sin thus came because of the transgression, and nature was bound by an evil bond on account of the decision, while the evil spirits invisibly are at work, because of this the Logos of God, out of merciful compassion, has set us free by becoming man. He also has commanded that one should not contemplate that which is against nature, nor work evil, but avoid it as much as possible and hold fast only to the virtues and commandments. If something evil chances to come in a human way, we must throw it off and hasten to subordinate the more wicked to the stronger good, and subject the flesh to the spirit by [230] exercising virtue and doing good works. For as we know, human nature has been bereft of the good works, having become barren through transgression. Indeed, the voice of the crying word became the voice according to the conscience of each one who transgressed, as it were crying out of the secret recesses of the heart: prepare the way of the Lord [cf. Jer 43:3; Mk 1:3]. Therefore, the explicit and clear preparation of the divine way constituted change and correction of living and reasoning for the better, and for the cleansing of the polluted former living and reasoning. Indeed, the way of the Lord, the good, royal and glorious way, is the life of virtue. In such a life in which the Word [Logos] works the way of salvation in each one, He dwells in us through faith and tarries among us through the various laws and teachings pertaining to both virtue and knowledge [cf. Eph 3:17]. Indeed, the paths of the word are the various kinds of virtues, the various ways of life according to God, and the pursuits of living according to God. The people who honestly pursue virtue according to God's will, make these paths straight. For the divine Word does not proceed in the paths which are not straight, even if the divine Word would find the way to some degree prepared. For instance, were one to fast and thus avoid the inflammatory diet of the passions and do other things which are able to contribute to the expulsion of wickedness, he would have prepared the way. But if he practices these things for the sake of vanity, or greed, or to please men, he has not provided for God to walk in his paths. For the way of the Lord is virtue, and the way of the straight path is without guile. Furthermore, as Scripture says: "the valley shall be filled." The flesh of each one, which has been inundated by the strong current of passions, is to be set right and lifted up through good works. Therefore, let us with great joy send far off every vice which rises up against virtue, "and every proud obstacle to the knowledge of God" [2 Cor 10:5]. Being converted by the Holy Spirit, let us journey on the way of the Lord by directing the members of the body by His divine commandments and freed from passions of every sort, [231] desiring the true life. Thus, surely, we shall see the salvation of God by becoming "pure in heart" [Mt 5:8]. Through true faith and works which proclaim faith, we prepare the divine ascent [reign] of the Word.

### [2. Concerning Grace and Works]

Moreover, we should especially know that grace not only of itself works in the saints the knowledge of the mysteries, but also that grace works in the worthy ones, who have powers by nature, the capability of receiving the knowledge. The one, then, needs the other; grace needs works, and works need grace. As light needs sight and sight needs light, the soul needs the body  and the body needs the soul. Then, clearly, both [grace and works] are those things which lead to salvation; it is unambiguously necessary for one to have both—correct faith with [good] works, and works of virtue by faith. One must believe without hesitation. For with doubt and hesitation in faith, faith is not complete. Also, if faith has once been accepted, it is further deepened by searching to investigate it. For simplicity of the faith is stronger than rational proofs. Also, simple faith is stronger than the faith which is not simple—immeasurably stronger. For when one searches the depths of faith, it rises in waves, but it becomes tranquil when considered with a simple disposition.

### [3. Idle Faith and Faithless Work]

Therefore, since it is undoubtedly and completely sure that we must believe without doubt, only this remains, that which it is necessary to seek with all one's might and is to be found by every means. What in reality is this? It is this: that we may attain salvation with all that we do. For idle faith and works without faith are both rejected in the sight of God. Let us consider what has been said in the light of the following: for God, who has shown himself to us as being of three hypostases, has also shown this most evident way to us. And, indeed, know also that faith, hope, and love [cf. 1 Cor 13:13], the golden threefold rainbow, when kept by us, effects salvation for us.

### [4. Faith in Hope and Love]

And now we will elaborate at length: "Now faith is the assurance of things hoped for, the conviction of things not seen" [Heb 11:1]. In faith, the impossible is possible; weakness becomes strength; suffering is painless; and the perishable, imperishable; and the mortal, immortal. [232] Indeed, "this is a great mystery" [Eph 5:32]. Hope is a wealth of unthinkable riches, and without doubt it is a treasure beyond treasures. Love is the source of faith, a depth of mercy, a sea of humility, and exaltation of holy souls, a likeness to God, as far as is possible for humans. Apart from these three it is impossible to find salvation. The three greatest witnesses of the past in our midst are sufficient to confirm the matter.

### [5. The Apostles on the Means of Justification]

Come thou, Peter, leader of the venerable Apostles, and thou, John, the most beloved in Christ, and thou, James the Just, the first bishop of Jerusalem, bear witness concerning what has been said. Peter in the first chapter of his Second Epistle cries out in this manner and solemnly testifies thus:

> for this very reason make every effort to supplement your faith with virtue, and virtue with knowledge, and knowledge with self-control, and self-control with steadfastness, and steadfastness with godliness, and godliness with brotherly affection, and brotherly affection with love. For if these things are yours, and abound, they keep you from being ineffective or unfruitful in the knowledge of our Lord Jesus Christ. For whoever lacks these things is blind and shortsighted [2 Pet 1:5-9].

Moreover, the Son of Thunder [the Evangelist John] in the first chapter of his First Epistle says:

> 'that God is light and in him is no darkness at all. If we say we have fellowship with him while we walk in darkness, we lie and do not live according to the truth; but if we walk in the light, as he is in the light, we have fellowship with one another, and the blood of Jesus his Son cleanses us from all sin' [1 Jn 1:5-7]. 'He who says he is the light and hates his brother is in the darkness still. He who loves his brother abides in the light, and in it there is no cause for stumbling' [1 Jn 2:9-10]. 'He who does not love [his brother] remains in death. Any one who hates his brother is a murderer, and you know that no murderer has eternal life abiding in him' [1 Jn 3:14-15].

Also, in the third chapter of the same Epistle: "but if any one has the world's goods and sees his brother in need" [1 Jn 3:17], etc., and [John says] many other things concerning love.

[6. Saint James on the Relation of Faith and Works]

Also, the brother of God [James] in the 2nd chapter of his Epistle agrees saying:

> What does it profit, my brethren, if a man says he has faith but has [233] not works? Can his faith save him? If a brother or sister is ill-clad and in lack of daily food, and one of you says to them, 'Go in peace, be warmed and filled,' without giving them the things needed for the body, what does it profit? So faith by itself, if it has not works, is dead. But someone will say: 'You have faith and I have works. Show me your faith apart from your works, and I by my works will show you my faith.' You believe that God is one; you do well. Even the demons believe — and shudder. Do you want to be shown, you foolish fellow, that faith apart from works is barren? Was not Abraham our father justified by works when he offered his son, Isaac, upon the altar? You see that faith was active along with his works, and faith was completed by works, and the scripture was fulfilled which says, 'Abraham believed God and it was reckoned to him as righteousness'; and he was called the friend of God. You see that a man is justified by works and not by faith alone, as we said a short time ago. For as the body apart from the spirit is dead, so faith apart from works is dead [cf. Jas 2:14-24, 26].

[7. Intercorrelation of Faith, Hope, and Love for Salvation.]

Let us consider whether it has not been said in vain, that apart from faith, hope, and love, it is impossible to be saved. For as we, indeed, need the eyes of our body for viewing visible things, so doubtless we have need of faith for the study of the divine things. For as knowledge of the matters comes according to the proportion of the accomplishments of the commandments, so also the knowledge of the truth comes according to the measure of the hope in Christ [cf. Jn 7:17]. And as, indeed, it is meet to worship nothing else than God, so one should not hope in any other than God alone who is the One who cares for all [cf. Mt 4:10]. As he who has hope in man is accursed, so blessed is he who rests in God. And just as the memory of the flame does not warm the body, in the same manner faith without love does not effect the light of knowledge in the soul. Indeed, it is impossible for love to be found apart from hope. Hence, the [234] Holy Fathers say one thing is permanent: the hope in God. All other things are not in reality, but merely thought. He who has fastened his heart on the power of faith has nothing without works. And when one has nothing, he limits everything to faith. Indeed, the power of faith is in good works. And he who has been deprived of love, has been de--prived of God himself. One ought to strive in such works and also hope in Him. For if you ask yourself or another true Christian on what ground the ones being saved have hope of salvation, he would by all means say that we hope only in the mercy of God. But this is the forbearance of God. For if He would not endure evil for us, no one would be saved, since no one among men is without sin. "If even his life on the earth should be but one day on the earth" [Job 14:4-5]. Therefore, if we have the hope of salvation in the forbearance of God, this hope of salvation, indeed, is given only to those who endure the evil and not to those who bear malice. Let us then, as far as possible, be patient, piously forgiving others who have trespassed against us; and then the Heavenly Father will not only forgive us, but He will bestow upon us life everlasting in Christ.

[8. Religious Awe and Obedience Presupposed for Good Works]
Therefore, wherever religious awe of divine things and obedience to the words of the Holy Fathers are abandoned, there no good works can be built up, nor the true faith which proves itself by good works. In other words, how would we be worthy of the beatitudes, which are laid up hidden in the faith if we are persuaded only by evidence according to human reason. Why did the Gentiles "become futile in their thinking and their senseless minds darkened; and claiming to be wise, became fools?" [Rom 1:21]. Is it not because they had refused obedience to the preaching of faith and followed the dictates of this reasoning? Isaiah lamented bitterly concerning such men as being condemned. "Woe unto those who are wise in their own eyes and shrewd in their own sight!" [cf. Is 5:21]. For the Godhead, as it seems to the illustrious Athanasios, is not delivered to us by demonstration in words, but by faith and by pious and reverent use of reason.[66] And the Apostle Paul preached concerning [235] the redemptive cross "not with eloquent wisdom" [1 Cor 1:17], "but in demonstration of the spirit and power" [1 Cor 2:4]; and, thus, he [Paul] tells of the "man caught up into Paradise" who heard powers "that cannot be told,[67] which man may not utter" [2 Cor 12:4]. How will one believe by reasoning the truth of the Holy Trinity, who has not simply believed?

Do you see how all the divine teachers repudiate curious reasoning and throw it all out of the household of God? For anyone who has lost what he had before seeks to find it. Yet he who has lost nothing but has kept in completeness that which he possessed from the beginning does not seek it anymore, but merely keeps well that which he possesses. We, then, have learned to keep the faith and not be seeking after many things. We, by the grace of the Holy Spirit, have lost nothing, and we seek nothing; the search after a faith [that has not been lost] is self-defeating. Therefore, just as the one who believes does not seek, likewise neither does the one who seeks believe. The one who continues to seek has not yet found, nor has he truly and steadfastly believed as he should. Where there is seeking, there is no faith; and there where faith exists, there is no need for seeking, but there is a need of the fruits of faith, which are good works. For he who is convinced by words can also be induced to adopt a different opinion. But he who is convinced by faith fortifies himself and is a confirmed believer. Therefore, we do not seek to hear the polluted words and those that are sought in faith but which do not refer to the common meanings to see if they [hearing] agree, but only to prove if they are in accord with the enunciated dogmas of the Church—even if it happens that they negate all the doctrines of philosophy. For we have not been guided to the truth by words of wisdom, nor have we been initiated to any discernable degree into the mystery of the Trinity, nor, indeed, have we learned any other doctrine from it [philosophy] than the dogmas of the faith. For the matter of philosophy, as you well know, is ontological. But the end purpose of theology is He, who is above all beings and creator of everything. It is, then, neither necessary to think of the faith as an art, nor subject to criticism that which has been approved by theologians, but to continue in those matters which the spiritual preachers have made clear. For if we would rely upon our own reasoning, we would be in danger of sinking in the chaos in which Anaxagoras fell. May Christ the King preserve us from it.[68]

[9. Saint John Chrysostom—Works Are Indispensible]

[236] In addition, Saint Chrysostom, also, in interpreting the six days of creation in his fourth homily [On Genesis], proves that works are indispensable:

> Therefore, I ask, let us not become careless about keeping the commandments, but let us control our thoughts, First, then, let us try to win over our neighbor with love [brotherly affection] [cf. Rom 12:9f] and according to the blessed Paul, 'outdo one another in showing honor' [Rom 12:10]. For this is, indeed, what holds together and preserves our life; and in this we are distinguished from the animals and the beasts, that we can, if we will, keep the appropriate order in us, and show great concord with our fellow men, and restrain our thoughts, and crush anger, that untamed beast, and always have before it the struggle of the awesome judgement. For it is not fitting for us to simply spend the time without purpose; but every day and hour we should have before our eyes the judgement of the Lord, and also those things which can give great assurance, and those things which emphasize punishment. And thus recalling these things in our minds, let us overcome our base passions. Let us restrain the temptations of our flesh and 'put to death,' in the words of blessed Paul, 'What is earthly in you' [Col

3:5] that we may be able to receive the 'fruit of the Spirit: love, joy, peace, etc.' [Gal 5:22]. For the grace of God makes us more sturdy than a diamond and in every way invincible, if we would will it. Let this be the difference between a Christian and the ungodly person: that he [the Christian] wishes to bring forth the fruit of the Spirit. Let us not pride ourselves in name only, nor be conceited on account of external appearance. But even if we would possess the things, we should not be greatly conceited, but rather should we humble ourselves even more. Scripture says: 'when you have done all, say we are unworthy servants' [Lk 17:10]. If we would think thus and be concerned about our own salvation, we will be able to benefit ourselves and also rescue from the future hell those who have us for their teachers, so that when we accomplish with strictness this course of life, we may be deemed worthy [237] of God's love for mankind in the future age.[69]

Therefore, one cannot find consolation in that [future] life, who has not in the present life cleansed himself of sins. 'For in Hades,' Scripture says, 'who will give to thee praise?' [Ps 6:5; cf. Sir 17:25]. And rightly so! For this [life] is the time of toil and of contests and of wrestling, and the future life is the time of wreaths and of rewards and of prizes [cf. 1 Cor 9:24]. Therefore, let us struggle as we still continue in the stadium so that in time, when it is proper, we may receive the wreath and accept the rewards of the toils with assurance. This is not merely said...but we wish to remind you each day to remember to carry out good works so that when you have been perfected and accomplished and shine in the virtue of the manners of life, 'that you may be blameless and innocent children of God without blemish' [Phil 2:15; Mt 5:14] and 'shine as lights in the world, holding fast the word of life, so that in the day of Christ' [Phil 2:16] we may be proud, that even when you are merely manifest, you have benefited those who associate with you and those who communicate with you in conversation by sharing in a spiritual fragrance and excellent manner of life which are characteristic of you. For just as it happens that keeping company with bad persons is injurious to those who associate with them, it is as the blessed Paul says: 'bad company ruins good morals' [1 Cor 15:33].

In like manner, also, keeping company with good persons greatly benefits those who associate with them. Therefore, our Master who loves mankind has allowed the good to associate with the wicked, so that the latter will benefit some from this association and not remain continually in wickedness; but having before them a

constant reminder, they will reap more benefits from their association with the good persons. For such is the power of virtue, that
even those who abandon it do greatly respect it and render great
praise for it [virtue] as also do those who are evil. Let us give heed
concerning matters of virtue before it is too late, and we unwittingly punish ourselves. May it not be so. Do you see that there is need
for works and, indeed, for vigorous works and most excellent?
Now, indeed, the discussion concerning these matters is sufficient.[70]

Let us hear, therefore, the matters concerning the sacraments.

### [D.] CONCERNING THE SACRAMENTS

[238] For the fourth subject we shall discourse concerning the holy
sacraments of the Church in general; and, in particular, we shall take up,
God willing, also the discussion concerning the matters that would make
them more explicit for you.

### [1. First Three Sacraments: Baptism, Chrismation, and Eucharist]
No Christian would contradict[71] the fact that the life in Christ is truly
constituted by what is believed through the sacraments, and that it
receives from them [sacraments] its beginning and, furthermore, is
perfected [by them] in the future; and we would arrive at the day in
which the flesh does not obstruct the light, concerning which Paul also
says: "my desire is to depart and be with Christ" [Phil 1:23], who enjoins
the perfect and the highest happiness of those longed for. We shall briefly state, therefore, by which method the Church of the faithful has
handed down the instruction in them [sacraments], through which "we
live and move and have our being" [Acts 17:28] in Christ.

### [a. Baptism]
Baptism, therefore, bestows being and subsists completely in Christ.
For when it [baptism] receives those who are dead through sin and the
corrupted ones, it leads them into life. Moreover, through these
sacraments, just as through small openings, the sun of justice enters into
this dark world and illuminates those who are worthy. For he who has
not been reborn by water and the Spirit, cannot enter into life [cf. Eph
2:1; Jn 3:5]. We also die His death so that we may rise up in the resurrection [cf. Rom 6:5] and become heirs of the kingdom, being crowned
thrice in triple immersions when the hymn of the Holy Trinity is chanted.
However, we do not use the [method of] the triple affusion [pouring of
water]. For in early [Christian] times they did not baptize by aspersion by
using their own hands to sprinkle water on the candidates to be baptized, but by three immersions [in water], following the teaching of

the Holy Gospels which says: "he went up immediately from the water" [Mt 3:16], thus indicating that he had gone down [into the water] inasmuch as He went up [from it]. Behold the immersion and not aspersion [sprinkling or affusion]. Furthermore, interpreting the 50th Apostolic canon which reads: "if any bishop or presbyter does not perform the one initiation with three baptisms," the wise John Zonaras says: "the canon says that the three baptisms mean the three immersions."[72]

### [b. Chrismation]

We are anointed with chrism that we may become communicants of the royal chrismation, that is, of deification [sanctification]. Indeed, concerning chrismation, not only Dionysios the Areopagite speaks at [239] length (a man most worthy of esteem and faithful, who is mentioned in the Acts, chapter 17:34, where it says that "some men joined him [Paul] and believed, among them Dionysios the Aeropagite," who became a pupil of the blessed Paul and archbishop of Athens, and concerning whom the Church has written many encomia, but also Symeon [of Thessalonike], the translator, a man of letters and faithful, who wrote biographies of the saints and martyrs, whose martyrdom which we send having personally transcribed), but also the holy synods [concerning chrismation]. For the forty-eighth canon of the Synod of Laodicea says: "They who are baptised must, after baptism, be anointed with the heavenly chrism and be partakers of the kingdom of Christ."[73] Also, the Synod in Carthage [A.D. 257] in Epistle 70 mentions that chrismation is necessary and indispensable.[74] Furthermore, the Sixth [Ecumenical] Synod in its 95th canon says:

> For, inasmuch as the Christians are called anointed as partaker of the Holy Spirit, by the anointing of the holy chrism, they also, by necessity, are anointed by Him [the Holy Spirit]. Therefore, also, from that which is spoken during the anointing, henceforth, the partaking of this divine gift is necessary; for the one anointing says, 'the seal of the gift of the Holy Spirit, Amen.'[75]

But, also, John Chrysostom, in his discourse in which he discusses the Holy Trinity, says:

> It was the power of oil and sanctification; the chrism was one, but the gifts are three; the power is one, but the anointings are three; for they anointed priests, kings and prophets; such, indeed, is every Christian who is baptized. A prophet, as seeing 'what no eye has seen, nor ear heard' [1 Cor 2:9]. A priest, as being obliged to offer himself up 'as a living sacrifice, holy, acceptable to God' [Rom 12:1]. And a king, suffering as the son of the absolute sovereign God and heir of His kingdom.[76]

For the chrismation imprints the first seal, which we received in the soul by divine inspiration. Therefore, it bears the power and the fragrance of the Spirit [cf. Gen 2:7], and it is a sign of Christ. Read, even in the Old Testament in the 30th chapter [cf. Ex 30:22f], and see what the Lord said to Moses, foretelling and preparing for it [chrismation]. Taking occasion from this word of God, the divine Dionysios, as well as the holy Synods and all the other saints who wrote concerning it [chrismation], wrote relying on this biblical statement. Therefore, do not be surprised, [240] that in what you have written on baptism, you do not mention chrismation. Indeed, the Church of Christ, progressing by His grace, has discovered much in the divine utterances and foundations with which she has been adorned. Since Paul does not write everything, nor even his disciple, Dionysios, and after them many other luminaries of the Church of Christ, who have been moved in the Holy Spirit, it is not right to think that what they did not write should be discarded. Although the main sacraments are baptism, and Holy Communion, and without them it is impossible to be saved, yet it was the Church which handed them down, also, with all the others, I say, up to the seven, as we shall further state. Concerning these, other writers also write at length in a marvelous manner, reporting the ecclesiastical orders. But Symeon the Archbishop of Thessalonike also wrote concerning these as well as other ecclesiastical subjects. And Mr. Stephen Gerlach, who is wise in ecclesiastical matters, has his [Symeon's] book. Therefore, first we cleanse ourselves [in baptism] and then we are anointed [by Chrismation]. And thus cleansed and fragrant, we are accepted at the table of the Lord "until Christ be formed in you" [Gal 4:19].

### [c. The Holy Eucharist]

Holy Eucharist, the body and blood of Christ, preserves and sustains this life and health. For the Bread of Life grants salvation to those who have been created and keeps them alive. We live in Christ when we worthily receive Communion as He said: "he who eats my flesh and drinks my blood abides in me, and I in him" [Jn 6:56]. Indeed, the bread becomes the body of Christ, and the wine and the water are changed into the blood of Christ by the descent of the Holy Spirit who changes them [in a mystical manner] beyond reason and thought. Also, the bread of oblation, as well as the wine and water, through the *epiklesis* [invocation] and the descent of the Holy Spirit, are changed supernaturally into the body and blood of Christ; indeed, they are not two, but one and the same. Yet, the bread and wine are not a type of the body and blood of Christ; by no means. For this the body of the Lord is deified inasmuch as the Lord himself has said that this is not a type of my body, but *the* [His] body, and not the type of my blood, but *the* [His] blood [cf. Mt 26:26-28]. Also, before this He [the Lord] said to the Jews that: "unless

[241] you eat the flesh of the Son of man and drink his blood, you have no life in you...For my flesh is food, indeed, and my blood is drink, indeed" [Jn 6:53-55]. Therefore, let us draw near with all reverential fear and pure conscience and undaunted faith; and it shall truly be with us as we believe without doubting. Indeed, let us honor it [the Eucharist] in all purity of soul and body. For those who worthily partake in faith it becomes the forgiveness of sins and life ever-lasting and a guard of soul and body. But for those who participate unworthily and without faith it becomes everlasting damnation.

### [i. Bread and Wine]

But if some called the bread and the wine antitypes of the body and blood of the Lord [cf. 1 Cor 11:27-29], as the God-bearer Basil said, they did not call them as such after the consecration, but before the consecration of the Oblation. We, therefore, call them antitypes that later will become not as truly the body and blood of Christ, but rather that now we partake through them the divinity [Godhead] of Christ, and later in a spiritual manner [we partake] only by seeing them.

### [ii. Leavened Bread]

Moreover, we offer it [the bread of Oblation] not as unleavened, but as leavened, which in truth is bread; for thus the saints of the East, Chrysostom as well as others, interpret and prove that it is necessary to offer not the unleavened, but leavened bread. But a discourse concerning this subject is a major one and requires a lengthy dissertation. We will not elaborate now, but we will discuss the matter when it becomes necessary.

### [d. Other Sacraments: Ordination]

Ordination, also, imparts the authority and the power of Him who instituted it, which we receive through the priesthood. Through the priesthood all religious ceremonies are performed for us, and there is nothing holy without the priest.

### [e. Marriage]

Also, marriage is a gift of condescension from God for the procreation of children, as long as everything remains, to the consummation of time. Indeed, this also is a sacrament of God, and for this reason He blesses marriage inasmuch as our life does not begin with His blessing.

### [f. Confession]

Penance [repentance] again activates our restoration from falling into [242] sin by repentance, the confession of iniquities, and the separation of ourselves from evil. This is a great gift for those who fall into sin after receiving Baptism. Indeed, repentance is even included in the vows of the monks.

### [g. Holy Unction]

Holy [oil] unction has also been handed down as a sacred rite and a sign of divine mercy, which is granted to those who repent from sin for their deliverance and sanctification. Therefore, it absolves from sins and heals sicknesses. Furthermore, James, the brother of our Lord, in the 5th chapter [of his Epistle], bears witness concerning it [holy unction] saying:

> Is any among you sick? Let him call for the elders of the church, and let them pray over him, anointing him with oil in the name of the Lord; and the prayers of faith will save the sick man, and the Lord will raise him up and if he has committed sins, he will be forgiven [Jas 5:14-15].

In this, also, he speaks concerning confession, as well as prayers and supplication of the faithful.

### [2. Sacraments Handed Down by Christ and the Apostles]

Indeed, all these sacraments were also handed down by Christ, as well as His holy Disciples. For inasmuch as we are dual, consisting of a soul and a body, these also were given to us in a dual manner, just as He is himself God and man; and just as He, indeed, sanctifies our souls spiritually by the grace of the Spirit and by visible means, that is, through water, oil, bread, and the cup, etc., which are sanctified by the Spirit, He [the God-man] consecrates us and our bodies and also completely bestows salvation upon us.

And the above, concerning the seven sacraments of the Church, we briefly state and piously hold. And now it is time to speak concerning the invocation of saints in what follows.

### [E.] THE INVOCATION OF SAINTS

Proceeding to the fifth [article] concerning the invocation of the saints, you say that you imitate their faith, their patience and everything else that works toward salvation; and yet you deny any invocation of them and their intercession to God [on behalf of humans], and you [243] refuse to venerate them or their icons or honor them in churches and offer them spiritual memorials, fearing lest you transfer the honor which belongs to God alone to His creations.

### [1. Invocation for Help]

Indeed, concerning the above, we say with the grace of God that it is necessary to invoke the saints, for they are able to help; and as for this, there are many proofs.

And first, read the word of God in the 42nd chapter of the book of Job:

> After the Lord had spoken these words to Job, the Lord said to Eliphaz the Temanite, 'Thou hast sinned and thy two friends; my wrath is kindled against you and your two friends, for you have not spoken of me that is right, as my servant Job has. Now, therefore, take seven bulls and seven rams, and go to my servant Job; and offer up for yourselves a burnt offering, and my servant Job shall pray for you,' etc. [Job 42:7-8].

We learn from this that the just intercede and pray for us and not for the living alone, but also for the dead, as in the case of the dead man who was thrown on the grave of Elisha according to 2nd Kings [13:20]. Furthermore, the Church of Christ calls the saints living ones as if they were alive and in the hand of God, and refers to their death as if it were asleep; for they toiled in the present age, and they shall live to the end of time. For God is life, and those who are in the hands of God are alive. That God has dwelt in them, through their mind and in their bodies, the holy Apostle [Paul] corroborates by saying: "do you not know that your body is the temple of the Holy Spirit?" [1 Cor 6:19]. Why, then, are not the living temples of God to be honored? When they were living, the saints publicly witnessed for God. Christ opened up many redemptive sources for us. Through the invocatons of the saints, demons are driven out, sicknesses are banished, temptations are averted. And the gift from God is from above by invocation through the beneficent angels who are immediately sent to those who invoke their names.

### [2. Sacred Relics]

Moreover, their sacred relics in many ways are the source of beneficences. And let no one doubt this. For if water in the desert flowed as a fountain from a flint rock, and water [flowed] from the jaw-bone of an ass for the thirsty Samson, is it unbelievable that such may also occur [244] from the relics of martyrs? Not in the least for those who know the power of the saints from God and their veneration.

### [3. The Honor of Saints]

Honor should then be rendered to the saints as friends of God, as His children and heirs, as the theologizing voice says: "but to all who received him...he gave power to become children of God" [Jn 1:12], so that they are not slaves but sons and heirs [cf. Gal 4:7]. What would one do in order to find one guardian who is a mortal king, and who would speak in his behalf? Should they not be honored, then, they who are the guardians of the entire Christian populace, who offer petitions to God in our behalf? Yes, they should be honored by erecting churches dedicated to God and bearing their names, but offering fruitfulness entirely for the glory of God by spiritually and divinely conferring honor to their memory through whom God is served and who, indeed, by serving Him, rejoice in psalms and hymns and spiritual odes. We raise up icons in their honor, for they are living examples of virtue, and we should imitate their virtue. Let us truly honor the icon, not as God, God forbid, but mainly and truly as the Mother of God; the Prophet John, as Forerunner and Baptizer [of Christ] who was an Apostle and martyr; the rest of the Apostles, as eye-witnesses of Him and His works; the martyrs of the Lord from every order, as soldiers of Christ who also drank from His cup [of grief] and who shared in His passion and His glory. Therefore, let us imitate their manner of life, their faith, their love, their hope, that we may with them share the crowns of glory.

### [4. The Veneration of Icons]

Behold, therefore, when we venerate their icons; and let no one find fault with us, for, indeed, we venerate each other as being created in the image of God. And, furthermore, Saint Basil says that: "the honor paid to the image passes on to the prototype."[77] Also, the people of Moses, by encircling the tabernacle, worshipped the icon which represented the heavenly order and the whole of creation; for God said to Moses: "and see that you make them after the pattern for them, which is being shown [245] you on the mountain, etc." [Ex 25:40]. Furthermore, the Holy Scriptures say that the Lord said: "you shall fear[78] the Lord, your God, and shall serve him" [Dt 6:13]; and "you shall not make for yourself a graven image" [Dt 5:8]. Yes, truly, all those are the laws of God. But God, teaching this, has taught us in Deuteronomy:[79] "The Lord spoke with you...out of the midst of the fire, etc." [Dt 5:4]; "you shall not bow down to them or serve them" [Dt 5:9] from which we learn, for the purpose is one, that we do not worship the creation instead of the creator. Neither do we offer the adoration of worship to any other but to God alone. Therefore, Scripture throughout combines worship with adoration. Therefore, we also know, beloved, that honor is owed to God alone; but relative worship differs as much as to say that the lie differs from the truth. Hence, we venerate the holy icons in a relative worship; but we worship God alone by [worship] of adoration.

### [5. Saints as Helpers]

Truly the saints are capable of much, who by grace are gods, as the Psalmist [David] also says: "God has taken his place in the divine council in the midst of the gods" [Ps 81:1] which Gregory [of Nazianzos] interprets [as quoted by John of Damascus] as[80] "dividing the worthiness." And it is worthy to believe that [according to John of Damascus]:

> [the saints] while living were filled with the Holy Spirit, and when they died the grace of the Holy Spirit did not depart, but remained in their souls, in their bodies, in their graves, in their images and in their holy icons.[81]

Did not Solomon know the divine law which declares: "you shall not make for yourself any graven image?" [Dt 5:8]. How then did he, Solomon, erect the Temple, and as the book of Kings says, make cherubs and oxen and lions and many as such [cf. 3 Kg 6:23ff]? Is it not then more honorable to adorn all the walls of the house of the Lord with figures of the saints, rather than with figures of animals and trees and carved graven images and palm trees and other such similar figures? The holy icons are open books in the churches of God to call God to mind and to honor Him. For he who honors the martyr and the other saints, honors God; and he who honors the Mother of the Son, primarily [246] honors Jesus himself. For there is no other God for us, but one, He who is known and worshipped in Trinity.

### [6. Saint John]

Although we say, "O Saint John intercede for us," and "all Holy Theotokos [Mother of God]," and "Holy Angels," yet before all we cry out, "O Lord of Hosts, be with us, for besides Thee we have no other helper in adversity. Have mercy upon us, O Lord of Hosts." Observe the most true and perfect purpose of the Church, how it beseeches God to come as a help and calls upon His mercy? For He is the blessed and only Master, as it is written.

### [7. Saint Epiphanios (c. A.D. 315-403)]

Further, you cite Saint Epiphanios,[82] who supposedly rejected the holy icons, writing against the Collyridians [a female cult], which made and offered idolatrous cakes to [the Virgin] Mary. Certainly, the Virgin is not God, and none of the Christians would say that she is, yet she is worthy of honor and is holy and a servant of God, as she says of herself: "behold, I am the handmaid of the Lord; let it be to me according to your word" [Lk 1:38]. Nevertheless, Saint Mary is truly the Theotokos [Mother of God], as having been deemed worthy to receive in her bosom the Son of God and God. For He who existed before all ages, was born of this very woman and appeared to us as God and Man. Therefore, primarily and truly, Saint Mary the Ever-Virgin is the Theotokos [the Mother of God], but she is not God; for we Christians know no other God, save Him the true God who is praised in Trinity. Know, therefore, that this *Homily Against the Collyridians,* although it refutes a very evil heresy, as we said, nevertheless, it did introduce iconoclasm. For even the good is not good when it is not done well.

### [8. Saint John the Damascene (c. A.D. 675-749)]

Hence, also, even before us Saint John the Damascene, in his *Second Treatise on the Sacred Images*, detected the above to be spurious, adulterated and fictitious, and he completely refuted them. Hence, he said:

> If however, you say that the blessed Epiphanios had clearly forbidden us our icons, know that the discourse is fictitious, either because someone else used the name Saint Epiphanios, as it happens that such things do occur; or because they are the work of the heretic Epiphanides of similar name. For a Father [such as was Epiphanios] does not dispute against the other Fathers [of the [247] Church]; since all have been partakers of the One [and the same] Holy Spirit. And witness is His Church which was adorned with icons, until the fierce and savage Leo the Isaurian gnashed his teeth [cf. Acts 7:54] and confounded the Church of Christ. Others also revolted against it [the church], and greatly disturbed the flock of Christ, and attempted to make the people of God drink polluted subversion, etc.[83]

### [9. Icons Should Not Be Worshipped]

Indeed, it has been proven that it is necessary to render relative worship to the holy icons, as we have said, but not worship of adoration. Moreover, that the supplication of the saints is heeded [by God], you may further read in 2 Kings, chapter 18 and 19. It says that Sennacherib said through Rabshakeh: "do not let your God on whom you really rely deceive you" [2 Kg 19:10]. Then proceed with the following, for then said the Lord: "For I will defend this city to save it for my own sake and for the sake of my servant David" [2 Kg 19:34]. And if this was not so, God would not have left others to intercede. Furthermore, He also prepares for it, which was done during the time of Moses, also. For God said to him: "I will blot them out..." [cf. Ex 32:32f], so that He [God] would lead him [Moses] to supplicate in their behalf. And he did this, not that He has need of supplication, but that we would not become worse by being saved so simply. For this reason He also gave the gift of prayer, as Paul says: "the Spirit himself intercedes for us with sighs too deep for words" [Rom 8:26]. And for this reason, also, He frequently told David and another person to be reconciled to one another, thus preparing their reconciliation. For this same reason He also said to Jeremiah: "Do not pray for the welfare of this people, for I will not hear" you [Jer 14:11f], not because He [God] wanted him to stop interceding [for them], for He greatly desires our salvation, but in order to frighten them. And, indeed, the Prophet perceiving this did not stop interceding.

[10. Saint Cyril on the Prophet Daniel]

Furthermore, Cyril, who was great in wisdom, interpreting the Prophet Daniel, says that intercession will also take place at the time of the [second] coming of the Lord, [Parousia, the day of Judgment], and angels will be interceding for some. No less the Lady [Virgin Mary] will be interceding for the world, as will the saints, also. However, not simply for everyone, nor for anyone who died in a sinful state, no indeed! For God has once and for all shut out His mercy for them [the unrepentant sinners]. Consequently, God has spoken out against them thus: "Even if [248] Noah, Daniel and Job were in it...they would deliver neither [their] sons nor daughters" [Ezek 14:20], but those only for whom the intercession will also be acceptable, that is to say, for those who through repentance have been able to change their life, but who could not completely erase the stains of sins. And now, yes, even now when the Judgment Day is impending. But there will be no interceding after the time when the visible world will be dissolved, and each one is carried away to his particular place. However, intercession occurs now through the priests and the just servants of God who are interceding and who accomplish much.[84]

[11. Saint John the Damascene Concerning Icons]

Moreover, Saint John the Damascene in his *Third Treatise on the Sacred Images* says:

Who was the first to make an icon [image]? God himself first begot His only begotten Son and Logos, a living image of himself, an exact image of His eternity. And He created man in His image, after His likeness [cf. Gen 1:26]. And Adam saw God and heard the sound of His feet walking 'in the cool of the day,' and he hid himself in Paradise [cf. Gen 3:8f]. Jacob also saw and wrestled with God [cf. Gen 32:24f]. Therefore, it is apparent that God appeared to him [Jacob] as a man. And Moses, too, saw God as the back of a man [cf. Ex 33:24]. Isaiah, too, saw God as a man sitting upon a throne [cf. Is 6:1]. And Daniel saw one who came in the likeness of man, 'like a son of man and he came to the Ancient of Days' [Dan 7:13]. Yet no one has seen the nature of God, but rather the pattern [type] and the image of what will be. For the Son and Logos of God, the invisible One, was to become truly man, so that He would be united with our [human] nature and be seen on earth. Therefore, all have worshipped who have seen the pattern and the image of the future, as Paul the Apostle said in his Epistle to the Hebrews, chapter 11: 'these all died in faith, not having received what was promised, but having seen it and greeted it from afar' [11:13f]. Shall I not, then, make an image [icon] of Him who has appeared for me in the nature of flesh? And shall I not, also,

worship and honor Him by honoring and venerating His image
[icon]? Abraham saw not the nature of God, for 'no one has ever
seen God' [Jn 1:8], but the image of God, and [Abraham] 'fell
[249] [on his face]' [Gen 17:3] and worshipped. Joshua, the son
of Nun, saw not the nature of an angel, but the image. For the
nature of an angel cannot be seen by human eyes, 'and [Joshua]
fell [on his face to the earth] and worshipped' [Jos 5:13f]. Similarly, Daniel also [worshipped] [cf. Dan 7:13]. Indeed, an angel
is not God, but a creature and a servant of God and an assistant;
and he [Daniel] venerated him [angel] not as God, but as an assistant
and minister of God. Shall I not also make an icon of the friends of
Christ? And shall I not venerate, not as gods, but as icons of the
friends of God? For neither Joshua [the son of Nun], nor Daniel
worshipped the angels who appeared as gods. Neither do I worship
the icon as God, but by means of the icon and the saints, I render
worship and honor to God, through whom I respect His friends and
hold them in reverence. God did not unite with the nature of angels,
but He united with human nature. God did not become an angel, but
God became, by nature and in truth, man: 'for surely it is not with
angels that he is concerned but with the descendents of Abraham.'
[Heb 2:16].

## [12. Saints and Angels]
He [God] did not become the Son of God hypostatically through
the nature of the angels; but He became the Son of God hypostatically through the nature of man. And angels did not partake of, nor
did they become sharers of divine nature, but rather in operation
and grace. But men partake of and become sharers of divine nature
when they receive [in Communion] the holy body of Christ and
drink His precious blood. For the Godhead united hypostatically,
and the two *natures* united hypostatically in the body of Christ,
which is received by us [in Holy Communion], are inseparable. We
partake of both natures, that of the body physically and that of
the Godhead spiritually; and more specifically each person partakes
of both without their being confused hypostatically. For first we
are conceived, and then we are united by intermixture of the body
and blood. How, then, are they not greater than the angels, who
sincerely guard the union [with God] by keeping the commandments? Our [human] nature was made a little lower than the angels
[cf. Heb 2:7, 9], because of the death and the dullness of the body.
[250] But because of God's benevolence and His spiritual relation
to man, it [human nature] became greater than that of angels. For
angels are present in fear and terror, while it [human nature] is
seated on the throne of glory in Christ, and they [angels] shall

also again be present and trembling on the day of Judgment. They [the angels] have been spoken of by Scripture as not laying down with, nor as communicants of the divine glory; they are 'all ministering spirits sent forth to serve for the sake of those who are to obtain salvation' [Heb 1:14]. Nor will they reign together, nor be glorified together, nor be seated at the table of the Father; but the saints are sons of God, and sons of the Kingdom, and heirs of God, and fellow heirs with Christ [cf. Rom 8:15-17].

### [13. Adoration of Prototypes]
Therefore, I honor the saints and I glorify His servants and friends and fellow heirs. The servants I glorify by nature; the friends, by preference; and the sons and heirs, by divine grace, as the Lord says to the Father [cf. Jn 17:6-19]. Therefore, having spoken about the icons, let us also speak about worship.[85]

Thereupon, the Saint [John the Damascene] speaks about it [worship], and subsequently he speaks of the various manners of worship:

How many objects of worship we find in the Scripture, and in how many ways we may offer veneration to these objects; also, that Jacob bowed in worship over the head of his staff, which was indeed a typology of the Savior [cf. Heb 11:21], just as the tabernacle was a typology of the entire world; and the golden Cherubim, formed of cast metal, as well as the Cherubim [depicted] in the curtain separating [the holy place from the Holy of Holies] was made of woven material. Thus, we venerate the precious form of the Cross which is the likeness of the physical character of my God, and also of her who gave birth to Him, and likewise of His attendants, and all the revered objects which are used in serving God, such as the holy Gospels [books], the patens, the chalices, the censors, the candelabra, and the holy altars. For observe how God brought the kingdom of Belshazzar to an end when he commanded that the people be served from the sacred vessels [cf. Dan 5:22-28].[86]

### [14. Hold the Traditions of the Church]
Therefore, brethren, let us stand on the rock of faith and on the tradition of the Church, and not remove the boundaries which our Holy Fathers have set. Thus, we will not give the opportunity to those who wish to innovate and destroy the edifice of the holy, catholic and apostolic Church of God. For if permission is granted to everyone who wants it, little by little the whole body of the Church will be destroyed. [251] Do not, brethren, do not, oh Christ-loving children of the Church of God; rather let us worship and adore the founder and creator, God,

who due to His nature alone is to be worshipped. Let us venerate the Holy Theotokos not as God, but as the Mother of God, according to the flesh. And let us also venerate the saints as the chosen friends of God, who have greater access to Him [God]. For if men venerate mortal kinds, who frequently are impious as well as sinners, also rulers and others, and according to the Divine Apostle: "Remind them to be submissive to rulers and authorities, to be obedient" [Tit 3:1], "pay all of them their dues," etc. [Rom 13:7], how much more is it necessary to worship the King of Kings, who alone is master over nature and also over the passions of His servants and kings? David, also, in Ps 44 says: "Thou didst make [me] them head of nations" [17:43; cf. Ps 18:43 RSV]. They [the saints] were given power over demons and sicknesses, and they shall reign together with Christ. Even their shadow alone drove away demons and sicknesses [cf. Acts 5:15-16]. Therefore, we should not consider the icon weaker and less honored than the shadow. For [the icon] truly is a sketch of the original. Brethren, the Christian is a person of faith. He who comes in faith gains much. But he who separates himself [from faith] is like a raging sea churned by the wind and blown about and who will receive nothing. All the saints by faith have pleased God: they who confirm it [faith] and prove it to everyone by good works.

[15. Accept Traditions of Church with Sincerity of Heart]
Let us accept, then, the tradition of the Church with a sincere heart and not a multitude of rationalizations. For God created man to be [morally] upright; instead they [humans] sought after diverse ways of rationalizing. Let us not allow ourselves to learn a new kind of faith which is condemned by the tradition of the Holy Fathers. For the Divine Apostle says, "if anyone is preaching to you a Gospel contrary to that which you received, let him be accursed" [Gal 1:9].

[16. Veneration of Those Portrayed on Icons]
We venerate, therefore, the icons not by offering veneration to the wood [or paint], but through them [icons] to those who are depicted [252] therein. "For the honor paid the image [icon] passes on to the original," as the blessed Basil said. May God satisfy you, the holy flock of Christ, with the above and deem you worthy to follow in the footsteps of the saints, of the pastors and teachers of the Church, to bring you forward to receive His glory in the splendor of the saints. And may it be that all of us might attain His grace by glorifying Him forever; for to Him is all glory, amen.[87]

[17. Icons—the Visible of the Invisible Ones]
Bringing these [statements] to a conclusion, therefore, Saint [John

the Damascene], having taught what was necessary, also adds corroborating statements of other saints, that of Dionysios, bishop of Athens from his *Epistle to John the Apostle*: "Truly, visible images are visible forms representative of the invisible." [88] There are many other similar statements in the writings of the *Ecclesiastical Hierarchy* and others. Saint Basil in his *Homily on the Martyr Barlaam* says: "Arise now, ye famous painters of the martyrs' struggles! Adorn by your art the mutilated figure of this officer of our array." [89] And a little further on he adds: "Also, let Christ be sketched on the canvas who bestows the reward in spiritual warfare." [90] Also, from his [Basil] *Homily On the Forty Holy Martyrs*: "For writers and painters often describe courageous acts of war, the former by adorning with words, and the latter by sketching on canvas, etc." Furthermore, many other admirable things have been interspersed throughout his discourses on the martyrs, as well as in his other exegetical discourses. In his interpretation of Isaiah, he says: "because he saw man, the image and likeness of God, not being able to turn to God, he vented his own wickedness against the image of God, just as when a man is angry, he flings stones at the icon. Because he is unable to throw stones at the king, he strikes the wood [of the icon] which bears the image [of the king]." [91] And conversely, everyone who honors the icon, clearly honors the original depicted. And he [Saint Basil] says much more concerning the icons.

### [18. Icons Not Adored as Gods]

Furthermore, Saint Athanasios from his writings to Antiochos in his answer to the 39th[92] [question] says:

> We, the faithful, do not worship the icons as gods. By no means as the pagans, rather we are simply expressing our relation to, and [253] the feeling of our love toward, the person whose image is depicted in the icon. Hence, frequently when the image has faded, we burn it in a fire, then as plain wood, that which previously was an icon. Just as Jacob, when dying, bowed in worship over the head of the staff of Joseph [cf. Heb 11:21] not honoring the staff, but him to whom it belonged, in the same manner the faithful, for no other reason, venerate [kiss] the icons, just as we often kiss our children, so that we may plainly express the affection [we feel] in our soul. For it is just as the Jew once worshipped the tablets of the Law and the two golden sculptured Cherubims not to honor the nature of the stone and gold, but the Lord who had given them. [93]

### [19. Saint Cyril of Alexandria (Patriarch ca. A.D. 412-444)]

Also, Saint Cyril, Bishop of Alexandria, in his address to the Emperor Theodosios said: "Indeed, the icons are as the originals; and, therefore, it is necessary to thus have them and in no other way." [94]

[20. Saint Gregory of Nazianzos (ca. A.D. 330-389) and Chrysostom]

Also, Gregory of Nazianzos from his second discourse, *Concerning the Son*, says: "For it is the nature of an image to be the copy of the original and of him whose name it bears." [95] Also, Chrysostom from his third *Homily on Colossians* says: "The image of the Invisible is itself also invisible, etc." [96] And you will also find in his other writings much more concerning honor given to images [icons].

[21. Severian, Bishop of Gabala (d. A.D. 408)]

Furthermore, from the discourses of Bishop Severian of Gabala in his *Homily on the Dedication of the Precious Cross,* it is worth listening to him saying:

> How is it, then, that the image of the accursed [the cross] brought salvation to the people who had suffered misfortune? Is it not, then, more plausible to say if someone among you is tormented that he should look up to heaven toward God or else to the Tabernacle of God, and he shall be saved? But overlooking these, he [Moses] simply planted and set up the image of the cross. Why, then, did Moses do this? He who said to the people: 'you shall not make for yourself a graven image, or any likeness of anything that is in heaven above, or that is in the earth beneath, or that is in the water under the earth' [Ex 20:4]. [O, Moses] That which you [254] forbid, you yourself do? That which you refute, you yourself make? You who have utterly destroyed the molten calf, do you yourself cast the bronze serpent? And this [serpent] not secretly, but openly and before everyone so that it was known to all? But he [Moses] says, 'I legislated these [laws] in order that I might eliminate the matters of impiety and draw the people away from idolatrous acts; but now I cast out of molten metal the serpent for a useful purpose as a model of truth. And just as I set up the Tabernacle and all objects in it, and I displayed in the Holy of Holies the Cherubim in the likeness of the invisible ones as a typology and foreshadow of things of the future, for this reason I also set a serpent on a pole for the salvation of the people so that by this experience I would prepare them for the image of the sign of the cross and the Savior and Redeemer [who on it would be crucified].

[22. Moses' Serpent: Invisible Symbol of Christ]

The fact that this reasoning is beyond questioning, dearly beloved, let us harken unto the Lord who assures us and says: 'And as

Moses lifted up the serpent in the wilderness, so must the Son of man be lifted up, that whoever believes in him should not perish[97] but have eternal life.[98] And just as the Lord says: 'he who does not honor the Son, does not honor the Father' [Jn 5:23], in like manner, he who does not honor the image [icon], does not honor the one depicted therein either. Moreover, harken to the Lord speaking to the Disciples about the saints in Matthew, chapter 10: 'he who receives you receives me' [Mt 10:40]. Consequently, he who does not honor the saints, does not honor the Lord himself; he who does not worship the Cross in adoration, can not rightfully worship the Crucified One either. Therefore, not because of the nature of the wood do we venerate all wood as Israel did, adoring the forests and the trees saying, 'thou art my God' [cf. Is 44:14-17]. We do not worship in this manner, rather we remember and write about the passion of our Lord and about those who have endured martyrdom for them [our Lord's sufferings], indicating the true feelings of our souls for the Crucified One and for His servants.[99]

[23. Quinisext Synod Concerning Icons (A.D. 692)]
Furthermore, [a canon] of the Sixth Synod at the time of Justinian, [255] concerning the Fifth Holy Synod [states]:

In some of the venerable icons a lamb is painted to which the Precursor points his finger, which is received as a typology of grace, indicating beforehand, through the Law of our true Lamb, Christ our God. Embracing, therefore, the ancient types and foreshadows as symbols of the truth and patterns given to the Church, we prefer 'grace and truth,' receiving it as the fulfillment of the Law. In order, therefore, that 'that which is perfect' may be delineated to the eyes of all, at least as colored expressions, we decree that the figure of the Lamb who taketh away the son of the world, Christ our God, be henceforth exhibited in the images, instead of the ancient lamb, so that all may understand by means fit the depths of the humiliation of the word of God, and that we may recall to our memory His polity in the flesh, His passion and His salutary death, and His redemption which was wrought for the whole world.[100]

[24. Seventh Ecumenical Synod on Icons A.D. 787]
Moreover, after all the above we are justified in reminding you, who know that the holy and Ecumenical Seventh Synod of the 407[101] Godbearing Fathers assembled in Nicaea during the reign of Constantine [VI] and Irene [his mother] against the Iconoclasts [who made war against the images]. There it was confirmed that the venerable icons

should be venerated and honored, and the holy images have been restored in the holy churches. Also, this holy Synod pronounced a severe penalty against those who reject the holy icons: "if one does not worship our Lord Jesus Christ depicted in an icon, according to the human form, let him be anathema."[102] For as the greatest theologian, John the Evangelist, says: "that which was from the beginning, which we have heard, which we have seen with our eyes, which we have looked upon and touched with our hands concerning the Word of life, we proclaim also to you" [1 Jn 1:13]. And the other Disciples [said]: "who ate and drank with Him" [Acts 10:41] not only before His passion, but also after the passion and the Resurrection. For this reason, then, we sketch and worship that which was seen and that which has been touched:

> As the Prophets beheld, as the Apostles have taught, as the Church has handed down and has received, as the Teachers have dogma-[256] tized, as the universe [ecoumene] has agreed, as grace has shown forth, as truth has revealed [as falsehood has been dissolved, as wisdom has presented, as Christ awarded], thus we declare, thus we assert, thus we preach Christ, our true God, honoring, also, His saints in words, in discourses, in writings, [in thought], in sacrifices, in churches, in icons, worshipping [absolutely] the former [Christ] as God and as Master, while the latter [the saints], because of Him, we honor as true servants and offer them relative worship [veneration].[103]

We venerate in absolute or true worship [latreia] to none, save only to God alone. Moreover, the Seventh Ecumenical Synod itself decreed that those who venerate [anything other than God] in the sense and meaning of absolute or true worship [latreia] are subject to anathema. It [the Seventh Synod] also anathematized those who accept the incarnate dispensation of God in lip service only, but who do not condescend to view it [Nativity] in icons; and for this reason they depict it by words alone, and, in reality, they are denying it [the Nativity]. The Synod then decreed, as its Acta read:

> And He [Christ] to be portrayed in icons as He was crucified, and as He was buried, and as He has risen, and as He did everything for us, as universal and salvatory works. For those of the Jews and the Greeks blaspheme when they criticize the immediate original, but they who do condescend to venerate the holy icons, blaspheme Him who has been portrayed through His own icon.[104]

Therefore, these teachings have been respectfully recalled to your attention, for you know, as diligent scholars, that you will be blessed only if you will heed these [teachings]. We earnestly pray that you, dear brethren, will prove to be emulators of those who have lived the godly life. We do not cease hoping that you may be deemed worthy through the mercies and grace of the Great and Chief Archpriest, Christ our true God, and through the intercessions of our most holy, pure, blessed and glorified Lady, Mother of God and Ever-Virgin Mary, and of the godlike angels and of all the saints, Amen.

## [F.] CONCERNING THE MONASTIC LIFE

And now for the sixth [article] of which you speak, that of the monastic life. We have been aware that, in particular, you do not find [257] fault with the occasional existence of some godly men, whom the order has called abbots and archimandrites. And again, in particular, after close observation and retrospection, that you do not approve of their manner of life, enunciating the instability of nature and its impossibility to endure being weighted down with unbearable burdens and confined as if in a prison.

[1. Dionysios (Pseudo) Areopagites on Monastic Life]

Answering these arguments we say that those abbots in the past also entered the monastic life of necessity by tonsure and prayer, and accordingly this procedure is still the practice up to now. And first, the disciple and successor of Paul, the great among divines, Dionysios the Areopagite, thus speaks in his *Discourse on Ecclesiastical Hierarchy*:

> The priest stood before the holy sanctuary, giving the benediction [*epiklesis*]; and the candidate stood behind the priest not bending his two knees, not even one, nor having the God-given words over his head, but simply the priest standing before him and praying the inaudible prayer for him. And the priest, having completed the benediction, proceeds before the candidate and, first of all, asks him if he renounces not only all worldly life, but also worldly thoughts. Following this he [the priest] instructs him concerning the angelic life, emphasizing that it is necessary for him to uphold a course of moderation. The candidate then makes his vow for all those; and the priest, making the sign of the cross over him and tonsuring, chants the holy beatitude of the Trinitarian hypostasis. Then, removing all the outer garments, he vests him with another [cassock], and along with the other clergy who are present, he embraces him [with the kiss of peace] and pronounces him a communicant of the divinely-instituted sacraments.[105]

And this we have from Dionysios.

[2. Basil the Great on Monastic Life]

Now, second, Basil the Great in his ascetic discourse, *On the Renun-*

*ciation of the World*, speaks in this manner using the Gospel text:

'Come to me, all who labor and are heavyladen, and I will give you rest' [Mt 11:28], says the Divine Voice, signifying either earthly or heavenly tranquility. In either case, He calls us to himself, inviting us, on the one hand, to cast off the burden of riches by [258] distributing to the poor and, on the other, to hasten to embrace the cross-bearing life of the monks by ridding ourselves through confession and good works of the burden of sins contracted by our use of worldly goods. How truly admirable and happy, then, is he who has chosen to heed Christ and hastens to take up a life of poverty and undistracted [by worldly concerns] of the monks. But, I beseech you, let no man do this thoughtlessly, nor promise himself an easy existence and salvation without a struggle. But rather let him train himself toward improving his fitness of endurance and tribulations, both of the body and soul, lest exposing himself to unforeseen wrestlings, he be unable to resist the assaults against him and find himself in full retreat to his starting point, a victim of disgrace and ridicule, returning to the world with a judgment of condemnation on his soul, etc.[106]

[3. Saint Basil on Marriage and Virginity in Relation to Monasticism]
Furthermore, this same Basil proceeding [in the same discourse] says:

For this reason, also, the benevolent God, who is solicitous for our salvation, ordained two states of life for men, I say, that of marriage and of virginity, that he who is not able to endure the hardships of virginity, he would have intimacy with a woman, etc.,[107]

which you, as intelligent persons, might read and gain a satisfactory understanding of the monastic life. And again [Basil], a little further on, elaborating on the same subjects in the same discourse [of marriage and virginity], emphasizes: "But you, the lover of the celestial policy, an active participant in the angelic life, and desiring to become a fellow soldier of the holy Disciples of Christ, brace yourself for the endurance of tribulations and enter manfully into the assembled body of monks." [108] Can you observe how clearly and openly the God-inspired theologian [Basil the Great] calls the life of the monks 'the angelic life'? And further on: "Hasten to imitate those who are already of disciplined habits, and do not wait to be taught each one." [109] And still further [Basil says]: "if you are young, either in flesh or in mind, fly from close association with those of your own age, and run away from them, as from fire; for the enemy has set many aflame, etc." [110] Thus, the Saint [Basil] speaks concerning this subject [monasticism], also; and we agree with him when he says, "Do not think that all who live in cells and in the solitary life, the bad as well as the good, are saved." [111]

### [4. Monks as Men of Violence of the Kingdom]
[259] Many, indeed, take up the life of virtue [of the monks], but few bear its yoke. The 'kingdom of heaven has suffered violence and the men of violence take it by force' [Mt 11:12]. [Our Lord] called violence the affliction of the body, which the Disciples of Christ voluntarily undergo in the denial of their own wills, and in the refusal of rest for the body in the observance of all the command-ments of Christ. If, then, you wish to take the kingdom of God by force, become a man of violence; bow your neck to the yoke of Christ [cf. Mt 11:30]. Bind the strap of the yoke tightly about your throat. Let it pinch your neck.

### [5. Ascetic Exercises for Monastic Life]
Rub it thin by labor in the virtues, in fasting, in vigil, in obedience, in silence, in psalmody, in prayer, in tears, in manual labor, in patiently bearing all tribulations which befall you at the hands of demons and men. Let not presumptuous thoughts induce you, as time goes on, to relax your toils, so that you may not be caught destitute of virtue, perhaps at the very moment of your departure, and be kept outside the gates of the kingdom. [112]

Observe that he [Basil] does not say anywhere that if you become op-pressed to forget it. Rather, a little later [Basil says]: "Advance in virtue, that you may become a companion of the angels." [113] And the Apostle [Paul] says: "forgetting what lies behind and straining forward to what lies ahead" [Phil 3:13]. And Saint Basil continues:

Spend your time in isolation not for days nor months but through-out the period of many years, chanting the praise of your Master night and day in imitation of the Cherubim. If you will begin thus, you will also thus end travelling the narrow path in the brief span of your asceticism [cf. Mt. 7:14]; you will, by the grace of God, enter into paradise. [114]

### [6. Not Only by Grace but by Asceticism Also]
Observe [how] through many ways, by the grace of God, we may enter into Paradise and not merely by grace only; for it would be a good thing if it were possible [to enter into Paradise by grace alone], but it is not. We need much more in order to enter into the kingdom. The present age is one of struggles, and you know how many things may occur in the strug-gles; but the future age is one of rewards. After the battles the rewards of victory follow. That this is a fact, and that there are two lives, Saint Paul witnesses also in the second chapter of his 2nd Epistle to the Corin-

thians.[115] Following in the wake of the above statements, the holy
Ecumenical Synods, also being stirred by the Holy Spirit, have accepted
[260] and confirmed them by formulating canons, a few of which we
shall mention in their defense.

[7. Ecumenical Synods on Celibacy]
The [7] canon of the Fourth Ecumenical Synod [states]:

We have decreed that those who have once been enrolled among
the clergy, or have been made monks, shall accept neither a military
charge nor any secular dignity, and if they shall presume to do so
and not repent so as to return to that which they had first chosen
for the love of God, they shall be anathematized.[116]

[8. Fourth Ecumenical Synod A.D. 451]
And again, the same Fourth Synod in the [24th] canon [states]:

Monasteries, which have once been consecrated with the consent
of the bishop, shall remain monasteries forever; and the property
belonging to them shall be preserved and shall never again become
secular dwellings. And they who shall permit this to be done shall
be liable to ecclesiastical penalties.[117]

[9. Sixth Ecumenical Synod A.D. 680-681]
Canon [4] of the Sixth Ecumenical Synod reads: "if someone has intercourse with a woman dedicated to God, let him be deposed, as one who
has corrupted a bride of Christ, if he is from the ranks of the clergy; but
if he is a layman, let him be excommunicated." [118]

Read, also, another canon [40] of the same Sixth Synod beginning as
follows: "Since to cleave to God by retiring from the turmoil of life is
very beneficial for salvation, it behooves us, not without examination, to
admit, before the proper time, those who choose the monastic life,
etc." [119] Also, the next canon [41] of the same Sixth Synod says:

Those who in cities or villages wish to depart to go into cloisters and
take heed for themselves apart before they enter a monastery and
practice the anchorite's life, should, for the space of three years,
in fear of God, submit to the superior of the monastery and fulfill
obedience fittingly in all respects, as is proper, thus showing forth
their choice for such a life, that they embrace it willingly and with
all their hearts; they are then to be examined by the superior of
the place, and then to remain patiently outside the cloister one year
so that their purpose may be fully manifested. For by this they
will show fully and perfectly that they are not grasping at vain
glory, but that they are pursuing the life of solitude for the sake
of what is truly and inherently good, etc.[120]

[10. Women in Convents]
Similarly, canon [46], subsequent to the one above, begins:

> Those women who choose the ascetic life and are settled in a con-
> vent, may by no means go forth from it. If, however, any inexorable
> necessity compels them to do so, let them do so with the blessing
> and permission of the Mother Superior; and even then they must not
> go forth alone, but with some older women of the convent.
> [261] However, they must not be permitted to sleep outside of the
> convent at all. And men also who follow the monastic life may
> themselves go forth upon urgent necessity with the blessing of the
> one in charge of the monastery, etc. Wherefore those who trans-
> gress this rule are to be subjected to suitable punishments.[121]

[11. The So-called First and Second Synod Held in the Church of the
      Holy Apostles in Constantinople A.D. 861]
Also, canon [2] of the First and Second Synod [states]:

> Because some men pretend to take up the life of solitude not in
> order to purely serve God, but in order that by virtue of the monas-
> tic garb [habit] they might assume the glory of appearing reverent
> and find from that a way of enjoying the abundance of pleasures
> connected therewith, and sacrificing only the loss of their hair,
> while spending their time in their own homes without fulfilling
> any service or status whatever of monks, the holy Synod has decreed
> that no one at all shall assume the monastic habit without the person
> being present to whom he owes allegiance, and who is to act as his
> superior or abbot, and who provides for the salvation of his soul,
> that is, a man who is truly God-beloved and of the head of a
> monastery, and who is capable of saving a soul that has but recently
> offered itself to Christ. If anyone be found tonsuring a person
> without the presence of the abbot under whose charge he shall be,
> that person [tonsurer] shall be deposed from office on the grounds
> that he is disobeying the canons and transgressing the monastic
> discipline, while the one who has been illegally and uncanonically
> tonsured shall be consigned to whatever subordination and monas-
> tery the local bishop may see fit. For irresponsible and unwarranted
> tonsure dishonors the monastic habit, as well as causes the name of
> Christ to be blasphemed.[122]

Observe that because of the wickedness of some, they did not stop them
from being monks but merely put them on trial and corrected them; and
they did not reduce, in any way, anyone who became a monk, again to
the rank of layman, rather they corrected those things which were not
proper.
   Canon [6] of the same Synod [states]:

Monks ought not to possess anything of their own. Everything that belongs to them ought to be consigned to the monastery. For Saint Luke says concerning those who believed in Christ and conformed to the monk's way of life: 'And no one said that any of the things which he possessed was his own, but they held everything in common, etc.' [Acts 4:32]...If anyone be found appropriating or claiming any possession...it shall be distributed to the poor...and he shall be chastened with a suitable discipline.[123]

### [12. Basil the Great on Monastic Life]

[262] Moreover, Basil the Great, in his *Canonical Epistle* to the same Amphilochios, bishop of Ikonion, and also in his Second Epistle [Canonica Secunda, canon 18], concerning lapsed virgins who after professing a chaste life before the Lord make their vows vain because they have fallen under the lusts of flesh, concurs by teaching, healing, correcting, and doing as much as is mentioned in what follows in this canon.[124] Therefore, it becomes apparent from the above canons what exactly the monastic life entails [that is]:

[a] from the canon which instructs those who return not to demand anything of value;

[b] that those consecrated to a monastery are not transferrable to another;

[c] that those who have been greatly chastized for having had intercourse with women dedicated to God; and women who are to be in the convent, who are the overseers and the sponsors, and also the authority of the salvation of the soul; and also the monks must not own any possessions and be cenobitic. The monks must reside in the monasteries, and be absent from the midst of worldly cares. And above all, of what Saint Basil also writes and clarifies, citing rules and regulations of the monastic life and who wrote the treatise on *Ascetics* concerning virginity, as well as other great and holy, truly excellent treatises.

Indeed, also, many other Fathers of our Church have written on the renunciation of the world and about the monks and what the true ascetic should be. But it would be too tedious to write about all these things.

### [13. Reaffirming of Monastic Life]

To all this you may wonderingly say that neither in the Old nor in the New [Testaments] was the monastic life lived. However, be assured that in those times also, there existed such a way of life, save that it was practiced in theory, as Elijah and Forerunner in the Old, and the Disciples of Christ themselves, being celibate and living a cenobitic life, also running the risk of being separated from Christ, were models of such a life, as we learn from the Gospel and Epistle texts. Indeed, the later Holy Fathers, in what is now by the grace of God, passed on to the Orthodox faith not some new religion which they invented, nor some contrived, strange and unusual manner of life, but the truly angelic, the holy and admirable life. Therefore, [the phrase], "Let no one disqualify you," etc. [Col 2:18], was not said by Paul concerning this matter; for as Chrysostom explains in saying: "There were some who maintained that we must be brought near by angels, not by Christ."[125] And this is for [263] this purpose. Again, the verse, "Train yourself in godliness" [1 Tim 4:7], does not have such meaning [that is, through the angels], as Chrysostom says:

> This has been by some referred to as fasting; but away with such a notion! For this is not a physical, but a spiritual exercise. If it were physical, it would nourish the body; whereas it [fasting] wastes [the body] and makes it lean so that it is not physical. Hence, he is not speaking of the discipline [exercise] of the body. What we need, therefore, is the exercise of the soul. For physical exercise has no profit but may benefit the body a little. But the exercise of godliness yields fruit and advantage here and now and in the future.[126]

### [14. Exercise]

Since it has been proven from what has been said that the pallet-beds [beds on the ground] and the fastings are not physical, but spiritual, exercises which also provide benefits, then it becomes necessary for all, and especially for the monks, to adorn themselves with them. For it behooves us not to confess God on the one hand, and on the other to deny Him by [lack of] works.

### [15. Fastings and Prayers Necessary]

Since the fasts and the prayers are necessary, hearken unto the Lord who says in the 2nd chapter of the Gospel according to Saint Luke: "And there was a prophetess Anna...She did not depart from the temple, worshipping with fasting and prayer night and day" [Lk 2:36-37]. Also, hear Paul in the 7th chapter of his *First Epistle to the Corinthians*: "that you may devote yourselves to fast and prayer" [1 Cor 7:5].[127] And also, the 6th chapter of his *Second Epistle to the Corinthians* [reads]: "in watchings, in fastings" [2 Cor 6:5, KJV]. And if someone would like to elicit similar testimonies from the Scripture, he will easily find many others. For one will deny that the snow is white, but this is admitted without proof of witnesses.

## [G.] CONCLUSION

[1. Invitation to Accept Orthodox Faith without Innovations]

Finally, having understood [Greek] Orthodoxy from the Holy Scriptures, come enter into it with all your souls, O wise and sagacious men, and put far away from you every irrational innovation, which the host of Ecumenical Teachers and of the Church has not accepted. For thus, both you and we will be worthy of blessings. You, as obeying your leaders and submitting to them [cf. Heb 13:17] and not "disputing about words which does no good" [2 Tim 2:14]. And we, as having spoken in the ears of those who have listened and sowing in the good soil [cf. Lk 8:8]. And since we have agreed on almost all of the main subjects, it is not necessary for you to interpret and understand some of the passages of the Scripture in any other way than that in which the luminaries of the Church and Ecumenical Teachers have interpreted. They themselves [260] interpreted Scripture according to Christ our God, who is truth itself. And we, that is, our Church, keep these truths and uphold them. For nothing else is the cause of dissention than this and only this, which when you correct it, we will be, with the grace of God, in agreement; and we will become one in the Faith, the glory of God. For having researched diligently some of the passages of Holy Scripture, which you referred to in your first and second letters which you sent to us, we saw clearly that you had misinterpreted them, perhaps in following your new teachers. For this reason we again entreat you to understand the passages as the Ecumenical Teachers of the Church have interpreted them and which interpretations the seven ecumenical synods and the other regional ones have ratified. For as we have already said, it is not necessary to rise up and remove everlasting boundaries which the Fathers have established, so that we will not violate the definition which was mentioned at the beginning of the Sixth Synod and be subject to penalties. Therefore, if up to the present something has been violated, you who are prudent may correct it from now, and you will be worthy of praise by God, as well as by men and by us. For to err is human, but the correction is angelic and salvific. May you take care of this, also, so that the grace and the mercy of God be with you.

In the month of May, Indiction 7, 1579.

Jeremiah [Archbishop of Constantinople]

## NOTES

1. The Greek term μετριότης (mediocrity) cannot be translated literally without debasing the person using the term. The English *humble servant* is implied, and therefore used here.

2. Athena, the goddess of wisdom in Greek mythology, sprang forth from the aching head of her father Zeus, fully dressed and armed with weapons of war.

3. NPNF Ser. 2, vol. 14, 374.

4. Cf. S. Stevenson (ed.), *Cyril's Letter to John of Antioch*, 19.108 in *Creeds, Councils and Controversies* (London, 1972), p. 293 (with corrections).

5. PG 26.533; C. R. B. Shapland, *The Letters of St. Athanasius Concerning the Holy Spirit* (London and New York, 1951), pp. 64-65.

6. PG 37.25.

7. *Discourse Against the Arians*, 3, 3; PG 26.468; cf. NPNF Ser. 2, vol. 4, 363. *The Synods 41*; cf. NPNF Ser. 2, vol. 4, 472.

8. *Epistle to Serapion, 1.20;* PG 26.529-676; Shapland, *The Letters*, pp. 117-18.

9. Pneumatomachi = Adversaries of the Spirit.

10. *Epistle to Serapion* 1, 15; cf. Shapland, *Letters*, pp. 95-98.

11. *Acta et Scripta*, p. 160.

12. Jeremiah's use of ταὐτά and αἴτια, ἐπί ταὐτοῦ τό ταὐτόν is probably an adaptation of the geometrical axiom τῳ αὐτῳ ἴσα καί ἀλλήλοις ἴσα, i.e., things equal to the same thing are equal to each other. Also cf. Gregory of Nazianzos, PG 36.85 and 89 for use of ταὐτό in reference to the Godhead.

13. Cyril of Alexandria *Epistle 17*, i.e., *Third Letter to Nestorios*, PG 77.117.

14. See original manuscript referring to the method of treating the subject matter. Jeremiah used the dialectic method to prove that their conclusion is absurd.

15. The article before "Rome" in the text is plural dative instead of singular genitive.

16. Extract from the *Declaration of Faith*, used by the Greek Orthodox Church on the Sunday of Orthodoxy (First Sunday in Lent); cf. NPNF Ser. 2, vol. 14, 555.

17. J. Hardouin, *Acta Conciliorum*, 6, 344 (hereafter HAC).

18. NPNF Ser. 2, vol. 14.

19. *On the Spirit*, PG 32.46; cf. NPNF Ser. 2, vol. 8, 29.

20. The text mistakenly records this as Psalm 93.

21. *Psalm 96*; PG 55.607-08.

22. The Second Ecumenical Synod, *Article 8 of the Creed*; cf. NPNF Ser. 2. vol. 14, 163.

23. *Third Ecumenical Synod of Ephesos*, canon 7; cf. NPNF Ser. 2. vol. 14, 231.

24. *Fourth Ecumenical Synod of Chalcedon*, canon 1; cf. NPNF Ser. 2, vol. 14, 267. The quotation cannot be found as a canon, therefore, the addition of canon 1.

25. This in not a direct quotation.

26. This is not a direct quotation; cf. NPNF Ser. 2, vol. 14, 240.

27. *Sixth Ecumenical Synod in Constantinople*, canon 1; cf. NPNF Ser. 2, vol. 14, 360.

28. *Seventh Ecumenical Synod in Nicaea*, canon 1; cf. NPNF Ser. 2, vol. 14, 555.

29. St. Silvester (A.D. 314-335).

30. Cf. Shapland, *The Letters*, pp. 64-65.

31. *Discourse on the Holy Spirit*, PG 26.1191.

32. Ibid.

33. St. Cyril of Jerusalem, *Discourse on the Holy Trinity*, NPNF Ser. 2, vol. 7, 125.

34. Ibid.

35. Pope Damasus, *Epistle to Paulinus, Epistle 4*; PL 13.362; cf. Theodoret, *Ecclesiastical History, 5, 11.*

36. Pope Agathon, *Epistle to Herodius and Tiberius, Augustae, Epistle 3*, PL 87. 1219D.

37. Ibid.

38. *Homily 24*, PG 32.616. Reference in text is incorrect.

39. Text incorrectly refers to Gregory's *Second Discourse Concerning Peace*. The correct reference is his *Third Theological Oration (29) On the Son*, PG 36.76; NPNF Ser. 2, vol. 7, 301.

40. Ibid.

41. *Fifth Theological Oration*, PG 36.141; cf. NPNF Ser. 2, vol. 7, 320; LCC vol. 3, 194-214.

42. PG 52.825.

43. The reference *Theonymeae* in the text is misplaced here. *Theonymeae* or *On the Divine Names* is the work of Dionysios referred to below. The quotation of Gregory of Nyssa cited here is from his discourse *On Common Notions*, as identified in the next note.

44. Gregory of Nyssa, *On Common Notions*, PG 45.180. Cf. J. N. D. Kelly, *Early Christian Doctrines*, p. 265; F. Oehler, *S. Gregory, Bishop of Nyssa, Writings* (Halle, 1858-59), 2, p. 226; R. Seeberg, *History of Doctrines*, trans. Charles E. Hay (Grand Rapids, 1952), 1, pp. 227, 233.

45. The reference *On the United and Distinguised Theology*, in the text is incorrect. The quotation is from the *Theonymeae (On the Divine Names)* as indicated in the next note.

46. Dionysios Areopagite, *Theonymeae (On the Divine Names)* chapter 2, PG 3.641.

47. St. Augustine, *Epistle to Maximinus*, PL 42.710-42.

48. St. Gregory the Thaumaturgos, PG 46.912-13.

49. St. Jerome, *Epistle to Pope Damasus*, PL 22.355-57; cf. NPNF Ser. 2, vol. 6, 18-20.

50. St. Nilos, "On the Holy Trinity," in the *Praktikos* chapters on prayer. Cistercian Studies Series 4.

51. St. John Damascene, *Exact Exposition of the Orthodox Faith*, 1.8; cf. PG 94.832-33, and NPNF Ser. 2. vol. 9, 11.

52. Note that the next article on baptism is not mentioned.

53. St. John Chrysostom, *Commentary on Ephesians, Homily 4*, PG 62.31; cf. NPNF Ser. 1, vol. 13, 65-66.

54. *Commentary on Romans, Homily 5*, PG 60.425; cf. NPNF Ser. 1, vol. 11, 362.

55. Ibid.

56. *On Baptism*, bk. 2, PG 31.1537; cf. St. John Chrysostom, *Commentary on Hebrews, Homily 12.3*, PG 79.361 A.

57. St. Anastasios of Sinai, *Questions and Answers*, Question 95, PG 89.733.

58. Heraklitos, *Frag. 118*.

59. *On the Structure of Man*, PG 30.17, 29f.

60. *That God Is Not the Cause of Evil, Homily 7*, PG 31.345B.

61. *Exact Exposition of the Orthodox Faith*, PG 94.968-72.

62. St. John Chrysostom, *On Obscure Prophets, Homily 1.4*, PG 56.171.

63. St.Maximus, *To Anastasios the Monk*, PG 90.137.

64. *Exact Exposition of the Orthodox Faith*, PG 94.968-72.

65. The text mistakenly refers to chapter 47. The correct reference is chapter 30.

66. St. Athanasios, *To Serapion, Epistle 1*, PG 25.530-676; cf. Shapland, *Letters*, p. 114.

67. Ἀρρήτων δυνάμεων instead of the biblical ἄρρητα ῥήματα (2 Cor 12:4).

68. Anaxagoras (500-428 B.C.) in 432 B.C. was condemned to death for undermining religion by teaching theories of astronomy.

69. *Genesis, Homily 4*, PG 53.47-48.

70. *Genesis, Homily 5*, PG 53.49-50.

71. Ἀντιρεῖ from the verb ἀντιλέγω = contradict.

72. RPS 2.66; cf. Karmires, Μνημεῖα, 1, p. 210.

73. *Canon 48*, not 47 as in text. Cf. NPNF Ser. 2, vol. 14, 154.

74. The Synod of Carthage (A.D. 275) issued no canons but wrote epistles. See Epistle 70 in NPNF Ser. 2, vol. 14, 578; Alivizatos, Ἱεροί Κανόνες (Athens, 1949), p. 221; RPS 2, 309.

75. *Canon 95 of Quinisext Council*; cf. NPNF Ser. 2, vol. 14, 405; Alivizatos, Κανόνες, pp. 113-14.

76. *Second Corinthians, Homily 3*; cf. NPNF Ser. 1, vol. 12, 290.

77. *On the Spirit*, PG 32.45; cf. NPNF Ser. 2, vol. 8, 28.

78. The Greek text of the Septuagint has φοβηθήσῃ = fear, but a variant reading has προσκύνησις = worship, which Jeremiah preferred in his text.

79. The reference in the text was incorrect and has been corrected.

80. Gregory of Nazianzos, *Homily 40, 6*, PG 36.365.

81. Gregory of Nazianzos as quoted by John Damascene in *On Icons, Homily 1, 19*; cf. PG 94.1249.

82. *Homily Against the Collyridians*; PG 42.749f.

83. *Oration 2*, PG 94.1257.

84. This thought led to the formulation of purgatory in the Roman Church; it introduces a difference between guilt and punishment or penance.

85. St. John Damascene, *Oration 3*, PG 94.1345-48.

86. Ibid. 94.1353.

87. Ibid. 94.1357, 1360.

88. Ibid. 94.1360; cf. Dionysios Bishop of Athens.

89. Ibid. 94.1360; cf. St. Basil, *Homily 17, On the Martyr Barlaam*, PG 31.489.

90. Ibid.

91. Ibid. Cf. St. Basil, *Homily 19, On the Forty Holy Martyrs*, PG 31.508-9.

92. Ibid. *39th Question to Antiochos* is correct and not Question 37 as text indicates; see PG 94.1365.

93. Ibid.

94. Ibid. PG 94.1368; cf. St. Cyril of Alexandria, *Address to Emperor Theodosios*, PG 76.1153.

95. Ibid. PG 94.1368; cf. St. Gregory of Nazianzos, *4th Theological Discourse on the Son*, PG 36.129; NPNF Ser. 2, vol. 7, 317.

96. Ibid. PG 94.1368; cf. St. John Chrysostom, *Colossians, Homily 3*; NPNF Ser. 1, vol. 13, 270.

97. The phrase "should not perish" is not recorded in the RSV translation.

98. St. John Damascene, PG 94.1364; cf. Severian, Bishop of Gabala, *Homily on the Dedication of the Precious Cross*.

99. St. John Damascene, PG 94.1388.

100. *Canon 82, Quinisext Synod*; cf. NPNF Ser. 2, vol. 14, 401, with corrections.

101. Other historians record 350 Fathers, others 367 Fathers.

102. Cf. Karmires, Μνημεῖα, p. 205.

103. Ibid. pp. 205-6.

104. Ibid.

105. PG 3.533.

106. PG 31.625f; FC vol. 9, 15 (with corrections).

107. Ibid.

108. Ibid. PG 31.629; cf. FC vol. 9, 18 (with corrections).

109. Ibid. PG 31.636; cf. FC vol. 9, 22 (with corrections).

110. Ibid. PG 31.637; cf. FC vol. 9, 23.

111. Original text in Migne has χρηστούς instead of ἀχρήστους.

112. Ibid. PG 31.645; cf. FC vol. 9, 30 (with corrections).

113. Ibid. PG 31.645; cf. FC vol. 9, 31.

114. Ibid. PG 31.648; cf. FC vol. 9, 31 (with corrections).

115. The text incorrectly refers to the 7th chapter instead of the 2nd chapter.

116. *Canon 7 of the Fourth Ecumenical Synod*; cf. RPS 2, 232; *Rudder* p. 251; NPNF Ser. 2, vol. 14, 272.

117. Ibid. RPS 2, 271; NPNF Ser. 2, vol. 14, 284.

118. *Canon 4 of the Sixth Ecumenical Synod*; cf. NPNF Ser. 2, vol. 14, 364.

119. Ibid. *Canon 40*; cf. RPS 2, 397; NPNF Ser. 2, vol. 14, 384.

120. Ibid. *canon 41*; cf. RPS 2, 401; *Rudder*, p. 338; NPNF Ser. 2, vol. 14, 385.

121. Ibid. *canon 46*; cf. RPS 2, 414; *Rudder*, p. 346; NPNF Ser. 2, vol. 14, 387.

122. *Canon 2, the First and Second Synod* (A.D. 861); cf. RPS 2, 654; *Rudder*, p. 457 (with corrections).

123. Ibid. *canon 6*; cf. RPS 2, 667; *Rudder*, p. 461 (with corrections).

124. Ibid. *canon 18*; cf. RPS 4, 140f; NPNF Ser. 2, vol. 14, 236.

125. St. John Chrysostom, *Colossians, Homily 7*, PG 62.344; cf. NPNF Ser. 1, vol. 13, 288.

126. Ibid. *On 1 Timothy, Homily 12*, PG 62.561; cf. NPNF Ser. 1, vol. 13, 445.

127. "Fast" is not found in RSV.

*Chapter 5*

# THE SECOND THEOLOGICAL EXCHANGE:
# TÜBINGEN TO CONSTANTINOPLE

*[A.] The Letter from the Tübingen Theologians to Patriarch*
*Jeremiah [II] in Response to the Second Answer*

To the All-Holy Patriarch of Constantinople, the New Rome with the title Ecumenical, the Most Reverend and Most Beloved Lord Jeremiah.

### Greetings in Christ the Savior

[261][1] Nothing could have happened to cause us more bitter sorrow, nothing to cut with deeper grief into our souls, All-Holy Lord Patriarch, than for us to receive the report that truly Your Holiness has been removed from the highest office of governing and directing the Eastern Churches and that Your Holiness no longer occupies that illustrious position which the piety, wisdom, and eloquence of Your Holiness adorned. But Your Holiness does not need to hear consoling words from us in this misfortune nor a soothing of the wound. Indeed, Your Holiness from long ago has become accustomed by your own steadfastness and magnanimity to pay no heed to any wind whether favorable or contrary. Your Holiness knows that the worth of men does not depend on the titles of dignity that they bear, but on the virtue and wisdom that shines in them. In addition to this, it ought to be thought a most highly prized treasure for one to be protected by a good conscience, and by the recollection that he has done nothing wicked nor blameworthy; but, on the contrary, that he has done many good and noble deeds. For neither envy nor death itself could ever blot out the fame of a person whose true virtue is held up for deserved praise, and whose name is good and indelible before God and men. But enough of this! Lest we appear to distrust the courage and the genius of Your Holiness. Now we are sending a reply to the treatise of Your Holiness, which we received in the month of May of last year. We have derived it from, and have structured it on, the foundation of the Holy Scriptures. We hope that Your Holiness will read it kindly, graciously, and in Christian love. For certainly Your Holiness,

215

[262] pious as you are, will not reject our reply, but will gratefully receive it, recognizing that its contents have been selected from the divine treasures. Your Holiness also knows very well that the opinions of all men should be brought under the test and judgment of the prophetic and apostolic Scriptures, because they are a lamp unto our feet. Moreover, those shining luminaries of the Church, those invincible heroes, who with absolute concern and earnestness spent their entire lives in the assiduous study of the divinely inspired writings, likewise led us directly to these sources of living water. This is how they intended their writings to be read by us and be accepted by us, since they received their aroma from those blessed fountains and streams. Nor did they hesitate to subject their writings to the critique of all men, with the one condition that they desire to judge these writings according to the wholesome and ever-living fountains of Scripture. Wherefore, we once again appeal to Your Holiness, as much as we can, to excuse us because of the late arrival of our reply. We have been so busy with our everyday tasks that we were barely able to breathe freely. Only with difficulty could we find enough leisure time from our many occupations to satisfy either our own desires or the desire of Your Holiness [to answer]. For that reason may Your Holiness favorably receive these reflections of ours, and consider them worthy of careful study. We, on our part, will, by the grace of God, be most willing ministers to Your Holiness for every good and pious service, as much as our weakness will enable us. Finally, we warmly entreat Jesus Christ, who in His love for men has redeemed every human being, to guide all of us in a fatherly fashion by His Holy Spirit for the honor and glory of His most reverend name, and to make us vessels of mercy, that we may reign together with Him forever and ever. Amen. Let us enjoy the affection of Your Holiness, most honored Sir, and may Your Holiness be of good health.

From Tübingen, the Nativity of the Holy Forerunner and Baptizer John, in the year of the universal salvation, one thousand five hundred eighty.

Eberhard Bidembach, Doctor of Theology and Abbot of the Monastery at Bebenhausen, signed.

Jacob Andreae, Doctor of Theology, Provost of the Church at Tübingen and Chancellor of the University, signed.

John Mageirus, Theologian, Provost of the Church at Stuttgart, the capital city of Wittenberg, signed.

Jacob Heerbrand, Doctor of Theology, and Professor of the Church and University at Tübingen, signed.

Theodore Schneff, Doctor of Theology, Professor in the Church and University at Tübingen, signed.

> Lucas Osiander, Doctor of Sacred Theology and Ecclesiastical Councilor of the Ducal Court of Wittenberg, signed.
> Stephen Gerlach, Doctor of Theology and Professor at Tübingen, signed.
> Martin Crusius, Professor of Greek and Latin Language and Culture at Tübingen, signed.

In addition, let Your Holiness know that the books of the Holy Fathers and the other books for which Your Holiness has asked, which have been printed and well bound by us, will arrive shortly. Moreover, Master Stephen Gerlach has faithfully carried out everything that Your Holiness has asked of him with reference to some of us, and we in turn have respectfully expressed and are expressing our thanks to Your Holiness.

1. Pages here are incorrectly numbered.

*[B.] The Second Reply from the Tübingen Theologians to the*
*Second Answer of Patriarch Jeremiah [II],*
*Translated into Greek by Martin Crusius.*

[264] The fact that Your Holiness, Most Holy Sir Patriarch, being involved in many and most important tasks, nevertheless, thought it worthwhile not only to read, but also to give a most kind answer to our book which was sent you, helped us to appreciate the extraordinary kindness of Your Holiness to us, and reverent loyalty to God.

We were not at all displeased that Your Holiness set forth openly and clearly [those positions] which you hold, although in some points not in agreement with ours. However, again we have been convinced that Your Holiness, excelling in kindness and affection, will be willing to listen, if we would counter by stating our reasons and their basis as briefly as possible.

They [our reasons] are by no means satisfactory among us, nor in any way are our conclusions final. We assuredly would never attempt this [to set forth our reasoning], nor anything else, out of a desire to create difficulties for Your Holiness, or to disrupt your most holy tasks and labors. But devoutly, without malice, and out of love for the truth would we humbly discuss such matters of great importance in order that Your Holiness might be well informed [concerning them]. We are not compelled by arrogance nor by contentiousness, but by good intention and most sincere motives to express another opinion and judgment concerning those [subjects which will follow]. And thus we continue believing until we might be subsequently taught the truth and the good from the Holy Words. We would have replied sooner if we also had not been bound by the many and heavy responsibilities of our order and pastoral duty. Nevertheless, we earnestly wish, respectfully, to entreat Your Holiness' calm demeanor and with gentle spirit to deem it worthy to accept these replies from us.

[265] Therefore, in answering we will keep the same order as in your treatise which has arrived. We will pursue only those articles on which you and we are not in complete agreement; those in which we agree we will omit for the sake of brevity. May God, the Prince of Peace, lead us to complete agreement concerning all parts of the divinely revealed teaching, and to teach them [with the same interpretation and understanding].

As an authoritative principle underlying our former treatise, we have prepared the theory concerning the standard and rule according to which all the religious controversies should be judged and analyzed. If there is no agreement on both sides concerning that which is being judged, nothing would aptly be accomplished. We have made note of your opinion that we recognize the holy and divinely inspired Scripture as the only standard and rule, by which it is necessary to examine all the doctrines of religion and faith. We have, in additon, brought to the fore distinct proofs that the writings of the Holy Fathers, and the dogmatic definitions of the synods cannot have the same power and authority as the Holy Scriptures, but they will be greatly acceptable in so far as they are in agreement with Holy Scripture. For though we know absolutely nothing that makes uncertain those dogmas which are contained in the three symbols, the Apostolic, the Nicene, and that of Saint Athanasios, nevertheless, in the decrees of some other synods, we are of the opinion that some of them [decrees] are not found to be consistent with the sacred writings.

In addition, we suggest that it is dangerous to present something to the Church of Christ to believe in which is not based upon indisputable scriptural witnesses as on solid foundation. We have proved also by the apostolic texts that the Holy Scriptures are not imperfect so that their imperfection should be completed either from the patristic writings or from the decrees of the synods. However, everything which the Christian person must know in order to attain everlasting life is included in the Scriptures. Moreover, we had declared that the Scriptures are not so unclear [266] that they could not be understood by comparison and examination of identical and like passages, and could not be explained with proper disclosure by the Holy Spirit. For that which is said in a somewhat riddle-like and obscure manner is unfolded more fully and clearly in other places [in Scripture]. For an obscurity which is sometimes not in the original language of the Scriptures, but in the translations, we advised that it is necessary to return to the sources of the Hebrew language for the Old Testament, and to the Greek text for the New Testament. When the two languages, by the Spirit's good guidance in us, have been restored from idiomatic into the pure language, we think that much light is shed for a clear interpretation of the Holy Scriptures. Therefore, we consider that none of those passages which bring forth the true knowledge of God, as well as sincere piety, will fail the one who believes and he who sincerely tries to do that which should be believed and should be done by us, as set forth in the sacred writings. Because all those beliefs [mentioned above] are thus held, we have prepared the scriptural proofs as well as those proved by the most renowned and great John Chrysostom.

### [A. THE FATHERS AND SCRIPTURE]

To these [subjects mentioned above],[1] Your Holiness has answered thus: [we] will converse further on this for edification [ourselves] being confirmed by divine witnesses, as the God-bearing Fathers have accepted them [cf. Eph 4:29]. For there is a canon, an unchangeable decree of the holy and Ecumenical Sixth Synod, which postulates that we accept the Holy Scriptures as the approved teachers of the Church have expounded them. And those who would interpret such teachings should not of themselves cunningly contrive superfluous interpretations. Indeed, this decree is found in the 19th canon, which reads literally thus:

> And if any controversy in regard to Scripture shall have been raised, let them not interpret it otherwise than as the luminaries and teachers of the Church in their writings have expounded it; and in these let them glory rather than in composing things of their own, lest through their lack of skill, they may have departed from the bounds of propriety.[2]

This is the answer of Your Holiness. And we answer thus:

There is indeed no doubt on our part, unless we are greatly mistaken, [267] that all who contrive superfluously in themselves, attempting in vain to succeed [in interpreting Scripture], because of lack of experience, fail to interpret correctly. For it is necessary then to follow the Holy Scriptures in revealing light rather than pursuing the glory of superfluous wisdom. In the Scriptures, indeed, only the glory and the honor of God, as well as the salvation of the Church, should be sought.

We do not think that it is superfluous to contrive in oneself if a person with a pious heart who prays beforehand goes on to learn the Holy Scripture and to practice it from his heart. If one embraces this plain and genuine meaning, which is revealed as the entire result of logic and reasoning, from the more obscure to the more clearly evident in the same Scripture when we are speaking concerning the same matter and professing the same as the faithful interpreters, he will conclude the same by comparing and by examining such meaning of the Scriptures, which is in conformity and agreement with the entire Divine Scriptures. But even if with earnestness and with grateful heart we take advantage of the expositions and writings of God-bearing Fathers, inasmuch as they correctly interpret them, nevertheless, neither when they themselves forbid anyone after them to attempt to interpret the Holy Scriptures, nor when they require all the others to be bound by their interpretations and claim absolute authority over them [the Scriptures], could we be justly blamed if we cannot always follow their explanations and interpretations. For some of them (and let no friends of the Fathers think that we deprecate their greatness), and we say some of them, and, indeed, those of the Greek language were not found to be altogether learned in the Hebrew language. Wherefore they did not interpret many passages of the Old Testament in a manner in which they should have. Moreover, with some interpretations of the New Testament one could justifiably find fault at times. And Your Holiness, we need not wonder about the reason. For although the Evangelists and Apostles wrote [their books of the New Testament] in Greek, yet they did not entirely depart from the Hebrew manner of speaking and idiomatic [expressions]. And, indeed, to such a degree that not even they who had [268] thoroughly trained their intellect in the Greek could understand if they had not also learned and studied the Hebrew [language]. Therefore, with a thankful heart we too make use of the gift of languages for a clear explanation of the Scriptures. The Lord in these last days [cf. Heb 1:2] carried back this very gift to the Church, so that when we are now dealing with more obscure verses, we return to the clear springs of Hebrew and Greek languages. The Lord did not exhort us to turn to the literary work of the Fathers; but Jesus, the most wise and most benevolent, expressly commanded us to search the Scriptures (that is, the teachings of the Prophets). And our Heavenly Father commanded us to listen to His beloved Son [cf. Jn 5]. Christ bids us go to listen to His Apostles, having said to them: "he who hears you hears me" [Lk 10:16]. We earnestly endeavor to comply with these ordinances; we go to those most clear springs of Israel, so that we might draw the clearest water, which is unmixed with human opinions and traditions, and will renew our souls. Indeed, we do not disdain the most illustrious luminaries of the Church (God forbid that we be so disrespectful), rather we honor Christ, the Prophets and the Apostles above the Fathers. And who could justly blame us for this? They are the best and the truest interpreters of their own words. They understood very thoroughly and most accurately that which they had in their mind, and that which they had in mind they were able to state most clearly and most explicitly. They [Christ, Prophets, Apostles], in disclosing the divine mysteries, nowhere overlooked, nor failed to see; nor did one differ from or disagree with the other in any manner.

### [1. Scriptures Inspired, but Fathers
### Disagree among Themselves]

Now, the eternal and admirable agreement and continuity of the God-inspired Scriptures is so great that a pious soul, which might at times be tempted and grieved, is able without fear to anchor safely in them [Scriptures], as in a calm and peaceful harbor. Moreover, the interpretation and exegesis of the Fathers do not in every respect agree with each other, but one of them interprets that which is written in this way, and another in that way. Also, one may observe that sometimes one and the same Father understood a certain scriptural passage very differently and incorrectly, which could not escape Your Holiness, who has studied so very [269] carefully not only the Holy Scriptures, but also the readings of the Fathers. For instance, the book of Genesis [reads]: "Dan shall judge his people" [Gen 49:16]. Gennadios, on the one hand, says that this means that the government of the tribe of Dan, which comes through Sampson who, by a woman who treacherously plotted against him as a serpent, shall fall as a horse [cf. Gen 49:17ff]. Cyril, on the other hand, says that the

renowned and admirable group of the Apostles who had been destined to
lead and judge the faithful is indicated. Also, Hippolytus, the holy martyr among the saints, had taken this to refer to the betrayer Judas as being from the tribe of Dan. Theodoretos again [interprets the verse in
question] in reference to Christ, whom the anti-Christ plotted against.
Again [another example], in the First Epistle to the Corinthians: "if any
man's work is burned up, he will suffer loss, though he himself will be
saved, but only as through fire" [1 Cor 3:15]. Theodoretos, the
aforementioned, understands it thus: "if any man's work is burned up, he
will suffer loss...but only as through fire," instead of the work of the
wicked listener being burned up as through fire on the day of the
Parousia of the Savior, "though he himself will be saved," that is, the
teacher, for He is not the cause for the listeners to turn away toward the
worse. If someone (he says) does not wish to apply [the phrase] "but only
as through fire" to "work," but [apply it] to the teacher, let him understand it in this manner, that it will not inflict punishments for those on
the one hand, and on the other hand, he will be saved, as tested by fire if,
indeed, his manner of life is in accordance with the teaching. However,
Chrysostom [interprets it] in this manner:

> He shall suffer loss; lo, here is one punishment. But he himself shall
> be saved, but so as by fire. Lo again, here is a second [punishment].
> And his meaning is: He himself shall not perish in the same way as
> his works, passing into nought, but he shall abide in the fire. He
> calleth it, however, 'Salvation,' you will say; this is why he added,
> 'so as by fire'. Since we also used to say: It is preserved in the fire,
> when we speak of those substances which do not immediately burn
> up and become ashes.[3]

This, then, is what they [the Fathers] have said.

### [2. Conscience Rests on Scriptures Which Presuppose
### Prayer and God's Grace]

For the conscience of man is not at ease if we do not fathom the true
meaning of the Scripture from the Scriptures themselves, which are in
harmony with themselves in every point. Nor, indeed, can our faith be
supported with confidence in any interpretation, whatever it may be,
which could not be proved by a harmonious agreement within the Scriptures themselves. In addition, if there were no other interpretation of the
Scriptures than that of the Fathers, could it be held that all those
members of the Church are mistaken who, throughout their entire
[270] life, were not fortunate enough to obtain a commentary of the
Fathers, but who with earnestness and in true fear of God, read the Holy

Scriptures? Were it so, then the nineteenth canon of the Sixth Synod would not bind us to the interpretations and expressions of the Holy Fathers in such a way that it would not be lawful for us to study with devotion and faithfully teach others the true and genuine meaning of the Scriptures, by the grace of God, from the infallible continuity and harmony of the God-given Scriptures. For by doing so, we do not contrive superfluous things as vain persons, but we wish to rest our conscience in a calm and tranquil spirit. Let God who knows the hearts of all men be [our] witness. Wherefore, entreating Your Holiness, honorable sir, we request you to enter into the same manner [of study] with us, and carefully scrutinize and assess the words of the Sacred Writings (what they are able and what they are not able to support). Do not tolerate the diverse or opposing interpretations and explanations [of Scripture] of the Fathers, which are obstructed and limited. The true and unadulterated meaning can become clearly ascertained, wherever there is a collation and comparison of the Scriptures. If a disagreement still exists over some parts of the divine teaching, it will easily come to an agreement with the assistance of the grace from above. However, let us pass over to the subject concerning the procession of the Holy Spirit.

## [B.] CONCERNING THE PROCESSION OF THE HOLY SPIRIT

### [1. Agreement on Godhead of the Holy Spirit]

To begin with, we are very pleased that Your Holiness does not differ with us concerning the eternal Godhead of the Holy Spirit, nor concerning the distinction between the three hypostases, but only concerning the procession [of the Holy Spirit]. In addition, we also understand that you allow nothing to detract from the grandeur and Godhead of the Son of God, even though you say that the Spirit proceeds from the Father alone. And we would hope that the long standing difference of opinion between the Latin and the Greek churches would at long last come to an end, provided that the truth concerning that teaching be preserved. Therefore, to this purpose to which we might offer a small contribution according [271] to our ability, allow us to examine the solutions which you have brought over against our beliefs, so that it will be made clear to you whether you have satisfied us or not. It will become evident from this discussion with whom of the two [you or us] the other should agree with.

### [2. Disagreement on Procession and Sending of the Holy Spirit]

Your Holiness, then, indeed thinks that we are mistaken in this, that we do not distinguish between the eternal procession of the Holy Spirit, and His being sent in time. And hence, it is not right to mention those things which have been written in the Scriptures concerning the sending forth of the Spirit or the bestowing of His [Spirit's] gifts, which occurred at Pentecost, to prove that it is an eternal procession of the Holy Spirit from the Son. We, also, are not at all ignorant of this distinction between the eternal procession and the sending in time, between the essence of the Spirit and His gifts. Indeed, we know this also, that the one no less is the preparation for the other. Otherwise, why does the Son send the Holy Spirit to the Apostles on the day of Pentecost no less than does the Father, except for this: that the Spirit himself, to whom the gifts belong, proceeds from the Son, as well as from the Father? Thus, there is one and the same grandeur in this matter, that of the Son and of the Father, each of whom sends the gifts of the Spirit to the hearts of the faithful, seeing that the Spirit is proceeding from both. Moreover, even Your Holiness has brought forth many passages of the Scripture, desiring to prove the procession of the Spirit from the Father. These passages, concerning the sending of the Holy Spirit in time, declare most clearly, according to Your Holiness' understanding, that the sending in time is distinct from the procession before the ages.

It is for this reason that even now the testimonies from the Scriptures which we have provided remain invincible: the Holy Spirit proceeds from the Son no less than from the Father, and the sending of the Spirit is by the Son no less than by the Father. Moreover, we bring to the fore other strong proofs which establish the emission of the Spirit from the Son. Because of this emission [for instance], the Holy Spirit is called by the Scripture "the finger of God" [Lk 11:20], that is, that most operative [272] virtue and infinite power of God. If we would not declare that such a great power and inexplicable greatness also proceed from the Son, we shall be forced to postulate that the Son of God has become deficient in eternal power and sovereignty, which is absurd. For how is it possible that "all things were made through him," according to John [1:3], if the same eternal virtue and power (which is the Holy Spirit) was not proceeding from the Son, also? To this question, and concerning our other points carefully presented then, we find no reply in your writings.

### [3. Correctness of Misinterpretations of the Latins]

Concerning those things which the Latins in the past have said and concerning their disproof, even though we believe that you do not differ with any of them and even though these reasons have not been presented by us, we will, nevertheless, state without difficulty what we believe concerning them.

[4. First Argument of the Latins (Not Accepted):
Without the Filioque the Holy Spirit Is Inferior]

The first argument of the Latins, which in form and manner was presented by you, is not acceptable to us. No, indeed, but from him who proceeds from the lesser (as it is in John 10:30: "I and the Father are one"), we also obviously conclude that the Holy Spirit is to proceed from both [Father and Son] and this because of this reason. The Father, indeed, is the first hypostasis of the All-Holy Trinity, for He is the origin, source, and cause of the others [Son and Holy Spirit]. And the Son is the second [hypostasis], by reason of origin but not of time, being posterior to the Father and anterior to the Holy Spirit. Also, the Holy Spirit is the third [hypostasis], being posterior to both [Father and Son] by reason of origin.

If this is not taken as a premise, no order will exist between the Son and the Holy Spirit by reason of origin, nor would the reason be apparent by which the Son is placed as the second, or the Spirit as the third person of the Holy Trinity. And yet order, and not disorder, exists amid the hypostases of the Holy Trinity. This also has been clearly testified by the Holy Scriptures and the God-bearing Fathers. Thus, taking this under consideration, we declare that since the Father and the Son are one, that is, by reason of essence, and the Son comes before the Holy Spirit by reason of origin, it follows that it is not likely for the Spirit to proceed from the essence of the Father, if He [Spirit] does not simultaneously proceed from the Son. Unless, indeed, we would want to separate the Father and the Son, tearing asunder one from the other as to essence, saying that the essence of the Father, from which the Holy Spirit [273][4] proceeds, is one thing and that of the Son is another, which has been separated from the essence of the Father, from which [essence of the Son] the Spirit does not proceed. This, then, we say would be heretical.

[5. Second Argument of the Latins (Not Accepted):
Without the Filioque, Two Spirits Would Exist]

Neither do we approve of the second argument of the Latins, unless someone will define its major premise thus: Whatever belongs to the Father, belongs also to the Son, save that of begetting. For the Scripture and the more ancient Fathers denied only this begetting of the Son. The minor [premise] holds that the characteristic of the Father is to be the emitter of the Holy Spirit. Therefore, this characteristic is of the Son also; if not, we would assume two Holy Spirits, one inspired by the Father, and the other by the Son. For the Holy Spirit is the characteristic of the Son also, not for any other reason but that of breathing, as it will be shown in the following pages.

[6. Third Argument of the Latins (Accepted):
Without the Filioque, the Son Could Not Breathe on Disciples]

However, we accept the third argument of the Latins, which is a proof of the following, that is to say, [a proof] of the former by the latter, and proof of the cause by the effect. For if the Holy Spirit would not be proceeding from the Son also, He [the Son] could not give the Spirit to the Disciples by the breathing. Now then, because He [the Father] blew Him [the Spirit] into them, for this reason [the Spirit] proceeds from Him [the Son] also. For the sending in time and this proceeding presupposes eternity as a cause.

[7. Filioque Presupposed as a Gift for the
Forgiveness of Sins]

But that which opposes us, according to Saint Chrysostom, is that He [the Son] gave to them [Apostles] the gift of forgiving sins, and not the Spirit. But this weaving of words cries out against this reasoning. For the Holy Spirit is distinguished from each one of them [the gift and the breathing]; that which He [the Son] gave through the breathing and the gift to forgive sins which He [the Son] granted to them [Apostles] through the spoken word. First, He [the Son] breathed the Holy Spirit, and then He gave to the Disciples the power to forgive sins through the spoken word.

Saint Augustine is of the same opinion as us, in additon to other Fathers whom, for the sake of brevity, we pass over. Saint Augustine wrote more accurately concerning the doctrines of Christianity than he [Chrysostom]. He [Augustine], in the second book, *On the Holy Trinity*, says: "that physical breathing was not the essence of the Holy Spirit, but a proof through a proper emphasis that the Holy Spirit proceeds not only from the Father, but from the Son as well." [5] For who would come to such a madness as to say that, indeed, the Holy Spirit, whom He [the [274] Son] gave by breathing, was to be one person, and He, whom He sent after His Ascension, was another. The fact that He [the Son] sent the same Holy Spirit, the third hypostasis of the most venerable Trinity, after the Ascension, we will proceed to prove is not only unreasonable to assert (as it seems to you), but rather is impious to deny. For Christ says in [the Gospel of] John, chapter 14: "but the Counselor, the Holy Spirit, whom the Father will send in my name, he will teach you all things, and bring to your remembrance all that I have said to you" [Jn 14:26]. Who would not understand these [words] except he who is destitute of reason, as referring to the gifts of the Holy Spirit, but not to His hypostasis? Also in John, chapter 15: "but when the Counselor comes, whom I shall send to you from the Father, even the Spirit of truth, who proceeds from the Father, he will bear witness to me"

[Jn 15:26].

If, indeed, it is unreasonable to say that the hypostasis of the Holy Spirit has been given to the Disciples, then foolishly would one construct anew [the fact] that the hypostasis of the Holy Spirit proceeds from the Father. However, only the gifts of the Spirit, which [gifts] proceed from the Son also, prove Him [the Son] to be the Cause of the Cause, that is, of the Holy Spirit.

### [8. The Filioque and the Hypostasis of the Holy Spirit]

It is evident from those words of the Lord that the hypostasis of the Spirit was sent by the Son to the Disciples, and thus He [the Spirit] proceeds from Him [the Son] as well. For although the procession [of the Spirit] and the giving by breathing are not the same, yet the one is presupposed and induced by the other because it is caused by it. And because we disavow that the procession and the giving are one and the same, accordingly your concept (that the begetting and the proceeding are the same) is absurd. This is not our opinion; rather it is a figment of your imagination. Furthermore, what you say, that if it is necessary that the Holy Spirit proceeds also from the Son since He [the Spirit] is given by Him [the Son], it follows that the Spirit emits himself also because He [the Spirit] gives and sends himself. We do not accept this sequence as absurd. For in the same manner the Son did not send himself. The same John in [his Gospel] chapter 7, says: "I have not come of my own accord; he who sent me is true" [7:28]; and John in chapter 8: "for I proceeded forth and came from God; I came not of my own accord, but he sent me" [8:42, KJV]. Thus, the Holy Spirit neither gives nor sends [275] himself. But this is a divine dispensation and order of things, so that, indeed, the Son [is sent] by the Father, while the Holy Spirit [is sent] by both [Father and Son]. But neither [is sent] by the Spirit except the Son inasmuch as He became flesh. For even from the sayings of Christ (as you think), that is: "when the Counselor comes" [Jn 15:26], and he "will come," and "when the Holy Spirit has come upon you" [Acts 1:8], it does not follow, therefore, that He [the Spirit] sent himself. For it would be as if someone would say: "if when the mailman will come from Tübingen, and the mailman shall come, and when the mailman having come, you will receive letters, then the mailman has sent himself." It is said that he has sent himself where there is no one, and even though when he consents to the sending, he is said to be sent. Therefore, the Lord distinctly adds: "when the Counselor comes, whom I shall send to you from the Father" [Jn 15:26], and nowhere is it written that the Spirit has sent himself.

[9. The Son Sends Both Himself and the Spirit,
but Neither Sends the Father]

Moreover, you argue that if the Holy Spirit does not give and send himself, the authority of the Son and that of the Spirit is then divided, because the Son sends both himself and the Spirit, but the Spirit sends neither himself nor the Son. On the one hand, we have proven by what has been said before that the Son did not send himself. The Father, on the other hand, being the origin and source of both the Son and the Spirit, has the authority to send either one (the divine things have this particular order). Neither the Son nor the Spirit sends the Father. Also, since according to the ninth chapter of the Third Ecumenical Synod [A.D. 431] the Holy Spirit is peculiar to the Son, and according to Basil the Great He [the Spirit] is the image and word of the Son, for this reason He [the Son] has the authority to send His own Spirit, whom He himself [the Son] breathes and He [the Son] has emitted as His own image. We do not read the reverse, that the Son was sent by the Holy Spirit, save [in the case] of the Incarnation. Consequently, the sending is not a shared and fundamental authority, but merely an authority of dignity and order: the one of begetting [belonging] to that which is begotten, and the other of the emitting [belonging] to that which is emitted.

[10. The Fourth Argument of the Latins (Accepted):
The Receiving and Sending of Spirit Proves the Filioque]

We likewise accept the fourth argument of the Latins with which they prove that by the receiving and the sending of the Holy Spirit, the Holy Spirit proceeds from the Son as well. You assert in your argument that it does not necessarily follow that if one sends something, he then is the [276] cause of its existence. Indeed, we agree with you that this is true among human beings. For the master sends the servant, although he is not the cause of his existence. Nevertheless, the sending is the result of one's authority over him who has been sent for some particular purpose. Of course, the master sends the servant because he has power over him, but not the opposite, i.e., the servant [does not send] the master. The same procedure [is to be found] in divine matters. For, indeed, what is the cause of the sending of the Son and the Holy Spirit by the Father, while the Father himself is not sent by either of them, save that He is the cause of each of them? Moreover, this cause is the reason [for the relation] of the Son to the Holy Spirit: the sending by the Son, but not the Son [sent] by the Spirit. Because He [the Spirit] is God, it is acknowledged that at no time has He been sent, save only by the Father, as it is evident from the Gospel according to John [16:14-15].

[11. John 16:14-15 Presupposes the Filioque]

With regard to your previous remarks: "he will take what is mine"

[Jn 16:14] (which you interpret as "he will take what is my Father's"), we answer that this interpretation is not completely wrong, but it is grossly forced. Indeed, Christ himself refutes this by saying: "all that the Father has is mine; therefore I said that he will take what is mine and declare it to you" [Jn 16:15]. Nor does the Lord in the Gospel, concerning His Father at any time whatever, suggest such a thing even by the omission of a word. Epiphanios, at least, writing against the Sabellians, quoted this passage in reference to the hypostasis of the Son but not that of the Father, saying:

> The Father, truly having begotten the Son, and the Son truly having been begotten of the Father, is personally subsisting without beginning and eternal; and the Holy Spirit, as truly of the Father and the Son, being of the same Godhead, proceeding from the Father, and forever receiving from the Son.[6]

In this passage three things that take place are worthy of notice: first, by making a distinction between the divine hypostases, [Epiphanios] clearly declares the procession of the Holy Spirit from the Father and Son. Second, he then says that the Holy Spirit is receiving from the Son, contrary to what is believed by you. Third, he [Epiphanios] affixes the adverb *forever* [ἀεί] by which we necessarily conclude that if the Holy Spirit [forever] is receiving from the Son, He also proceeds forever, that is, from eternity from the Son. For whatever the hypostasis is among the holy persons, it receives something from the other [hypostasis], that is, it is understood that He [the Spirit] is receiving it [the hypostasis] with his *being*.

[12. The Holy Spirit Receives His Essence from the Son Also]

[277] For nothing happens to the divine hypostases in time. And further, from whatever [source] it receives anything, it is necessarily from that [source] that it also has its essence. For *being* of itself, whatever it is, is everything; and if it does not have being from itself, neither can it receive anything from itself. Indeed, the Holy Spirit received from the Son, as Christ himself says. It would follow that if He received from himself, then He has being from himself. And then later if the Lord will say: "He will take what is mine and declare it to you" [Jn 16:14], it would not, however, follow in this case that it is one thing which receives and another which is received. For this is true for things in the present age in which by virtue of essence there is order; later on [there is] subject, occurrence, formation, and division. Now this [development] which has no place among the divine persons, that is, the receiver as well as that which has been received, is entirely the same thing, as, indeed, the mind, the understanding, and the intelligible. According to this manner [of thinking], the Son, receiving His being from the Father, is the same as He

who has been received. Even when the Lord uses a verb in the future tense [in the Gospels], He is speaking in human terms. For the Spirit received nothing in time, but through the procession He has received everything that He has, that is, He [the Spirit] exists.

But thus it is necessary for one to accept those words of Christ (according to the interpretation of Augustine) in order to understand that He [the Holy Spirit] does not have existence from himself. For to listen is to know Him [the Spirit], and to know is to exist. Therefore, because He [the Spirit] is not from himself but from Him from whom He proceeds, from whom His existence originates, the knowledge is from Him and the listening from Him. And reversely, from whom is the listening and the knowing, from Him, that same one, is the existence. Yet the listening and knowing is in Him [the Spirit] from the Son (for He says: "he will take what is mine"); consequently, also from the Son is the existence [of the Spirit]. Then the Holy Spirit eternally listens because He eternally knows. Therefore, the Holy Spirit heard from Him [the Son], and hears, and shall hear. We should not be troubled that the verb [of the above verse] is in the future tense. If, indeed, that hearing is eternal, then the knowing is also eternal. This then [the above] is according to Saint Augustine.

### [13. The Filioque Not According to Time but by Virtue of Reason]

Just as it is said, not accurately but in human terms, that the Holy Spirit is receiving from the Father and the Son, seeing that He is and has existed from them and His coming into existence, He [the Spirit] possesses everything, so that it is not said correctly that the Spirit is receiving himself, since truly both are the same: that which receives and [278] that which has been received. For this reason the undivided Spirit is not subject to division or synthesis. To this you bring the argument that if the Spirit was to receive His own existence, how is it that He has not yet received being? We have said that Christ is speaking on matters of the future [the Spirit] in human terms. Indeed, the Spirit having received nothing in time, it is not possible to be understood even in a split second of time in which the Spirit did not exist or was found to be non-existent. So the Spirit received His essence before all time, according to which everything is from the Father and the Son through the procession.

### [14. The Fifth Argument of the Latins (Accepted): Not Only Does the Holy Spirit Proceed from the Father, but from the Son Also]

Now, less do we judge the fifth argument to be true. It is the argument which the Latins prepared, that the Spirit proceeds from the Father and the Son, for both are called Spirit. For the Holy Spirit is thus denoted from the [word] breathing (as we shall state below); nor could it be properly understood without Him who is breathing himself. Therefore, only because of this is the Spirit the property of Him from whom He proceeds, that is, He who is breathed. Yet He is also the Spirit of the Son. Consequently, He [the Spirit] proceeds from the Son. It is for this reason that the Holy Spirit is referred to as being breathed, that is, the one emitted, and thus an effect in relation to the Son as emitter, as breather, and cause so that the Spirit could not be, nor be called, His own Spirit if not for the breather.

Therefore, your answer would in no way stand when you say that the Spirit, which if called by that name, is not indicative of the relation it has with the Father and the Son, since the Holy Spirit, being named by a slight change from the word *breath*, is the most impossible to be understood apart from him who breathes himself. Not even the Father (as you incorrectly think) is said to be the main cause, emitter, source, and origin of the Spirit (if, indeed, with such titles the Father is mentioned by the creatures); but rather because of Him who breathed, and because of the Spirit, having been breathed by the Father, He is not called origin, cause, source, or the emitter mainly to say that He [the Spirit] becomes that which is emitted, effected, and originated. And this may be possible to others, but not for the Holy Spirit. So the matter which has been concluded by you is unsubstantiated, for it is by logic against the Spirit, that is, the breath which is to have relation toward its own breath. Hence, in the thirty-second Psalm [32:6] the Holy Spirit is called the "breath" of the Lord's mouth  not for any other reason than [279] that it is from the mouth, that is, of the essence, of the Lord, breathed. Basil the Great, referring to it in his *Fifth Homily Against Eunomios*, distinctly witnesses. writing thus:

> For neither the Son, [they said] nor the birth, is the property of the Godhead, but to bring forth for human similarity. Therefore, similarly, the appellation of the Spirit, also. Wherefore, the Holy Scripture has made use of it [the appellation] for the Holy Spirit, which [the Scripture] has demonstrated differently than from God, since it is not necessary to declare it also by the same similarity, as it has been said.

### [15. The Holy Spirit Proceeds from the (Mouth) of God, Therefore, the Filioque Is True]

What then is this human similarity if not that just as spirit or breath come from the human mouth, in like manner the Holy Spirit [comes] from the mouth, that is to say, from the existence of God? For this reason Basil, a little later, writes:

> God begets not as a man, but truly begets; and the offspring brings

forth a word of himself, not a human one, but brings forth a word truly from himself, and sends forth the Spirit through the mouth, but not as in the human manner, since God has no physical mouth.[8]

### [16. The Same Attributes of the Father and Son Verify the Filioque]

Therefore, the Father is called origin, source, cause, and emitter of the Holy Spirit, for He [the Father] is the one who breathes [the Holy Spirit]. In like manner the Son should be called the origin, source, cause, and emitter of the Holy Spirit since He [the Son] is the one who breathes the Holy Spirit. That the Son is He who breathes Him [the Spirit] is clear from this, that He is called also Spirit of the Son, who [Spirit] according to the Scriptures and Basil the Great is said to be different from the breathing, doubtless because of the procession from the mouth of God.

### [17. The Son Is Not the Son of the Holy Spirit but of the Same Essence]

Nor is He [the Spirit] called Spirit of the Son (as it seems to you), for He proceeds with the Son from the same source, since as the Son He then would be the Son of the Holy Spirit, which your own Damascene [John of Damascus] and other [Greek] Orthodox Fathers deny. Nor has your use of quotations of Saint Cyril which you have set before us proved anything against us. Cyril only wanted to prove this against the heretics, that the Holy Spirit is of the same essence with the Father and the Son, but not a creature or anything that was made according to the impious claims of Macedonios, Eugenios, and other blasphemers.

### [18. The Father with the Son Are Emitters of the Holy Spirit]

And in no way does it conflict with logic (even though you may think [280] so) that the two are emitters of the one, we mean, the Father and the Son [emitters] of the Spirit. Rather nothing, therefore, is more reasonable, not even by nature is it more agreeable and suitable than to proceed the one from the two, a fact which is shown by an infinite number of examples. Indeed, it is a matter of perfection that the Father with the Son, but not without Him, is to emit the Holy Spirit, who is inferior to the Son by origin, and through the Son, in the Spirit, is to proceed toward the external, and without them not to create anything. And even though the two, the Father and the Son, emit the one, the Holy Spirit, yet they do not emit Him [the Spirit] as two, separately and distinctly, but they emit Him as one conjoined together; and the primacy of the emission returns to the Father, who indeed has given this perfect power of breathing to the Son through the begetting as Augustine in book fifteen in *The Holy Trinity* says: from whom the Son has [power] to be God; certainly, from the same He has the [power] so that the Holy Spirit proceeds from Him [the Son] also.[9]

[19. The Holy Spirit Proceeds from the Father and the Son
as by One Closely Conjoined]

In addition to the above, in no way do we wish to propose that the Holy Spirit proceeds from the Father indirectly, that is, by the intercession of the Son, but from both together as by one closely conjoined. For no order of essence exists in matters of the divine. And this argument of yours has a place only in matters which have been ordered because of the essence. For in such matters it is the related and the unrelated, it is the indirect and the direct. But among the intelligible and the divine there exists a very simple union, and the persons of the Trinity are believed to be distinguished from each other not in essence, but in person, that is, in being. Therefore, the entire Father is in the entire Son and in the entire Holy Spirit; and the entire Son is in the entire Father and in the entire Holy Spirit; and the entire Holy Spirit is in the entire Father and in the entire Son. They cannot accept any separation, for there is no order that exists in them because of essence. And consequently, just as there exists an order in the Trinity because of origin, in like manner there is a first, and middle, and third; yet there is in no way a division or separation by virtue of the unity and singleness of the existence. Thus in no way at all is it necessary for them to be separated from each other in whom the middle is indeed found because of origin and not of essence. For only those which differ in essence and have been received in the middle appear to be divided.

[20. The Father and the Son Are of the Same Essence but
Not without the Son Emitting the Holy Spirit]

[285][10] Consequently, we do not simply declare that the Son is the cause of the Holy Spirit because He [the Son] is of the same essence as the Father. Therefore, whatever absurd things you have assembled on this matter, they are not conclusive for us, nor for the opinion we hold. But we unite together these two in an inseparable bond; and because the Son is by origin prior to the Spirit and of the same essence as the Father, we conclude and say that it is not possible for the Father to emit the Holy Spirit from His own essence without the Son, if we would not therefore intend to cause the Son to be of a different essence than that of the Father. Nor is it permitted for you to conclude that. Consequently, the Holy Spirit also begets the Son with the Father, for He is of the same essence as the Father. For the Spirit, being second to the Son by virtue of origin, cannot concur with the Father in the begetting of the Son, and much less [the Spirit] be with the Son also the cause of the Father where indeed the Father precedes both. The Father is the origin and cause of both, bringing each forth from His own essence. Consequently, not only

should the participation in the essence be considered in this very mystery, but also the fellowship of the hypostases by virtue of the precedence of the origin, the theory which rejects all the absurdities which you concluded from the unity of the essence does not comply with the order of the persons according to the sequence of their origin.

### [21. By Virtue of Birth the Son Was Granted the Power of Procession of the Holy Spirit]

In view of this then, we are not denying at all whether the Father is the prime origin and source from which all things flow, while the Son and the Spirit as the cause are caused from it [the source which is the Father] according to Gregory the Theologian. But we add that this power is granted to the Son necessarily through the begetting, so that the Holy Spirit being of the same essence as the Father has been able to proceed afterwards by reason of the origin of each, who [the Spirit] would breathe from the Father and the Son, according to Epiphanios in his *Discourse on the Ancoratos.*[11]

### [22. The Illustration of the Tübingen Theologians in Contrast to Jeremiah's Illustration of Two Streams]

In reference also to your illustration concerning the two-directional streams arising from one overflown fountain, we place against it another similar to it which is much more fitting to that mystery, that of the sun, which is the cause both of light, and of illumination. Wherefore, certainly not without His innate light, but by it He illuminates the world so that the illumination will be reflected from both. In like manner, the Father is the origin and the cause of the Son and of the Holy Spirit, and [the Father] is the emitter of the Spirit not, however, without the Son who [286] preceded the Spirit by origin. And to all this we further set forth that the Holy Spirit proceeds directly from both together, as from one essential source, however the two differ as to being but not to the substance in essence, so that the Father and the Son do not risk becoming one hypostasis in number by virtue of the one activity of emission (as if the three hypostases of the Trinity, by virtue of the singular activity of the creation, would not be confined within the unity of hypostasis). Again, there should not be two prime origins. Neither should one be placed after the other. Whenever, indeed, the Father and the Son are one essential being and conjoined together by virtue of the emission, and the Son is referred to as the begotten of the Father, who is the cause of the begetting from whom [the Father] the Son has, according to Augustine, the gift, the Spirit is to proceed from Him [the Son] also.[12]

Therefore, from what has been said, Most Holy Sir, you see that we do not think wrongly, nor will any absurd teaching result (as it seems to you) from what we think, but all things [that we hold] agree with the Holy

Scripture and have exceedingly great conformity with one another.

### [23. Different Interpretations of John 15:26]

Indeed, we notice how much Your Holiness seizes upon the Word of Christ: "but when the Counselor comes, whom I shall send to you from the Father, even the Spirit of truth, who proceeds from the Father, he will bear witness to me" [Jn 15:26]. Yes, we too, of course, believe in that saying; but we cannot see how it follows if someone would thus say: that because the Holy Spirit proceeds from the Father, He [the Spirit] does not proceed from the Son. For the procession of the Spirit from the Father does not negate the procession from the Son. For in like manner, just as Christ does not deny that He is the true God when He says: "and this is eternal life, that they know thee the only true God, and Jesus Christ whom thou hast sent" [Jn 17:3], thus neither does He deny the procession from the Son when He says that the Holy Spirit proceeds from the Father. Therefore, this saying must upset the procession from the Son to such a degree that it is rather a preparation for it. For if He [the Spirit] proceeds from the Father, in every way He also proceeds from the Son, for the Father and the Son (each of whom on account of origin precedes the Spirit) are one in essence, as it was stated earlier above.

### [24. Development of Previous Illustration of
### One Source for Two Rivers]

[287] And again [we will comment] concerning related matters that you brought to the fore. For you say that from one source two rivers will flow, and from one root two branches will grow; and you relate those to the ineffable mystery of the most Holy Trinity, as perhaps, thus, from one source of the paternal Godhead the other two persons exist—that of the Son by the begetting, and that of the Spirit to the procession. But it ought to be known that such a mystery which is at hand, as great as it is, cannot be developed fully by such illustrations, nor indeed be established [by them]. For neither does Holy Scripture make use of such illustrations in order to unfold this mystery, nor again [does Scripture] thus have the matter of the mystery of the Holy Trinity taught unskillfully as with a source [fountain] or a tree. If, however, such a great matter would be strengthened by illustrations skillfully contrived, it would not be wanting in examples to confirm our opinion, such as, for instance, men and women in union who give birth to a human being; and he who is born exists no less from the father than from the mother, nor no less from the mother than from the father, as if (so to speak) he proceeds from them. But even if this illustration (of which there would be more were we not concerned with brevity—and it would not be difficult to find and present them) might render our true belief concerning the procession [of the

Holy Spirit] more clearly, yet we never established our faith on it.
Therefore, not even those illustrations which you have presented have
such an intention that someone would consider them more effective than
the proofs which we have provided from the Divine Word. It is necessary
for much stronger arguments than those which have been presented
hitherto to confirm that the procession [of the Spirit] is from the Father
alone.

[25. The Two Persons Proceeding from Another—the Holy Spirit]

Again, it seems to you that it is much more proper and more
reasonable for us, along with the Greeks, to relate the duality under the
monad and to derive two persons from one origin, that of the Father,
than for a third, the Holy Spirit, to proceed from two persons making
the duality as the origin of the monad. And you say that this latter is full
of absurdities. Therefore, again we offer other arguments which might
prove our opinion, that is, that the Latins are illogical and absurd. But
[288] we, Reverend Master, know that in matters of faith there is nothing
to be rejected which conflicts with the axioms of the philosophers and
seems strange to human reasoning unless it is contrary to the profound
witnesses of the Scriptures.

[26. Two Kinds of Absurdities]

For there are two kinds of absurdities. One, indeed, concerns Christianity, that is, that which contradicts the Holy Scriptures, and the other,
that which human reasoning cries out against. Concerning the latter
kind, we have nothing further to say; but overcoming every obstacle, we
simply believe what is taught by the God-inspired words, even though
they may appear to be most inconsistent with all human logic. For such is
the religion of the Christians which is opposed to the judgments of the
most acute men and the deepest thinking philosophers. It is more just,
therefore, for human philosophy to obey the word of God, than for the
Divine Word to yield to human wisdom even when expressed by the most
accurate proofs (which remain without the witness of the Holy Scriptures). For Paul, concerning the matters of the Christian faith, writes
thus:

> For the weapons of our warfare are not worldly, but have divine
> power to destroy strongholds. We destroy arguments and every
> proud obstacle to the knowledge of God, and *'take every thought
> captive to obey Christ,'* etc. [2 Cor 10:4-5].

With these words this Apostle indicates, as do also the other Apostles
of Christ, this kind of teaching, which in many ways contends against
human understanding and logic. Our opinion, therefore, is to be captive,

as well as kept under the yoke, so that we may adopt the mysteries of the faith; and in obedient faith we might be able to believe in Christ our Lord. Nor would we be able to hold irrefragable much of our Christian worship if we would accept it by paying attention to the cunning contrivances and the enigmatic syllogisms of the philosophers. So that we do not seek in the chapter concerning the procession of the Spirit what is reasonable or irrational, familiar or strange, but rather what the Holy Writings teach us, or what they reject. And up to now, not one scriptural proof has been produced which denies the procession from the Son, also. [289] And since whatever we have brought forth from the Scriptures concerning the procession of the Spirit from the Son also has not yet been refuted, it is not possible for us to abandon the opinion that we hold.

### [27. The Prepositions: *Dia* Versus *Kai*]

Some absurd matters have also been brought forward. Some seem to think that from this [the procession] occurs, if we would say that the Spirit proceeds from the Father through [dia] the Son. But for us it is not customary to speak thus, for we say that the Spirit proceeds from the Father and [kai] the Son. According to this word, the Spirit does not happen to be nearer to one person or to the other. And this is our opinion, and that which has been proposed to us [by you] is completely rejected as absurd. Moreover, if in this manner we were to overlook the absurd, we would be pleased if it were possible, there might spring forth from the reason concerning the procession of the Spirit from the Father alone a double absurdity. Indeed, it is one thing to place the Spirit nearer to the Father than to the Son, and another to create an inequality of the hypostases between the Father and the Son if, indeed, the Spirit would proceed from the Father alone and not from the Son, also.

### [28. Without the Filioque There Would Be Two Christs]

Again, you hold this opinion, and this absurdity is the result: that there is a risk that there shall be two Christs and not one. For at the baptism of Christ, the Son of God would send the Holy Spirit to the Son of God if the Spirit did not proceed from the Father alone but from the Son, also. But, beloved and most honorable ones in the Lord, be informed that most great is the distinction between the procession of the Spirit, concerning which we are now discussing, and that of the visible manifestation of the Holy Spirit in the form of a dove. For the former, that of the procession, exists from eternity and is hidden, which is not revealed save through the Divine Word. Neither has it ever been seen by anyone through human eyes. The latter, the manifestation itself, occurred in the course of time and from it the Holy Baptizer was first informed that this, indeed, was the true Messiah who baptized with fire. Indeed, these were his words. He [John] said:

I saw the Spirit descend as a dove from heaven, and it remained on him. I myself did not know him; but he who sent me to baptize with water said to me, 'He on whom you see the Spirit descend and remain, this is He who baptizes with the Holy Spirit.' And [290] I have seen and have borne witness that this is the Son of God [Jn 1:32-34].

### [29. The Doctrine of the Filioque Is Witnessed by the Descent of the Holy Spirit at the Epiphany]

And after that it was declared by that manifestation that the mighty gifts of the Holy Spirit were to be poured on the human nature of Christ (because of the hypostatic union of the two natures in Him). That vision or epiphany of the Holy Spirit at the time of the baptism of Christ does not establish two Christs, the one sending, the other receiving the Holy Spirit; but rather it confirmed that which has been said by the Holy Forefunner concerning Christ: "for he whom God has sent utters the words of God, for it is not by measure that he [God] gives the Spirit, etc." [Jn 3:34]. Although, it is obvious that the Holy Spirit is given in measure to other holy men so that one is to receive some gifts from the same Spirit, and another is to receive more or fewer [gifts of the Spirit]. Concerning this the divine Apostle Paul adds much more in the First Epistle to the Corinthians. And the Spirit has been given to Christ, being man not in measure, but He indeed received all the gifts of the Spirit. In order that this might be made publicly manifest to all, the Holy Spirit, in a visible manner like a dove, descended upon the Lord. Therefore, that epiphany was neither descriptive of the procession of the Spirit from the Father alone, nor did it conspire in that absurdity, just as if we were perpetrating false tales concerning two Christs.

### [30. Not Mere Theory, but by the Incarnation of the Word Is the Standard of the Filioque]

Another absurdity opposes our belief, that is, our saying that the Spirit proceeds from the Father and Son, that two rather than one are the primacy or origin introduced. Here we diligently request that you carefully remember that we now are in theory familiar with the mystery of the All-Holy Trinity. Meanwhile, we are changing the contemplation of the Incarnation of the Logos, and are examining (insofar as it is possible and to the degree that the Holy Scriptures bring to light) which are the differences between the hypostases as they are studied each in themselves. In this case we grant to the Father this: to be the source of the Godhead, but outside of time so that we will not place the Son after the Father [in time]. Furthermore, we never attribute the primacy to the Father alone (in spite of what we have said concerning the source or the origin) so that we may not make the Son inferior to the Father.

[31. There Is No Discrimination of Persons in the Holy Trinity]

[291] For if, indeed, the three hypostases are of equal honor among themselves, [then] the primacy or origin is doubtless to be accounted not only to the Father, but also to the Son and to the Spirit. If, however, only the Father takes title to primacy, then neither the Son nor the Spirit would have equal honor with Him. All these diametrically contradict the Holy Scriptures and our faith. Therefore, when the primacy is attributed to the Father, this in itself is not denied or withheld from the Son and the Spirit, but it is common to all three hypostases. Indeed, it [the primacy] is distributed in the true single tri-hypostatic God in contradistinction to the fabricated gods, that is, idols which were worshipped impiously by the pagans. Neither is it [this primacy and worth] affixed to the Father alone to the exclusion of the Son and the Spirit. Therefore, nothing less is introduced by us than the origin of only one true God and not the sovereignty of many gods, although in the meantime we hold forth that the Holy Spirit proceeds not only from the Father, but also from the Son.

[32. Some Fathers of the Church on Both Theories of the Filioque]

Then again, witnesses are brought forth in your treatise, the Godbearing fathers who have shone forth in the Church as the sun. Yes, indeed, some of the bishops of the Elder Rome[13] have declared that the Spirit proceeds from the Father alone, that is, Athanasios, Gregory the Theologian, Pope Silvester of Old Rome, Pope Damasus, Pope Agathon, Basil the Great, Gregory the Thaumaturgos [Wonderworker], Chrysostom, Gregory of Nyssa, Dionysios the Areopagite, and in addition, the hierarchs Zacharias, Leo, and Benedict. We grant, therefore, that most of these have distinguished themselves and are of high esteem in the Church of God, and we salute their most beneficial endeavors, and we acknowledge gratitude to God for the excellent gifts which He has granted to them. But we cannot see how these quotations from them [their writings] which you have brought to the fore contradict what has been said by us. For they say the same as does Christ, that is to say, that the Holy Spirit proceeds from the Father. We, indeed, have never denied this, nor will we ever deny it (to say the same thing as the Lord). For it is one thing to say that the Spirit proceeds from the Father, and another [292] [to say] that *He does not proceed from the Son, also.* The abovementioned fathers and hierarchs say the first part, but they do not say the second, and far from it. Consequently, they do not oppose our opinion either. Rather, they agree with us. Hence, it is sufficient to draw the conclusion from that which you have provided in their own words that they declare that the Holy Spirit is not foreign to the Son, but rather the Holy Spirit is of the Son. What else do they wish to say than that the Holy Spirit is of like manner and life to the Son as He is to the Father, and no less that He proceeds from the Son (indeed, whose characteristic it was from the beginning) as He does from the Father? Only Cyril among those ancient Fathers emits Him [Holy Spirit] from the Father alone. But just as we admire the other writings of such a great man, in like manner we do not think that it is right, on the contrary, that one or two of his utterances may carry more weight or have more authority than ours, which on the other hand we have built upon the foundations of the God-inspired Scriptures. We have the same reply also concerning practices of some persons who have adorned the throne of Elder Rome, who received them from Nilos and Damascenos, of whom no one has had such arrogance as to demand that his own words be believed rather than the firm proofs from the sacred words [of Holy Scriptures].

[33. Some Latin Fathers in Favor of the Filioque]

Moreover, if it should happen that human authority and opinions would prevail and supercede to such a degree so that what seems proper and is pleasing to them is dogmatized, it would be easy for us to produce [as witnesses] the most illustrious Latin Fathers, the brilliant illuminators of the Church, to oppose the above-mentioned writers. For what could you say in opposition to Saint Augustine? The Fifth [Ecumenical] Synod fully accepted him. It is truly obvious that this great man held the same opinions which we do: that the Holy Spirit proceeds both from the Father and the Son. Who is he who does not regard those ancient wise men, who so avoided condemning our doctrinal teaching, that claims he [293] is worthy of receiving it? For if anyone should delete the procession of the Spirit from the Son as heretical foolery, they could not for any reason cite Saint Augustine as a worthy authority. But in this instance it is by no means so, for they have accepted his opinions. It would be easy for us to bring forth witnesses of other most trustworthy Latins. But inasmuch as neither faith nor conscience, in reference to the sacred mysteries, do not firmly depend upon the witnesses of men, indeed, we did not wish to bother you further with those writings by the Latins, but rather, indeed, what we well know and what is not unknown by you: that all the greatest Latin Fathers are entirely [in agreement] with our opinion.

[34. Some Greek Fathers Could Be Interpreted as Favoring the Filioque]

Moreover, the Fathers of your Church hold the same opinion with us, even though they might differ somewhat in expression. Athanasios, then, in his writings, *Concerning the Dispensation of the Incarnation*, says that David chanting to God said: "for with Thee is the fountain of life; in Thy light do we see light" [Ps 36:9, RSV]. For he knew that the Son existed together with God the Father as the source of the Holy Spirit. (For the Greek Fathers in the chapter concerning the Holy Trinity the terms source, origin, and cause have the same meaning.)

Cyril [c. 370-444], in his first writings to Palladios, [says], "if indeed the Spirit is from God and Father, in truth (and, indeed,) also from the Son, the Spirit is poured out from both, that is from the Father through the Son." [14]

Epiphanios [c. 315-403], in his writings in *Ancoratos* [states], "the Father truly begot the Son, and the Son was truly begotten of the Father, existing in a hypostasis which is his own, without beginning and timeless-ly, and the Holy Spirit truly being of the Father and the Son, of the same Godhead...ever proceeding from the Father and receiving from the Son." [15]

Among them Basil the Great in his fifth homily, *Against Eunomios*, agreeing, calls the Holy Spirit "a true and natural image of God and Christ." [16] For this is (according to the second oration of Nazianzos, *Concerning the Son*) the nature of an image: "to be the reproduction of its original, and of that whose name it bears." [17]

Cyril [of Alexandria] also [writes] in the *Thesaurus*: "in the same man-ner as the Son is a most accurate image of the Father (for He who receives Him, [the Son] has [received] the Father also) [cf. Mt 10:40]. Thus, following the same figure of the analogy, He who received the im-age of the Son, that is, the Spirit, has by all means [received] the Son through Him and the Father in Him. How can the Holy Spirit be counted among the creatures if He is an identical image of God the Son?"[18] And Athanasios also [declares] in his *Epistle to Seraphion*: "As the Son is in [294] the Spirit, as in his own image, so also the Father is in the Son." [19] Again, the same [Athanasios says] to Serapion in *Concerning the Holy Spirit*: "then shall be revealed the lawless one whom the Lord Jesus Christ shall slay with the Spirit of His mouth" [2 Th 2:8].[20] To this passage, in an ancient large manuscript volume of the writings of Athanasios the Great, which is in our possession, the following old note has been appended: note that the passage is not found now in the same wording in the Apostle's [Epistle], but "whom the Lord shall consume with the Spirit of His mouth" [KJV]. It was considered by some that the words "Jesus Christ" should be deleted, although I do not know what they had in mind. That this was written thus from the very beginning by the Apostle is obvious from what has been said here [in this quotation] by this same saint [Athanasios], and also by what Saint Chrysostom in his *Epistle to Theodosios* and Basil the Great in the first homily in his *Ascetical Works* likewise commented upon this passage. Moreover, the passage also is thus laid down by the Latin [Fathers] in the idiom of the Holy Scripture. Moreover, observe [above] that Athanasios the Great has accepted this passage in reference also to the Holy Spirit, but not to any of the other spirits. These then [are our comments] with regard to this omission [i.e., of Jesus Christ]. For us, where the note writer says that by some the words "Jesus Christ" have been deleted and he does not know what they had in mind, it seems that they were deleted with an evil intent because from them it follows that the Holy Spirit proceeds from the Son also, since this Spirit is the Spirit of the mouth of Jesus Christ.

### [35. Latin and Greek Fathers Misled]

But enough concerning your Greek Fathers who, as we hope, you will allow us as worthy of your leniency the right to judge for ourselves. For you yourself and even the Latins have agreed when you said concerning them that Dionysios of Alexandria, Methodios, Pierios, Pamphilos, and others had been diverted from the truth. And furthermore, you considered them worthy of forgiveness because of the weakness of human reasoning and because of the tendency among all men to slip into errors. Therefore, let us read the books of all the ancient writers so that under their examination and judgment the God-given Scriptures may be researched as with a Lydian stone.

### [36. The Ecumenical Synods Do Not Oppose the Filioque]

Still further you state that the decrees of the seven ecumenical synods oppose our doctrine concerning the processions of the Spirit. But this does not seem so to us.

For, indeed, the First [Ecumenical Synod] (which was summoned at [295] Nicaea for the first time) teaches: The Holy Spirit comes forth from the Father and is peculiar to the Son, but it [the Synod] does not deny that the Spirit proceeds from the Son, also. There was not even at that time any doubt concerning from whom the Spirit proceeds; but rather, concerning the divinity of Christ.

The Second [Ecumenical Synod] states that the Spirit proceeds from the Father, but it does not teach that He proceeds from the Father alone.

The Third and Fourth [Ecumenical] Synods stood to ratify the First (the First Synod does not contradict us).

The Fifth, Sixth, and Seventh [Ecumenical Synods] declare nothing specifically concerning this matter, but only exhort that the preceding Synods be kept unshakeable by all. From this it is obvious that although the aforementioned Synods did not bear forth distinctly and clearly our opinion, yet neither did they reject it nor refute it.

Therefore, such being the case, Most Holy Sir, since these matters which you have selected to refute our orthodoxy do not satisfy our souls, nor relieve our consciences, and our beliefs, which we have presented from the venerable holy irrefutable Scriptures, have not as yet been disproved but even now stand correct, we remain hopeful that by offering your Christian-like manner of love it will not be difficult for you to neither seek irrational obstinacy nor any willfulness to judge us harshly because we are unable to agree with and subscribe to the opinion which you introduce.

## [37. Conclusion]

Therefore, we rather have good hope that when you examine and scrutinize wisely and accurately those points about which we wrote to you to the best of our ability and in good conscience, you might in good time, with the grace of God, concur with our opinion and agree with us. Besides, when we each also agree with the true and eternal divinity of the [296] Holy Spirit and on the emanation of the same Spirit from the Son also, it does not in the least diminish His divine nature but rather, on the contrary, strengthens it. Moreover, not even in the least does it detract from the Father His glory and majesty, which remain absolutely pure even when the Holy Spirit is believed to proceed from the Son, who is of the same essence as the Father.

## [C.] CONCERNING FREE WILL

In the chapter concerning the subject of free will we agree, indeed, with you that man is not to be turned back to God by force nor by compulsion. Furthermore, we also know this, that the true virtues advance not by the interweaving of the elements, nor from the temperament of man. And you most truthfully said that evil is [the result] of deliberate preference and of nature.

### [1. Man Is Free To Choose Evil but Not the Good]

We disagree with your understanding that man has the power either to choose the good or, nevertheless, is capable of choosing evil. Although, if indeed human nature had remained in man's original purity and goodness, he would, by all means, have an equal choice of the good or the evil. But now when the entire soul and mind of man has been depraved by original transgression and throughout the ages since has been perverted in such a manner "that (according to Moses) every imagination of his heart was only evil" [Gen 6:5] (as one reads in the Hebrew sources of Scripture), man can by himself choose evil; but he is no wise master in choosing the good. By thus saying, we have given an account concerning spiritual things which have to do with the glory of God and the eternal salvation of man. For although it may be written that God is to foreordain good and evil, life and death, as well as to exhort us to stretch out our hand for what we desire, it should not be concluded from this that a man who has not been reborn has the power to choose the good rather than evil. For, indeed, the Lord requires many things from us in His law which we cannot do. And He also requires as He leads us that we have knowledge of our wickedness and natural corruption so that we might take refuge in the divine mercy, which is offered to us through Christ the [297] Savior. It is for that reason that we consider diligently what a man (that is, a man who has not yet been reborn or who is spiritually dead) can do himself and by his own strength for his own conversion.

### [2. How and When Grace Helps]

If, therefore, we have understood correctly your opinion, you state that the grace of God leads, on the one hand, because of the inherent weakness of a created being; on the other hand, our will and preference follows it [grace] not because we are forced, but because we have free will. And indeed the former is called the primary and most pleasing will and benevolence, being from God; while the second is called the secondary and conceding will resulting from us. You think, then, a man (himself being too weak to return to God by his own power), first moved by the primary divine grace, tends at the beginning to the good; and then the will of man enters which prefers the good and which knows how to seek after the desirable. This will exists for us so that we might be able to choose or reject, that is, the good which has been recommended and pointed out [to us]. Indeed, this is the way that the occasion is given to us to be saved by our will, which prefers the good rather than the evil, since the will would be able either to choose or to reject the good. Wherefore it is for this reason that indeed you make God the author of our conversion, and you declare the human will as the supplementar.

### [3. Grace Alone Works Out Repentance]

Therefore, we are of the opinion that man, that is to say, a man who has not been reborn or who is spiritually dead, for his own [conversion] is incapable of doing anything whatever for himself. And it is not only necessary that the grace of God precede, but ONLY it completes the entire work of the return to God. And we deny that there is power in the will of man of itself able to choose the good, since it is of God when he will return and be reborn. Hence, we say that man is not only too weak to make his own return, but also that he is completely incapable [of doing it]. Concerning the return of man [to God], we attribute everything solely to divine grace and absolutely nothing at all to our own ability or will.

### [4. Holy Scripture Works Out Repentance]

[298] And this opinion is best acknowledged by the Holy Scriptures. This will be made apparent when we observe carefully the steps by which our Lord takes up and finalizes our return. Let us consider [the case of] an ungodly person who lives an unrestrained and wicked life, but who returns again to Christ. This must be shown to him: that his mind has been corrupted in such a manner that he now takes pleasure in iniquities, and he rejects the good. He should be taught the Divine Law in order not only to overpower the innate perversity within himself, but also his evil practices which sentence him to physical and everlasting punishments. And unless the Lord touches his heart with the Holy Spirit, he will laugh

contemptuously and look with scorn upon those exhortations and threats. Or when the temptation is aroused in him by satan (which until then lay dormant, according to chapter 4 of Genesis), and when it increases greatly, and when he enrages the wrath of God against himself, he will fall miserably into despair, saying with Cain: "my crime is too great to be forgiven" [Gen 4:13].[21] Behold the power of man! See what tensions man has when he is abandoned by God on the one hand, or on the other when he depends entirely on himself. When a man is separated from the Holy Spirit, he cannot choose to follow either one of these on his own power. But on the contrary, because of the power of the Holy Spirit (by means of the Divine Word), truly, when his [man's] heart has been touched and becomes reformed as well as renewed to the end that he is persuaded to comply, he then will become conscious of his own sins by virtue of the Divine Law. And he will greatly blame himself, and he will be very displeased with himself, and he will seek a way by which he might escape everlasting condemnation, and, on the other hand, how he again might be reconciled to God. These thoughts are not the result of human ability, but arise from the activity of the Holy Spirit, who makes use of the ministry of the law and reproves sins, as when Christ witnessing Him said: "he [the Counselor] will convince the world concerning sin" [Jn 16:8]. For this purpose was the Law given according to Paul, "since through the law comes knowledge of sin" [Rom 3:20]. This, then, is the first step toward salvation.

[5. Knowledge of Sin Should Lead to Knowledge of Christ the Savior]

It does not indeed suffice the miserable sinner to become conscious of sins if he does not recognize Christ as the Savior. For if Christ is not [299] recognized, such consciousness of sins ends and may change into despair. Wherefore the Apostle [Paul] orders that the Corinthian who had seriously sinned be deemed worthy of grace and forgiveness, lest he be overwhelmed by excessive sorrow [cf. 2 Cor 2:5-7]. Indeed, the Gospel concerning Christ should be presented to the sinner who recognizes his sins and who trembles at the word of God [cf. Is 66:2] so that his contrite heart may be healed. He should be taught that the Father has placed the iniquities of us all upon the shoulders of the Son, "who was wounded for our transgressions," so that "with His stripes we are healed" [Is 53:5].

He should be shown: "the lamb of God, who takes away the sin of the world" [Jn 1:29]. He should be shown the serpent lifted up [by Moses in the wilderness] [cf. Jn 3:15] which becomes a typology of the Crucified Christ. And the repentant one should be exhorted to gaze intently upon the Savior Christ through eyes of faith so that he will not die an eternal death. The comforting thought of John the Apostle should be brought to his attention, "that the blood of Jesus His Son cleanses us from all sin" [1 Jn 1:17]. Beyond this should be the witness of Peter concerning Christ saying: "to him all the prophets bear witness that every one who believes in him receives forgiveness of sins through his name" [Acts 10:43].

And even if all these examples be continuously spoken into the ears of a man who has fallen and who is troubled by the realizations of the wrath of God, unless the Holy Spirit touches and illumines his heart on the condition that he not only must believe that they are true but also that he must put them into practice, he must make them part of himself and must truly be edified by them, then they will be spoken to him completely in vain and to no avail. For such a person may believe that all these things are indeed true, yet he is not sure that all apply to him as being greater than his offence against God, or when he dares to hope for forgiveness. And if, indeed, the Holy Spirit will stir up his heart and raise his hopes in the Savior Christ and make the Gospel of the absolution of sins echo in his heart, then indeed this man will be revived as if from [300] death and will approach Christ at the throne of grace as a suppliant; and he will attain remission of all sins which he has committed. Which of all these things come from man and have not rather been achieved by the All-Holy Spirit?

[6. Man Can Escape God, but Cannot Come to Christ Alone]

Therefore, a man who has yielded to his own particular ability, not being incited by the Spirit, may flee from God; but he cannot approach Christ. For the Lord distinctly says: "no one can come to me unless the Father who sent me draws him" [Jn 6:44]. Hence David prays: "create in me a clean heart, O God, and put a new and right spirit within me" [Ps 50:10]. And the Apostle Paul declares that man is dead in his own nature through his trespasses [cf. Eph 2:1]. Wherefore, just as a dead man cannot contribute in any way to raise himself up, in the same manner the sinner is not of himself able to return to God, but has need of divine power to rise from the death of sin before he could instinctively consider or choose anything good. (Christ says): "For apart from me you can do nothing" [Jn 15:5]. For were we not implanted into Him through faith, we could not bear fruit of ourselves [cf. Rom 7:4]; for we are dry and fruitless branches. "That which is born of the flesh is flesh" [Jn 3:6], as Christ says. Carnal man, then, not having been illuminated by the Spirit, although able to commit sin and also to accept as well as execute the carnal desires, is not able to choose the good (in spiritual matters); "for the mind that is set on the flesh is hostile to [the will of] God and [it does not submit to God's] law." And by nature we are "sold under sin" [Rom 7:14] and are its slaves; nor can we be free unless the Son sets us free [cf. Jn 8:32,, 33, 36]. Indeed, only when we believe in Christ can we become partakers of freedom. However, to believe in Him is not our own work, but it is the gift and work of God within us, according to Paul: "for it has been *granted* to you that for the sake of Christ, you should not only *believe in Him*, but also suffer for his sake" [Phil 1:29]. Indeed, for these reasons, most honorable Sir Patriarch, let us offer glory to God as beloved students of godliness in Christ who is the only author of our [301] return as well as of our salvation. Let us not from henceforth attribute anything, whatever it may be, to our own will. This [the will] does not take precedence as the creative cause for the return of man, otherwise the Scriptures would so state. Rather it [the will] is an object and a material thing in which the Holy Spirit acts by means of the ministry of the Divine Word. This much then concerns the conversion of man which is the second step of salvation.

### [7. Regenerated Man Attributes Achievement of Good to God's Grace (Rom 7:18-19)]

And now we consider what the nature of man is after the conversion, where it will become apparent also among those who have been reborn and who have been converted, that all the achievements are to be attributed to God and not to man (if, indeed, one considers [the matter] correctly). We would not deny that the person who has already been converted has the power to will the good, as the Apostle Paul said: "I can will what is right" [Rom 7:18]. But let us listen again to the same Apostle finishing what he started to say. He says: "but I cannot do it [the right]. For I do not do the good I want, but the evil I do not want is what I do" [Rom 7:18-19]. Oh, the weakness of free will, even for those who are worthy of returning [to God]! On the one hand, man is able to will the good; but on the other, he is not able to exercise it. Let us listen furthermore to the Apostle [Paul] who speaks concerning how great the power is to do good for those who have been renewed by regeneration. He said: "for I delight in the law of God, in my inmost self, but I see in my members another law at war with the law of my mind and making me captive to the law of sin which dwells in my members" [Rom 7:22-23].

The restored man, however, has the power to will the good in such a manner although he is not able to perform as much good as he would like. Where does the power come from to him who has already been restored to will the good and also to be able to perform the good? We will state this clearly again in the words of the same saint [Paul] rather than our own. He says: "God is at work in you, both to *will* and to *work* [Phil 2:13]. What then is our part in all this? Nothing. For the good that we will, God works in us. And what good we do consequently is not our work, rather it is that of God in us. Experience itself witnesses strongly that this is the way it is.

### [8. Even for the Regenerated, God Wills and Works the Good]

For the Lord did not say that He would withhold the guidance of the [302] Holy Spirit from us, and we would run aground in every sort of

(and whatever?) wickedness. David was contaminated by adultery as well
as by murder, and Peter denied by oath his own Savior, Christ. And yet,
what kind of men were they? Certainly not of the common lot, but of the
most illustrious, each of whom was regenerated and returned to the
Messiah Christ. Therefore, the Christian person is similar to a small child
who walks on very weak feet under the guidance of its father walking in
its own manner, and it falls down instantly when the father takes away
his hand from it. If, however, a man who has already been raised from
the death of sin and has returned to God cannot of himself will the good,
then even though God sets his heart in motion to will [the good], without
God's activation he [the Christian] is unable to perform it [the good].
What then would he who has not yet returned [to God] do, being still
under the death of sin? Behold this is the third step. Moreover, that
which moves our hearts not to scorn the divine threatenings is from
God. For us to believe in the Gospel is from God. To delight in the law of
God, when we have already returned to the Lord, is from God. To do
some good work is from God. We are not competent to reason
something of ourselves [cf. 2 Cor 3:4] as coming from us, since our com-
petence is from God. And yet these are not fictions of our mind. It is certainly clear to you, from where we have chosen the scriptural evidence,
that certain Holy Fathers worthy of admiration, indeed, luminaries of the
Church, have not escaped our notice, i.e., Chrysostom and Basil, who
have just so much free will to dispense on us as you also think it should
be dispensed. And it should be known that these most excellent [Fathers]
(and we ask that no anger should occur because of it), who were willing
to prove that man was not forced to commit sins, nor were they tempted
to justify themselves before God in order that they might not appear to
condemn man unjustly, proceeded somewhat beyond what was
necessary. Indeed, they do not demand of us to depend upon their
authority more than we should. Wherefore, for that reason, Most Holy
Reverend Sir, we will accept that teaching of ours which is prophetic and
apostolic. And we will support firmly that [teaching] which assigns to
[303] God perfect glory and honor and diminishes within us the wretched
humanoid. Therefore, let us not be fearful lest we, who think along these
lines, humiliate ourselves beyond moderation before the Almighty, supposing that we are bestowing on Him more honor than befits Him.

## [D.] CONCERNING JUSTIFICATION BY FAITH
## AND GOOD WORKS

It is greatly necessary, even more than anything else, to diligently seek
and to be fully informed concerning how we are justified before God so
that we will receive true justification which being armed with we might
stand steadfastly before the judgment [seat] of God. For no one is able to

condemn those who have been justified by God, as the Apostle [Paul] testifies in his Epistle to the Romans, chapter 8 [cf. 8:33]. Also in Romans, chapter 5 [is stated]: "therefore, since we are justified by faith, we have peace with God" [Rom 5:1].

Indeed, in the article concerning justification you have presented many things which for us also are beyond any doubt. Concerning these we shall now make a brief recapitulation, but later we shall consider [the points] where we are in disagreement.

### [1. Those in Agreement]

There is no doubt that we should make every effort in order not only seriously outwardly to live according to the commandments of God, but rather also to consider how best to conduct ourselves according to the Divine Law and spiritually in order not to transgress with our deeds and words, or even with the desires of the heart, the Law of God (which is spiritual and should be understood spiritually). The many exhortations of the Divine Apostles were made for this purpose to awaken in us [the desire] to do good works. We are pleased, indeed, to confess that they who do not perform good works are not sons of God. Indeed, we further concede that the good works should be done not out of arrogance or any such reason, but the virtues should minister to the glory of God and the welfare of [thy] neighbor. Again, it is irrefutable that everyday progress in true godliness, which is not contemptible, should be made. In addition to those, we teach that he who is subject to some human weakness, even if he has been overtaken by some transgression, should repent so that he [304] may be reconciled to God, and be more careful thereafter in order that we not be conquered by sin. Moreover, we often cry out to our listeners that the faith which does not result in good deeds and works is not a true faith. For how could a tree be sound which does not bear good fruit [cf. Mt 7:16]? Neither do we say that a faith which thus remains fruitless of virtues pleases God, just as, indeed, we agree with you that works without faith also displease Him. Yes, indeed, we unite together in an indissoluble bond of faith, hope and love; and we believe that one who is lacking one of these is not a Christian either. "And without faith it is impossible to please him [God]" [Heb 11:6], according to the saying by the Apostle [Paul] in Hebrews, chapter 11; and without hope no one is able to be saved or to escape the evil of despair. Furthermore, if someone would speak in the tongues not only of men, but also of angels, but not have love, what would such a person be but either "a noisy gong" or "a clanging cymbal," as it is written in First Corinthians, chapter 13 [1 Cor 13:1].

### [2. Saint Paul Versus Saint James on Justification]

Moreover, the belief is credible which says that it is understood from works (to the degree that it is possible by human reason to know concerning man) who are the ones justified in faith before God, just as surely as we conclude that a tree is sound by its good fruits [cf. Mt 7:16]. Saint James also was of this opinion when he declared: "that a man is justified by works" [Js 2:24]. But if according to the passage [in your answer] his words should be understood [as you do], they would be diametrically opposed to what was written by Paul. But he [James] has not used either the [word] faith, nor [the word] righteousness by name with the same meaning as Paul. Therefore, in view of the fact that among the sacred words nowhere is there seen such a discord and strife of meanings, it is not becoming to accuse the Adelphotheos [Saint James] of corrupting the thought of Paul. Undoubtedly, he wished to weaken the false opinion of the hypocrites who thought that faith is any knowledge of the life of Christ; and furthermore, they boasted of a faith without works. Saint [James] then, correcting their error, points out that if they only boast of a faith in events of history, they will not advance [spiritually] more than the demons [cf. Js 2:19] who also know the deeds and the [holy] passion of Christ.

### [3. Foolish To Magnify Works by Leaving Out Faith]

[305] Moreover, it is a foolish boasting to magnify works at the expense of faith. Rather, then, it is necessary to do this just as the tree is recognized from the fruits [cf. Mt 7:16f]; so also justifying faith, which is hidden in the heart, must be measured by the evident righteousness of a good conscience just as a man is known to be alive from his breathing. And these things are clearly seen from the words of the Apostles. He [James] says: "show me your faith apart from your works, and I by my works will show you my faith" [Js 2:18]. He also presents as an example the holy Abraham, who was so ready to serve the Lord [cf. Js 2:21] that he would not even spare His only-begotten, by which his faith was tested and became manifest.

### [4. Justification by Faith in Reconciliation with God]

But on the other hand again, when the beatified Paul speaks concerning righteousness, he handles it as something else. For he seeks at least not that we might appear justified in any way before men, but how we might be reconciled to God so that He will forgive our sins, make us His sons, and enroll us as heirs of the heavenly kingdom. This, then, is what justification according to a holy person means, that is, when God does not reckon us [cf. Ps 32:2] as if we were sinners, but brings us justified before Him. Therefore, the context of Romans 4 leads to this [conclusion] saying: "so also David pronounces a blessing upon the man to whom God reckons righteousness apart from works: 'blessed are those whose iniquities are forgiven, and whose sins are covered; blessed is the man against whom the Lord will not reckon his sin, etc.' " [Rom 4:6-8; cf. Ps 32:1-2]. For we know with Paul that a man who is judged and reckoned as just before God has received remission of sins and life everlasting [cf. Rom 3:24f] through faith. This we believe and confidently hold: that Christ has fulfilled the Law on our behalf and by His passion has blotted out our sins and, indeed, through faith alone without the works of the Law, whether being inspired spiritually within or externally displayed. This is our opinion which is based upon the most clear and sure witness of the Scriptures. For the beatified Paul in this manner publicly addressed the Antiochians in Pisidia concerning Christ in chapter 13 of Acts:

> Let it be known to you therefore, brethren, that through this man [Jesus] forgiveness of sins is proclaimed to you, and *by Him* (Christ) [306] *everyone that believes* is freed from everything from which you could not be freed by the law of Moses [Acts 13:38-39].

Also, in the 10th chapter of Acts concerning Christ Peter said: "to him all the prophets bear witness *that everyone who believes in Him receives forgiveness* of sins through his name" [Acts 10:43]. And in like manner, Christ concerning himself, in John 3 [says]: "for God so loved the world that he gave his only begotten Son, that *whoever believes* in Him should not perish, but have eternal life" [Jn 3:16]. Even Paul also excludes the works of the Law, whatever they might happen to be, from justification by faith, saying in the 3rd chapter of Romans: "for we hold that a man is justified by faith, *apart from works of law*" [Rom 3:28]. What could be said more clearly and more brilliantly than that? Observe, Your Holiness, Most Reverend Sir, that Paul is assigning to faith [the attribute] that it justifies. Observe that Peter is assigning to faith [the attribute] that it confers on man the forgiveness of sins. Observe that Christ is assigning to faith [the distinction] that He makes us sharers of eternal life. Observe that Paul excludes the works of the law whether spiritual or carnal, regardless of the matter of justification. And since in Paul it is the same to be saved and to be justified (as the passage which has been cited concerning the sanctification of man indicates), we see this very great Apostle separate justification with such great clarity from all works and, on the other hand, sanction faith alone. He says: "for by grace you have been saved *through faith*; and this is not your own doing (it is *the gift* of God), *not because of works*, lest any man should boast" [Eph 2:8-9]. The above, therefore, we thus simply know and state concerning the justification of sinful man by God.

### [5. Jeremiah's Argument]

Let us now compare this with your opinion which is as follows:

Perfecting, as far as it is possible, the Law according to the spirit...

we shall be justified...But the others, who worship according to the physical aspect of the Law, completely fall away from divine grace, not receiving the perfection of the grace of the spiritual Law which cleanses the mind from every taint.[22]

And on another page:

The Word [Logos] of God by His love for mankind has set us free [307] by becoming man. He also has given commands that one should not contemplate that which is against nature, nor commit sins, but desist as much as possible and hold fast to virtues and the commandments. And if something human chances to happen, cast it off and hasten to subject the evil to the good and to enslave the flesh under the spirit by virtue and exercise of the good.[23]

And again after some pages: "for it is impossible for one, then, to find consolation there [future life] who has not been cleansed from his sins in this present life."[24] Thus, indeed, Your Holiness, is the above contained word for word in your writing.

## [6. A Bad Tree Cannot Bear Good Fruits]

How then these statements can agree with the scriptural references we have cited we are not able, for our part, to see. And how would it be possible for us, who are perfecting the Law, that is, performing good works, to become perfectly just while, indeed, we truly do not practice good works anymore if we were not already justified? For "nor can a bad tree bear good fruit" [Mt 7:18], as Christ himself indeed bears witness. For in what manner could he, who has not yet become righteous, nor reborn, nor yet been raised from the death of sin, act justly? And if one has not yet been reconciled, how could works please God? Because it is necessary for a man to please God first before his works could please Him. Therefore, we are not able to become perfectly just in the presence of God or be justified through perfection in the Law. However, it is necessary for us to be perfectly just rather than to be justified through faith before perfecting the Law according to the Spirit.

## [7. God's Law Cannot Completely Accomplish Justification]

But yet it is not possible for us to perfect the Law of God according to the Spirit, nor fulfill it spiritually. For according to Paul: "the law is spiritual" [Rom 7:14], demanding of us not only obedience which appears externally and dignified manners which even the pagans might display, but also that the entire mind within us be applied and conform to the Divine Law to such a degree that not even our intentions and thoughts, in which there is no good, be expressed. Since God especially looks steadfastly at the heart, certainly neither do the secret things of our hearts escape Him. Wherefore, He [God] does not consider that the Law is to be perfected by the person who now only seems to live blamelessly, but in the meantime whose soul is secretly scorched by impious passions even though he might have been reborn and this unwillingly happens to him.

[8. The Law Promises Life for Those Who Completely Obey It]

[308] If, therefore, we would wish to be justified by the perfection of the Law, in very truth the possibility of our salvation will have vanished. For the Law does not promise life to those who will keep some of its details, or to those who will fulfill the whole body of the Law. On the contrary, it [the Law] threatens an eternal curse on all who will not give themselves up completely to obedience to the Law. It states: "cursed be everyone who does not abide *by all* things written in the book of the Law, and *do* them" [Dt 27:26; cf. Gal 3:10]. Also, James [says]: "for whoever keeps the whole law but fails in one point has become guilty of all of it" [Js 2:10]. Consequently, those who are seeking to be justified by God through the fulfillment of the Law shall not receive justification from the Law, but a curse. Whence, it follows that we should take refuge in the grace and mercy of God so that we might be freely justified through faith in Christ, but not through works of the Law. Moreover, for instance, the Law says: "you shall love the Lord your God with all your heart, and with all your soul, and with all your mind. This is the great and first commandment" [Mt 22:37; cf. Dt 6:5]. But who among men (with the exception of Christ) has ever been found able (unless, perhaps, he has thus not known himself) to say that he has completely loved God in this manner? And not being able to achieve the first and great commandment, how could we be justified by perfecting the Law? How could one love God with all his heart, and with all his soul, and with all his mind when he has not yet been reconciled to God, when he has not yet been justified, when he has not yet been renewed with the Spirit of God? For even those who have been reborn and justified in this age do not have such perfect love. If, then, the mind which is set on the flesh is hostile to God [cf. Rom 8:7], by what device can a man who thinks in terms of the flesh, who has not yet been converted, who has not yet been justified, who hates God, love Him? And if he does not love God but hates Him, in what way can he fulfill the Law? And if he does not fulfill the Law, let some one say in what way can he be justified by the Law. For our love is not the source of faith, but rather faith (in which we believe that God will expiate us [309] through Christ) is the source of love, so that God is loved by us for this reason that He first loved us. For John expresses it thus: "we love [Him] because he first loved us" [1 Jn 4:19]. Therefore, from what has been said it is concluded that it is impossible for a man to be rendered just before God by the power of the Law if, indeed, he cannot fulfill the

first commandment; neither can he fulfill all the others [command-ments].

### [9. Works of the Law Are a Step toward Grace]

If, however, the Lord sometimes sends men to the Law (who are asking what they have to do to inherit eternal life [cf. Lk 10:25]), He does not do this with the intention that we might be justified by completely keeping the commandments of the Law. But rather He was contriving that they recognize their own sins and their indifference to the Law. And then when they have firmed up many of their failings and are convinced of their own righteousness, they might take refuge in the Mediator Christ. For this reason not only did He send them to the Law, but very often He spoke concerning himself, saying: "*whoever believes in me* [shall]...*have eternal life*" [Jn 3:16; cf. 1 Jn 5:11], by which words He assigns [us] to seek salvation not by the keeping of the Law, but by believing in Him.

### [10. Christ Alone Works Salvation and Not Man's Good Works]

In addition to all this, it is a matter lacking merit that our salvation be divided between us and Christ, as if we are able to absolve our own sins together with God in such a manner that a part of the achievement of the Mediator Christ would be attributed to us, also, and that it might happen to be said that we would in some way also be saviors, which would be an extreme absurdity. For the honor is owed *only* to the Mediator Christ and absolutely to no one else. For He himself says through the Prophet Isaiah thus: "*I, I am he*, who blots out your transgressions for my own sake, and I will not remember your sins" [Is 43:25]. Certainly no one of us is He and *I*, who speaks through the Prophet. Christ alone is the Mediator and He who blots out the sins. We are also taught the same by the Apostle John who said that: "*the blood of Jesus Christ* his Son [of God], cleanses us from all sin" [1 Jn 1:7, KJV]. And lest one consider only the pristine transgression and not the personal sins, let him hear from [310] the same [Saint John], who shortly afterwards adds the following: "my little children, I am writing this to you, so that you may not sin; but if anyone does sin, we have an advocate with the Father, Jesus Christ the righteous; and *he is the expiation* for our sins, and not for ours only but also the sins *of the whole world*" [1 Jn 2:1-2]. Therefore, by no means, Sir, Most Holy Patriarch, do we ascribe to man any power whatsoever to atone for sins, save only to the God-man Christ. Nor anyone else, who may shine by whatever great purity of life, would we seat upon the throne of Christ; for we acknowledge Him, the One and only *expiator* [cf. Rom 3:24f], "whom God put forward as an expiation by his blood to be received by faith" [Rom 3:25], "that whoever believes in him should not perish but have eternal life" [Jn 3:16].

[11. Conclusion: Justification Witnessed by the Lamp of Scriptures]

This is our opinion, All-Holy Sir, concerning justification by faith and good works. In this opinion we follow not by reckonings of appearances, nor by proofs of logic, nor by superfluous syllogisms; but rather we follow the lamp of the Word of God. Nor do we reject the exhortations of the Holy Fathers and preachers of the spirit, but in truth we highly honor them, inasmuch as they closely follow the God-inspired Scriptures. But above all, we harken to Him who is our overseer, concerning whom the Father proclaimed: "this is my beloved Son, with whom I am well pleased: *listen to him*" [Mt 17:5]. Moreover, we also listen to His Apostles concerning whom He said: "he who hears you *hears me*" (Lk 10:16]. We hope that those Holy Fathers whose testimonies you have cited thought better in their mind than what they sometimes uttered in words, when they stirred to use a stronger word in reference to good works. We also urge our congregation, frequently and wholeheartedly, and exhort and persuade them to demonstrate their faith by good practices and virtues; but if they do not fall back upon divine grace, they will be destroyed forever. And even though all do not travel the journey by equal steps in accordance with piety and virtuous manners, yet we feel that our ministry is not fruitless, while God is giving the increase in which the chosen are eager in their souls concerning true guilelessness and piety.

[311]          [E.] CONCERNING THE SACRAMENTS

[Careful Discernment of Traditions]

It is apparent to us from your treatise in the chapter concerning the sacraments of the Church that you have greater regard for the traditions of the Church which you have received by succession, from hand to hand; and nothing of all that you have inherited from your fathers do you willingly concede. Moreover, we ourselves also think that it is not outside the sphere of rudeness, or rather to say impiety, that some refuse to practice or quietly neglect that which has been handed down piously and correctly by those before us. Yet we are justified to make a discernment between traditions so that some [traditions] would not creep in under this respected name which have not been ordered by the Apostles, nor by those who immediately succeeded them, but have crept into the Church of God gradually by human self-made religion. For we are able to find such traditions and ethos in the Church from some hints in the Holy Scriptures which we understand were in use even at the time of the Apostles in the Early Church. These we do not reject at all, but we gladly practice them if indeed they are useful to the needs of our time. In view of this, moreover, we are not unaware that even after the [time of the] Apostles, by good intention, it was necessary to enact many laws in the Church which served well those particular times. Indeed, there were good reasons for such enactments. We neither condemn them, nor do we profanely reject them. However, just as those very good men who ordered such rules did not have in mind to establish eternal laws for all later generations, we also think that it is our duty to use Christian freedom in these matters and not to take on the yoke of abiding by them as entirely necessary. Indeed, it often happens that the Church is burdened more than is necessary by traditions and is not only sinking, but lately the most important and rather indispensable traditions are deemed less than worthy of keeping and practicing so that the people who are dealing with incidentals will do the work less skillfully and carelessly. Yes, indeed, some traditions have been inserted into the Church not because they are Apostolic, but rather because they adversely oppose the teaching of the Old and New [Testaments] and the examples of the Prophets, as well [312] as of Christ and the Apostles. Concerning these we will comment later when we come to the appropriate place. Therefore, to dismiss and to void such traditions is a matter of piety worthy of praise and God-pleasing; it is a correction and a reforming of our churches. We do not disregard such traditions as a desire for innovation, certainly not; but since we cannot accept them in good conscience and practice them, we have banished them from our churches, just as we do not again depend upon those traditions which contain nothing impious yet are not based upon the cornerstone of the Divine Word. We are truly afraid lest, even though out of conviction we shall not build upon them, the time might somehow come when this will cause our conscience to fall into conflict; nor do we doubt that our harkening and obedience would not be accepted by the God of all if we would diligently strive to practice the traditions which He himself left for us which are inscribed in each of the Testaments and which concern all who follow.

## [1] Concerning Baptism

### [a. Three Sprinklings Versus Three Immersions]

We learn from your previous treatise that there is an ethos indeed among the Eastern Churches to baptize by three immersions. And we in the Western Churches sprinkle water thrice on the baptized, but we have not been accustomed to immerse in water. Nevertheless, we do not find fault with your usage, just as we have no doubt concerning the ancient origin of that ethos. And although in some of the northern churches in Germany some sixty years ago, more or less, the same method of baptizing was in common use, we do not sanction it since it was voided by some there. However, if such custom was practiced among us, we would not change it, but we would continue it. Moreover, among our churches (insofar as is known from the memory of the elders and from those who have reliably recorded the ecclesiastical events) the custom prevailed for many hundreds of years that the candidates for baptism were not immersed into the water, but that water was poured or they were sprinkled three times (that is, in the name of the Father and of the Son and of the [313] Holy Spirit). And if, indeed, we would consider stopping it [the method of triple sprinkling] and introduce the triple immersion instead, we would perhaps cause a great scandal among those who were baptized up to the present time differently and would suspect that they were not baptized correctly, nor even brought into the Church of Christ lawfully. Therefore, either they would feel doubtful concerning their own salvation, or they would want to repeat the baptism. If the former, then they might be inclined to scorn the divine name (which was invoked at baptism); if the latter, it would offer the occasion for complete despair. And yet according to the peculiar nature of the middle ground, being neither good nor bad insofar as it is put to use by the Christian freedom, a few would be scandalized; but many more would be edified, even though fortified by true faith and piety.

[b. No Difference between Immersion and Sprinkling]

Nevertheless, we believe this to be a neutral and moot question, whether one is baptized by three immersions or three pourings. For nothing is clear and certain either in [the words] of Christ or the Apostles that this should be taken as a command in those books which have uncontested authority (for a Christian man, who does not have illicit thoughts). Moreover, this sacrament is not debased in the least, nor are the essentials in it decreased whether, indeed, the candidate for baptism is sprinkled by water or, indeed, is immersed into water. For the element of the sacrament remains, indeed, so that man is baptized by *water* and not by wine or any other liquid, and the word of the Lord also remains so that the baptism is administered in the name of the Father and of the Son and of the Holy Spirit. Therefore, with us the ceremony is completely and exactly according to the ordinance of Christ, and a person is reborn of *water* and Spirit in the manner concerning it in which we were initiated by the Savior. Therefore, we are of the opinion that it is not right that the difference in the manner concerning baptism, which certainly in no way destroys the essence of the sacrament, provides an occasion for schism among those who bear the name of Christ. And if you seek, you might perhaps find in the very ancient Greek books the practices which show that to dip has not only been said concerning immersion, but also concerning sprinkling. However, concerning the external [form] and the improvisation of this ceremony, as we also said above, we shall give ac- [314] count to no one; and we would hope that there would be no further grave doubt among the Christians concerning matters of religion. To that extent further, we do not doubt that we, who believe in the Savior Christ and thrice (we say in the name of the Father and of the Son and of the Holy Spirit) have been sprinkled by water, are recognized by you as being truly baptized Christians and not required to be regenerated by a second baptism.

### [2.] Concerning Chrismation

[a. Chrismation Not Clearly Mentioned in Holy Scriptures (Jn 2:20, 27)]
Insofar as what concerns chrismation [confirmation], let us hope, Most Honorable Master, that we might be able to agree together as easily concerning it [chrismation] and with baptism. You state that you not only use chrismation, but you also find it to be greatly beneficial and you perform it. Wherefore, you literally say thus: "we are anointed with the chrism so that we might become communicants with the royal chrism of deification." The words indeed are a few, but you know, being most wise, what great meaning they express. However, we would not assign such meanings to chrismation. And for what reason? Because the Divine Word teaches nothing concerning chrismation, much less would He affirm that it has such power. John the Evangelist, it is true, makes mention of chrismation when he says: "you have been anointed by the Holy One" [1 Jn 2:20], and a little later [when he says]: "the anointing which you received from him abides in you" [1 Jn 2:27]. But know that the Apostle says this not concerning the anointing with oil, but concerning the Holy Spirit with whom all who are indeed Christians have been anointed that they might attain the kingdom of heaven. Moreover, the anointing with oil has nowhere been attested to in the New Testament, nor do they deny it; and not only do they agree that Paul had written nothing concerning it, but they also do not in any way connect the institution of chrismation with Christ or any Apostle. And among other things you say thus: "indeed, the Church of Christ, progressing by His grace, has *discovered* much in the divine utterances and foundations with which she has been adorned," etc.[25]

### [b. Chrismation—An Invention of the Church]
From these words it becomes clear that chrismation is an *invention* of the Church. Therefore, just as it is permitted to the Church to institute something for purposes of discipline within it, in like manner it was never [315] granted to it to form new sacraments or new forms of worship. And the human inventions are ill spoken of in the Scriptures. For the Lord has most severely declared to neither add to His Word, nor to take away from it [cf. Mt 5:18; Rev 22:18f]. Nor again must it be thought that the whole Church should be forever led by that which was invented by some self-appointed religious persons and on pretense of a divine and spiritual revelation were stealthily ushered into the Church. For what is necessary for its [the Church] salvation has all been revealed in the Holy

Scriptures and has been emphatically commanded by Christ and the Apostles.

### [c. Chrismation Is Not Witnessed by Christ or Apostles, Therefore Not Necessary]

Therefore, since chrismation has neither witness nor example from Christ or from the Apostles, it is clearly not necessary for salvation. Neither do we have the conviction that some gift of the Holy Spirit is given to us through chrismation. Why then would we convince ourselves of this, not having the word of God, proclaiming such a thing by anointing with chrismation? Wherever, therefore, there is no divine proclamation, neither is there room for a true conviction. And they who are convinced by a person without the promissory word (because of this) are tempting God rather than honoring Him. Indeed, we would not be able to receive any benefit from the baptism, or from the Lord's Supper, or proclaim it for ourselves unless these ceremonies were from God and constituted by the manifest word of God. Therefore, we think that we do not harm the salvation of our souls, even if we should omit chrismation, if in the meantime we gladly receive those sacraments which God has clearly ordered.

### [d. Tradition of Chrismation by Pseudo-Dionysios]

Regarding that Dionysios the Areopagite who holds and recommends that chrismation is an Apostolic tradition, we say [that] we are not unaware that a Dionysios Areopagite became a holy man (who is mentioned in the Acts of the Apostles [17:34]) and was a disciple of Apostle Paul, who while teaching in Athens converted him to Christ. But that this Dionysios who became a disciple of Paul has written the book which bears the name of Dionysios, we are not able to put it in our mind to [316] believe it. For Clement of Alexandria, who lived many generations after Dionysios the Areopagite who was a disciple of Paul [cf. Acts 17:34], is referred to in that book. It is certain, therefore, that this book was written by another person who lived after the time of Clement of Alexandria. Moreover, there are also many things in that book which contribute little to the true knowledge of God and to piety, and he who has written profusely concerning ceremonies and customs is superfluous. Moreover, if the details are carefully examined, it will easily be seen that it was not motivated by the teacher Paul, whose epistles are entirely different from this book of Dionysios. Therefore, we beseech Your Holiness, All-Holy Sir, to accept without disagreement our sincerely truthful frankness. For the above was said out of necessity, not out of insolence toward anyone, but merely to set forth the truth.

### [e. Synods and Fathers Do Not Claim Chrismation a Sacrament]

Moreover, the Synods of Laodicia and Carthage have no such authority so as to enable you to either institute a new sacrament or to confirm it, which was neither ordered by Christ nor by His Apostles. Chrysostom, an otherwise holy man and a most powerful speaker by common opinion and custom which had already been deeply rooted in the Church and brought forth as if by a torrent, also accepted chrismation. And accordingly, since the piety of this man has been recognized, if in his time a correction and purification of religious matters would have been proposed for the purpose of washing out human innovations which crept into the Church but had been again rejected, there is no doubt among us that he [Chrysostom], being of such God-pleasing character, would simply not oppose; but rather he would take up the work, advance it, and strive with all his power to perfect it.

### [f. Old Testament Anointings: A Prefigure of the Holy Spirit]

Further, the anointings of the Old Testament did not mean chrismation with oil; but they prefigured the more rich gifts of the Holy Spirit, some of which are common to all Christians, while some others are directed toward those whose toils the Lord uses for particular callings for the edification of the Church. And still others [were given] more wonderful gifts, such as those distributed to the Apostles on the day of Pente-
[317] cost and later to some others for the establishment of the teachings of the Gospel. Wherefore, the anointings of the Old [Testament] do not refer to the New [Testament]. Indeed, in the Old [Testament] they were shadows of what is to come, according to the Apostle [Paul]; and in the New [Testament] they were the body itself [cf. Col 2:17; cf. Heb 10:1]. Therefore, we should not in the least leave the body to pursue the shadows today and begin or look for new anointings without the Divine Word.

### [g. The Holy Spirit Is Granted through Baptism]

Indeed, not even for this reason are men deprived of the grace of the Holy Spirit, even if they do not make use of the anointing with oil. For the Spirit is given through baptism. Therefore, the Apostle [Paul] also calls baptism not only the "washing of regeneration," but lo, "*and renewal in the Holy Spirit*" [Tit 3:5]. As to the granting to us of the Holy Spirit at baptism, we also are renewed by Him [Holy Spirit]. And indeed, also, as we listen to and eagerly study day by day the word of God, the gifts of the Spirit increase in us; and as we continually and fervently pray, the grace of God increases, according to Christ: "if you then, who are evil, know how to give good gifts to your children, how much more will the heavenly Father give the Holy Spirit to those who ask him!" [Lk 11:13].

By grace, then, we know God through the Word and the two sacraments which were instituted by Christ, who abundantly gives us everything necessary for our salvation. However, all others which are not founded on the Divine Word, we omit without offending anyone or sinning.

### [3.] Concerning the Lord's Supper

#### [a. Agree That the Body and Blood of Christ Should Not Be Given Separately]

And we agree with you in this: that you believe the body and the blood of Christ are truly present in the Holy Eucharist. And we point out that we rejoice greatly for those who believe concerning this sacrament by human reasoning rather than by the Word of God and who suppose that the body as well as the blood of the Lord are far removed from Holy Communion; for they cannot comprehend in their own mind how Christ is, for instance, at the same time in heaven and on earth. Thus, indeed, [318] we believe that the body and the blood of Christ are truly eaten and drunk together with the bread and the wine in the Holy Supper so that, however, the bread and the wine are not up to this time changed. For the Apostle Paul calls that sacrament "bread" saying: "as often as you eat this bread" [1 Cor 11:26]. And a little later [He says]: "whoever, therefore, eats the bread or drinks the cup of the Lord in an unworthy manner" [1 Cor 11:27]. Therefore, we have learned from the Apostle that the gifts of the bread and wine retain their own essence so that indeed he who eats this bread, truly eats at the same time the body of Christ; and he who drinks the wine from the cup, truly drinks at the same time the blood of Christ. Saint Irenaios, a man of the most ancient writers of the Church, whose teacher was the All-Holy Polycarp, who in turn became a disciple of John the Evangelist, accepted the words of Paul with this meaning. Wherefore, this Irenaios, among the saints, says that the Holy Eucharist consists of two realities: one from earth and the other from heaven. And indeed, that from the earth he understands as the species of bread and wine; and that from heaven, as the body and blood of Christ.[26]

#### [b. The Bread and Wine Are Unchanged but Are Carriers of the Real Body and Blood of Christ

Wherefore, just as in baptism the substance of the water is not changed but the grace of the Holy Spirit is present together with the water and acts to regenerate, so it also occurs in the Lord's Supper. The substance of the bread and wine remains unchanged; but together with the bread and wine the body and blood of Christ are present and distributed not only to those who are worthy, but also to those who are unworthy. Indeed, in this manner it is done so that (as the Apostle witnesses) both receive the body and blood: the former, the worthy ones to salvation, while the latter, the unworthy ones to condemnation. In addition, it is indeed known by everyone that the Word of God receives His own body from the flesh and from the blood of the most blessed Virgin Mary. If, however, the bread should be changed into the body of Christ and the wine into the blood of Christ, the Lord might run the risk of having two bodies, the one received from the flesh and the blood of the Ever-Virgin and the other which was transubstantiated from bread and wine. Moreover, if such a change should happen to occur, it would follow from this that whatever might happen to the bread and the wine in the Holy Supper, it would be imperative that the same change might happen to occur in the body and blood of Christ.

[c. Irrational Consequences of Change into the Real Body
and Blood of Christ]

Certainly in the same manner, as we say, if indeed a part of the bread [319] which was sanctified should be thrown into the fire (which has been maliciously done by impious persons, as is witnessed by history), the body of Christ would be consumed by fire. However, if the wine should be poured out from the cup and swallowed up by the earth, the blood of Christ would be spilled [sacreligiously] and swallowed up by the earth; and in either case it is an absurdity. Yet by expressing it in this manner, we in no way deny that the body and blood of Christ is truly present in the Holy Eucharist. For in this, being supported by the Divine Word, we vehemently oppose those among us who speak against it. For we truly believe that the bread and wine are present together with the body and blood of the Lord and are distributed to all the communicants. For then, indeed, at that time the Lord's body and blood are distributed when we conform to this commandment of Christ: "Eat ye, drink ye." And when it is not eaten nor drunk, then we believe that the bread and the wine have not been united mystically with the body and blood of Christ, for without this utilization the bread and wine in themselves are not sacraments.

[d. The Water in Wine in the Eucharest Is Not Witnessed in Scriptures
Nor by the Apostles]

You, moreover, are also accustomed to mixing water with the wine in the cup which we omit. For the Gospel writes, and Paul who described the Holy Supper has made no mention of water, whatsoever. Indeed, we think that it is more appropriate to the [underlying] meaning not to mix in water. For just as the more pure and undiluted the wine is, the more it delights the hearts of those who drink it, in the same manner is the blood of Christ, just as in the case of the most undiluted wine which truly gladdens and revives our souls. For mixed wine is not highly praised in the Holy Scriptures as the Prophet says: "your wine mixed with water" [Is 1:22]. Nevertheless, we say this with the following thought: that it is necessary to seek in Holy Communion the recovery and cure of the body, and not that one is impious if he should mix a little water with wine, but rather that we might give the reason for which we hold the opinion that such a mixture is not necessary, since there is no mention of it in the Scriptures.

[e. Leavened Bread Versus Unleavened Bread (cf. 1 Cor 5:5)]

[320] Similar to this is your use of leavened bread in the preparation of the Holy Eucharist, while we use unleavened bread. And you, indeed, are of the opinion that the leavened is truly and correctly called bread, as if it is not proper to call the unleavened rightfully bread. And we say that the flour which has been mixed with water and kneaded truly becomes bread, whether mixed with leaven or not; for otherwise the Israelites would not be eating bread throughout all the Passover because it is not allowed to offer leavened bread. Moreover, since our Pascha is Christ, that True Lamb, who in the Holy Supper becomes our meat, we with good reason use unleavened bread not only to remind ourselves of the faultlessness and purity of that heavenly bread, but forthwith also so that we may be alerted to cleanse the old leaven of evil and wickedness and then celebrate the Passover with the unleavened bread of sincerity and truth at the exhortation of Paul [cf. 1 Cor 5:5f]. Certainly not for any reason whatever would we wish to quarrel with anyone over this. We are merely concerned that one will hold the correct opinion concerning the essence and the use of the Christ-instituted Supper.

[4.] Concerning Ordination or Priesthood

[a. Ordination Not Numbered among the Sacraments]

We do not number the ordination of the ministers of the Church (for thus we call our priests) among the sacraments which have been instituted by God to assure the faith of each person who believes in Christ (concerning the forgiveness of sins and life everlasting). However, we do not allow anyone the authority to teach in church or to administer the sacraments if they have not been called rightfully into the ministry of the Church and granted the necessary gifts concerning the sacred duties. We are aware, further, that the Church of God cannot be instituted without suitable ministers. For it is declared by the Apostle [Paul] that they should be stewards of the sacraments of God. Just as there is need of a steward or a master for those in the house, in like manner the Church also has need of ministers [cf. 1 Cor 4:1f]. Therefore, again it is apparent [321] that God works through the service of the ministers so that persons return to the Lord to be justified, to be reborn, to become rich in good works, to endure the temptations and sorrows calmly, and to be saved when they die, provided that the churchmen perform their duties proper-

ly and neither adulterate the teaching of the Divine Word, nor become
sluggish concerning their own duties.

### [b. Piety and Education Needed for Ordination]

Moreover, we examine their education as well as their gifts and their
manner of life. Then we determine whether to allow them to teach and to
administer the holy sacraments. Nor do we assign them to churches
before they are found to be approved. Furthermore, they are installed in
the churches by prayers, which are made in prescribed words which are
heard by all over him, who shall minister to the church and who also with
bended knee prays alone that he receives the Holy Spirit to set him with
God over all the church as befits his calliing. And he is earnestly ordered,
while the entire assembly is listening, to execute his work faithfully,
diligently, and faultlessly so that in time he will be able to give an account
before His judgment seat to the Chief Shepherd, Jesus Christ. In addition to this, appropriate psalms and hymns are piously offered for the
work at hand, and the overseer (with some of the pastors of the church
who are present) place hands upon him, according to the practice of the
Ancient Church. In this manner he [the candidate] is consecrated in the
Lord and God on the condition that he henceforth diligently care for His
Church. We omit the anointing and the other customs since we find
nothing of the sort in the Book of Acts of the Apostles, although in this
book not only once, but many times there is mention made of how the
ministers of the churches were ordained. We doubt if the ordination of
ministers has need of their great attention (of which no great multitude is
found), unless a description of them would have been left by the
Apostles, who indeed ordered what is proper to be done in the Church
even for lesser matters, and undoubtfully in the Acts [of the Apostles],
would be seen an example of such [anointing]. We, indeed, acquiesing
with the customs that the truly Ancient Church practiced, do not doubt,
[322] but believe, that our ministers of the holies have been canonically
called, ordained, and sanctified by our Lord Jesus Christ to feed his
flock, even though the external oil has not been applied, but only the oil
of the Holy Spirit which is not deficient in them.

### [5.] Concerning Marriage

### [Marriage Not Numbered among the Sacraments]

Nothing in this chapter differs from your teaching as understood by
us, save this: that we do not understand what proof you offer from the
Scriptures so as to validly call marriage a sacrament, since there is not a
trace of it there. Neither is there a confirmation made as in the true
sacraments where the forgiveness of sins and the grace of God takes
place. And if in Ephesians 5 Paul calls it [marriage] a great mystery, he

understands it symbolically, comparing Christ and the Church to marriage, as the words of the Apostle bear witness when he says: "this is a great mystery, and I take it to mean Christ and the Church" [Eph 5:32].

### [6.] Concerning Penance

#### [a. Confession Not Numbered among the Sacraments]
Your Holiness declares that the component parts of repentance are the return, the confession of sins committed, and withdrawal from the evil. Moreover, you think that the monastic figure is included in the sacrament of penance. What we know concerning all of this we shall make clear with brief testimonies which are in harmony with the Scriptures.

It is, indeed, quite definite that there is a great need for repentance. For the impenitent "are storing up wrath for [them] yourselves on the day of wrath when God's righteous judgment will be revealed. For he will render to every man according to his works" [Rom 2:5-6]. And Christ, when hearing of the murder of some Galileans, said: "But unless you repent you will all likewise perish" [Lk 13:3]. And true repentance is the return to God of those who are exceedingly doubtful among us. For those who turn their backs on the Lord [cf. Jer chs. 2 and 32] (according to the expression of Scripture) and pursue their own contrivances and the desires of the flesh (neglecting in the meantime the word and the com- [323] mandments of God) are entering by the wide way that leads to destruction [cf. Mt 7:13]. Therefore, all whosoever with the prodigal son [cf. Lk 15:11f] return to the heavenly Father, asking with humility of heart for forgiveness of sins, shall obtain salvation. Indeed, we seek such a return to God (as does Your Holiness, also) together with such a true conviction in the divine mercy that the Father in heaven, through the Mediator Christ, will freely grant us forgiveness of our sins; and we will be received again into grace. For those who have truly repented for committing sins, but who lack the courage to receive pardon, are in danger of having hopelessness hang over them. Also, they who afterwards refrain from committing evil, but who hesitate to ask for forgiveness, do not love God, but from the depth of the heart despise Him. Hence, they do not truly perform good works which are pleasing to God, but that which is defined as hypocrisy. For how can those things, which are done by one who secretly hates God, please God? And those who love God through faith know that they have received forgiveness of sins, as Christ declares concerning the sinful woman: that it is judged by her great love that her many sins are forgiven [cf. Lk 7]. Therefore, in the description of repentance, that is to say, of the return [to God], the faith concerning the forgiveness of sins through Christ should not be passed over in silence.

[b. Confession to Minister Optional, Enumeration of Sins
to Minister Not Necessary]

Moreover, concerning the confession of sins, we also are prepared to admit that it is necessary for a person to confess them. But to whom? To God who is able to heal the wounds, as the great luminary of the Church, Chrysostom, teaches. And just as we do not forbid anyone to confess his sins either in part or all (as many as he is able to remember, or as many as burden his conscience) to the minister, in like manner we do not force anyone by any law to make such an enumeration of sins. For what reason? Because we have no law or commandment of God concerning this whatsoever. So we do not urge such a confession as if it is necessary [324] for salvation or for attaining the forgiveness of sins. We are satisfied if someone, in general terms and sincerely, will confess to the minister of the church that he is a sinner who feels deep sorrow for his sins, who believes in Christ the Mediator as the Expiator of sins, who desires to correct his life for the better, and who pleads for the forgiveness of his failings. Furthermore, the whole assembly of the people, before it is time to receive of the Lord's Supper, is accustomed to making such a general confession of sins while the minister leads the assembly with words in which they confess before God with humility, admitting guilt of many sins and beseeching forgiveness. After this confession (both private and public) absolution of sins follows. In this manner the Israelites by the Jordan confessed their sins, saying that they offended God grievously and in many ways and they earnestly besought forgiveness [cf. Mt 3]. For if it was necessary for John (as well as the Apostles at Pentecost) to hear and to carefully examine the sins of each one (of so many thousands who streamed together toward him), how would this be accomplished or how long a period of time would it take for those confessions? Not even one hundred celebrants of the sacraments, nor even indeed the one Saint and Forerunner [John] would suffice for such a multitude of confessions.

[c. Enumeration of Iniquities to a Confessor Not Mentioned
by Christ or Apostles]

Wherefore, since neither Christ nor the Apostles have ordered anywhere that iniquities should be enumerated one by one to the confessor, we do not deem it worthy to place such a strangle-hold on consciences [cf. 1 Cor 7:35], to make one think that sins will not be forgiven if each one is not confessed to the priest. Sometimes sins are committed by some people for the following reasons: because they do not trust the confessor (and especially those who are not able to keep silence) without risk to their life, and some could be found who would rather die than make known to another their own shame. Such persons would be obsessed by despair if they would hear that their sins would not be forgiven unless they confessed them to a priest.

### [d. Confession before God Is Sufficient]

Therefore, we believe that confession before God suffices for salvation. God knows our iniquities very well and forgives those who repent. Concerning such confession, we have a worthwhile and the sweetest [325] promise that: "if we confess our sins, he is faithful and just, and will forgive our sins and cleanse us from all unrighteousness" [1 Jn 1:9]. Furthermore, David says: "I said, I will confess my iniquities to the *Lord* against myself; and thou forgavest the ungodliness of my heart" [Ps 131:5]. From so many examples of true repentance, which are recorded in the Book of Acts of the Apostles, nowhere is anyone found enumerating every one of his sins. For these reasons, concerning this matter, we by custom employ it [confession]; and above all, it is obvious that it occurred in the practice of the primitive Church also, since it is impossible not to have been done (if we believe in the holy Psalmist, as indeed we should,) who said: "but who can discern his errors?" and immediately again: "clear thou me from hidden faults," O Lord [Ps 19:12].

### [e. Sincere Repentance Is Rejection of Sins]

And then, seeking after true repentance and the abstinence from evil, you correctly say if you accept this as the fruits of repentance. For Saint John the Baptist calls the withdrawal from evil fruits of repentance, saying: "bear fruit that befits repentance" [Mt 3:8]. For to abstain from sins and to be eager to do good works is an indication that we have sincerely repented, just as good fruits is an indication of a sound tree. For those who proceed shamelessly in their own iniquities while boasting of repentance, however, do not repent; but they mock God more. We are not here discussing those who indeed have good intentions but because of the weakness of the flesh, in time fall back again into sins. For you know that it is not necessary to include those among the hopeless, but they should be restored in a spirit of gentleness [cf. Gal 6:1].

### [f. Repentance Does Not Include Monastic Life]

You say that the monastic order is also not included in the sacrament of penance. This seems to us to be otherwise. For the God-inspired Scripture introduces only one and the same way and manner of true repentance for all Christians. It does not offer various types of repentance. If, therefore, the manner of life of the monks were some part of repentance, it would become necessary for all Christians to adopt the monastic [326] estate, which even you would not recommend. If, indeed, it is a genuine repentance, it can be effected without monastic solitude which endangers this sort of life, making it something different from that of repentance. Nor is it easier for him to repent who is not a monk and who embraces the monastic life. However, concerning the monastics, we will again speak in the proper place and at greater length.

### [7.] Concerning Holy Unction and Last Rites [Anointing]

And you believe that holy unction also was handed down as a sacred ceremony and as a sign of divine mercy which grants redemption and sanctification to those who turn away from sins, therefore, to offer deliverance from sins and to raise up from weaknesses.

### [a. Holy Unction Not Numbered among the Sacraments]

Most Holy Sir, it is not known to us that this oil has been handed down with the sacraments for great purposes. We cannot convince ourselves [of this]. For nowhere is it recorded that the Lord ordered that last anointing in the manner that He set forth the sacraments of baptism and Holy Supper. It is known to us that the Apostles, for the first time (before the Lord's passion), were sent to anoint with oil many that were sick and to heal them [cf. Mk 6:13]. This has reference to the miracles of that time; but when they ceased, naturally such an anointing also came to an end [cf. Jn 9:4-5]. And just as the clay from the spittle with which the Lord anointed the eyes of the blind man is not a sacrament, in like manner neither is the oil with which the sick are anointed, so that by miracle they might receive the cure of the body (just as that blind man regained his sight). Nor is that oil a sign of the divine mercy because for such external signs of divine mercy, it is necessary to have a definite and clear divine promise such as that concerning baptism (so that we might express it by an illustration): "he who believes and is baptized will be saved" [Mk 16:16]. But no such [promise] is reported in the Holy Scriptures concerning the oil of unction. Indeed, faith cannot take something external and accept it as a mark of divine mercy, which does not have a Divine Word upon which it is based. Nor, again, is it necessary that oil be granted for redemption and sanctification of a man who turns away from his iniquities.

### [b. Holy Unction Not Necessary for Redemption for those Already Sanctified by the Holy Spirit

[327] For, lo, those who turn to the Lord with a true resolve are already saved because they are sanctified by the Holy Spirit who is dwelling in them as temples of God [cf. 1 Cor 3:17]. For concerning the forgiveness of sins, as Peter testifies, it assuredly occurs to all who believe in Christ [cf. Acts 10:43]. Also, concerning the Corinthians who repented ("And such were some of you") he said, "But you were washed, you were sanctified, you were justified in the name of the Lord Jesus Christ and in the Spirit of our God" [1 Cor 6:11]. The Scripture says nothing concerning granting of oil to these, neither did Paul in any of his

epistles mention anything about oil, even though he made mention of minor matters which add something to true piety. Nor, again, does James say that forgiveness of sins is granted to those who have been anointed by this oil; rather these are his words: "Is any among you sick? Let him call for the elders of the church, *let them pray* over him, anointing him with oil in the name of the Lord; and the *prayer of faith* will save the sick man, and the Lord will raise him up; and if he has committed sins, he will e forgiven" [Jas 5:14-15]. Here the prayer of faith was added to effect the forgiveness of sins from the faith of the sick man, that is, who is also praying. And the anointing with oil was the wondrous recovery of the sick body to its previous health, which in the then primitive church had happened to many by confirmation of the Gospel preaching. But today, when the Gospel has already been substantiated by miracles, we see no one among all of them who has found relief or has been restored to health because of that final anointing. Therefore, when the miracles abated, we contend that the use of the means through which in the past miracles were performed also abated. Moreover, since the use of the oil is no longer necessary in the church, while the sacraments are eternally necessary in the church, for this reason, therefore, we do not include this final anointing among the sacraments.

### [c. Ministers Called upon to Pray for the Sick]

And although we omit this anointing, nevertheless, we omit nothing which brings salvation to the sick. But if one of us is dangerously ill, the minister of the church is called who, with other pious persons gathered [328] there, also exhorts him who lies ill to acknowledge his sins, and also become contrite and place his complete trust in Christ, and take up a true improvement of life as long as God allows him to remain in the present life. Then, after a general confession of offenses there follows the absolution, and the sick person is deemed worthy to receive Holy Communion based on his own faith. Delightful consolations of the Divine Word are placed before him concerning the forgiveness of sins, concerning eternal salvation which Christ has reserved for us, concerning the resurrection of the dead, and concerning the forthcoming never-ending blessedness following the afflictions of this present life. Devout prayers are offered for the sick person, for the salvation of the soul and of the body. Moreover, there are those who remain with him (especially when it seems that death is rather near) who give courage to his faith with holy supplications and pray with him and for him up to his last breath. Indeed, we believe that this is the most salvitic anointing of all, which truly conveys man to life eternal.

### [8. Conclusion: Baptism and Eucharist Alone Are Sufficient]

Therefore, those two sacraments concerning which Christ himself is

270 AUGSBURG AND CONSTANTINOPLE

legislator, baptism and the Lord's Supper, suffice for us. For they have a divine promise given: that when we use them piously, we shall receive forgiveness of sins and be sanctified. These two sacraments were legislated by Christ in order that they should continue in the Church in uninterrupted use until the last day, up to the time when the Lord shall return to judge the living and the dead [cf. Mt 25:31-32]. With these two sacraments not only our souls, but also our bodies are sanctified in order to become holy temples of God [cf. 1 Cor 3:16-17]. With these [two sacraments] our faith is confirmed, our hope is nourished, our love is kindled, and Satan is driven away; the world together with the flesh are fought against. We give thanks with all our heart to our Savior and Lord Jesus Christ for these two [sacraments] in order that His most benevolent dispensation deemed it worthy to help our weakness through such obvious sacraments.

## [F.] CONCERNING THE INVOCATION OF THE SAINTS

### [1. Invocation of Saints Not Found in Scripture]
[329] We do not invoke the saints, for we do not find even one divine command nor example concerning this in the God-inspired Scriptures. Rather, Isaiah says that Abraham and Israel (the chief patriarchs of holiness) do not know the things which were done by us on earth [cf. Is 63:16], from whence the Prophet also forthwith takes refuge there in the direct help from the heavenly Father [cf. Is 63:16].

It should be known, then, Reverend Sir, that the reasons by which you endeavor to support the invocation of the saints (and we beg you may accept it calmly) do not ease our conscience, nor do they satisfy our mind.

### [2. Scriptural Interpretation Opposed to Invocation of the Dead]
You believe that the saints should be worshipped because they can help the unfortunate mortals, and you think that this can be proved by words and by examples. To each one of these we respond with God's help, however briefly and firmly, and say: Job, by prayer to God, achieved the forgiveness for those with whom he conversed, and he did this while still living on earth [cf. Job 42]. But we are not speaking about this. Therefore, it is necessary for the living to pray for the living; and consequently, they can accomplish something. For we also pray for one another; and we are convinced, or rather, we perceive by reality that our prayers shall be heard. Therefore, this example cannot properly be applied to the saints who have died. For the saints, when they die, even if they indeed live in the presence of God according to the testimony of Christ, yet it does not follow from this that they know specifically each thing that was done by us on earth, as-it is much clearer from the above-mentioned testimony of Isaiah rather than if it would be denied.

That when a dead man came in contact with the bones of the Prophet Elisha, he returned back to life, is not something that is unknown to us [cf. 2 Kg 13:21 RSV]. But with this sign the Lord intended that even when the Prophet died, his ministry would continue so that the Israelites would not hesitate, lest they feared that everything which He had foretold through Elisha when he was alive was not liable to happen. But nowhere do we find that more dead persons were brought to life by his bones. Nor again, did they, who had thrown the dead body of Elisha into the grave (through fear and anguish at the sight of the marauders), invoke the Prophet to resurrect the dead man, for certainly nothing of this kind entered into their mind [cf. 2 Kg 13:21]. Consequently, we cannot see how the invocation of the saints could be established by this miracle.

[3. Honor of Saints Accepted, but Not Invocation nor Intercession]

[330] We do not deny that it is necessary for the saints to be honored because of God abiding in their bodies, and who indeed became temples of God. But to honor and to invoke are two things that differ from each other. The temples of God should be held in honor but not invoked. Rather it is God who abides in His own temple who should be invoked. We truly believe that this is the lawful honor suitable for the saints, as members of Christ: to think and speak well with respect concerning them, to exalt their faith, hope, love, and to project them as examples to be imitated on appropriate occasions. However, this is far removed from invocation.

[4. Scriptures Do Not Mention the Sending of Angels Either]

If this were the case, the holy angels would be sent to those who invoke their names. We do not recall having ever read this in the Holy Scriptures. Even when we invoked God to send His angels to guard us in His paths, lest at some time we strike our foot against a stone [cf. Mt 4:6; cf. Ps 91:11-12], and to surround the Lord's angels about those who fear God and free them from dangers, as we have been taught by the book of Psalms, Scripture does not teach that it is necessary for the angels to hasten and help; rather, indeed, in the [Book of] Revelation of John the Theologian it is forbidden to worship them [the angels] [cf. Rev 22:8f]. Athanasios the Great says:

> Creature does not worship creature, but a servant, the Lord, and a creature, God. Thus, Peter the Apostle hinders Cornelius, who would worship him, saying: 'I too am a man' [Acts 10:26]. And when John would worship an angel in the Apocalypse [Book of Revelation] he hinders him saying: 'You must not do that! I am a fellow servant with you and your brethren the prophets, and with those who keep the words of this book. Worship God' [Rev 22:9]. Therefore, to God alone appertains worship; and the very angels

know that though they excel other beings in glory, yet they are all creatures and are not to be worshipped though worthy of the Lord. Thus, when Manoah, the father of Sampson, was wishing to offer sacrifice to the angel [he] was thereupon hindered by him saying: 'Offer not to me, but to God' [cf. Jg 13:16].[27]

And this, indeed, is what Saint Athanasios [Bishop] of Alexandria said. But continuing further, the Book of Judges adds that from the rock in the desert from which water flowed as a fountain for the Israelites who were thirsty, Sampson quenched his thirst from the water which flowed from the jawbone of an ass [cf. Jg 15:15-19].[28] From the above it is concluded that from the relics of the martyrs, in many ways, good works occur whatever they are.

### [5. Relics of the Saints Not Accepted]
[331] But we, O Blessed Ones, cannot in any way see how this follows from the above, that is to say, what the connection is between that rock and the ass's jawbone, and the relics of the saints. Further, we do not seek [to find] what God can work either through the rock or through the relics of the saints, but what He wills. And just as the will in God is His power, the opposite is not true, that is, that the power in God is His will. For God does not make all that He is able. It is for this reason that it is necessary to look steadfastly at His expressed will. Moreover, even if one example would be shown to us from the Holy Scriptures, that God wills to benefit something when one of the deceased saints is invoked, we would gladly and without excuse agree with Your Holiness concerning this subject.

### [6. Saints As Heirs and Sons of God Accepted]
We know that the saints are indeed the children and heirs of God, yet in view of this we do not regard them as being invoked or worshipped. For it is indeed imperative that the only-begotten Son of God be invoked, as the good Proto-martyr Stephen taught by his own example. But that the other sons who were adopted by God should be invoked, this we have not read anywhere in the Scriptures.

### [7. Erection of Temples in Honor of Saints Not Denied, but Not Understood]
We do not deny that the saints make petitions to God for the Church militant on earth, but certainly in such a manner so as to not know specifically by which burden each one has been oppressed. For Paul says in Romans 8 that the whole creation has been groaning for our redemption [cf. Rom 8:22]. But they should not be invoked for this reason, inasmuch as "Abraham does not know us," according to the Prophet [cf. Is

63:16]. Concerning [your belief] that the saints should be honored by erecting churches in honor of God in their name, we cannot see how this can be justified. For, indeed, we do not oppose erecting a church in honor of God, that is, so that the Gospel of Christ may be taught in it and the divinely instituted sacraments may be lawfully administered in it. But we cannot understand how it is one and the same thing to erect a church in honor of God and to erect a church in honor of one of the saints. For churches should be erected in honor of God and not of men, so that God may be worshipped in the churches but not men.

### [8. Commemorations of Saints Accepted]

Moreover, All-Holiness, you declare that the memory of the saints should be honored appropriately, that is to say, by psalms, hymns, and spiritual odes by which when God is worshipped His servants rejoice.[29] But also icons should be made of them [the saints], so that we might [332] imitate their virtues. Indeed, it is not necesary to imitate their virtues as we have already testified above; nor is it necessary on that account to erect icons of them, although we do not deny that we may have icons if for the purpose of remembrance alone, but not for worship. Moreover, we take it to be not unwarranted to extol their virtues and their struggles in hymns as well as their illustrious deaths which they suffered for Christ. But we should never accept to attribute to them in the hymns that which alone belongs to the Mediator Christ. We rather believe that the saints would not be delighted with such praises, as when the honor of the Messiah was attributed to John the Baptist, the saint declined this honor most firmly [cf. Mt 3:13f]. Paul and Barnabas also would not tolerate in the least to be offered divine honors by the people of Lystra as can be seen in the Acts of the Apostles [cf. 14:11-15]. Nor, indeed, should honors be tendered to the saints, by which honors God in particular is served and honored, so that we do not transfer to the creatures the honor which is owed to God alone.

### [9. Virtues of Saints Are Imitated in Hymns and Prayers, but Not Portrayed on Icons]

You are of the opinion that it is necessary to pay due honor and worship to the icons of the saints because we also worship one another as being made according to the image of God. But it should be known that the honor which a living man affords to a living man is a civil or common honor, which absolutely does not attribute divinity to man. Nor do we tender civil worship to the image of the ruler but to the ruler himself. Therefore, the civil honor which a man tenders to another is not properly transferred to the icons. Never in the least did the saints demand whatsoever honor and worship of their own icons. Therefore, the honor toward the icon never passes over to the original [depicted therein].

Neither God nor the saints are properly honored in this way, since nowhere in the Holy Scriptures has this way been revealed to us. For this reason this is superfluous and unlawful. The Jews did well to worship round about the tabernacle; and they worshipped God in the tabernacle (as also later in the temple) who proclaimed expressly in their local dialect to present himself to them and to harken to their prayers. The Jews did not worship anything or anyone else (whosoever was truly living [333] piously) save only God himself (who truly abides in the tabernacle which they knew from His own testimony). Consequently, the custom of worshipping the icons cannot be based on this example.

### [10. God Alone Is To Be Worshipped]

To the word of Christ: "you shall worship the Lord your God and him only shall you serve" [Mt 4:10; cf. Deut 6:13], you answered that you forbid such worship because in that case either we would be worshipping creation rather than the Creator, or because of bondage and servitude, we would be offering worship to creation. And you think that the worship is withheld while the relationship is not broken. And yet, whoever has revealed matters pertaining to his soul to some saint and has rid his soul of these matters by worshipping him [the saint] or prostrating himself before the icon, repeating from memory his troubles and asking for help, assigns to that saint to listen to the groaning of the heart and, indeed, to know his inner self and help in time of need. In addition, he attributes to the icon something of the divine nature and heavenly majesty. The Lord in the Old Testament has sternly forbidden that no image (none whatsoever it might be) should be worshipped. For He knew that by this means that something divine is attributed to the icon which actually it does not have. Therefore, we cannot see how when the saints are invoked, or when their icons are worshipped, this can be called merely relation and not worship. For there, no difference occurs in matters even though one might place various names on them as a pretext. For they know that worship belongs to God alone. Therefore, most assuredly it behooves us to worship only one God, the Father, the Son, and the Holy Spirit, and to worship Him *alone* so that we do not have a misdirected piety which would divert us into superstition. For it makes no difference to God whether one worships a statue or an icon. He did not order either one, nor are they acceptable anywhere in the Scriptures.

### [11. Psalm 82:6 Does Not Apply to the Saints]

Moreover, the passge of the Psalm, "I say, you are gods, sons of the most high, all of you" [82.6], was not correctly transferred to the saints. For the Lord in the Psalm is speaking to the civil judges, chiding them harshly because they are not carrying out the work of justice, although [334] they are representatives of God on earth. Consequently, they were called gods because they were obliged to exercise justice and to respect the rights of the entire populace on earth. Whereby, these Psalms here impose dreadful threats that all the cities be overthrown unless they carry out what is necessary more earnestly in the future. But that this does not apply to the saints in heaven, we hope that you yourself will understand, if you will accurately contemplate the entire connection and agreement of the Psalm.

### [12. Saints Filled with the Holy Spirit Accepted, but Not through Icons]

Further, you say that the saints are filled with the Holy Spirit (which most truly is also believed by us) and not even when they are deceased does the grace of the Spirit depart from them (which if this is meant concerning their souls, we do not deny), but it is in their souls and their bodies and their characteristics as well as in the holy icons. If we see these latter statements confirmed by the God-inspired Scriptures, we shall be ready to accept and receive them. But if they cannot be proved by the Prophetic and Apostolic writings, we cannot be criticized for any folly or rashness if we abandon them to those who introduced them.

### [13. Solomon's Cherubim Is No Example]

We know that Solomon made the Cherubim, but nowhere in the Scriptures do we find that they were worshipped. This example, therefore, confirms that it is lawful to make icons, and we do not argue the point; but that they should be worshipped, we do not agree.

Moreover, the contention that he who honors a martyr (in some way) honors God, and he who honors the Mother of Jesus, honors Jesus himself, we might not deny if such an honor is understood in the same sense as that which belongs to the saints, as we have commented previously. But if divine honors are offered to them, we are of the opinion that as much honor is taken away from God as that which is given to the saints. For God does not wish to give His glory to another.

### [14. Intercession of the Saints Not Mediation between God]

The following pretext is also presented as an apology in defense of the invocation of the saints: that even if someone should beseech the intercession of saints, yet above all God alone is known as the helper. But know that if the discussion concerns intercession and petition to God, then we have a mediator and intercessor who sits at the right hand of the Father, Jesus Christ, interceding for us (as Apostle Paul testifies in Romans, chapter 3). Nor do we need to intercede for a saint to provide an intercession for us inasmuch as the beloved Son of God (to whom the Father would not deny anything) faithfully intercedes for us. And [335] generally speaking, we do not deny that the saints pray for the

Church, as we mentioned previously. For this reason we judge that the saints should not be invoked for the reasons we have stated a short while ago.

### [15. Epiphanios on the Invocation of the Theotokos]

Moreover, Most Holy Master, we marvel at the statement of Saint Epiphanios which prevents the Most Holy and Blessed Theotokos from being invoked, which we were given to understand as being spurious (according to the supposed opinion of the Damascene). We say we marvel, for we are not unaware that some foreign elements have crept into the writings of the Fathers, who if they were alive today, would claim that these were not theirs. However, the entire style in the writings of Epiphanios and the entire vocabulary prove that nothing has been adulterated. And, indeed, there is harmony among all the parts. Yes, indeed, the Holy Father [Epiphanios] who agrees unquestionably with the Holy Scriptures proceeded to write the above quotation, since he was not able to find any trace of worship of the Ever-Virgin in the entire Holy Scripture. For if Christ wanted to be honored through the worship of His Mother, the Apostles by all means would have left us either a command pertaining to it, or at least an example in their books.

### [16. Epiphanios' Interpretation of John]

Furthermore, this same Epiphanios, writing to Bishop John of Jerusalem (whose letter the blessed Jerome translated into the Latin language and from which translation the following passage we retranslated into Greek), states the following:

> Travelling to the holy place called Bethel, I came to a villa called Anablatha. And as I was passing, I saw a church there in which a lamp was burning. Entering in order to pray, I found there a curtain hanging on the doors on which was portrayed the image of Christ or of one of the saints, for I do not rightly remember whose image it was. Seeing this and being loth that an image of a man should be hung up in the Church of Christ contrary to the teaching of the Scriptures, I tore the curtain asunder. I advised the custodians of the place to use it as a winding-sheet to bury some poor dead person in. [336] And I beg you (he said to Bishop John) to advise the presbyters not to allow hereafter such curtains to be hung in the Church of Christ, because it is contrary to our faith.[30]

This, then, is from the good Epiphanios.

### [17. Interpretation of Passage on King Hezekiah Is Not an Intercession, but a Desire of the Lord]

For if the Lord said to pious King Hezekiah (when the Assyrians demanded of him to surrender to the city of Jerusalem), "For I will defend this city, to save it for my own sake, and for the sake of my servant David" [2 Kg 19:34; cf. Is 38:6], this cannot be seen as a special intercession of the saints and their worship and invocation. For the Lord did not say that He would save the city through prayer, that is, through the intercession of David, but that He [God] wills it. "Since in the past I promised to my servant David to keep this kingdom and the city among his descendents as long as they would continue in the true religion, for this reason now I will confirm that promise; and for the glory of my name I will defend it against the blaspheming Assyrians." This is the true meaning of that passage which does not indicate some type of intercession of the saints.

### [18. The Example of Moses]
Moreover, we know that Moses through prayer was to restrain God from freeing the Israelite people in a cruel manner [cf. Ex 12], and from the passage where the Lord was to have said to Jeremiah concerning these people [cf. Jer chapters 11 and 14], that they were not worthy. But the supplication for the living and that for the dead is not the same, nor is any other supplication made for further supplications. This we proved above while dealing with the intercessions of Job.

### [19. Cyril's Interpretation Not Accepted]
Furthermore, we cannot accept the opinion of Cyril (a person who dealt with the other matters in the Church of God very differently) that there will be an intercession in the final coming of the Lord, when the Most Blessed Virgin Mary and angels and saints will intercede for those who were able to repent before they died, but who were not able to have all the stains of sins cleansed. For those who truly believe in Christ [cf. 1 Jn 1:7] are cleansed by the blood of Jesus Christ, the Son of God, from all sin whenever they might come to the end of their life. Also, in Christ "all the prophets witness that everyone who believes in Him, receives forgiveness of sins through His name" [Acts 10:43]. But not even Christ, [337] who describes in detail among other things the nature of that last Judgment Day, mentions anything concerning such supplication. But instead He says that the goats which have been placed at the left hand shall be sent away into the eternal fire [cf. Mt 25:41], while the sheep which will be placed at His right hand shall inherit the kingdom of heaven [cf. Mt 25:34]. Nor is there here a distinction at all between the sheep, some of which were completely cleansed, while others' sinful stains have not been sufficiently cleansed. Consequently, that intercession was not on any scriptural foundation, and being without foundation, it falls.

[20. Man Created in God's Image Accepted,
but Not the Worship of Icons]

Consequently, the reasons which have been advanced by the good John of Damascus, on the assurance that the icons produced cures, are weaker if such a confirmation existed. He said: "God created man in His own image." We agree. Is this, then, the reason that icons should be worshipped? [The Damascene] said "God begot the Son, His true image." Is it for this reason that the painted icons should be worshipped? "God," he says, "appeared to have been portrayed as man." And what then? Is it for this reason that a painted icon should be worshipped? "Whatever it is, would I" (he said) "not honor the icon of my Savior?" Honor Christ (we say), who is the image of the invisible God. If, however, you think you are reverencing Christ because you reverence His portrait [icon], remember Christ saying: "in vain do they worship me, teaching as doctrines the precepts of men" [cf. Mt 15:9]. But "I worship them" (he [Damascene] says) "not as gods, but their images as friends of God." [31] But do good to your neighbor who has been made in the image of God, then Christ on that day will say to you: "as you did it to one of the least of these my brethren, you did it to me" [Mt 25:40]. It is much better to minister to these living holy icons of God (who go back and forth before your very eyes every day, and who seek your help or counsel). And it is much better to lighten their needs with good deeds rather than honor painted icons which neither see, nor hear, nor feel anything. If someone would, in a friendly manner, respectfully discuss these matters with that very virtuous Damascene, we think that he might accept them without much difficulty.

[21. Worship of Icons Not Found in Scripture]

We are not able to find in the Holy Scripture up to this day any [338] lawful manner to worship the icons. Also, it is not possible to justify the old but unworthy-of-praise custom, which was cleverly contrived to appease the conscience of man concerning the gravity of such a matter, because it is not substantiated by any Divine Scriptures.

[22. Difference between 'To Profane' and 'To Adore' Sacred Vessels]

We know that the impious monarch Belshazzar of Babylon was punished because he profaned the sacred vessels, which of old were taken out of the temple of Jerusalem, and drank freely from them with his concubines to extol the golden and silver and wooden and stone gods as an insult to the true God [cf. Dan 5:1-4]. But we do not see how it follows from this that it is necessary to worship the form of the cross, chalices, patens, and the books of the Gospel. It is one thing not to profane the sacred vessels, which are dedicated to the service of God, and another to worship such vessels. The Lord did not will that His vessels be profaned, nor did He order them anywhere to be worshipped.

### [23. Boundaries Set by Fathers Not Altered]
Nor do we for this reason shift the boundaries set by the Holy Fathers, even if we cannot accept everything which has been introduced into the Church in the name of traditions; rather we therefore carefully seek out and dig up the boundaries which the Prophets, Christ, and the Apostles set down. We limit ourselves within them so that we will not be led astray more than we should.

### [24. Examples of Kings Cannot Be Applied to Saints]
Further, Your Holiness offers this, also: that if honor is offered to kings and rulers who frequently are impious, then the heavenly magistrates, that is, the saints, should be worshipped much more. The honor about which we spoke above, we do not deny to the saints; but we desist from worshipping them. For what reason? Because the Lord ordered that the king should be honored [cf. 1 Pet 2:17], but He did not order that the saints should be worshipped. And He would not tolerate the angels being worshipped [cf. Rev 22:9]. In thinking thus we are not instituting a new faith, nor are we condemning the traditions of the Holy Fathers which conform to the Divine Words [Holy Scriptures]. Consequently, the threat does not apply to us: "If anyone is preaching to you a gospel contrary to that which you received, let him be accursed" [Gal 1:9]. This is our only prayer: that everything which has been taught [339] by the Prophets and Christ and His Apostles be included in the true faith and not depart, not even as far as the width of a fingernail, from these ancient, most steadfast, Prophetic and Apostolic traditions.

### [25. Claim of Not Worshipping Material of the Icons is a Pretext]
Again, even the excuse, which states that worship is not offered to the material of the icon but to the person who is depicted in it, is not able to gloss over the worship of icons. For the pagans in the past were able to use the same pretext; and indeed they used it declaring that they offered worship not to the material of the icon, but to the divine person who was depicted in the material. In vain do they, with toil and sweat, hold on to the fostering of the icons so that it might appear from the Holy Scriptures that God wishes himself and the saints to be honored and reverenced in the icons and in images.

### [26. Writings of Dionysios Not Convincing]
And what esteem and authority should be given to that book which has been inscribed and has circulated under the name of Dionysios the Areopagite has been clearly made known by us previously so that iconolatry had need of stronger support and defense [that provided

by Dionysios].

### [27. Portrayals of Martyrs Accepted As Examples]
We do not forbid the portrayal of the martyrs' sufferings of the saints, so that by their examples we might be encouraged to equal their bravery and perseverance in the true faith. And many such writings are seen by us every day. But we neither demand, nor do we recommend, the invocation of the martyrs, because this is superfluous for the reasons which we have so often repeated.

### [28. Jacob Did Not Worship His Staff]
Jacob the Patriarch did not worship "the top of his staff" [Gen 47:31]. Why? For what reason would he worship his staff or its top? But neither is there mention there of an icon which the saint might have worshipped. But even if in the Epistle to the Hebrews the Apostle [Paul] had followed the common and modern spoken Greek translation (for nothing was distorted here in this case), the Hebrew source in truth has it thus: "that Israel worshipped turning toward the head of his bed" [Gen 47:31]. That is, the patriarch withdrawing himself apart from his son Joseph, worshipped the Lord and thanked Him for so many benevolences which he had received beyond all expectation. But what have all these to do with recommending the worship of icons?

### [29. Some Fathers Were Respected but Some Were Admonished]
[340] We espouse the most holy efforts and writings of Cyril, Gregory of Nazianzos, Chrysostom and such others; but, nevertheless, we require them [the writings] to be subjected under the scrutiny of the God-given Scriptures. We thus understand them to have been good and reasonable men, so that we would not hesitate to gladly yield to them if they had been advised by others who had taught better.

In using the testimony of Severian [Bishop of] Gabala we see nothing to confirm the granting of honor to the icons.

### [30. Example of Worship of Father and Son Cannot Be Applied to Icons]
Further, it is said that just as the one who does not honor the Son does not honor the Father, in like manner, also, the one who does not honor the icon does not honor the one who is portrayed. But most of this comparison is dissimilar so that this argument follows no logical sequence. What then? The Father and the Son in the most Holy Trinity are one in essence. Thus, in all likelihood he who does not honor the one will not honor the other either. But the icon and the one portrayed in it may not be one in essence so that it may be possible to honor God and to honor a holy man also (at least lawfully), even though his icon may not be honored. Therefore, none of that which follows these has any connection

with the text where it says: that he who does not honor the saints does not honor the Lord himself either, and he who does not worship the cross does not worship the Crucified One either.

### [31. Invocation of Saints and Reverence of Icons of Saints Not Commanded by Christ or Apostles]

Moreover, the Sixth and Seventh [Ecumenical] Synods are not of such great esteem as to have the authority in the Church of God to introduce new forms of worship without the sanction of the Divine Word. Neither can it be denied that many of the canons which have been decreed in some Synods are not entirely applicable to the rule of faith of the Divine Word. Therefore, since neither the Prophets, nor Christ, nor the Apostles ordered the invocation of the saints or the reverencing or the worshipping of their icons, no one perhaps is able on this account to condemn us for impiety because we only omit that which God himself in His own words did not require of us.

### [G.] CONCERNING MONASTIC POLITY OR LIFE

### [1. Monastic Life Is Permitted]

[341] None among us is forced to be tied down by the bonds of marriage, but is permitted to live either a monastic life, or to be a citizen among the people. One is merely required to hold the right opinion concerning the faith, and remain in it, and live blamelessly. Indeed, lately, concerning monastic conduct, which is practiced in many villages in Europe, one can see we justly judge much that is blameworthy. For many believe in this wise, that by this manner of conduct they are able to wipe out their sins. This belief is an insult to the saving work of the Savior Christ. Moreover, many are of the opinion that by such a manner of life they are much better than the other Christians who are doing the proper things in their civil and financial life and who worship God. But this opinion is immersed in pharisaic hypocrisy. And consequently, all who have at some time embraced the monastic life have placed a snare on their conscience so that they are convinced that it is no longer lawful for them to be freed from such a life except with a great stain of guilt, even if they might indeed happen to be acquitted from it. Moreover, the greatest of all reasons which makes us not take the monastic life seriously is this: that it is not commanded by God, and it is stripped of the Divine Word which would recommend it. And indeed, to spend all the time of one's life in such a manner lacks the approval of the Divine Words and rather engenders great danger for souls. And on the other hand, everyone is not well fitted for celibacy. The Savior says: "not all men can receive this precept" [Mt 19:11]. But the Apostle Paul also said: "For it is better to marry than to be aflame with passion" [1 Cor 7:9]. It is truly unquestion-

able that there are very few who have the gift of self-control. We see in
the words of the Apostle himself an almost infinite number of persons
who are confined within the monasteries. For the promise of self-control
is not sufficient for the Lord unless it is achieved so as to be completely
acceptable to His grandeur.

### [2. Dionysios on Monastic Life Is Not Accepted]

Not even, indeed, would that spurious Dionysios, the supposed
Areopagite, who writes much concerning the making and sanctifying of
monks, quiet the consciences. For we proved above that this writer was
[342] not the same as the Areopagite who was a disciple of [Apostle] Paul
mentioned in the Acts of the Apostles [cf. ch. 17].

### [3. Basil on Monastic Life Exaggerates Its Value]

We know Basil became a great admirer of the monastic life. But there
are times when even the most renowned men, in judging, overlook some
things (which you yourself have said beforehand in your book happened
to many of the Fathers who wrote in Greek and Latin) so that, consequently, nothing on earth is found absolutely perfect and blessed in
everything. Therefore, we demand divine and not human evidence
without purpose.

### [4. The Kingdom Is Rather for Sinners]

When Christ says, "the kingdom of heaven has suffered violence, and
men of violence take it by force" [Mt 11:12], He is speaking about the tax
collectors and sinners and such other men for whom the matter of salvation seemed to be completely hopeless. They mentally repented so
seriously and, indeed, had such a zeal that others with whom they were
compared seemed cold and sluggish. Therefore, as if by violent force,
they were rushed into the kingdom of heaven, thrusting themselves into it
which seemed not to be prepared for them. Such then was that force and
violence of that sinful woman who when she repented sincerely, "wet his
[Christ's] feet with her tears, and wiped them with the hair of her head"
[Lk 7:38]. But this repentance from sins was not a promise for the
monastic life. Surely, this word of Christ has not been projected correctly to enhance the monastic manner of life.

### [5. Struggles and Rewards Not Only for Monks, but for All Christians]

Furthermore, we also know this: that the present time is a time of
struggle and the future one of reward. Yet not only do the monastics endure these struggles but, lo, also all of those who are in truth Christians.
For all are to struggle and fight in whatever state of life they may live,
whether they are leaders who teach in the Church or govern the affairs of
the state, or whether they are occupied with financial matters. For satan

attacks us, and the flesh brings upon various troubles; and the world, now enticing and now doing wrong and insulting, makes an attempt to draw us away from God. Saint Paul, then, in what he wrote in the Epistle to the Ephesians, prepared all Christians by equipping them for that battle. So, then, what the Holy Scriptures say concerning struggles is not correctly applied to monasticism. They [the Scriptures] do not then con-[343] firm, just as they do not recommend, its establishment.

[6. Dogmas of Synods Accepted if They Agree with Scripture]

We accept the dogmas of the Synods with open arms only when we see them agreeing with the God-inspired Scriptures. If, however, they lack scriptural proofs, we abandon them to those who have introduced them. And we do this without offense or insolence against those good men in whom there was a zeal for piety but who sometimes erred concerning the better selection and who sometimes built on the foundation of straw, which the Apostle [Paul] foresaw and foretold would happen [cf. 1 Cor 3:12f]. But we remember what has been written by him. He said to the Colossians:

If with Christ you died to the elemental spirits of the universe, why do you live as if you still belong to the world? Why do you submit to regulations, 'Do not handle, Do not taste, Do not touch'...according to human precepts and doctrines? These have indeed an appearance of wisdom in promoting vigor of devotion and self-abasement and severity to the body, but they are of no value in checking the indulgence of the flesh [Col 2:20-23].

Also, to Timothy, the same Apostle speaks about those who forbid marriage and "enjoin abstinence from foods which God created to be received with thanksgiving by those who believe and know the truth" [1 Tim 4:3].

[7. Scriptural Witness of Monastic Life Not Substantiated]

Demanding scriptural proofs concerning the monastic life from the Old and New Testaments, behold, Elijah the Prophet appears. But nowhere do we find him either praying for or promising monastic life or imposing upon another person to live such a life. He at one time withdrew to a high mountain, and to another again with other persons, as also was the case with the Prophet Elisha. Each one had his own disciples who were called sons of Prophets. Yet they did not live a celibate and monastic manner of life which is clear from the Scriptures. For one among those sons of the Prophet, when he died, left a widow woman and two sons when the Prophet Elisha [cf. 2 Kg 4], by a miraculous increase of oil, freed the sons from being given into slavery to a greedy creditor. John the Baptist, having been called by God for a particular mission, was living in the wilderness. But at the appropriate time, going out into the midst of the people [cf. Is 40:3f] and teaching the Church [the people] of God, he did not counsel anyone to pursue the life [344] of an ascetic or the monastic life; but he allowed each one to continue in the particular mode of life (if, indeed, it was decent in itself) in such a way that he neither forbade anyone to serve as a soldier, nor is he known to have advised anyone to live as a celibate. At times the Lord Christ taught in the desert. At other times He sought tranquility in the desert with His Disciples. And sometimes again He withdrew into the wilderness to pray more fervently or to avoid the bias of enemies; but the greater part of His life was not spent in the wilderness at all, but was reckoned among men. In additon, it is apparent that some of His Apostles (especially Peter) had wives. Paul also indicates that the Apostles had the right to travel about with their own wives [cf. 1 Cor 9:5]. Be that as it may, it has been proven that neither Elijah, nor the Forerunner, nor Christ, nor the Apostles, introduced or became examples in leading the life of monks. Therefore, some of the Fathers would have done well if they had been satisfied with the other kinds of life which were ordered and approved by God.

### [8. Paul in the Letter to Colossians Misunderstood]

Moreover, [regarding] the passage of Paul to the Colossians, concerning those who by a particular kind of conduct develop an angelic holiness, you are unable to understand that we are to be saved by angels. And this is clear from the connecting thoughts of Paul. He says: "let no one disqualify you, insisting on self-abasement and worship of angels, taking his stand on visions puffed up without reason by his sensuous mind" [Col 2:18]. Nothing is said here concerning those who have formed this opinion that our salvation is through angels, but it is ordered that we be on guard from those superstitious worshippers who pretend to live the angelic life. It is necessary for us to remember well this exhortation so that we will not, in pursuing the manner of life of angels, deviate from true godliness and innocence. We do not, indeed, doubt that we many, who have lived the monastic life and still live it now, will become good persons; but, nevertheless, we cannot see any firm foundation upon which that ascetic life has been built.

### [9. Paul on Bodily Exercise (1 Tim 4:8)]

[345] Also, Paul indeed says that "physical training is of some value," and in the meanwhile exhorts us to pursue godliness. He is not speaking, certainly, concerning the bodily exercises which are done for reasons of health. It is obvious then that at any rate they are beneficial and lawful.

Yet the Apostle did not admire the practices of fastings, of [sleeping on] beds on the ground, and such other practices which later became the objects of great admiration. But moreso, they are objects of grief rather than of benefit. For he wishes to spare the body and to deem it worthy of appropriate honor [cf. Col 2:23] on condition that we do not insult the flesh. This order has been given to all Christians, and not to a particular class of men.

[10. Fasting and Prayer Not Only for Monastic Life but for All]

The fastings and supplications of the Prophetess Anna were not in the least part of the monastic life. But that devout widow daily offered up prayers for all churches of God continually, and sometimes she fasted to help the prayers flow more ardently. But this might be achieved even by those who never professed to live the monastic life. So this matter is not correctly related to the subject of monastic life. And Paul, also, who orders that from time to time fasting be dispensed with, says very clearly, concerning those who come together in marriage, that he demands that they abstain from their nuptials for a season so that by means of fasting they will be able to pray with greater devotion for their own and the Church's salvation. Consequently, not even this testimony of the Apostle can be brought to support the monastic manner of life [cf. 1 Cor 7:5f].

[H.] EPILOGUE

These were, Most Holy Sir Patriarch, the comments with which we wished to reply to the writings of Your Holiness. Indeed, with respect, which we owe for the love and mercies of God, we pray that that which we have written in a more independent fashion, according to our Germanic and reverent, undisguised love of truth, Your Holiness will accept without difficulty. For it was not in our mind to intentionally insult or grieve anyone, but to frankly offer the reasons which we judged for ourselves to be the reasons your letter in some parts does not satisfy our [346] souls, nor make us peaceful. And, indeed, every innovation (as Your Holiness piously exhorts) we, of ourselves, reject; yet we judge those to be most ancient which have been handed down from the Prophets, from Christ himself, and from the Apostles. Anything, indeed, from their teaching, whatever it may be, which obscures all others by virtue of antiquity and certainty which could be proved to us, we will accept most gladly and most gratefully. Truly, we believe that the interpretation of the Scriptures, which is the most certain and most secure, is that which makes the Scripture interpret itself (that is, by dexterously placing the God-inspired words beside each other and comparing them by referring back to the sources of the Hebrew and Greek phrases as the most excellent counselor). When, therefore, there is a pious agreement between us on most of the articles of teaching, and Your Holiness' soul, which has a pious love for us, is disposed to better consideration, a hope possesses us that our writings which have been read and which have been closely examined by you will bring both sides to a much nearer agreement in the true religion. May this be accomplished by the unique tri-hypostatic God of all, the cause of sincere peace and devout love. Amen.

## NOTES

1. Ioannes Karmires, *Μνημεῖα*, p. 435.

2. *Quinisext Synod, canon 19*; cf. NPNF Ser. 2, vol. 14.344 (with corrections).

3. St. John Chrysostom, *Commentary On First Corinthians, Homily 9*; cf. NPNF Ser. 1, vol. 12, 51, PG 61.79.

4. Page numbers in *Acta et Scripta* at this point are incorrectly paginated: 273 is written as 277. However, continuity of the text is not disturbed.

5. St. Augustine, *On the Trinity, Bk. 2*; cf. PL 42.845-68.

6. St. Epiphanios, *Homily Against Sabellians*, PG 42.289f.

7. St. Basil, *Against Eunomios, Homily 5*, PG 29.733-36.

8. Ibid. cf. PG 29.736.

9. St. Augustine, *On the Trinity, Bk. 15.45;* PL 42.109.

10. Pagination of *Acta et Scripta* skips from p. 280 to p. 285. However, continuity of text follows correctly without any apparent omission.

11. St. Epiphanios, *The Firmly Anchored Man, Bk. 3.1, 72-74*; PG 43.17-236.

12. St. Augustine, *On the Trinity, Bk 15.48*; PL 42.1095; cf. *The Later Christian Fathers,* ed. H. Bettenson (Oxford, 1972), p. 228.

13. Only a few of these were bishops of Old Rome, the majority were Eastern bishops.

14. St. Cyril of Alexandria, *The Adoration and Worship of God in Spirit and in Truth,* PG 68.148.

15. St. Epiphanios, *The Firmly Achored Man, Bk. 3.1*; PG 42.486, 489.

16. St. Basil, *Against Eunomios, Homily 5*, PG 29.725.

17. St. Gregory Nazianzos, *The Fourth Theological Oration* (i.e., *The Second Concerning the Son*), PG 36.130; cf. NPNF Ser. 2, vol. 7, 317.

18. St. Cyril of Alexandria, *The Holy and Consubstantial Trinity, Homily 33*, PG 75.572.

19. St. Athanasios, *Letters Concerning the Holy Spirit*; Shapland, *The Letters*, p. 115.

20. Ibid. p. 76.

21. Gen 4:13 (RSV) reads: "My punishment is greater than I can bear."

22. Cf. "Second Answer" of Jeremiah, pp. 178-79.

23. Ibid.

24. Ibid., p. 185.

25. "Second Answer" of Patriarch Jeremiah II, pp. 188-89.

26. St. Irenaios, *Against Heresies, Bk. 4.18, 5*; cf. *The Ante-Nicene Fathers. Apostolic Fathers Justin Martyr and Irenaeus* (Grand Rapids, Mich.) vol. 1, 486 (hereafter: ANF).

27. St. Athanasios, *Against Arians, Discourse 2*, PG 26.152; cf. NPNF Ser. 2, vol. 4, 361.

28. St. John of Damascus, *Exact Exposition of the Orthodox Faith*, PG 94.1165; cf. NPNF Ser. 2, vol. 9, 87. *Note*: According to Judges 15:15, Sampson slew a thousand men with the jawbone and then threw it away. He did not drink water from it, but drank from the water that came from the rock.

29. The last two words προσήκειν and πράγμασιν are not in the Latin translation of the *Acta et Scripta*.

30. St. Epiphanios, *Letter to John, Bishop of Jerusalem*, PG 43.379-92; cf. *Epistle 51, Letter to Jerome*, PL 22.517; Quasten, *Patrology*, 3, p. 390.
31. St. John of Damascus. *On the Holy Icons, Oration 3.26*; PG 94.1343.

*Chapter 6*

THE THIRD THEOLOGICAL EXCHANGE:

CONSTANTINOPLE TO TÜBINGEN

*[A.] The Letter of Patriarch Jeremiah [II] to the Tübingen
Theologians Accompanying Patriarch Jeremiah's Third Answer*

This letter is to be handed to the most erudite and esteemed Germans.

Jeremiah, by the mercy of God, Archbishop of Constantinople, New
Rome, and Ecumenical Patriarch to those who truly recognize the terms
of friendship, may you, most wise Germans, fare well.

In the commotion and confusion which recently confronted our
Church, many (both the inhabitants of this city and some absent far
away, being greatly concerned for what happened to us and pretending
to show their friendship), in any event, persuaded us that the misfortunes
of the times were painful and severe. Truly, they are ignorant, since gain
comes from the temptations to those who are attentive, according to the
word of the Lord: "for it is necessary that temptations come" [Mt 18:7],
so that the father of such temptations will inherit the woe. Yet your letter
to us, indeed, being full of wisdom and ingenuity yet denying anything of
the kind, also became the cause of many other good things. Truly, this
letter of consolation, showing both wisdom and grandeur, proved to all
persons that it is necessary for friendship to be preserved steadfast and
true not only in good things, but especially during misfortunes. It proved
this not simply with words alone, but also with deeds: by your sending to
us booklets, a favor which, good fortune failing, we have no hope of
repaying. Commending you for the intention, we admire the manner
[348] of friendship. Above all, we share one gift: that we declare always such a steadfast and sincere love for one another. May you remain strong in health, most wise and dearly beloved gentlemen, through
the true love in which God also is pleased. We also send you our answer
to those questions you have requested in writing.

> Jeremiah
> Month of May, Indiction 9

## [B.] The Third Answer of Patriarch Jeremiah [II] of Constantinople to Tübingen in the Year 1581

Jeremiah, by the mercy of God, Archbishop of Constantinople, New Rome, and Ecumenical Patriarch.

[349] O most wise German men, the book you sent to us has arrived. In it you again set forth supposedly plausible reasons and evidence, saying that you have not completely received satisfaction from our answers sent in response to your previous letters. You also say that somehow not even your thinking has been set straight not only from Holy Scripture, but neither from the Holy Fathers of the Church each after having been taught the truer and the better.

### [A. CONCERNING THE PROCESSION OF THE HOLY SPIRIT]

But after saying this you bring in Saint Augustine in book 2, *On the Trinity*,[1] and you strongly maintain that the Holy Spirit proceeds not only from the Father, but also from the Son himself. And you decide that the Holy Greek Fathers agree with you in the matter of the procession of the Holy Spirit from the Son, even though they differ in literal expressions. They are Athanasios in his treatise, *The Incarnation of the Word*;[2] Cyril [of Alexandria] in his *First Treatise to Palladios*;[3] Epiphanios in the Homily *Ancoratos*;[4] Basil the Great in his fifteenth epistle *Against Eunomios*,[5] who agrees with them; [Gregory] Nazianzos in the *Fourth Theological Oration*, which is the Second *Concerning the Son*;[6] Cyril [of Alexandria] again in *Thesaurus*;[7] and Athanasios again in his *Letters to Serapion*.[8] We wonder, then, if indeed by abandoning the obvious and explicit passages of Scripture and the Fathers, which distinctly state and submit that the Holy Spirit proceeds from the Father alone, which may have another meaning and have been understood by them [the Fathers] in another way, you might have changed to serve your own purpose! Accordingly, indeed, is also the matter of sending forth, which according to [350] Augustine, as well as to the truth of the matter, has nothing in common with the procession. And the same is true concerning the many other passages which these Fathers have of necessity and fittingly used in speaking against those who alienated the Spirit from the essence of the Son. They surely did not use them with the intention of showing that the Holy Spirit proceeds from the Son also. For this reason we had purposed to remain absolutely silent in response to your replies and give no answer to you. For you have quite plainly altered Holy Scripture as well as the interpretation of the above-mentioned holy men according to your own will. We have Paul to exhort us: "a man who is factitious,[9] after admonishing him once or twice, have nothing more to do with him"

[Tit 3:10]. However, since by silence it might appear that we agree with you and that perhaps you correctly hold and understand these matters, we run the risk of having it thought that Holy Scripture and these holy men [Fathers] agree with you on this subject. By defending them we reiterate these matters again, although we have been well informed by your letters that you will never be able to agree with us or rather, we should say, with the truth.

## [1. The Orthodox Position Concerning the Procession of the Holy Spirit]

First of all, then, let it be made known as much as possible what are the causes of deviation. After that if this Orthodox opinion of ours concerning the Spirit could be proved by the discourses on the Holy Spirit, and in like manner piety, also, so that it is known what it is, then we shall be able to avoid the deviations as much as possible. Therefore, concerning the procession of the Holy Spirit, it ought to be stressed above everything else that "spirit" is not only a name attributed to many others, but also to the Holy Spirit himself. This is a unanimous voice. For it implies that the graces of the Spirit are many and various in kind. For they are called "spirit of truth," "of sonship," "of grace," "of wisdom," "of prudence," "of knowledge," "of piety," "of will," "of might," "of fear," and of many other such graces as it seems to John the Damascene, to the esteemed Gregory, and to Isaiah the Prophet. It also signifies, indeed, the Paraclete himself, one of the Holy Trinity, that is, the Holy Spirit.

## [2. Verification of the Procession of the Holy Spirit in Holy Scripture]

[351] Nevertheless, the voicing of the procession, although it is attributed in a particular way to the Holy Spirit who transcendentally manifests His unutterable procession, even we are aware is common to others in Holy Scripture. For it [the procession] harmonizes all of His recorded divine operations, as it has been declared throughout Holy Scripture and, indeed, just as the word "birth" befits the Son. For the Holy Fathers of Nicaea say that Holy Scripture says concerning the Son: "I will extend peace to here like a river" [10] [Is 66:12], which proceeds from the true life of the Godhead of the Father. As the Holy Gospel says, the multitudes "wondered at the gracious words which proceeded out of his mouth [the Lord's]" [Lk 4:22]. And the Psalmist says: "O God, when thou didst go forth before thy people" [Ps 67:7]. And somone else states that "the Spirit of the Lord began to go out [proceeded] with him" [Jg 13:25]. And if someone would correctly contemplate what things belong to causes, he would find the reason for procession truly common, just as a line proceeds from a point, a reflection [cf. Heb 1:3], a ray from the sun, a stream from its source, and as wet vapor proceeds from wet bodies of water. Consequently, when you hear in the Scripture that the Son is the source of the Spirit, or [He] sends, or gives or [does] anything similar

to these, do not understand by these terms that He [the Son] brings forth the hypostasis of the Spirit, that is, the very person of the Spirit. For that person proceeds from the Father alone, that is to say, He [the Spirit] has existence from the Father. But you believe that the gifts of the Spirit are granted to Him because He is of the same will and of the same essence as the Father. And again, when you find one or another of the Holy Fathers saying that the Holy Spirit proceeds from the Father through the Son, you use this as a general rule, and you seem to understand that procession means to send through, and to be sent, and to be given. Although they [the Fathers] were uprooting the heresy which alienates the Spirit from the Son, at the same time, as it has just been said, they also wanted to demonstrate the oneness of nature and the true relationship of the Spirit to the Father and the Son. And the Fathers, as one might say, have spoken accordingly.

### [3. Misunderstanding of the Gift and the Sending]

[352] Indeed, it is necessary to closely scrutinize and observe that many of the more naive have actually overlooked and, as they should not have, misunderstood. This has caused a turning away from the true faith, wrongly supposing that the "gift" is the hypostasis and that the "sending" is the existence, which they are not. Observe the power of what has been said. Except that they must be explained in greater detail to become clearer and substantiated by more witnesses, the reasons may become more credible. I say that all the gifts of the Holy Spirit are called spirit, having the same name as the Spirit who bestows them. Hence, when the Holy Spirit grants the gift of sanctification to someone so as to have the body and soul holy, the gift which has been given is called spirit of holiness, as Paul says: "set apart for the Gospel of God which he promised beforehand through his prophets" [Rom 1:1-2], according to the spirit of holiness [cf. Rom 1:5].

If one receives the power and the gift of the Holy Spirit to believe in the promise of the good which shall be given in the future, he has received the spirit of promise. Therefore, Paul says: "[you] were sealed with the promised Holy Spirit" [Eph 1:13]. And if the Holy Spirit grants the gift to someone to believe in the Scriptures, even though he does not know it, this gift is called the spirit of faith, as Paul says: "since we have the same spirit of faith" [2 Cor 4:13]. There is a gift called spirit of sonship, as the same Paul says: "for you did not receive the spirit of slavery to fall back into fear, but you have received the spirit of sonship, when we cry, 'Abba! Father' " [Rom 8:15]. If one is meek and humble of heart, he has received the gift of the spirit of gentleness, as Paul says: "you who are spiritual should restore him in a spirit of gentleness" [Gal 6:1]. There is a gift called spirit of eagerness, as Paul says: "since you are eager for manifestations of the Spirit" [1 Cor 14:12], that is, for gifts. There is a gift of love, as Paul says, that you received: "a spirit of power and love and self-control" [2 Tim 1:7]. And also Isaiah says: "there shall come [353] forth a shoot from the stump of Jesse, and a branch shall grow out of his roots. And the Spirit of the Lord shall rest upon him" [11:1-2]. Thus, the name of the hypostasis [person] of the Spirit himself is in this [verse], and in the previous [Paul's verse] are the names of the gifts as follows: "the spirit of wisdom and understanding, the spirit of counsel and might, the spirit of knowledge and piety, and the fear of the Lord" [Is 11:2].

Can one make an expanded interpretation of Scripture? If the meaning were hidden and obscure, the Holy Spirit would allow that the meanings which are hidden be disclosed to someone, and this person would receive the spirit of revelation, as Paul says: "I pray to God that he may give you a spirit of wisdom and of revelation" [Eph 1:17]. Indeed, God, wishing to show that just as He sends to one who teaches the spirit of wisdom, in the same manner He also sends the spirit of understanding to one who is learning so that he may understand the will of God. For the sake of wisdom He has a mouth for preaching and teaching, and for the sake of understanding He has a heart for learning. David says: "my mouth shall speak wisdom and the meditation of my heart shall bring forth understanding" [Ps 49:3]. He who acts with knowledge has received the spirit of knowledge; he who serves God in words and in works becomes rich in the spirit of piety. For true knowledge is the brightness of the soul, and certainty is by nature the work of all knowledge. Yet sometimes the teacher does not know how to pass on knowledge, for he has not received it. For one does not receive all things, so that he does not think that he has the gift from nature. One receives the gift of teaching in order that he will not willingly boast about matters in which he is found to be inadequate. Another person who is not able to teach may give good advice, and he who lends to others may be found to be borrowing elsewhere. The spirit of wise counsel is given to one who gives advice. The spirit of power [ability] is given to him who accepts the advice in the same way that the one who gives advice receives the gift to say what is useful. So that he who receives the counsel receives the gift of power to accomplish that which is advantageous. There is the gift of spirit of the fear of God. Each one of these gifts is given in proportion to the individual need.

### [4. God Promises the Gift of Loving Kindness]

[354] Elsewhere, God promises to give the gift of loving kindness: "I will pour out on the house of David...and the Spirit of grace and compassion" [Zach 12:10], that is, the gift of loving kindness [cf. Tit 3:4]. Again [God] bestows the gift of humility, wherefore while the three youths were praying even as they were walking on fire, because they were

just, they confessed themselves to be sinners before God.[12] They were chanting as saints, but at the same time they were confessing that they were sinners. Because they were just, they humbled themselves and received the spirit of humbleness, the gift of humility. For this reason, when they recognized the gift, they said: "Nevertheless, let us be accepted in a contrite heart and an humble spirit." [13] When he who receives the whole gift is filled with grace, it is said that he has received the spirit of fulfillment. Thus, the Apostles had the spirit of fulfillment, as it is written: "Paul, filled with the Holy Spirit" [Acts 13:9]. David also asks for "a steadfast spirit" [Ps 15:10], which leads one to honesty, and again, a governing spirit [cf. Ps 51:12],[14] the gift which governs the passions and enables the soul not to be a slave of the passions. And certainly the above is sufficient to prove the equivalence of the names of the spirit. However, the subject concerning the procession [of the Spirit] shall be explained by the following.

[5. The Procession Is Twofold: without Beginning and in Time]
We know, indeed, that the emanation of the Holy Spirit is twofold and not single. We have this assurance concerning the Spirit from the Scriptures as cited above. Therefore, the first [the hypostasis] being incomprehensible and ineffable, thus is certainly without beginning; and the other is [being sent] in time. For the holy [Prophet] Joel and, yes, also blessed Peter receiving it from him said: "and it shall come to pass afterward that I will pour out my spirit on all flesh" [Jl 2:28; cf. Acts 2:17].

[a. Saint Gregory the Theologian]
About the uncaused emanation, as in the case of the birth of the Son, Gregory the Theologian says: "in the beginning He was uncaused, for what is the cause of God?" [15] And again, concerning the same [uncaused]: "He has His being from beyond all time and being beyond all cause and reason." [16] And the other emanation [of the Spirit] is that of [355] cause, because the Lord says in the Gospel according to John: "when the Spirit of truth comes, he will guide you into all the truth" [Jn 16:13]. Moreover, the first, as uncaused, is therefore not beneficial to others; but the latter, as caused, is beneficial to others. Hence, Paul in his Epistle to Titus says: "he saved us...but in virtue of his own mercy, by the washing of regeneration and renewal in the Holy Spirit, which he poured out upon us richly through Jesus Christ our Savior" [Tit 3:5-6].
The first [emanation of the Spirit] is of the divine nature and not the result of the will, about which indeed the theologians, concerning the birth of the Son, also speak. But the latter [emanation], through the benevolent willingness, proceeds to us from God. For this is a gift. Yet it is not without the will of the Giver. For this reason Saint Paul, writing to the Hebrews, says: "while God also bore witness by signs and wonders

and various miracles and by gifts of the Holy Spirit distributed according
to his own will" [Heb 2:4]. Again, the first emanation [uncaused] cannot
possibly also come from the Spirit. For it is impossible for the Spirit to
proceed in person from himself. The latter emanation [of procession in
time] is also from the Spirit. For as Moses, from among the Prophets in
behalf of God, says: "I will take some of the spirit which is upon you and
put it upon them" [Num 11:17]. And [Prophet] Joel also says: "I will
pour out my spirit on all flesh" [Jl 2:28]. Furthermore, from the Apostles
[Saint Peter], the chief among them, says: "you shall receive the gift of
the Holy Spirit" [Acts 2:38], and John [says]: "by this we know that we
abide in him and he in us, because he has given us of his own Spirit" [1 Jn
4:13]. Also Paul, who spoke for Christ, says: "God's love has been
poured into our hearts through the Holy Spirit which has been given to
us" [Rom 5:5]. And the fact that the Apostles spoke of this emanation,
concerning which the Prophets also spoke, is obvious from what has
already been said; and it will also become clear from what will further be
said by the Teachers [of the Church].

### [b. Saint Chrysostom]

For Saint Chrysostom, interpreting the verse, "It is not by measure
that He [God] gives the Spirit" [Jn 3:34], [said]:

> For in this place he means by Spirit the operation of the Spirit, for
> this is that which is divided; but Christ hath all. Its operation is
> [356] unmeasured and entire. Now if His operations are un-
> measured, much is His essence [unmeasured].[17]

Also elsewhere, interpreting from the Psalms the verse, "grace is poured
upon your lips" [Ps 45:2], he [Chrysostom] offers these comments: that
all grace was poured out on that temple, for he said, "for the Father does
not give the Spirit by measure to that temple, yet we have a small portion
and a drop from that grace." For he says [further]: " 'from his fullness
have we all received' [Jn 1:16], as if someone would say, from that which
has overflowed, from that which is left over." And afterwards he
[Chrysostom] said: "God poured out His gift. The Godhead has not been
poured, but His gift. 'Grace is poured upon your lips.' Grace has been
poured out, not He who bestows the Grace."[18]

And again [Chrysostom continues]:

> He [the Psalmist] did not say, I [the Godhead] give the Spirit, but:
> 'I will pour out my spirit on all flesh' [19] [Jl 2:28]. And the grace
> which is given to so many parts of the world is a part of the gift and
> a guarantee. [The Holy Scripture] says: 'He [God] has put his seal
> upon us and given us his Spirit in our hearts as a guarantee' [2 Cor
> 1:22], which means, the part of the operation. For, indeed, the

Paraclete is not divided. Therefore, that temple received that operation and also gave it to the worthy ones from a reservoir.

And elsewhere [Chrysostom says]:

It is necessary for the heretics to understand which names of the Holy Spirit indicate His nature and which [names] interpret His grace. For they [the heretics] who exploited the truth [cf. 2 Cor 2:17] confused everything and ran afoul of the truth.[20] For the Holy Spirit is one thing and another is the gift; a king is one thing, and another is the gift of the king.[21] If you hear someone saying: 'I will send to you the Holy Spirit,' do not understand this to mean the Godhead. For God is not sent. These are names which indicate the operation.[22]

### [c. Saint Gregory the Wonder-worker]

Gregory the Wonder-worker also, in *A Declaration of Faith* which he had by revelation [from the blessed John the Evangelist], has instructed thus: "There is one Holy Spirit deriving His subsistence from God and being revealed by the Son, that is, to mankind."[23] The former [subsistence] concerns the everlasting emanation, and the latter [being made manifest to men] concerns the emanation in time.

### [d. Saint Cyril of Alexandria]

Bishop Cyril of Alexandria also, in the interpretation of the Holy Symbol [Creed], says: "that the Holy Spirit, on the one hand, is poured out, that is, He proceeds from the God and Father." This concerns the ineffable emanation. "And on the other hand [the Holy Spirit] is granted to the creation through the Son," and this concerns emanation [in time].[24]

### [e. Saint Augustine]

[357] Saint Augustine also, in his work *On the Trinity* [says]:

Nor is he less than they because they are givers and he given. Though given as a gift of God, He is, as God, the giver of himself. The Spirit who said: 'blows where it wills' [Jn 3:8] cannot be held to lack power over himself. And similarly the Apostle says: 'all these are inspired by one and the same Spirit, who apportions to each one individually as he wills' [1 Cor 12:11][25]

### [f. Saint Gregory of Nyssa]

Gregory of Nyssa also, in his *Discourses Against Eunomios*, [says]: "the Holy Spirit...having the same cause of His being from the God of all, as the only-begotten Light, and having shone forth in that very Light, and not being divisible by duration, nor by an alien nature, from the

Father or from the only-begotten [Son]." [26] Here the division is shown clearly: on the one hand, the existence of the Spirit by procession from the Father, and on the other hand, emanation from the Son is understood by His appearing [on Pentecost] to us. And not because of this or that reason are they both one and the same, but the former implies this [existence].

### [g. Saint Basil the Great]

Basil the Great also, knowing of such an emanation of the Spirit and that it was of the Spirit, says in his refutation *Against Eunomios*:

> The Holy Spirit...is subject to further increase, being most perfect. This is the reason that all things in Him are perfect: love, joy, peace, forbearance, goodness, wisdom, understanding, will, security, piety, knowledge, sanctification, salvation, faith, operation of powers, gifts of healing, and many other virtues similar to these. He [the Spirit] has acquired nothing of himself but has everything from eternity as the Spirit of God, and has become manifested from Him [God]. Also, He has cause from Him [God] as the source of himself, and was derived from thence. Therefore, He also [the Holy Spirit] is the source of the aforementioned good things. But that which originates from God is a real person; while the others [aforementioned goods], which derive from God, are his operations. [27]

And again, in the same *Refutation* Saint Basil continues:

> Just as the Father is said to have distributed the operations to those who are worthy of receiving them and the Son distributes the various gifts to those who are worthy of the diakonia [ministry], in like manner the Holy Spirit is witnessed distributing the gifts to those who are worthy of receiving the gifts.... Observe how here also the operation of the Holy Spirit has been coordinated with the operation of the Father and the Son. [28] For when everything is [358] wrought by God through Jesus Christ in Spirit, I see that the operation of the Father and of the Son and of the Holy Spirit is not divided. [29]

### [6. Grace—Operation of the Holy Spirit]

### [a. Saint Athanasios the Great]

Athanasios, the most proficient in conformity with the above, also refers everything to the one God, the Father, in his *Letters to Sarapion* saying:

> The blessed Paul, knowing this, does not divide the Trinity as you

do but teaches its unity when he wrote to the Corinthians concerning things spiritual: 'Now there are varieties of gifts...but it is the same God who inspires them all in every one' [1 Cor 12:4, 6]...For the gifts which the Spirit divides to each are bestowed from the Father through the Word [Logos]. Indeed, all things that are of the Father, are of the Son also. Therefore, those things which are given from the Son in Spirit are gifts of the Father. And when the Spirit is in us, in this himself is the Father. And thus it is: 'I and the Father will come to him [men] and make our home with him' [Jn 14:23]. This again the same Apostle taught when he wrote to the Corinthians in the Second Epistle as well, saying: 'The grace of the Lord Jesus Christ, and the love of God and Father, and the fellowship of the Holy Spirit be with you all' [2 Cor 13:14]. For this grace and gift that is given, is given in the Trinity from the Father, through the Son, in the Holy Spirit. And just as the grace given is from the Father through the Son, so we can have no communion in the gift, except in the Holy Spirit. For it is when we partake of Him [Spirit] that we have the love of the Father, and the grace of the Son, and the communion of the Holy Spirit himself. Consequently, it is clear from the [above] that the operation of the Trinity is one. For the Apostle does not mean that the things which are given are given differently and separately by each person, but that what is given is given in the Trinity, and that all things are from the one God.[30]

Indeed, the Evangelist Luke also in Acts, speaking on the subject concerning this emanation, says: "And there appeared to them tongues as of fire, distributed and resting on each one of them. And they were all filled with the Holy Spirit" [Acts 2:3]. And further [he says]: "Now when Simon saw that the Spirit was given through the laying on of the Apostle's hands" [Acts 8:18]. And later on [he says]: "While Peter was still saying this, the Holy Spirit fell on all who heard the word" [Acts 10:44]. And the most holy Paul in his First Epistle to the Corinthians says:

To each is given the manifestation of the Spirit for the common [359] good: to one is given, through the Spirit, the utterances of wisdom; and to another, the utterance of knowledge according to the same Spirit; and to another, faith by the same Spirit; to another, gifts of healing by the one Spirit; to another, the working of miracles; to another, prophecy; to another, the ability to distinguish between spirits; to another, various kinds of tongues. All these are inspired by one and the same Spirit, who apportions to each one individually as He wills [12: 7-11].

Also, Peter, the chief [of the Apostles, says] in Acts: "Being therefore exalted at the right hand of God, and having received from the Father the promise of the Holy Spirit, he has poured out this which you see and hear" [2:33]. And also: "Can anyone forbid water for baptizing these people who have received the Holy Spirit just as we have?" [Acts 10:47]. And the Lord, being mindful of both of the emanations of the Spirit, says in the Gospel according to John: "But when the Counselor [Paraclete] comes, whom I shall send to you from the Father, even the Spirit of truth, who proceeds from the Father, He will bear witness to me" [15:26].

Indeed, then, in saying "when he comes," He indicated the dominion of the Spirit while He emphasized emanation in time in saying, "Whom I shall send to you from the Father," that is, that the Holy Spirit is not rivalling God. Because of us He [the Son] presented this emanation, for He [the Spirit] was sent to us. And with the additon of "who proceeds from the Father," He [the Son] bequeathed in a manner befitting God the eternal and uncaused emanation of the Holy Spirit, which it is indeed. Thus, the emanation of the Spirit is twofold: that of being and that which is called. The former [emanation], for reasons of explicitness, has been correctly called first and hypostatic and of being, while the latter [emanation] is [called] second and communicative of operation. Again, the only cause of the first emanation is the Father. The cause of the second emanation [sending] is the Son and the Holy Spirit himself. Accordingly, none of the Teachers of our Church said that the Holy Spirit proceeded personally from the Son, or that He [the Spirit] has existence from the Son or is an emission of the Son. None of them have ever stated that the Son is an emitter or a cause of the Holy Spirit. All of them declare that to be poured out, and to gush forth and to proceed, and to shine forth, and to be sent, and to be granted, and to be given all come through Him [the Son]. And they [the Teachers] were not unaware that these terms are suitable to express the communication of the emanations [of the Holy Spirit].

[7. Discerning between Sending and Procession of the Holy Spirit]

[360] But they [the Teachers] say that the originating of the Spirit from the Son, the pouring, the shining, the listing [as the wind], the sending, the granting, the giving, and the many other similar expressions are the same as the proceeding from the Son. Therefore, if the emission of the Spirit is the same as the giving, then He who emits must be the giver of that which is emitted; and the giver is He who emits that which is given. Consequently, the giving of the Spirit is an emanation of operation, and the emission is an emanation of being [hypostasis]. But being [hypostasis] and operation are not the same. Consequently, to be given is not the same as to be emitted. Again, if the giving of the Holy Spirit is the same as the procession, then either through the giving, which is com-

municable, the procession will also be communicable; or through the procession, which is incommunicable, the giving will also then be incommunicable. Yet the former, the holy giving, is communicated; while the latter, the procession, remains incommunicable. But the communicable is not the same as the incommunicable. Consequently, the procession is not the same as the communicable.

Again, if the pouring out of the Holy Spirit is the same as the procession, then either through the procession which is invisible, the pouring out will also be invisible; or through the pouring forth, which is visible, the procession will also then be visible. But the former [the pouring forth] was seen by thousands, while the latter [the procession] remains invisible. Therefore, the visible and invisible are not the same. Consequently, the procession is not the same as the pouring out. And furthermore, if the gift of the Holy Spirit and the procession are the same, then through the procession, which is single, the gift will also be single; or through the gift which is diversified, the procession will also be diversified. Moreover, the former, the procession, is single; while the latter, the gift, is diversified. But single and diversified are not the same. Consequently, the procession is not the same as the gift. Again, if the sending of the Spirit and the procession are the same, either through the sending to us which occurs in time, the procession to us shall also be in time, and was and is, and truly is, or through the procession, which was not made to us now, nor before the establishment of the world. Nor will the sending of the Spirit ever come to us. Nevertheless, the sending to us occurs, and the procession in itself was, and is, and shall be, and it truly is. [361] Consequently, the procession is not the same as the sending of the Spirit.

Again, if the personal procession of the Spirit is the same as the grace which is given to us, then either through the procession, which is personal, the grace will also be personal; or through the grace, which is common, the procession will also then be common. Moreover, grace comes forth from the three persons [of the Holy Trinity], but the procession of the Spirit is not from three [persons]. Consequently, the procession is not the same as the grace. Again, if the sending of the Spirit and the procession are the same (the sending which is given for us through the goodness of God), then the procession will also be given to us through His goodness; or if the procession is without cause, then the sending shall also occur without cause. But certainly the sending occurs for a cause when it occurs. And the procession of the Spirit occurs eternally and is not through any cause. Consequently, the procession is not the same as the sending. Indeed, if the sending of the Spirit is the same as the procession, certainly it is not the one and the other. Indeed, not only is the Holy Spirit sent by the Father, but also the Son himself is sent. Consequently, the sending of the Son will also be the same as His birth, and the same as the procession of the Spirit. However, the Father has not begotten the Son as a being [hypostasis] by sending and by giving Him, and by abiding in us through the Spirit. Nor, consequently, does He [the Father] cause the Spirit to proceed as a being by sending and by giving Him, and by abiding in us through the Son.

### [8. The Son Is Sent by the Holy Spirit As Well]

And in the same manner, indeed, we have to say the same concerning the Son and concerning the Spirit. Inasmuch as the Holy Spirit is not only sent by the Son, but also the Son is sent by the Spirit, and if the sending and the procession of the Spirit is the same, then surely the sending and the birth of the Son will be the same. However, the Spirit does not beget the Son by sending and giving and abiding Him in us. Nor, consequently, does the Son in the sending and in the giving of the Holy Spirit cause Him [the Spirit] to proceed as a being. Therefore, if the eternal procession of the Spirit occurs by cause, then the eternal birth of the Son will be by cause.

He who would say concerning Him [Son] that He was without cause in the beginning, does not speak the truth. Indeed, if He for whom these were caused is greater than He who is the cause, then the Spirit has [362] His existence because of us. Consequently, we are superior to Him as far as the final cause is concerned. And then who could possibly enumerate the many irrational conclusions which follow such reasoning? But yet, if the person of the Spirit, existing eternally and inseparably in the Father, is the same as the gift given to us in time and communicatively, [then] His eternal existence is the same as His being given to us. For not only the Father and Son are giving Him [Spirit], but He also gives himself, and of himself. Consequently, the Holy Spirit proceeds himself in person.

Furthermore, it could not be thought of, even by the demons themselves, that the Son together with the Father begets himself and is the cause of His own birth. How could we then believe that the Holy Spirit personally creates himself and is the cause of His own procession? And which place of damnation could cast forth such a thought? If, indeed, on the one hand, the eternal procession of the Holy Spirit is not personally from himself, for it is illogical for Him to proceed from himself as it has been proved, on the other hand, the giving to us is from the Spirit also. Consequently, the person of the Spirit is one thing, and the gift is another; the giving of the Spirit is one thing, and His existence is another.

But that which greatly deceives many persons is that whenever the Holy Fathers speak concerning that which has been given or concerning the gift, they know that He [the Spirit] is not only from the Father, but is also given from the Son. Thus, He [the Spirit] proceeds from the Father through the Son, and He is bestowed by the Father through the Son, and He is made visible by the Father through the Son, and many similar [statements] which the Holy Fathers have laid down. Many persons who hear them [the Holy Fathers] but do not understand that these statements are not said concerning the person of the Spirit, but concerning the gift, or perhaps because they have some eagerness concerning the Holy Spirit, although not in full knowledge, immediately understand the giving as the procession and the gift as the person of the Spirit. Hence, they think that the dogma is fortified by these utterances, and a lone wall reaching the sky separates them from us.

### [9. The Varieties of Gifts]

But, of course, the circle of Teachers is able to persuade them from such a belief. Rather Paul, who speaks for Christ, is sufficient, indeed, [363] to confirm for all, saying: "varieties of gifts, etc..." [1 Cor 12:4]. Now, to the one is given this gift through the Spirit; to the other, another gift; to another person, still another gift; and to the other, yet another. And to all of them [Paul] imposes the word as a conclusion: "All these are inspired by one and the same Spirit, who apportions to each one individually as he wills" [1 Cor 12:11]. Thus, grace is a matter of will and not of nature. Therefore, the variety [of gifts] is a matter not of persons, but of operations. Moreover, just as God who activates the operations is not an operation, but the person of the Father himself, so too the Lord who apportions the ministries is not a ministry, but absolutely the person of the Son himself. In like manner the Spirit who apportions the gifts is not a gift, but the person of the Holy Spirit himself. If, however, the person and the gift of the Holy Spirit is the same, then the giving of the Spirit and the procession would be the same. Consequently, the ministry of the Lord and the Lord himself would be one and the same, and also the operation of God and God himself would be the same, since the person who would apportion the gifts would be the same as He who is apportioned.

But the Divine Apostle divides this opinion in order to show that the person who apportions is different from those who are to be apportioned. Thus, with a piercing voice he [Paul] says: "All these are inspired by one and the same Spirit, who apportions to each one individually as He wills" [1 Cor 12:11]. That is to say, on the one hand, those things which are apportioned are many and diversified, and on the other hand, the person who is apportioning them is one and the same and single. And, therefore, just as the Father in granting gifts to human beings does not bestow himself personally on someone, and just as the Son in giving powers to those who are worthy does not give himself personally to anyone, in like manner, also, the Holy Spirit, who distributes the common gifts of the Father and of the Son and of himself to the faithful, does not grant himself to anyone personally. However, the Holy Fathers speak of these common gifts in the singular, i.e., spirit, and giving, and grace, and gift, and charisma; and in the plural, i.e., spirits, and charismata, and givings, and gifts, and graces. Also, the gifts which are imparted by one of the persons of the Holy Trinity in particular, and the gifts which are granted by two persons whomever [in the Trinity], one might say, and the gifts which are given by the three persons are given to those who are worthy directly from the Spirit, but not directly from the Father and the Son.

[10. Nature of the Trinity, the Hypostases and Operation Differ]

[364] But certainly falsehood brings forth tempests and chaos and darkness. Let the Teachers of the truth witness that nature in the Holy Trinity is one thing and persons [hypostasis], another and operations, still another.

John the Damascene says: "However one must know that operation is one thing, and what is operative [acting] is another.... Operation, then, is the efficacious and essential activity of nature. And that which is operative is nature, from which operation proceeds. That which is operated is the effect of the operation. And the operator is the person who performs the operation, that is, the hypostasis [subsistence]." [31]

Gregory the Theologian [says]: "The person who begets is distinct from the act of begetting. He who wills is distinct from the act of willing, the speaker is distinct from the speech, or else we are all vindictive. Therefore, the former is the mover, and the latter is the motion." [32]

Also, Saint Justin the Philosopher and Martyr says: "If to exist is one thing and to be contained in is another, and the essence of God exists, then the will is contained in the essence. Consequently, the essence of God is one thing and His will is another." [33]

Also, Saint Maximos says: "None of the beings has existed without natural operation. For the Holy Fathers explicitly say that no nature whatsoever exists nor is known to be without this essential operation." [34]

And Cyril of Alexandria says: "If to give birth is the same as creating, then the birth-giver will be the creator of that to which birth is given. Also, he who is the creator will also be the one who gives birth to what has been created. But the creating is an operation, and the giving birth is of nature. Yet nature and operation are not the same. Consequently, the giving of birth is not the same as the creating." [35]

[11. Nature and Divine Operation Are Not the Same]

Therefore, operation is one thing, and person [hypostasis] is another, while the essence is still another. Just as nothing gives birth to itself, thus nothing causes itself to proceed in the matter of existence. The person who gives birth is distinct from that which is born. He who causes procession is distinct from him who proceeds. The Son is one thing, and the birth of the Son is another. The Spirit is one thing, and the procession of the Spirit is another. The existence of God is one thing, and the condescension of God is another. And this is what we have to say concerning the procession of the Holy Spirit.

## [B.] CONCERNING FREE WILL

[365] Concerning free will, it is first necessary, according to us, to consider that evil is not in beings, nor does it have its existence from God. Observe that Scripture also says: "And God saw everything that He had made, and behold, it was very good" [Gen 1:31], and not merely good, but "very" good. What then is evil? It is an innate disposition of the indolent soul having the tendency to oppose virtue and to fall away from the good. Therefore, do not examine evil externally, nor imagine some pristine nature of wickedness, but rather let everyone reckon himself the leader of iniquity in himself. For whatever happens, some things always come to happen to us by nature, such as old age and sickness, while some others happen by chance of themselves, as incidents without reason; and others happen because of us, such as controlling our passions, or condemning sensual pleasures, or withholding wrath, or encouraging an irritated person, or speaking the truth or telling a lie, being agreeable, respecting the customs, and being moderate, or being pompous, or boasting. Wherefore, do not search elsewhere for the origins of those which you are master of. But know that the main evil has received its origin from voluntary failings. For, indeed, if it was involuntary and not from us, there would not be such a great fear threatening those who commit crimes. Consequently, the punishments of the courts would not be needed for the criminals who deserve to be repaid like for like.

Furthermore, the wise Solomon says: "for God created man to be immortal, and made him to be an image of his own eternity. Nevertheless, through envy of the devil, death came into the world" [Wis 2:23]. Therefore, inasmuch as man was created in God's image, man is a ruler and not a slave. For God says: "Let us make man in our image... and let them have dominion"[Gen 1:26]. He [God] did not say, let us be enraged, let us eagerly desire, and let us grieve, for the passions had not been included in the image of God, but rather the thought is the master of the passions. "Man in the image of God" refers to the inner man. But you may say, why does He not speak to us concerning reason? He [God] said [366] that man was created according to the image of God. Is reason then a man? Harken to the Apostle [Paul] who says: "Though our outer nature is wasting away, our inner nature is being renewed every day" [2 Cor 4:16].

How can I know man? One is he who is seen, and the other is he who is

hidden in whom he is seen, i.e., the invisible inner man. Therefore, we
have an inner man, and we are dual. For certainly that which has been
said is true, that we are within ourselves. Just as the body is an instrument of man, it is also an instrument of the soul. Man is primarily a soul
[created] in the image and after the likeness [of God] [cf. Gen 1:26].[36]
The former [image], we have through creation; the latter [likeness], we
achieve by free choice. In the first creation it exists within us to become
the image of God. However, the "likeness of God" may be achieved by
our free choice. Thus, then, the likeness by choice exists in us potentially,
and it becomes a reality by our personal endeavors.[37] If the Lord when
creating us had not said: "let us make" and "after our likeness," and if He
had not granted to us the ability to develop "into His likeness," we would
not have received the "likeness to God" by our own power. Therefore,
He created us with the potential to be similar to God. In granting us the
ability to resemble God, He permitted us to be the workers of our
likeness to God, so that the realization of "our likeness" would not bring
praise to anyone else [other than God]. In order that this miracle might
become mine and not of another, He bestowed upon me [the power] to
become like Him, to become "after His likeness." For by being created in
the image [of God], I have the gift of reason, but I attain the condition of
being in the likeness as I develop into a Christian: "be perfect, as your
heavenly Father is perfect" [Mt 5:48].

Have you observed where the Lord renders to us the gift of being
created after His likeness? For "He makes his sun rise on the evil and on
the good, and sends rain on the just and on the unjust" [Mt 5:45]. If,
therefore, it is so, there is nothing to prevent man, after the Fall by the
[367] sin [of Adam and Eve], from turning aside from evil, which is
foreign [to him], and doing the good and choosing the virtuous because
he has free will. Neither does anything spoken by Moses negate completely the choice of the good. Indeed, he points out that there is evil
which naturally besets man before the flood and after the flood, the
lustful desire, or any such thing. God, indeed, granted it [free will] for
our use, but we misused it for evil. And the Hebrew [interpreters], instead of "intently bent," placed "the nature of man" as inclined toward
evil from his youth [cf. Gen 8:21]. And it is also understood by them in
this manner: that the figment of the heart, that is to say, the rational free
will, is to pursue and sensually delight in evil things from one's youth.
However, man was not created to enjoy sensual satisfaction, but for the
procreation of children, and not for fornication, but to control the passion, and not for calumny.

That man had the power after the Fall to choose the good, shall be
made evident by the following: for unless this was so, David would not
have said, "Draw near to him, and be enlightened" [Ps 34:5]; and another
Prophet, speaking in behalf of God, "Return to me...and I will return

to you" [Zach 1:3]; and another, "Jerusalem, Jerusalem...how often would I have gathered your children together...and you would not!" [Mt 23:27]. And the Lord in the Gospel says: "If any man would come after me" [Mt 16:24]. This is evident more explicitly in the Parable of the Sower: "A sower went out to sow his seed" [Mt 13:3]. He did not say "to plow," because plowing would force us to bring forth. Also, the Parable of the Prodigal Son says: "But when he came to himself he said, 'How many of my father's hired servants have bread enough and to spare?' " [Lk 15:17]. Peter also says: "Christ also suffered for you, leaving you an example, that you should follow in his steps" [1 Pet 2:21]. From all these, indeed, it is evident that it depends upon us if we are to rise and to [368] follow. We have also the power to choose the good, but no less the evil. We need but one thing, that is, the help from God so that we may achieve the good and be saved. Without this we can accomplish nothing, according to [John]: "For apart from me you can do nothing" [Jn 15:5], and other similar texts [from the Gospels]. Thus, concerning this matter [of free will], the above suffices.

## [C.] CONCERNING THE SACRAMENTS

But since you are content with some of the sacraments, even though you have dangerously distorted and changed the written teachings of the Old and New [Testament] to you own purpose, you further say that some of them are not sacraments, but only traditions, not having been established in Holy [scriptural] Texts. But you oppose them in every way, just as chrismation, which was accepted even by Saint John Chrysostom. Some others you drag along as does a torrent. And then you call yourself theologians!

## [D.] CONCERNING THE INVOCATION OF SAINTS

### [Confession and the Monastic Life]

You reckon the invocation of the saints, their icons, and their sacred relics as futile. You reject their veneration, taking as a pretext the Hebrew source. Moreover, you also reject confession to one another. In addition, you reject the angelic, monastic life. And about these matters we say that the Holy [Scripture] passages concerning them have not been interpreted by such theologians as you are, for neither Saint Chrysostom nor any other of the blessed and true theologians interpreted as if they were dragged along by a torrent. But, indeed, he [Chrysostom] and the holy men after him, being full of the Holy Spirit who performed supernatural miracles while they were living and after they died, interpreted [the Holy Scriptures] as they did; and they received such traditions, and [369] they handed them down successively and gave them to us as indispensable and pious [sacraments]. Some of these even Old Rome also keeps and acquiesces with us. From whence have you reckoned better than Old and New Rome? Indeed, have you forsaken the interpretations of the true theologians and considered your own as more preferable? From the source of the Hebrew tradition we learn from history that contempt for the holy icons and sacred relics had its origin from the Hebrews. The schisms of the Lutherans there, which are many and various, were indeed caused and spread by some Hebrews, as it has been broached abroad feigning piety. And already, as you see, they have taken root and have opened the way for more evil as day by day they grow worse. Being completely not in communion with them [the Hebrews], we covet and, indeed, unshakably, the sacraments of our Church. We closely adhere to the teachings which have been uttered by the successors of the God-preaching Holy Apostles. We consider their interpretations as more precious than all the gold and gems. Indeed, we invoke the all-holy saints not as saviors and redeemers, God forbid, for only One is the Savior and Redeemer, the Christ; but we who are sinners and in the midst of evils hold them forth as intermediaries who have completed the journey of life in a holy and satisfactory manner and have departed to God, and who richly intercede for us. And of course, we are not committing sin by continually pursuing this aim. For by venerating their holy icons and their relics which cause thousands of healings to those who on occasion approach in faith, we reap extraordinary beneficences from them, and we are illumined in soul and body. We confess also to one another, according to the Holy Scriptures. We revere the monastic and angelic life. We pray that those who lift up these burdens do not turn back at all, if indeed they would choose to be properly prepared for the kingdom of heaven.

## [E. EPILOGUE]

[370] Therefore, we request that from henceforth you do not cause us more grief, nor write to us on the same subject if you should wish to treat these luminaries and theologians of the Church in a different manner. You honor and exalt them in words, but you reject them in deeds. For you try to prove our weapons which are their holy and divine discourses as unsuitable. And it is with these documents that we would have to write and contradict you. Thus, as for you, please release us from these cares. Therefore, going about your own ways, write no longer concerning dogmas; but if you do, write only for friendship's sake. Farewell.

Jeremiah, Patriarch of Constantinople
Issued in the year 1581, June 6

Protonotarios Theodosios

## NOTES

1. St. Augustine, *On the Trinity*, PL 42.845-68.
2. St. Athanasios, *The Incarnation of the Word*, PG 25.95-198.
3. St. Cyril of Alexandria, *First Letter to Palladios*, PG 77.44-50.
4. St. Epiphanios, *The Ancoratos*, PG 43.17-236.
5. St. Basil the Great, *Against Eunomios, Homily 5*, PG 29.725.
6. St. Gregory of Nazianzos, *Fourth Theological Oration*, cf. NPNF Ser. 2, vol. 7, 317.
7. St. Cyril of Alexandria, *Thesaurus of the Holy and Consubstantial Trinity*, PG 75.572.
8. St. Athanasios, *Letters to Serapion*, PG 75.9-656.
9. The KJV has "heretic."
10. River of peace refers to the Son.
11. Patriarch Jeremiah's text has "the mouth of the Lord."
12. *S of 3 Y*, vs. 5-6 amd 25-26.
13. Ibid. vs. 15.
14. The RSV has "willing" spirit.
15. St. Gregory Nazianzos, *Third Theological Oration, 29.19*, PG 36.100; cf. NPNF Ser. 2, vol. 7, 308.
16. Ibid. *30.11*; cf. NPNF Ser. 2, vol. 7, 313.
17. St. John Chrysostom, *Commentary on the Gospel of St. John*, PG 59.174; cf. NPNF Ser. 1, vol. 14, 104-05.
18. St. John Chrysostom, *On the Holy Spirit*, PG 52.826 N.B. A comparison with the original quotations recorded here, indicates that Jeremiah includes his own comments within the quotations. An attempt was made in the translation to separte the "comments" from the words of Chrysostom.
19. Ibid. p. 820.
20. Ibid. p. 819.
21. Ibid. p. 820.
22. Ibid. p. 825.
23. St. Gregory the Miracle-worker. *Exposition of Faith*, PG 10.985; cf. H.B. Swete, *The Holy Spirit in the Ancient Church*, p. 148.
24. St. Cyril of Alexandria, *The Third Letter to Nestorios*, PG 77.117.
25. St. Augustine, *On the Holy Trinity, Bk. 15*, PL 42.1091; cf. LCC trans. J. Burnaby. *Augustine: Later Works*, vol. 8, bk. 15.165 (with corrections).
26. St. Gregory of Nyssa, *Discourse Against Eunomios*, PG 45.369; cf. NPNF Ser. 2, vol. 5, 70.
27. St. Basil the Great, *Against Eunomios, Bk. 5*, PG 29.772.
28. Ibid. *Bk. 3*, PG 29.664.
29. Ibid. *Bk. 5*, PG 29.761. N. B. Bks. 4 and 5 of *Against Eunomios* are acknowledged to be works of Didymos the Blind; cf. Quasten, *Patrology*, 3, p.88.
30. St. Athanasios, *Letters to Serapion*, PG 26.600, 1421-24; cf. Shapland, *The Letters of Athanasios*, pp. 141-42.
31. St. John the Damascene, *Exposition of the Orthodox Faith, Bk. 3, 15*, PG 94.1048.
32. St. Gregory the Theologian, *On the Son, Oration 3*, PG 36.13; cf. NPNF Ser. 2, vol. 7, 303.
33. St. Justin the Martyr, *Quest. Christian. ad Graecos*, PG 6.1432.
34. *Acta Maximi*, PG 90.123.
35. St. Cyril of Alexandria, *Thesaurus of the Holy and Consubstantial Trinity*, PG 75.312.
36. St. Basil the Great, *On the Structure of Man*, PG 30.17.
37. Δυνάμει = potential, ἐνέργειᾳ = reality.

Chapter 7

# THE THIRD THEOLOGICAL EXCHANGE:
# TÜBINGEN TO CONSTANTINOPLE

*[ The Third Reply of the Tübingen Theologians
to Patriarch Jeremiah II]*

A reply to the third patriarchal answer by Martin Crusius, translated into
Greek, in the month of December 1581, to those around [with] the
Patriarch of Constantinople, Master Jeremiah,

Grace to you, and peace from God our Father and the Lord Jesus Christ.

### [Salutation]

[371] Most Holy Sir, with pure heart and sincere love we shared in
your suffering of distress and confusion, which had overtaken Your
Holiness in the previous time, and we earnestly strived by consoling to
lighten that calamity. In the same manner now when, with the grace of
God, tranquility prevails again and when matters have improved for the
better, we sincerely rejoice with Your Holiness that with the grace of
God, the previous order and service have been restored in the Church.
Furthermore, we entreat God, the Father of our Lord Jesus Christ, that
the Greek Churches, with the assistance of the Holy Spirit and under the
diligence, wakefulness, and faithful care of Your Holiness, will tend
most salvifically the Holy Gospel of Christ, so that they acknowledge the
Chief Shepherd Christ as their only Savior and publicly express their
thanksgiving toward Jesus Christ by good works, which He has ordered
so that having honorably finished the course of the present life and having kept the faith, they will receive the righteous crown of everlasting
life. May it be so.

Now, then, we come to your response to our booklet and briefly, as an
[372] epilogue, duly inquire into it not afflicted with obstinacy and difficulties (which are truly far from us), but drawn together by necessity to
briefly witness to the truth (for in our preceding two writings we made
known our position at length), and to make it known to you that our
booklet will not today or ever be revised.

[1.] Concerning the Procession of the Holy Spirit

Since we offered [the proof] on this subject, among the many and other proofs, that the Holy Spirit is sent not only by the Father, but also by the Son, it necessarily follows that the Holy Spirit proceeds not only from the Father, but also from the Son. You, however, think that the entire solution of this subject depends on this: you separate His gifts and His activities from the essence of the Spirit. And you surmised this from the many references from the Holy Scriptures and the Holy Fathers. But we need none of these arguments. For it is not our purpose to doubt you, nor to disagree with you concerning this matter. For we were teaching the same in our Churches up to now, following in this respect Saint Paul who says: "Now there are varieties of gifts, but the same Spirit; and there are varieties of services, but the same Lord; and there are varieties of working, but it is the same God who inspires them all in every one" [1 Cor 12:4-6]. Indeed, we reckon thus. Just as the Father would not send the Holy Spirit unless the Holy Spirit proceeds from Him, neither would the Son send the Holy Spirit unless the same [Holy Spirit] would proceed from the Son also. For if the sending and the procession are not one and the same thing (as we know from the past that the sending depends on the procession), and if one is able to send the Holy Spirit in time, the same Spirit proceeds also from Him [one who sent Him] before all ages. Again, since the Spirit is a power of God who is above all, we do not rashly and on purpose conclude that this power, nonetheless, proceeds [373] from the everlasting Son of God or from the Father. Besides, it is because in the God-inspired Scriptures the Holy Spirit was named Spirit not only of the Father, but also of the Son. Up to the present time (and we request you not be angry) we have not received any solid and satisfactory reply to these proofs and others which are in our writings.

[2.] Concerning Free Will

Concerning the free will of man, human ability in spiritual matters, we understand that you consider man as being in such a condition and, as such, in which and as such as he was before the Fall when he still retained the image and the likeness of God. Then you write in conclusion (which we greatly admire) that he is the master of his passions. And, indeed, an extraordinarily great perversion and distortion took possession of the nature of all men after the Fall of the human race, as the renowned Moses testifies, saying: " The wickedness was *intently* brooding over evil all the days" [Gen 6:5]. The Septuagint version says: ἐπιμελῶς (*intently*), which is interpreted by Favorunus as *continually* and earnestly. And in the Hebrew text (for one must always go to the source and the original language of the Holy Scriptures, since we do not wish to be mistaken concerning the truth in which the interpreters have erred in many places) is this small word ‏רק‎ (ra'k), which as the experts of language know, is translated as *only* (μόνον). Then, by nature the human heart is *only* in evil from youth, and all the days [i.e., continually]. And it is no wonder.[1] For Adam became a father not in sinlessness as before, but after the Fall; and he begot not in the image and likeness of God, but in his own appearance and image, that is, Adam begot sinners as he was himself a sinner. And this finds in Paul's words an irrefutable proof: "not that we are sufficient of ourselves to claim any thing as coming from us" [2 Cor 3:5]; "for God is in you, both to will and to work" [Phil 2:13]. And Christ, also, delineates for us the corruption and the wickedness of [374] the human heart when He says: "for out of the heart come evil thoughts, murder, adultery, fornication, theft, false witness, slander" [Mt 15:19]. These are lurking, indeed, in the hearts, and at times and on occasions they are cast forth (unless they are hindered by the Holy Spirit) because "we were brought forth in iniquity, and in sin we were conceived" [Ps 51:5]. So that they who compare the powers of man, which were acquired after the Fall, with those powers which existed before the Fall of Adam, are of the same opinion as we: It is as if a man who has reached the lowest point of poverty might strive to become very rich from the great riches he had in the past. But many such powers, which existed before the Fall, truly possess the daily experience; and for this power some boast with such big words, who either do not comprehend sufficiently what great perfection the Law of God demands from us, or they do not sufficiently recognize their own natural corruption and weakness.

### [3.] Concerning the Sacraments

And now concerning the sacraments. We recognize two: that of baptism and that of the Lord's Supper. For we know from the Scripture writers that they have been instituted by Christ. Rightfully these are called sacraments because they have visible elements which were established by the Lord for this purpose, and which were set forth as promises concerning the forgiveness of sins and life everlasting. Surely, our faith can be established on these two sacraments. But the others which do not have the same definition are cast out naturally from the enumeration of the true sacraments.

### [4.] Concerning the Invocation of Saints

We admire the holy men who have been endowed by God with such [375] extraordinary and remarkable talents. We endeavor to imitate their faith, their hope, their love, their patience, and their other virtues. But we neither invoke them, nor worship them; nor do we worship their relics or their icons, for we have learned from the Holy Scriptures to worship God alone. On this matter it does not escape your notice in the least that the words to worship (λατρεύειν) and to serve (δουλεύειν) are to be used differently. Indeed, service (δουλεία) is found to be delegated not only to the creatures, but also to God [cf. Dt 6; Mt 4] as in Matthew 6: "You cannot serve God and mammon" [Mt 6:24], and also in 1 Thessalonians: "to serve a living and true God" [1:9], and vice versa. Worship (λατρεία) is not only of God, but also of creatures. "Ye shall do no servile work on them" [Ex 12:16]. Worship (λατρεία) is servitude (δουλεία) upon payment, and the payment is the wage, says Suidas. Also, in John, chapter 2, according to Nonnus, a water-carrier knew he was a hired servant of the assembled crowd. Also, according to Xenophon in chapter 3 in *The Education of Cyrus*, even though someone is prepared to indict one to purchase a person so as not to worship (λατρεῦσαι) his own wife should she become a captive, this word λατρεῦσαι (worship) in what followed is interpreted by the word δουλεύειν (servitude) of this woman.[2] Neither do the saints claim such servitude from us, nor is it taught in the Holy Scriptures, nor is it necessary for the saints to be invoked, nor their icons to be worshiped. Rather, therefore, we are taught by the Scriptures that those who honor the icon thus should be punished, which is surely known by you. But neither is even one promise found to indicate that the worship and invocation of the saints is advantageous to men. But rather Isaiah teaches the opposite when he says: "For thou art our Father, though Abraham does not know us and Israel does not acknowledge us; thou, O Lord, are our Father, deliver us, thy name has been upon us from the beginning" [Is 63:16]. And if the saints do not know us, how can they hear our prayers? How can they help us? Therefore, we are content with the invocation of the one God, of the Father, and of the Son, and of the Holy Spirit, receiving from Him physical, as well as spiritual, blessings; and recognizing them, we remain debtors to Him and thank Him for His bounteous favors.

### [5.] Concerning Confession of Sins

[376] Again, we do not reject the confession of sins. For, indeed, we publicly confess our sins in the Church prior to communing of the Holy Eucharist, gratefully receiving remission of them; and, especially, we again make confession to the deacons prior to communing the Eucharist. We do not require in the confession to the priest the specific enumeration of all sins which one has committed. For such a confession, by the enumeration of each of the transgressions, would be humanly impossible according to: "But who can discern his errors?" [Ps 19:13]. Nor does Christ demand this from us. Therefore, we do not place such a burden on the Church. You know, indeed, the writing of Chrysostom, where it is affirmed that it is sufficient if we would confess our sins to Christ, if we would show our wounds to Him who is able to heal them. But we observe that you abundantly offer great honors and praises to the Holy Fathers, especially to the Greek Fathers, and frequently of late, depart from their teachings. So we also should not be blamed for doing the same when they

are led astray from the Scripture on which the Church is established.

### [6.] Concerning the Monastic Life

And now concerning the monastic life. We will believe that this manner of life is angelic when this eulogy is proved by the Holy Scriptures. But of this manner of life, being an invention of human cleverness (without the divine word and command), we justly prefer other callings and orders of life, which are God-commanded, to this one (we say this without insult to anyone). Human nature was created by God so that each one, according to his calling, will serve God as well as his neighbor. We forbid no one, however, to lead a celibate life. It is acceptable to us only if one conducts his life purely before God.

### [377]                    [7.] Concerning Schisms and Heresies

We are surprised, indeed, that you are charging us, having grown with schisms and heresies in our Churches. For it is not necessary for you to suspect the Churches of error from the fact that some distorters of the Churches, who were disturbing them [the Churches], go astray and who because of this were driven out of the company of the Church. John says: "They went out from us, but they were not of us" [1 Jn 2:19]. Also, Paul did not despise nor condemn the Church of the Ephesians when he said to the presbyters themselves: "I know that after my departure fierce wolves will come in among you, not sparing the flock; and from among your own selves will arise many speaking perverse things, to draw away the disciples after them" [Acts 20:29-30]. Yet even though many will be scandalized by such disruptions, nevertheless, we are of the opinion that it is better for us to continue to carry these Churches, which struggle against the roving heretics, using the weapons of God, rather than those Churches which in external matters seem calm but in internal matters are afflicted, harboring great errors within them. For just as the bodies which outwardly exude bad juices are more healthy than those which do not achieve health because they happen to be weak from inherent fever, in the same manner it is also understood that the Churches which attack the heresies which have grown up in them and are driven out will be more sound than those which endure the errors caused by the sickness of mind and good judgment.

### [8.] Concerning the Jews

Concerning the Jews, they have completely nothing to do with us. We are thus separated from them. They are banished from the jurisdiction of most of our governors, and they are not allowed to reside among us. The great teacher, Luther, in his published books, has wisely and effectively refuted their godlessness for the public by trampling on it. Neither, again, could anyone honestly charge us with the errors of the Jews

THIRD EXCHANGE: TÜBINGEN TO CONSTANTINOPLE     313

because of our knowledge of the Hebrew language. For we have abso-
[378] lutely not learned their absurd opinions and unbelief, but merely
their language in the same manner as with the Greek language, [i.e.],
from profane Greek writers. We absolutely never accepted the pro-
faneness of the pagans. Therefore, those among you who slander our
teaching and confession of faith as having received our incentives from
the Hebrews have done us an injustice without cause.

### [9.] That We Are Not Heretics

We cannot bear to be called heretics, even though he who is thus calling us might be one of our closest friends. For we have not up to this day
ever been convicted for any error, not even one by the Divine Words. We
have always been ready to yield if axioms and usages, which have been
correctly concluded from the Holy Scriptures, might have been placed
over against us. But up to the present we have not seen anyone who has
done that, even with the assistance of divine grace, nor will we see it in
the future. Indeed, we embrace all the articles of the catholic faith, rejecting absolutely none of them, and we respectfully make use of the
sacraments which were instituted by Christ. And, again, we are zealous
concerning the solemn and innocence of life and polity. Who, then, on a
pretext, will reproach us concerning heresy?

### [10.] Concerning the Holy Fathers

We concede to that authority of the Fathers which they bestowed on
themselves, that is, by accepting what they have written in so far as they
agree with the God-given Scriptures. But for the rest which they produced and left behind we are in agreement with Basil the Great, who has
thus exhorted in *The Ascetics*.[3] He says it is necessary that they who hear
those who have been educated in the Scriptures should examine what is
said by the teachers and accept them if, indeed, they are in accord with
the Scriptures, but reject the others [not in accord with the Scriptures]
and avoid very urgently those teachers who persist in such doctrines. For
[379] our faith cannot be based upon those matters which have no foundation in the Holy Scriptures. Many thousands of Christian people, who
have been illuminated and guided by the Scriptures, have entered the
road leading toward everlasting life and have been saved, even before
these Fathers whose teachings the human traditions have defended came
to be born on earth.

### 11. Friendly Conclusion of Correspondence

And even if you ask us to no longer trouble you with such writings
(although we have conversed with you with much love and much kindness and with due respect), yet we are hopeful that the matters which
have been written to you by us up to now will in time be re-examined and

reconsidered more accurately and much better. If you will do this, with the help of God you will understand that our confession has been founded truly and undoubtedly and clearly on the Word of God, to which was added neither human glories, nor traditions, nor ancient customs. For only the Word of God, in the struggle of man who is afraid, is unconquerable, the only encouragement and strengthening of him who labors and is heavy-laden [cf. Mt 11:28].

Therefore, standing together with Your Holiness, Patriarch and Most Reverent Sir, we offer to the God of all, our true friendship which we have shown to you and which we will continuously afterwards keep. We wish Your Holiness, with all our heart, all that is best and a prayerful wish for salvation, and above all this, that the Holy Spirit will lead all the activities of Your Holiness, the honor of God, and the salvation of His Church, Amen.

[380] Jacob Heerbrand, Professor of Theology, Provost of the Church at Tübingen, Professor of the University, Interim Rector (signature).

Eberhard Bidembach, Doctor of Theology, Abbot of the Monastery at Bebenhausen, Councilor (signature).

John Mageirus, Theologian, Provost of the Church of Stuttgart and Ecclesiastical Synedry Councilor.

Jacob Andreae, Doctor of Theology, Provost of the Church at Tübingen, Chancellor of the University, and Councilor General of the Ducal Court (signature).

Theodore Schneff, Doctor of Theology, Provost of the Church at Stuttgart, Professor, and General of the Churches of Wittenberg (signature).

Lucas Osiander, Doctor of Theology, Wittenberg, and Ecclesiastical Councilor and Assessor.

John Brentius, Doctor of Theology, Professor of Exegesis University of Tübingen, and Trustee of young students endowed by the Prince.

Stephen Gerlach, Doctor of Theology, Professor at the University.

William Holderer, Theologian, Church of Christ at Stuttgart, and Ecclesiastical Assessor.

John Schoppsius, Theologian, Councilor of the Court of the Church at Stuttgart, Assessor.

Martin Crusius, Institute Professor of Greek and Latin at Tübingen (signature).

## FINISH

## NOTES

1. Lines 30 to 42 of page 373 of the *Acta* are missing from the Latin text.

2. The greater part of this passage in the Greek text is not found to be in the corresponding Latin text.

3. St. Basil the Great, *On Renunciation of the World*, PG 31.633; cf. St. Basil, *Ascetical Works*, vol. 1, 19-20.

*Chapter 8*

# THIRD EXCHANGE: PERSONAL LETTERS

## [A.] The Letter of Jacob Heerbrand and Martin Crusius to Patriarch Jeremiah [II]

[381] To the All-Holy and Ecumenical Patriarch, the Lord Jeremiah, Archbishop of Constantinople, the New Rome, our Most Reverend Lord.

Most Holy and Most Venerable Sir Patriarch, you have favorably received letters from Germans before this, and now again we have great hope, and we implore Your Holiness, that you will graciously accept this letter as well. The matter, briefly stated, is this:

Your Holiness received with such good will the little book of our faith, which we call the Augsburg Confession, that you regarded it as worthy of a long and friendly reply. We sent it to you in order, thereby, to defend ourselves against the slanders, which some of our opponents have been spreading among the Eastern [Christians]. Again, not too long ago a kindly and respectful answer (with Mister Lucas Osiander signing in place of Mister Jacob Andreae, who was travelling abroad in Saxony) has been sent from here to Your Holiness. We hope that this answer has already been given to Your Holiness. It may perhaps be that in both these booklets not all of the main articles of our faith, and not all the texts — probably briefer than necessary — have wholly satisfied the great intelligence and desire of Your Holiness. We, on our part, also believe from evidence of not indistinct signs that Your Holiness is seeking a clearer explanation and an exposition of all the main articles of our Christian teaching. For all these reasons, Your Holiness will now receive from us such a book which contains an exposition, sufficient for the present not only of the issues which have been in dispute between us and the Church of the older Rome, but also the remaining parts of the Chris-[372][1] tian teaching. I, Jacob Heerbrand, composed the little book in Latin four years ago in a methodical fashion for the sake of students of theology, and I, Martin Crusius, recently translated it as faithfully and as diligently as possible into your language, as a little book which has al-

316

ready received general approval both among us and in many other places and which has value for both churches and for schools. In this way I offer to Your Holiness my gratitude and service with heartfelt respect and honor, the same friendly disposition with which I, as a philhellene, began to write to Your Holiness four years ago, when our dear Gerlach came down to your city.

For that reason both of us, the above-named, with all due humility and respect, entreat Your Holiness to receive with fatherly spirit this letter and our study. Judge favorably, according to the wisdom which distinguishes Your Holiness, our concern for religion and for the truth. And through the love of Your Holiness, count worthy both us and this our book, which the other bishops will also read. It contains no condemnation of anyone, except of one who struggles against Christ and places himself above the Holy Scriptures and Christ and the truth and who is prepared for open rebellion. We gratefully tolerate the ecclesiastical degrees so far as they serve good order.

May Your Holiness, Most Reverent Sir, along with the venerable clergy of your Church, be of good health.

From Tübingen, October 1, in the year of Salvation 1577

> Jacob Heerbrand, Doctor of Theology and Professor of the Universtiy at Tübingen.
>
> Martin Crusius, Professor of Greek and Latin Languages and Culture at Tübingen.

### [B.] The Letter of Patriarch Jeremiah [II] to the Tübingen Theologians

[383] To the most wise men and theologians in Germany, Sirs Jacob Andreae, Jacob Heerbrand, Lucas Osiander, and Martin Crusius.

The Most Holy[2] Patriarch of Constantinople with wishes and prayers for your well-being.

Jeremiah, by the mercy of God, Archbishop of Constantinople, New Rome, and Ecumenical Patriarch.

Most wise and dearly beloved German men, Chancellor and Superintendent, Sir Jacob Andreae; Doctor of Theology, Sir Jacob Heerbrand; Churchman, Sir Lucas Osiander; and Teacher of our two languages, Sir Martin Crusius; sons in the spirit of our humble self, may grace and peace and mercy from Almighty God be with you. We received your letters of March 4 while travelling about Thessaly, and we took note of what you have written and welcome also your love in Christ. While we were on our travels, conditions did not allow me to give an adequate answer to the questions you raised. Also, since our return to Constantinople on May 26, time has not given us the opportunity to prepare our answer. The very excellent and scholarly Sir Stephen Gerlach, Embassy Preacher, is preparing to depart from here on the first of June, if God wills. (This has been confirmed by his Excellency, the Ambassador.) But we have not had the opportunity to answer. So we are letting you know [384] that the answers to the questions which you have raised will be completed by August and turned over to Sir Solomon, the wise ecclesiastic, in the service of the illustrious Ambassador, who will remain resident here and will send the reply to you. We thank you, Sir Chancellor, for your affectionate generosity, and because of the timepiece which we carry in our hand to remind us of the sender; and we pray to God that by His grace He may account you worthy of His kingdom. May He protect you all and guide you to all that is good.

Jeremiah

Month of May, Indiction 6,
In the year 1578, from Constantinople.

## [C.] The Letter of Patriarch Jeremiah [II] to Jacob Heerbrand

To the erudite, wise Sir Jacob Heerbrand, Teacher of Theology.

Jeremiah, by the mercy of God, Archbishop of Constantinople, New Rome, and Ecumenical Patriarch.

[385] Most wise, profound, and studious Sir Heerbrand, Doctor of Theology and Professor in the Academy in Tübingen, may the grace and peace of God be with you. In our general letter we gave the information that you further requested on certain matters. However, concerning the book of an outline of theology which you have compiled with great care, I have not as yet examined it because of insufficient time. At a later time, when we have given it sufficient study, we will send the proper witness with the help of God, whose grace and mercy may grant you a long and blessed life. Amen.

Jeremiah

Month of May, Indiction 6,
In the year 1578, from Constantinople

## [D.] The Letter of Patriarch Jeremiah [II] to Martin Crusius

To the most wise Sir Martin Crusius, the distinguished Teacher of our two languages.

Jeremiah, by the mercy of God, Archbishop of Constantinople, New Rome, and Ecumenical Patriarch.

[386] Most diligent and erudite Sir Martin Crusius, Professor of the Greek and Latin languages in Tübingen, may you enjoy good health under the protection of divine grace. Recognizing your diligence and eagerness in research, which is also shared by your colleagues, we aspired to send an answer to the questions which you raised. However, time has held us back due to our journeying abroad. Therefore, we inform you with a general letter that it will be completed in August and sent to you. May the God of all creation keep you by His grace, nourishing you with His gifts. We thank you also for the timepiece which you sent to me with the Lord Chancellor.

> Jeremiah
>
> Month of May, Indiction 6.
> In the year 1578, from Constantinople.

### NOTES

1. Page is incorrectly numbered; should be 382.
2. The title "Most Holy" does not seem to have been written by the Patriarch, but by the theologians who were his scribes. They show their hand in this.

# A SELECT BIBLIOGRAPHY

## Abbreviations

ACW         *Ancient Christian Writers, the Works of the Fathers,* ed. J. Quasten and J.C. Plumpe. Westminster, Md. and London,                               1946ff.

ANF         *Ante-Nicene Fathers. The Apostolic Fathers to A.D. 325,* ed. Grand Rapids, Mich., 1978.

ASTW      *Acta et Scripta Theologorum Wittembergensium.* Wittenberg, 1583.

FC           *The Fathers of the Church, A New Translation,* ed. R. J. Deferrari. Washington, D. C., 1947ff.

HAC        J. Harduin, *Acta Conciliorum.* Paris, 1717.

HCG        C. J. Hefele, *Conciliengeschichte.* 2nd ed. Freiburg, 1874, revised in French transl. by H. Leclercq, *Histoire des Conciles.* Paris, 1907ff.

LCC        *Library of Christian Classics,* ed. J. Baillie, J. T. McNeill, H. P. van Dusen. Philadelphia and London, 1953ff.

PG          J. Migne, *Patrologia Graeca.* Paris, 1857-66.

PL           J. Migne, *Patrologia Latina.* Paris, 1844-55.

NPNF      *A Select Library of Nicene and Post-Nicene Fathers of the Christian Church,* ed. by P. Schaff and H. Wace. Buffalo and New York, 1886-1900; reprinted: Grand Rapids, Mich., 1952ff. Ser. 1, Ser. 2.

## Primary Sources

*Acta et Scripta Theologorum Wirtembergensium et Patriarchae Constantinopolitani D. Hieremiae: quae utrique ab Anno MDLXXVI usque ad Annum MDLXXXI de Augustana Confessione inter se miserunt: Graece & Latine ab ijsdem Theologis edita.* Wittenberg, 1584.

Alivizatos, Hamilkas. *Οἱ ἱεροί κανόνες καί οἱ ἐκκλησιαστικοί νόμοι.* Athens, 1949.

Broadus, J. A. *The Homilies of St. John Chrysostom on the Epistle of St. Paul the Apostle to the Philippians, Colossians and the Thessalonians.* NPNF: ser. 1, vol. 13. Grand Rapids, Mich., 1976.,

Browne, C.G., and Swallow, J.F. *Select Orations of Saint Gregory Nazianzus.* NPNF: ser. 2, vol. 7. Grand Rapids, Mich., 1955.

Chambers, T. W. *The Homilies of St. John Chrysostom on the Epistles of St. Paul to the Corinthians.* NPNF: ser. 1, vol. 12. Grand Rapids, Mich., 1956.

Crusius, Martin. *Turcograecia.* Basel, 1584.

*Die Bekenntnisschriften der Evangelisch-Lutherischen Kirche.* 4th ed. Göttingen, 1959.

Gerlach, Stephen, Sr. *Türckisches Tagebuch aus seinen eigenhändig aufgesetzten und nachgelassenen Schriften, herfürgegeben durch seinen Enkel M. Samuel Gerlach.* Frankfurt am Main, 1674.

Gifford, E. H. *The Catechetical Lectures of St. Cyril of Jerusalem,* NPNF: ser. 2, vol. 7. Grand Rapids, Mich., 1976.

Göz, W., and E. Conrad, eds. *Diarium, 1596-1597 et 1598-1599.* Tübingen, 1927-1931.

Gross, Alexander, *The Commentary and Homilies of St. John Chrysostom on the Epistles of St. Paul the Apostle to the Galatians & Ephesians.* NPNF: ser. 1, vol. 13. Grand Rapids, Mich., 1976.

Hartranft, C. D. *The Ecclesiastical History of Sozomen.* History of the Church from A. D. 323 to A. D. 425. NPNF: ser. 2, vol. 2. Grand Rapids, Mich., 1976.

Jackson, Blomfield. *"De Spiritu Sancto," Hexaemeron & Letters of St. Basil the Great.* 1975. NPNF: ser. 2, vol. 8.

Karmires, Ioannes. *Τά δογματικά καί συμβολικά μνημεῖα τῆς 'Ορθοδόξου Καθολικῆς 'Εκκλησίας.* 2 vols. Athens; 1952-53.

Kidd, B. J., ed. *D. H. C. Documents Illustrative of the History of the Church.* New York, 1933.

Kimmel, E. J. *Monumenta Fidea Ecclesiae Orientalis.* Jenae, 1850.

McGiffert, A. C. *The Church History of Eusebius.* NPNF: ser. 2, vol. 1. Grand Rapids, Mich., 1961.

Mesoloras, I. *Συμβολική τῆς 'Ορθοδόξου 'Ανατολικῆς 'Εκκλησίας.* 2

vols. Athens, 1893-1901.

Michalcescu, J. Θησαυρός τῆς 'Ορθοδοξίας. Leipzig, 1904.

Migne, J. *Patrologia Graeca*. Paris, 1857-66.

_____. *Patrologia Latina*. Paris, 1844-55.

Moore, Wm., and Wilson, H. A. *Select Writings & Letters of Gregory, Bishop of Nyssa*. NPNF: ser. 2, vol. 5. Grand Rapids, Mich., 1952ff.

Morris, J. B., and Simcox, W. H., translators; Stevens, G. B., revisor. *The Homilies of St. John Chrysostom on the Epistle of Saint Paul, the Apostle to the Romans*. NPNF: ser. 1., vol. 11. Grand Rapids, Mich., 1975.

Nikodemos Hagiorites and Agapios Monachos. Πηδάλιον. English trans. D. Cummings as *The Rudder*. Chicago, 1957.

Percival, H. R. *Decrees and Canons of the Seven Ecumenical Councils of the Undivided Church*. NPNF: ser. 2, vol. 14. Grand Rapids, Mich., 1956.

Prevost, G. *The Homilies of St. John Chrysostom on the Gospel of St. Matthew*. Revised M. B. Riddle. Grand Rapids, Mich., 1969.

Ralles, G. A., and M. Potles. Σύνταγμα θείων καί ἱερῶν κανόνων. 6 vols. Athens, 1852-59.

Robertson, A. *Select Writings and Letters of Athanasius, Bishop of Alexandria*. NPNF: ser. 2, vol. 4. Grand Rapids, Mich., 1969.

Salmond, S. D. F. *John of Damascus: Exposition of the Orthodox Faith*. NPNF: ser. 2, vol. 9. Grand Rapids, Mich., 1955.

Schaff, Philip. *Creeds of Christendom*. Vol. 2: *The Creeds of the Greek and Latin Churches, with Translations*. New York, 1919.

_____. *The Homilies of St. John Chrysostom on the Gospel of St. John*. NPNF: ser. 1, vol. 14. Grand Rapids, Mich., 1956.

_____. *The Homilies of St. John Chrysostom on the Epistle of St. Paul the Apostle to Timothy, Titus and Philemon*. NPNF: ser. 1, vol. 13. Grand Rapids, Mich., 1976.

_____. *A Select Library of Nicene and Post-Nicene Fathers of the Christian Church*. Buffalo and New York, 1890-1900; Grand Rapids, Mich., 1952ff (Reprint of 1890-1900 edition).

_____. *St. John Chrysostom: On the Priesthood*. Trans. W.R.W. Stephens. NPNF: ser. 1, vol. 9. Grand Rapids, Mich., 1968.

Stevenson, J. ed., *A New Eusebius. Documents Illustrative of the*

*History of the Church to A. D. 337 Based on the Collection of B. J. Kidd.* London, 1957.

Stratenwerth, Gerhard, ed. *Wort und Mysterium, Der Briefwechsel über Glauben und Kirche, 1573 bis 1581 zwischen den Tübinger Theologen und dem Patriarchen von Konstantinopel.* Vol. 2: *Dokumente der Orthodoxen Kirchen zur ökumenischen Frage.* Witten, 1958.

Tappert, Theodore G., ed. *The Book of Concord.* Philadelphia, 1959.

Zenos, A. C. *The Ecclesiastical History of Socrates Scholasticus.* NPNF: ser. 2, vol. 2. Grand Rapids, Mich., 1956.

## Secondary Sources

Adney, W. F. *The Greek and Eastern Churches.* Edinburgh, 1908.

Allbeck, Willard Dow. *Studies in the Lutheran Confessions.* Rev. ed. Philadelphia, 1968.

Bainton, Roland H. *Here I Stand: A Life of Martin Luther.* New York, 1950.

Benz, Ernst. "Wittenberg und Byzanz," *Zur Begegnung und Auseinandersetzung der Reformation und der Östlich-Orthodoxen Kirche.* Marburg, 1949.

_____. "Evangelisches und Orthodoxes Christentum," *Zur Begegnung und Auseinandersetzung der Reformation und der Östlich-Orthodoxen Kirche.* Marburg, 1949.

_____. *Die Ostkirche im Lichte der protestantischen Geschichtsschreibung von der Reformation bis zur Gegenwart.* Munich, 1952.

_____. "Melanchthon et l'Église Orthodoxe," *Irenikon,* 29 (1956): 165-76.

_____. "La Confession d'Augsbourg et Byzance au XVIᵉ Siecle," *Irenikon,* 29 (1956): 390-405.

Bettenson, H., ed. *The Later Christian Fathers.* Oxford, 1972.

Bevan, E. R. *Holy Images.* London, 1940.

Bonis, K. G. «Γεώργιος-Γεννάδιος Κουρτέσης ὁ Σχολάριος,» *Νέα Σιών* (1953).

Boyle, Patrick, trans. *On the Priesthood by St. John Chrysostom.* Westminster, Md., 1955.

Bradow, King. "Eastern Orthodox Church." *Encyclopedia of the*

*Lutheran Church*. Minneapolis, 1965. Volume 1, 744-46.

Burnaby, John. *Augustine: Later Works*. LCC: vol. 8. Philadelphia, 1953.

Campenhausen, Hans von. *The Fathers of the Greek Church*. London, 1963.

_____.*Die Griechischen Kirchenväter*. Stuttgart, 1955.

Chytraeus, David. *Oratio de statu Ecclesiarum hoc tempore in Graecia, Asia, Africa, Ungaria, Boemia*. Frankfurt, 1580.

Clercq, Charles de. "La *Turcograecia* de Martin Crusius et les patriarches de Constantinople de 1453 à 1583," *Orientalia Christiana Periodica*, 33 (1967): 210-20.

Crusius, Martin. *Annales Suevici, Dodekas Tertia*. n.p., 1596.

Damascene, St. John. *The Holy Images*. Trans. M. N. Allies. London, 1898.

Dositheos, Patriarch of Jerusalem. *Τόμος ’Αγάπης*. Jassy, 1698.

Dyobouniotes, Konstantinos. «Θεοδόσιος Ζυγομαλᾶς,» *Θεολογία*, 1 (1923).

Engels, W. "Tübingen und Byzanz, Die erste offizielle Auseinandersetzung zwischen Protestantismus und Ostkirche im 16 Jahrhundert," *Kyrios*, 5 (1940-41).

_____. "Die Wiederentdeckung und erste Beschreibung der östlichorthodoxen Kirche in Deutschland durch David Chytraeus," *Kyrios*, 4 (1939-40).

Florovsky, Georges. "The Orthodox Churches and the Ecumenical Movement Prior to 1910," *A History of the Ecumenical Movement, 1517-1948*. Ed. Ruth Rouse and Stephen Charles Neill. London, 1954, pp. 171-218.

_____. "The Greek Version of the Augsburg Confession," *Lutheran World*, 6 (1959): 153-55.

_____. "An Early Ecumenical Correspondence of Patriarch Jeremiah II and the Lutheran Divines." *World Lutheranism of Today, A Tribute to Anders Nygren*. Stockholm, 1950.

Gass, W. *Symbolik der Griechischen Kirche*. Berlin, 1872.

Gavin, Frank. *Some Aspects of Contemporary Greek Orthodox Thought*. New York, 1962.

Gedeon, M. *Πατριαρχικοί Πίνακες*. Constantinople, 1885.

Gennadios (George Scholarios), Patriarch of Constantinople. *Confessio Fidei and Dialogus. Oeuvres Completes.* Eds. L. Petie, X. A. Siderides, and M. Jugie. 8 vols. Paris, 1928-36.

Georgi, Curt R.A. "Das erste Gesprach zwischen Protestantismus und Orthodoxie," *Eine Heilige Kirche*, 21 (1939).

Hardy, E. R., and Richardson, C. C., eds. *Christology of the Later Fathers*. LCC: vol. 3. Philadelphia, 1954.

Heineccius, J. M. *Eigentliche und Wahrhaftige Abbildung der alten und neuen Griechischen Kirche.* 3 vols. Lepizig, 1711.

Hofmann, G. "Griechische Patriarchen und Römische Päpste. Untersuchungen und Texte," *Orientalia Christiana*, 25. (Rome, 1932).

Ivanka, Ev. "Palamismus und Vatertradition in 1054-1954, L'Église et les Églises. Neuf siècles de separation," *Irenikon*, 2 (1955).

Jackson, Samuel M. *The New Schaff-Herzog Encyclopedia of Religious Knowledge.* New York, 1912.

Kabasilas, Nicholas. *A Commentary on the Divine Liturgy.* London, 1960.

Karmires, Ioannes. *Ὀρθοδοξία καί Προτεσταντισμός.* Athens, 1937.

_____. *A Synopsis of the Dogmatic Theology of the Orthodox Church.* Trans. G. Dimopoulos. Scranton, Pa., 1973.

_____. «᾿Επιστολαί τοῦ Jacob Parkethyme ἀναφερόμεναι εἰς τόν Πατριάρχην ῾Ιερεμία Β΄,» *᾿Εκκλησία*, 15 (1937).

Kelly, J. N. D. *Early Christian Doctrine. 2nd ed.* New York, 1960.

_____. *Early Christian Creeds.* London, 1967.

Korte, B. F. "Early Lutheran Relations with Eastern Orthodoxy." *Lutheran Quarterly*, 9 (1959): 53-59.

Krumbacher, Karl. *Geschichte der Byzantinischen Litteratur Handbuch klassischen.* (Munich, 1897).

Kypriou, Gedeon. *Βιβλίον καλούμενον Κριτῆς τῆς ᾿Αληθείας.* Leipzig, 1758.

Kypriou, P. *Chronicon Ecclesiae Graecae.* Leipzig and Frankfurt, 1687.

Landenberger, A. *Die Reise zweier würtembergischer Gesandschaftsprediger nach Constantinopel im Jahre 1573 und 1577, nach ihrem Tagebücher erzählt.* Wittenberg, 1888.

Latourette, Kenneth Scott. *A History of Christianity.* New York, 1953.

Legrand, E. "Notice biographique sur Gean et Theodose Zygomalas," *Publications de l'école*, 2 (1889).

Lueker, Erwin L., ed. *Lutheran Cyclopedia.* St. Louis, 1954.

Luther, Martin. *Dr. Martin Luthers Werke: Kritische Gesamtausgabe.* 2 vols. Weimar, 1884.

Mesolaras, I. *Ἰερεμίου τοῦ Β΄ καί τῶν Διαμαρτυρομένων Θεολόγων τῆς Βυρτεμβέργης τά γράμματα περί τῆς Αὐγουσταίας Ὁμολογίας 1576-1581.* Athens, 1881.

Meyer, Phillip. *Die theologische Literatur der Griechischen Kirche, im 16 Jahrhundert, in Bonwetsch-Seeberg, (ed.), Studien.* Vol. 3. Leipzig, 1899.

Michalcescu, J. *Θησαυρός τῆς Ὀρθοδοξίας.* Leipzig, 1904.

Moxon, T. A. *Chyrsostom on the Priesthood.* London, 1932.

Mystakides, V. «Ὁ Πατριάρχης Ἰερεμίας Β΄ ὁ Τρανός καί αἱ πρός τούς Διαμαρτυρομένους σχέσεις κατά τῶν ΙΣΤ αἰῶνα,» *Ἐκκλησιαστική Ἀλήθεια.* 1 (1880).

_____. Ὁ Πατριάρχης Ἰερεμίας Β΄ ὁ Τρανός καί ἡ προσωπογραφία αὐτοῦ,» *Ibid.*

Neve, J. L. *Introduction to the Symbolical Books of the Lutheran Church.* Columbus, Ohio, 1956.

Ostrogorsky, G. *History of the Byzantine State,* New Brunswick, N.J., 1956.

Palmieri, A. *Theologia Dogmatica Orthodoxa Ecclesiae Graeco-Russicae Prolegomena.* 2 vols. Florence, 1911-13.

Papadopoulos, C. Σχέσεις Ὀρθοδόξων καί Διαμαρτυρομένων ἀπό Ἰερεμίου Β΄ μέχρι Κυρίλλου Λουκάρεως,» *Νέα Σιών,* 21 (1926).

Papadopoulos, T. *Studies and Documents Relating to the History of the Greek Church and People under Turkish Domination.* Brussels, 1952.

Pfister, G. *Urtheil der Orientalischen Kirche und ihres Patriarchen zu Konstantinopel über die Augsburgische Confession mit einigen Bemerkungen.* Würzburg, 1827.

Pichler, A. *Geschichte des Protestantismus in der Orientalischen Kirche.* n. p. , 1862.

Pieper, F. *Christian Dogmatics.* 4 vols. St. Louis, 1950.

Piepkorn, A. C. "Andreae, Jacob," *Encyclopedia of the Lutheran Church,* 1, 1973.

Prestige, G. L. *Fathers and Heretics.* London, 1963.

Quasten, J. *Patrology.* Vol. 3. Westminister, Md., 1960.

Randell, J. H. *Making of the Modern Mind.* Boston and New York, 1926.

Renaudin, P. *Luthériens et Greco-Orthodoxes.* Paris, 1903.

_____. "Les Églises Orientales Orthodoxes et le Protestantisme," *Revue de l'Orient Chrétien,* 5 (1900), 6 (1901).

Sathas, K. *Βιογραφικό σχεδίασμα περί τοῦ Πατριάρχου Ἱερεμίου Β΄ (1572-1594).* Athens, 1870.

Schall, J. "Tübingen und Konstantinopel, Ein theologischer Briefwechsel aus dem Zeitalter der Reformation," *Blätter für Württembergische Kirchengeschichte,* 7 (1892).

Schweigger, S. *Eine neue Reisebeschreibung aus Deutschland nach Konstantinopel und Jerusalem.* Nürnberg, 1608.

Seeberg, R. C. F. *History of Doctrine.* Trans. Charles E. Hay. 3 vols. Grand Rapids, Mich. 1952.

Sellers, R. V. *The Council of Chalcedon.* London, 1961.

Shapland, C. R. B. *Letters of St. Athanasius. Re: Holy Spirit.* London, 1951.

Smits, E. "The Lutheran Theologians of the 17th Century and the Fathers of the Ancient Church." *The Symposium on Seventeenth Century Lutheranism,* 1 (1962).

Stanley, A. P. *Lectures on the History of the Eastern Church with an Introduction on the Study of Ecclesiastical History.* New York, 1873.

Steinwand, Eduard. "Lutheranism and the Orthodox Church," *Lutheran World,* 6 (1959): 122-39.

Steitz, G. "Die Abendmahlslehre der Griechischen Kirche in ihrer geschichtlichen Entwicklung," *Jahrbücher für deutsche Theologie,* 13 (1868): 679.

Stevenson, S., ed. *Creeds, Councils and Controversies.* London, 1972.

Swete, H. B. *The Holy Spirit in the Ancient Church.* Grand Rapids, Mich., 1966.

Tatakis, B. *La Philosophie Byzantine.* Paris, 1949.

Taylor, H. O. *Thought and Expression in the 16th Century.* 2nd ed. New York, 1959.

Wagner, Sister M. Monica. *St. Basil: Ascetical Works*. Washington, D. C., 1962.

Zachariadis, G. E. *Tübingen und Konstantinopel: Martin Crusius und seine Verhandlungen mit der Griechisch-Orthodoxen Kirche.* Göttingen, 1941.

Zankov, Stefan, *The Eastern Orthodox Church.* 2nd ed. London, 1930.

Zernov, Nicholas. *Eastern Christendom, a Study of the Origin and Development of the Eastern Orthodox Church.* London, 1961.

# INDEX TO SCRIPTURAL REFERENCES

## New Testament

### Matthew

## Old Testament

# GENERAL INDEX

## A

*A Declaration of Faith*, 295
Aaron, 52
Abraham, 52, 60, 138, 182, 270, 272, 311
*Ascetical Works*, 241
Acta et Scripta Theologorum Wintembergensium et Patrarchae Constantinopolitani D. Hieremiae, 7, 12, 15, 16, 17
Acts of the Apostles, 130, 251, 259, 264, 267, 273, 282, 297
Adam, 20, 48
Adelphotheos, See James, Saint
*Against Eunomios*, 241, 289
Agathon, Pope, 168, 239
Almsgiving, 137
Ambrose, 171
Ananias, 96
Anastasios of Mt. Sinai, and free will, 176
Anaxagoras, 184
*Ancoratos*, 241, 289
Andreae, Jacob, 7, 12, 13, 14, 16, 27, 29, 30, 107,149, 216, 314, 316
Anna, Prophetess, 285
Anointing, sacrament of, 50, 144-45
*Answer, First*, 14, 15, 17, 20
*Answer, Second*, 151
*Answer, Third*, 289
Anti-Christ, 222
Antioch, church at, 60; Synod

of, 71
Antiochians, 251
Antiochos, 199
Apocalypse, 27
Apollinarios, 112
Apostles, 8, 14, 29, 30, 106, 111, 115, 116, 136, 141, 149, 152, 220, 236, 249, 255, 256, 259, 266, 272, 279, 285, 289, 294, 306; decrees of, 72; honor of, 221; thirtieth canon of, 70; twenty-fifth canon of, 70; sixty-third canon of, 100
Apostle's Creed, 134
Apostolic Symbol, 109
Archimandrites, 203
Arians, 117, 153, 171
Arius, 165
Assyrians, 277
Athanasios (the Great), 120, 171, 239, 296; and the Holy Spirit, 240; and the procession of the Holy Spirit, 153, 154, 167, 241; symbol of, 219
Athenagoras, Patriarch, 23, 24
Athens, 151
Augsburg Confession, 14, 17, 22, 31, 316; apology of, 6; articles of, 6, 15; text of, 15; translated into Greek, 7; translation of, 8
Augustana, 17
Augustine, St., 169, 171, 220, 289; and filioque, 226; and

the Holy Spirit, 227; need
for, 225-27; not decreed by
Synods, 172; receiving and
sending of, 228; two Christs
without, 237; verification
of, 232
Florovsky, Georges, 17, 23
Forerunner, Holy (and Baptizer), 216, 238
*Formula of Concord*, 7, 113
*Fourth Theological Oration*,
289
Free will, doctrine of, 121-23;
nature of, 303

## G

Gaius, 130
Galatia, church of, 138
Gennadios, 221
Gerlach, Stephen, 14, 17, 217,
314
Germans, 288
Germany, 5, 28, 116, 256
God, *passim*
Gospel, of Christ, 48, 70, 149,
273
Great Entrance, 65
Greece, conquest of, 10
Greek Church, 8, 128, 223
Greek ecclesiastical writers,
116
Greek Fathers, See Fathers,
Greek
Greek language, 8, 116, 131,
149, 172, 220
Greek superstitions, 94
Greek writers, 313
Gregory, Pope, 13; and filioque, 15, 172
Gregory of Nyssa, 239; and
the Holy Spirit, 295; and the
procession of the Holy
Spirit, 169

Gregory the Theologian (Nazianzos), 61, 72, 73, 80, 200,
239, 241, 280, 289, 293; and
procession of the Holy Spirit, 153, 161-62; and righteousness, 127; and saints,
192-93
Gregory (Thaumatourgos) the
Wonder-worker, 169, 239,
295

## H

Hades, 31, 58
Hannah, 75
Hebrew, language, 116, 131,
219, 221, 285, 312; tradition, 306
Hebrews, Epistle to, 280
Heerbrand, James, 216, 314,
316, 317, 318
Heraclides, Prince, 9
Heraklitos of Ephesos, 176
Herod, 175
Hezekiah, King, 276
Hippolytos, 171, 222
Halderer, William, 314
*Homily Against the Collyridians*, 193
*Homily on Colossians*, 200
*Homily on the Dedication of
the Precious Cross*, 200
*Homily on the Martyr Barlaam*, 199
*Homily on the Forty Holy
Martyrs*, 199
*Homoousios*, 158
Hope, nature of, 181
Huss, John, 4

## I

Icons, due relative worship,
194; veneration of, 192

Orthodox Church, 3, 12; con-
tacts with Lutherans, 8;
teachings of, 9; teachings of
invoked by Luther, 10
Orthodox faith, 16; faithful,
174
Orthodoxy, 69, 173, 210
Orthodox Church, Eastern, 8,
12, 13, 14, 15, 17, 20
Ottoman Empire, 10

### P

Palladios, and the Holy Spirit,
241
Pammakaristos, Patriarchal
monastery of, 103
Pamphilos, 171, 242
Paraclete, 118,173, 290, 295;
See also Holy Spirit
Paradise, 205
Parousia, day of, 222
Passover, 144, 263
Paul, Saint (Apostle), 31, 39,
43, 49, 52, 53, 57, 67, 69,
76, 94, 107, 114, 115, 118,
119, 123, 125, 126, 134, 135,
136, 142, 147, 163, 164, 188,
205, 209, 250, 261, 281, 283,
284, 291, 292, 293, 296, 303;
and almsgiving, 137; and
faith, 251; and free will,
174; and freedom of will,
78-80; and human nature,
246; and justification, 179;
and marriage, 131; and redemption, 183; and righ-
teousness, 127, 135; and the
Holy Spirit, 238; on faith
and good works, 37; on the
Christian faith, 236
Paul VI, Pope, 23
Peace, Prince of, 218
Peloponnesos, 151

Penance, sacrament of, 48, 50,
57-58, 189; nature of, 132
Pentecost, day of, 130, 224,
260, 266
Peter, Apostle, 38, 43, 50, 54,
80, 110, 111, 115, 119, 125,
131, 147, 152, 271, 284, 297;
and justification, 181
Peter, Cardinal, 163
Peucer, Dr., 9
Pharisees, 38, 50
Philip, Apostle, 130
Philippians, Epistle to, 79
Photios, Patriarch, on proces-
sion of the Holy Spirit, 163-
64
Pierios, 171, 242
Pisidia, 251
Poland, Orthodox Church in,
17
Polycarp, 261
Pneumatomachians, 171
Pneumatomachos, 165
Pope, primacy of, 3
Prayers for the dead, opposi-
tion to, 135
Priests, and marriage, 91-92;
worthy of honor, 51-54
Procession, disagreement be-
tween Greek and Latin
Churches, 223-34
Procession and Latins, 224;
and sending, distinction of,
152
Prodigal Son, parable of, 305
Prophets, 29, 31, 43, 51, 106,
111, 113, 115, 149, 256, 270,
279, 281, 285; honor of, 221
Protestants, 6
Psalmist, 290

### Q

Queen City, 163

Printed in the United States
17423LVS00004B/43-102

1188750

Made in the USA